The Three-Year Swim Club

The Untold Story of the Sugar Ditch Kids and Their Quest for Olympic Glory

Julie Checkoway

ABACUS

First published in the United States in 2015 by Grand Central Publishing
First published in Great Britain in 2015 by Little, Brown

This paperback edition first published in 2016 by Abacus

13 5 7 9 10 8 6 4 2

A CIP catalogue record for this book
is available from the British Library.

ISBN 978-0-349-14191-6

Printed and bound in Great Britain by
Clays Ltd, St Ives plc

Papers used by Abacus are from well-managed forests
and other responsible sources.

MIX
Paper from
responsible sources
FSC® C104740

Abacus
An imprint of
Little, Brown Book Group
Carmelite House
50 Victoria Embankment
London EC4Y 0DZ

An Hachette UK Company
www.hachette.co.uk

www.littlebrown.co.uk

For all of Coach's swimmers

Okage sama de

Contents

Contents

PART FIVE: *Fall Seven Times, Get Up Eight*
(Nana korobi, ya oki) *(1944–1948)*

Figure it out for yourself, my lad,
You've all that the greatest men have had.

—From "Equipment," by Edward A. Guest,
in *Merit Badges: Life Work, Revised*
Handbook for Boys, 1927 edition

I do not know much about gods; but I think that the river
Is a strong brown god —sullen, untamed and intractable.

—T. S. Eliot, *Four Quartets*

Americanism is a matter of the mind and heart; Americanism is not and never was a matter of race and ancestry.

—Franklin Delano Roosevelt

Olympics First, Olympics Always!

—Motto of the Three-Year Swim Club

Swim swiftly.   —Soichi Sakamoto

The Three-Year Swim Club

Preface

20° 51' 44.7" N 156° 26' 58.3" W
—Coordinates of the irrigation ditch

20° 51' 22.4." N 156° 27' 10.7" W
—Coordinates of the Camp 5 pool

IN 1932, a reporter for the *Chicago Tribune* named Philip Kinsley visited Maui, and on approach by interisland aeroplane, he saw the place as a "sculptured green cup...rimmed," he wrote, "by white Pacific surf lines." The sides of that cup were the island's two great mountain ranges to the east and to the west, and at the top of one of those ranges was the famed volcanic crater Haleakala.

In March of 2012, some eighty years after Kinsley traveled to Maui, I, too, saw the island's lush peaks, but my destination was the very bottom of Kinsley's cup, the arid, golden lowland that gave Maui the nickname by which it's still known today: "the Valley Isle."

In Kinsley's time that flat valley was planted with 30,000 acres of sugarcane, and it was home to some 8,000 souls living in 13 segregated labor camps in a village called Pu'unene. Pu'unene is mostly gone now. It's still the site of Hawaii's last working sugar plantation, but it would take a forensic archaeologist to reconstruct the village as it existed in the 1930s. Pu'unene was then a beehive of life, with shacks and shops and red dirt roads, but now its footprint lies beneath the soil, plowed under into more cane fields. One plot of the old plantation is the 25-acre Pu'unene Shopping Center, the cornerstone of which is a 140,000-square-foot SuperTarget. Back in 1932, Philip Kinsley found the plantation at Pu'unene to be the very model of "enlightened feudalism."

To find Pu'unene now, the easiest thing to do isn't to look for Target; it's to sight on the horizon the two striped smokestacks of the Hawaii Commercial & Sugar Company mill that rise high above the tasseled cane. Over those stacks hang clouds of steam. Drive toward the stacks. Most tourists find them an eyesore, but to me, the stacks are a ragged kind of beauty: they are among the last pieces of a story that I'd grown afraid had passed away.

When I first heard of the Three-Year Swim Club, most of it, its stories and its people, had disappeared, and what little of it was left consisted of half-excavated bones that long ago had calcified into myth. There were a few original swimmers left; most were in their nineties and crisp of mind, but after years of "talking story" with each other—sitting together and emphasizing this moment or forgetting that one—the tale they told was a legend that went like this: in 1937, a schoolteacher in Pu'unene taught impoverished Japanese-American camp kids how to swim in the plantation's filthy irrigation ditches, and he challenged them to transform themselves into Olympians. That much was true, but was there was more that needed telling, and it was that *more* for which I'd come nearly three thousand miles to Pu'unene.

The school at which the teacher worked now houses county offices—and though just beyond its smudged windows and across the dusty road is the very ditch in which the Three-Year Swim Club had its start, if you stop and ask anyone nearby, no one will be able to tell you about the teacher or the children or the team.

Farther down that road, just past the abandoned Roman Catholic graveyard with its dark toothlike headstones, is the pool; it's on plantation land, but the sugar company hasn't kept it up. It's had no need to: no one really lives in Pu'unene anymore; after World War II, when the mill mechanized and laborers unionized, the camps emptied of workers who fled the island or moved on to real houses in a nearby subdivision known as "Dream City."

There's hardly any water in the old pool now, just what's gathered in the rain, puddles in which a couple of hopeful ducks skim the shallow surface and in which a wild black pig sometimes roams around. When I visited, I found the bamboo fence and the old bleachers gone, but the pool deck was intact, its zigzag pattern as perfect as if a team of masons had laid the brick and filled the joints with mortar only yesterday.

The pool's clubhouses, two of them, are standing, and on the outside walls is a set of hooks where rusty pulleys used to hang. Some seventy years ago, the children's teacher strung the pulleys' sheaves with lanyards and tied to one end of each of those ropes a heavy railcar wheel and to the other ends bamboo handles: the arrangement made a poor man's weight machine.

Knowing what the hooks and brick were once a part of, I couldn't help but see them all and the pool as symbols: the evaporating water, say, the ineluctable recession of the tale commencing in that very tank so many years before.

On the first afternoon I visited, I went there unseen, and, arriving stealthily, I stepped over two tipped plastic lawn chairs, making my way around oil barrels empty of their contents and slipping beyond an unchained gate onto the abandoned deck. I was trespassing, and in the last of the dim light, I noticed right away four planks of wood, each three feet long, and tacked above one another on a wall near where the pulleys used to be.

The planks had once been signs handpainted with the care of an amanuensis, but now on only two of the planks were words legible. In pretty script the topmost read *No Running*, and the next one down read *No Horseplay*, but the third and fourth had been erased by time and weather.

It grew darker still. There was no one around to hear or see me, and I felt in myself an impulse more brazen than trespass. The planks were held on by ancient, rusty nails. I scoured the deck for a tool of any sort, some way to gain leverage on the wood. A small crowbar would have done, a heavy stick, but I found nothing that could do the job.

Gently, starting at the topmost sign, I worked the tips of my forefingers around the edges of the wood until I felt that first resistance that occurs in the split second before a nail decides to give up the place that it's been sunk into for years. I felt the sweetness of the pull, the surrender of attachment. I gently pulled the wood some more. And then I heard the crack.

It wasn't loud; it was little more, say, than the sound of a twig breaking, but I knew for certain that I had separated a sliver of the plank from its place in the grain, and to me the noise was thunderous, and it stopped me cold. I felt the front of the sign for damage; finding none, I decided that the ruination was only in the back, and thus undetectable. When I stepped away from the wall, though, I was trembling. The weather hadn't changed, but I had. I stood in the dark like that for a long time. I was worse than a trespasser; I was a thief.

The plantation owns those signs, but who, I wondered, owns the disappearing story that, in part, they tell? The story of the teacher and the children lives now in so few places: on that weather-beaten wall, in scrapbooks filled with photographs. History isn't a sculptured cup; it's more like a sieve through which so many stories pass and disappear.

Over time I've learned that neither the teacher nor the children chose to write the story down because it was the tale of a team that no one felt he had the right to claim as his own. Each, instead, was content or, better said, resigned to the fact that the history of the Three-Year Swim Club would simply disappear.

I was a stranger to the story, but it seemed to me that someone ought to try to save it.

PART ONE

SUCH STUFF AS DREAMS

1932–1937

Each man has his own vocation. The talent is the call. There is one direction in which all space is open to him. He has faculties silently inviting him thither to endless exertion. He is like a ship in a river; he runs against obstructions on every side but one, on that side all obstruction is taken away and he sweeps serenely over a deepening channel into an infinite sea…He has no rival. For the more truly he consults his own powers, the more difference will his work exhibit from the work of any other.

—Ralph Waldo Emerson

Chapter One

TO RACE WITH GIANTS

ON FRIDAY, August 20, 1937, three thousand people brimmed the bleachers at the Waikiki War Memorial Natatorium—working stiffs and hoi polloi in general admission, swells in the reserved seats, and just outside the concrete walls, barefoot local kids climbed the hau trees for the gratis view, perched on boughs like avifauna in silhouette. On the deck, hacks from the *Advertiser*, the *Hawaii Hochi*, and stringers from the radio service puffed on Lucky Strikes and Laramies and bumped gums about celebrities that they spotted in the grandstand.

The Depression had dealt tourism a blow, but at last healthy, wealthy, and bohemian types were returning to Hawaii, lured by colorful brochures describing liquid sunshine and simmering volcanoes wreathed in misty clouds like angels' robes, a paradise where, it was said, it rarely rained, but when it did, the shower of it was brief, polite, and generous: it left behind a signature of double rainbows.

In the late 1930s, tourists had come back again, and the windows of the Royal Hawaiian hotel winked on in shades of ochre and gold. Lip-locking lovers perambulated on the seaside piers, and holidaymakers gathered at the shore for luaus under Maxfield Parrish skies. In town for the summer were the likes of Cliff Durant, the dashing racecar driver, and Charlotte, his—fourth—wife; the stars Jeanette MacDonald and Alice Faye had come to Eden in the lull between shooting pictures; and members of the moneyed class whose names appeared with regularity in Mainland society columns had arrived as well: the Dr. Andrew J. Timbermans of Columbus, Ohio; the Mr. and Mrs. Stocks of Philadelphia; and the eminent Professor Edward August Kracke, PhD, Harvard, historian of the late Sung dynasty. Even nine-year-old Shirley Temple, 20th Century Fox's biggest asset, had been toodling about the town, visiting the former royal palace, reviewing the scores of naval troops recently arrived at the Schofield Parade Grounds, and taking lessons on her brand-new *ook-kay-lay-lay*.

Hawaii, like the nation that possessed it, was in recovery. Before the stock market crash in '29, twenty thousand tourists traveled to the islands each year, and not just the well-heeled; even contingents of Shriners used to arrive at the Aloha pier for their national conventions and parade through the streets of Honolulu astride camels, elephants, and on little carts drawn by water buffalo.

The return to prosperity had been slow, though. On the campaign trail for reelection in 1936, Franklin Delano Roosevelt had called out to Mainland crowds at every whistle-stop that they looked happier to him than just four years before, but in truth not everyone had fared so well. A recession was on, workers were on strike in nearly every major US industry, even on Hawaii, and in the wake of a Supreme Court decision declaring FDR's reforms unconstitutional, the thirty-second president of the United States was in Washington, hanging on to the last shreds of his New Deal.

There were certain comforts, though, and on this night in Waikiki a festive spirit held sway. Even Liliuokalani Kawananakoa, the so-called "flapper princess," enjoyed the festivities; on Wednesday she'd shown up in a fabulous white skirt and jacket and had worn her dark, bobbed hair beneath a matching, au courant white hat.

At seven on the dot the Natatorium's incandescent lamps fizzed on, and the crowd stirred. In through a center arch marched the American Legion band followed by a scrum of grunting wrestlers, after whom spotlights spun to highlight the entrance of girls from the local pineapple cannery. On the far side of the pool, on all four of the springboards, lads from local swimming clubs performed a mass precision dive, the only low-spirited moment of which was when eight-year-old Sonny Boy Meyer had the wind knocked out of him and required resuscitation.

To Race with Giants

The Firemen's Glee Club crooned a round of a cappella tunes, and then, in a stadium darkened for the event, the men donned their leather helmets and rainproof coats and reenacted the search-lit rescue of a drowning fisherman, the successful completion of which was marked with streaming skyrockets.

A well-known stuntman, the 267-pound Hard Head Kalelua, climbed to the topmost level of the diving tower and, after toying with the crowd, pretending he might not jump, let loose a great Hawaiian war cry and flung himself into the air, sending up what the papers called "a mighty geyser of a splash."

The evening's honoree joined in the revelry, competing in an old-timer's fishing contest, reeling in a twenty-five-gallon barrel of gasoline; performing a "Chinese Triple Oar" trick with his brothers, three of them piled on one another's backs; and, although it was said that his heyday was far behind him, Duke Kahanamoku, the greatest swimmer of all time, performed a 50-yard exhibition swim at the age of forty-seven and in the very same trunks he'd worn while winning gold at the Paris Games in 1924.

There was—and arguably still is—no greater icon in the sport of swimming than Duke Paoa Kahanamoku. He was the most successful athlete of his time and the harbinger of Hawaii's Golden Age of Swimming. While the precise number of Olympiads in which he participated is in some dispute—some say three and others four—he competed as an amateur for longer than any other swimmer before or after him—twenty-one years in all—and even today, in the company of latter-day saints such as Mark Spitz and Michael Phelps, Kahanamoku looms larger than they for his pioneering technique and his enduring influence upon the sport.

Historians mistakenly remember Kahanamoku *only* as the father of twentieth-century surfing—no small accomplishment itself—but Kahanamoku made his greatest contributions in the swimming pool, and it has famously been said of him that he was to swimming "what Babe Ruth was to baseball, Joe Louis to boxing, Bill Tilden to tennis, Red Grange to football, and Bobby

Jones to golf." For centuries before him, people had mucked about in the water in all sorts of ways, but when Kahanamoku came along in 1911 and whizzed past the stunned spectators at Honolulu's barnacled Alakea Slip, he changed the way that human bodies moved through H_2O.

Kahanamoku was a speed demon and an innovator. He transformed what was previously known as the Australian crawl—a low-in-the-water technique derided by critics as a keep-your-head-in-the-sand stroke—into something faster and definitively American. He introduced the world to an efficient flutter called the Kahanamoku Kick, a six-beat sequence that coordinated the arms and legs, created less drag, and even today is considered the gold standard for freestylers. Equally, if not more, impressive as a person of color, Kahanamoku—who was variously described as "copper-hued" or "velvet-bronze"—broke down racial barriers in pools across the globe, competing in the same Olympic Games in which Jim Thorpe courageously crossed the color line in track and field.

Kahanamoku was born in Waikiki on August 24, 1890, to a Hawaiian family of eight other children: David, Bernice, Bill, Sam, Kapiolani, Mari, Louis, and the baby Sargent. His own given name, "Duke," had nothing at all to do with blue bloodlines; his father was a Waikiki policeman who had become enamored with the Duke of Edinburgh after the nobleman's visit to the Sandwich Islands in 1869. Kahanamoku preferred to be called Paoa, his middle name, because it connected him more directly to his family's Hawaiian past.

In Waikiki and beyond, though, Duke Kahanamoku became de facto royalty. His athleticism and charm made him the islands' best-loved son. People invited him to civic events and elected him to office because his quiet charisma and good looks made everything that much better, and they prominently pictured him on postcards and memorialized him in as many ways as was humanly possible. By 1927, Kahanamoku was as close to godliness as a human being could be in the Territory of Hawaii, where missionaries had long frowned upon the gods.

Kahanamoku was, at the very least, a demigod: sportswriters struggled with the ways in which he was, at once, divine, human, a piece of art, or an animal. At 6 feet 2, he seemed to have descended from the heavens or to be in the act of ascending to them. Those inclined to view humankind through the lens of eugenics found Kahanamoku's forehead to be noble, his body symmetrical, his limbs chiseled; he was as finely sculpted as Michelangelo's *David*. Still, as a dark-skinned Pacific Islander, he was, for some, of a baser, wilder origin: a species lower than human. His size 13 feet were large as a tropical jacana's; his eyes were dark as a sable's; his hair was a thick black mane. Abroad in the 1920s, in the streets of Paris, where the color line was fundamentally different than it was in both Hawaii and on the American Mainland—in Europe it was a time of greater freedom for an African-American expatriate community that included Langston Hughes, for example—Kahanamoku was fetishized by women and overtaken by mobs of flappers so large that gendarmes had to clear the way for him to walk. At home in Hawaii, the combination of the things that made Duke Kahanamoku attractive everywhere else made him a symbol of the new Hawaiian brand—familiar, exotic, and beckoning.

One generation after the arrival of New England missionaries, mid-nineteenth-century Hawaii's economy was built on pineapple and sugar, but by the time Kahanamoku came on the scene, *kamaainas*—whites who had lived in Hawaii for a generation or so—realized that the islands had plenty of other assets: tourism was ultimately the most enduring source of revenue.

The early form of the Honolulu Chamber of Commerce advertised Hawaii as a heaven on earth, and when Kahanamoku was at his peak as an athlete and even beyond, his image embodied the place.

But Duke Kahanamoku was a mere mortal, and by the end of his career, the Olympic great had not produced a literal or figurative heir to take his place on the starting block or in fresh copy. Back in 1920, a Hawaiian by the name of Pua Kealoha swam behind Kahanamoku in Antwerp, winning silver in the 100-meter freestyle. Another Hawaiian, Warren Kealoha, no relation, won back-to-back gold medals in the backstroke in 1920 and 1924. Buster Crabbe, who was not a native Hawaiian but who lived in the Territory, won Olympic gold in the 400-meter freestyle in Los Angeles in 1932, and two island brothers named Maiola and Manuela Kalili grabbed silvers at the same Games in the 4x200-meter relay.

But after Los Angeles, though, history just wasn't on Hawaii's side. That year, swimmers from the Japanese Empire surprised the world by arriving on the West Coast fit, formidable, and rigorously trained, and they promptly established an empire in the swimming pool. That was bad news for all American mermen, as they were called, but it was also the start of a complete shutout for Hawaiians: while, once, the US Olympic men's swim team had carried no fewer than eight Hawaiian swimmers, by the time of Hitler's carnival in Berlin in 1936, not one islander was on the US roster.

When Kahanamoku officially retired from amateur swimming, he tried his hand at lots of things. He'd given the movies and Hollywood a shot. But where it was easy for Caucasian swim stars like Buster Crabbe to become heroic spacemen like Buck Rogers and Flash Gordon or Johnny Weissmuller to became Tarzan, King of the Jungle, Kahanamoku's roles were of a lesser sort; mostly directors had cast him as a cigar-store Indian or a native tribesman.

In the late '30s, he had most recently run for the office of sheriff in Waikiki, and he'd won, although some people wondered how real the job was and how titular. He was Waikiki's unofficial greeter, too: when cruise ships docked at the Aloha pier, he met dignitaries and celebrities and showered them with leis. He was much loved and would be all his life. Not long before, a musician had composed a ditty in his honor; a new hula had been dedicated to him; a line of aloha wear now had his name on it; local sports promoters had commissioned a sculptor to immortalize him in a statue said to cost some $15,000. And the swimming competition that August night of 1937 was named especially for him. It was the first annual Duke Kahanamoku Outdoor Swimming Meet, an event the Honolulu Junior Chamber of Commerce had invented with the intention of reviving the sport of swimming as it had been in Kahanamoku's youth.

Friday was the second and final night of the competition, although on Wednesday, the visiting team had thoroughly swamped the local talent, and as for the prospect of a new Kahanamoku, there was nothing and no one yet on the horizon. What Kahanamoku thought of the sorry state of affairs was only revealed years later in an interview he gave to columnist Dick Hyland of the *Los Angeles Times*. Kahanamoku had once famously said that out of the water, he was nothing. In the Hyland interview he said he saw no one like him in the water. Despondent, he had taken to sitting alone tossing pebbles into the surf at a beach once known as Sans Souci; in French the term meant, loosely, "without care." The new generation had become soft and lazy, he said. He didn't see a chance for a revival.

If there wasn't a chance of the restoration of Hawaiian swimming in the islands, then there was equally as little a chance for it in the literal pool in which the night's competition was to take place. The War Memorial Natatorium had once been a gleaming place, the precious pearl of Waikiki. Some ten years before, in 1927, on an evening similar to this one, Kahanamoku himself had christened the tank. That auspicious night, madmen raced through the city's narrow alleyways honking their horns and parking pellmell on the nearby polo grounds just to be in time to see Kahanamoku perform a ceremonial swim and to emerge from the new tank to pronounce it a living dream.

There was, in fact, no other pool in history like the Nat. The tank was gargantuan, double the size of an Olympic venue—100 meters long and 40 feet wide, and it had cleverly been equipped with adjustable pontoons, so it was in that sense also the most ambitious swimming pool ever constructed: it could accommodate both American-style meets, which were measured in yards, and also European and Olympic ones, marked in meters. It was meant to become a draw for swimmers around the world who would compete with the generation of Hawaiian swim champions who were certain, from that vantage point in time, to come.

Its use was to be in the glorious future, but its purpose was also to serve as a permanent remembrance of the past. It was dedicated not to swimming heroes but to heroes who had devoted themselves to the American and

European cause, a kind of living memorial to any Hawaiian who had risked life and limb in the Great War.

The planning of the place had been the likes of a drawing room farce. It had taken its steering committee—a motley assemblage of local politicians, Daughters of the American Revolution, and sundry other interest groups and concerned citizens—years to agree on its design. First it was to be nothing more than a carved stone on hallowed ground; then it grew into something monstrously disproportionate. In the end, it was built in the Beaux Arts style, with three low concrete walls and a fourth wall—a facade adorned with urns and eagles—echoing the greatness of the Roman Colosseum, and it was hailed as an architectural triumph nonpareil. From a passing steamship, tourists looked out on the Waikiki shore and easily mistook the Nat for a gleaming white, half-submerged football stadium, and locals prized the place, because it was the first public swimming pool available to them for play; social reformers saw the pool as a great advancement in what had been Hawaii's particular form of segregation: most actual pools, until that time, had been connected either to exclusive white social clubs or to the fancy hotels.

Few knew it from the beginning, but the Nat, though always grand from the stands or the vantage of an arriving steamer, and a pleasure for locals to swim in, was an engineering disaster. Its San Francisco architects had never before drawn up blueprints for a pool, and while the public adored it and people swam in it for leisure, aside from its adjustability, it was wholly unsuited to sanctioned competition. It was the first ever pool to be built directly along a shoreline, and it jutted out to sea and was fed directly by the ocean. The blueprints of the place had been romantic, but when built, it was manifestly impractical. Open to the ocean, it was only as good a place to swim as the ocean was: a rough-water venue even at its best.

Furthermore, the tank's construction had first been long delayed and then rushed and shoddy. Within less than a year from when Duke christened it, the Nat became what one later critic called "a pockmark on the countenance of paradise." Its hazards were famous, countless, and almost too far-fetched to be real. Tides buckled its walls. Seaweed clogged its state-of-the-art filtration system.

To Race with Giants

For divers it was horrible. Most notably, in 1929, one of Admiral Byrd's most intrepid companions to the North Pole thought, during a brief sojourn in Honolulu, that it was not too great a risk to dive headfirst into the tank from the pool's 30-foot-high board, but he was rewarded for his stunt with a shattered shoulder—an injury more serious than any he had experienced during his adventures on terra firma.

Swimmers had it worse than divers, though. The tide sucked them off course, waves rendering lane markers useless. Competitors raced illegally in one another's lanes and, hence, risked disqualification for tangling hopelessly in the ropes. A bed of coral with pieces sharp enough to bloody up the knuckles and toes lined even the shallow end, and the water circulated so rarely in the tank as a whole that it became a viscous stew, in which a range of creatures made their habitat and through which one had to brace oneself in competition just to reach the wall.

Schools of fish, slithery eels, and even octopuses took up residence there. So did slimy blowfish. Bales of hard-shelled sea turtles popped up when least expected. On the other hand, like clockwork, exactly nine days after the waxing of a full moon, the tank filled with blooms of stinging jellyfish, and "blue rock," the poison that was used to kill them off, was a swimmer's toxic swallow. Most discomforting of all was a sharp-toothed barracuda with the charming habit not only of following swimmers during practice laps but turning simultaneously, and menacingly, with them as they pushed off at the wall. Swimmers have famously said that they achieved their best paces and broke world records in the Nat because their sole aim while in it was to get out of it as quickly as they possibly could.

One would have supposed, then, that the locals, who knew the tank's idiosyncrasies far more intimately than its visitors, would have had an advantage in the August competition, but in fact, the San Francisco swim team had proved to be easily victorious. Wednesday night's opener had been a total bust for the Hawaiians, and Thursday had been a day of rue and reckoning. The papers offered little solace: island hopefuls merely looked like hopeless slowpokes. The only bright spots, sports reporters pointed out, were a couple of scruffy kids from Maui who'd shown some moxie, but in the novice realm. It might be years before they'd peak, and even then, anyone who knew anything about swimming and Hawaii knew those kids weren't going anywhere. They were Japanese-American, *Nisei*—and at the bottom of Hawaii's heap of immigrants. They were the children of sugar plantation workers, and their future was in the cane fields, not in the swimming pool. Why the sorry lot had even bothered to spend what little money they could scrounge for interisland steamer fare was no little source of curiosity.

For the San Francisco "Flying O's" Club—the "O" was for "Olympian"— money was no problem. They'd been paid a fortune for the junket, because they were the first solid competition from the Mainland that Hawaiian kids had seen in years. Two thousand dollars in Junior Chamber of Commerce money had filled the O's club's coffers, buying first-class steamer tickets from the California coast not only for the swimmers but for the team's manager, a retired diver, who had enough moola left over to bring the missus along for a second honeymoon.

Upon arriving, the O's coach made it more than clear that the team intended to spend little time in the water challenging the local competition. Any swimming that they'd agreed to do was, he said, "incidental." It had been "ten long, lean years" since he and the boys had tasted the "papai and poi" of the Pacific, and they intended to take full advantage of the opportunity.

Indeed, by Friday night, they had. Their races on Wednesday had been, almost without exception, cinches, and they had returned two days later looking well-fed and tanned, the first-place trophy awaiting them at the judges' stand.

The aquacade reached its climax when a professional hula dancer by the name of Girlie McShane shook her ample hips awhile, and a local wrestler named Al Karasick, a former Pavlovan ballerino, demonstrated that he was as tough as he was delicate when he pinned an opponent pronto on the deck. Then, only one competition event remained, but that last race was meaningless on the whole, a fait accompli. The event was a middle-distance one—the 400-meter freestyle—and so, confident of themselves, the Flying O's had put in a sprinter and long-distance swimmer instead of anybody with middle-distance expertise.

The San Franciscans were Dick Keating and Ralph Gilman. Keating, a reigning Pacific Coast distance champion from Stanford, had broken his own record in both the furlong and the quarter on Wednesday night; and Gilman, a collegiate star and alum of the 1936 US men's Olympic relay team with a silver medal to his name, had raced against Duke Kahanamoku's younger brother Sam in the 100-yard freestyle. Sam Kahanamoku had attempted an ill-advised middle-aged comeback and Gilman outswam him by several body lengths. In the 4x200 team relay, the same race in which he'd medaled in Berlin, Gilman had been lightning in the water, leaving the other Hawaiians in his wide, white wake.

Dick Keating was dark-haired, towering, trim, and sinewy; and Gilman was blond, a 6-foot-2-inch mountain of muscle with shoulders as big as drumsticks. He looked amiable enough when on the deck—he had warm, dark eyes and a smile that seemed to be authentic—but in the water no competitor was to be taken as a friend.

There was only one other swimmer of note against whom the Californians were set to swim the final race, and he was notable for the fact that he was a most pathetic challenger. He was a boy from Maui, fifteen or sixteen at the most, and, like others on his sorry squad, he was at least a hundred pounds lighter than either Keating or Gilman, and had a face so thin that it made his ears, which weren't in truth that large, appear as floppy as the flaps on an aviator's cap.

He wore an old-fashioned, full-bodied black woolen swimsuit, one he had either cheaply acquired or obtained as a hand-me-down from an older kid, and even dry, the suit had clearly been waterlogged so many times that its narrow shoulder straps sagged down to reveal the concave chest not of an athlete but of an invalid. The boy's fragility was tragic to a depressing degree: the curve of his spine suggested that he suffered from scoliosis, and he was as bowlegged as a weaning colt, his feet disproportionately wide, the arches flat, the spaces between his toes gaping and spread out like a geisha's fan: he had clearly spent his life to date entirely barefoot.

When he proceeded slowly to the starting block, bystanders, who over the course of the long evening had breached pool etiquette and crowded the deck and taken over the blocks as seats, parted like a wave—in sympathy—to let him through. He stood alone among the crowd and looked as though he might be better off, rather than pulling himself up onto the block, if he were to stand still and collapse instead into a pile of unremembered bones.

Practically no one at the Natatorium knew much about the kid beyond his name and that he was a nobody. He was Kiyoshi Nakama, a schoolboy from a sugar plantation, and almost all the training he had done was in an 8-foot-wide and 4-foot-deep filthy irrigation ditch that snaked through the camps in which he and his teammates lived. He and the rest of the ragged island squad didn't even have a single towel to share between them, and their coach was a fifth-grade schoolteacher who didn't know how to swim.

The story only got worse the more you knew of it.

Just a few months before, the coach had set Nakama and all the Maui kids up for failure by filling them with nonsense about the future. Back home, both he and the swimmers had paid the price: they were a laughingstock to many, and now, as if he wished to court even more derision and disaster, the coach had the hubris to put his runt swimmer in a men's event.

The boy was smaller, weaker, and lived a life more deprived than any of his teammates. The story went that his father drank the family's money up; his mother beat both the father and the kid; and when the mother was tired of doing that, she beat the family's skinny pig until, one time, the thing collapsed right where it stood, dead, still tied up to a ragged rope. Sometimes the boy was so hungry he sucked on sugarcane for strength.

In his hand the Maui coach held a shiny stopwatch with which he planned to take the measure of his swimmer's pace and, in so doing, take the measure of a plan he'd hatched. A dreamer, the teacher had become possessed not long before of an idea of grand and possibly ridiculous proportion, and the race this night would be a test of whether he'd been right or whether he'd become a laughingstock back home.

His swimmer had no experience in a pool like the Natatorium or with men who were poised beside him now, world record holders, national champions, collegiate stars, Olympians. The boy's stiffest competition had been in local races with his own teammates and minor competitions with swimmers of his age back home on Maui. Recently, the boy had acquitted himself in a 440-yard event against a Honolulu college boy, and after he had done so, a few people, including the teacher, had sat up and noticed. Whether the boy's previous success had been a sign of talent or an accident of fate was what the teacher also wished to know this night, standing on the deck, listening for the pop of the starting gun, his finger poised upon the button on his stopwatch.

Now, on their blocks, Keating and Gilman shook out their enormous arms and legs, and in imitation Nakama did the same. Keating and Gilman leaned down, and Nakama did, too, curling his toes over the edge of the block and locking his arms behind him as they did, in the pose that in those years was customary for swimmers to take before the starting gun. Across the pool, the boy's coach was watching carefully. No matter what the crowd thought of the boy now, no matter what the boy thought or doubted deeply in himself—the kid had come tonight to race with giants.

The race was over from the plunge.

All the coach could do was watch the tragedy unfold, a dark disturbance in the pool. The salty water offered nearly zero visibility, and swimming without goggles, the boy might as well have been swimming blind between the primitive wooden lane lines. In the first lap, he was far behind, trailing Gilman and Keating by four body lengths, at least. He thrashed in the water with crazy kicks, with arms spinning like wheels gone off their axle, and for every stroke that Gilman and Keating took, the kid was taking two or three in an effort that was clearly unsustainable.

Ralph Gilman reached the wall after the first 100-meter lap, and Keating was right behind. Each pushed off the pads and started up again.

Gilman tore ahead, and Keating kept up with him. Nakama arrived at the wall—eons later, it seemed—and turned awkwardly, finding when he did that the Flying O's were a quarter-lap ahead and that it might as well just be a race between the California teammates now: Keating starting to struggle a bit to keep up, but Gilman carving effortlessly through the mucky tank.

There are worse things in life than watching an athlete fail miserably, but in the world of sport it's an ugly thing that dulls the edge of fandom. Everyone knows it's no good for the soul to stay with intention to witness another person's ruin, but at the same time, like a train wreck one sees coming, it's also a sickening spectacle from which it's hard to tear oneself away. Around the coach, the crowd was preternaturally silent, and what he heard inside his head was the deafening sound of a voice declaring him a failure.

On deck stood Duke Kahanamoku, serving as a judge, and he looked on attentively, his job to find irregularities of any sort in the proceedings, though the most glaring irregularity of all was the unfortunate matchup of a boy with men to whom the first was unequal. At the third lap, though, Duke Kahanamoku watched as the skinny boy pushed off at the wall and turned, somehow lurching forward, thrashing, then miraculously pulling up behind Dick Keating. Keating, who by the 200-meter mark had become unable to sustain his pace, fell back, and bit by bit and then by a body length, the boy had pushed the Californian out of the competition.

Gilman also struggled with the pace. As Nakama advanced on him, from high up in the bleacher seats the boy's teammates called his name out. In the water Nakama inched up farther, propelled by some force it seemed impossible he could have within him. He was a skeleton, a thing of emptiness, but now he sped along the surface of the water as if inside the shell of him he secretly possessed a powerful beating heart.

At the start of the fourth lap, with 100 meters to go, the very tone of the race changed. Then, with about 45 meters to go, the top of Nakama's head was even with Gilman's heels; at 40 to go, he'd advanced to Gilman's knee; and after the 35-meter mark, when he and Gilman were head-to-head in what looked to be a dead heat in the final stretch, the kid flew forward, most improbably.

Behind him in the water, Gilman lost momentum, rubbering up. On deck, the reporters dropped their cigarettes. In the stands, the spectators rose to their feet. Nearby, the coach leaned forward, and he shouted to the boy—the boy's name, syllables of now-revived belief. And from there it was—no overstatement—just the way things happen only in storybooks and in children's dreams. Giant Ralph Gilman fell behind the boy, and the Maui kid, though coughing up water and choking on air, reached across the longest stretch of water he had ever known, and he touched the wall.

Ralph Gilman came in from behind, far enough for the win to feel decisive but near enough to witness the Maui kid begin to sink below the briny surface of the Nat, at which point Gilman leaped over and with able hands fished the kid out of the drink, holding him tightly to his chest until he could deposit him safely once again upon the deck. The kid was wrung clean of life, but his concave chest rose and fell and rose and fell, and he was smiling as his teammates, as raggedy as he, stumbled down the concrete bleachers and slid toward him across the deck, nearly falling into the pool. From the cheap seats to the grandstands the crowd whistled and hooted, and Gilman, a gent, then backed away and let the kid have his moment.

The rest of Gilman's teammates rushed to the judges' table, appearing as though they might be lunging for their prize, but instead, they grabbed the enormous trophy, carried it over to the Maui kid, and tried to give it to him. He had earned it, they said. The kid, as much a gent as Gilman was, said thanks, but no: the O's had won the whole meet fair and square. His had been just a single race of many races.

Reporters gathered all around. *How do you feel, Kiyoshi? How do you feel, kid? What a race!*

This kid was still trying to catch his breath, and beside him his coach looked on. The coach knew better, but he didn't say a word: it wasn't just a race; it was the first of many challenges still to come, and it was the first proof of what was coming. Inside the boy beat a hummingbird's heart, but the kid could use it to push himself beyond the bounds of the bony cage that he inhabited, and he could lead the other children on the team to do the same: to swim upstream and toward the future. All of this the coach now knew to be true: the signs were good.

In the gallery and on the deck, the crowd whistled, hollered, and cried out: *Holy smokes!* and *Didja see that? Now, that was something else.*

The coach was a man named Soichi Sakamoto, and, silently, he agreed. What had just happened was something else, all right. Something no one had ever seen. It was something else, Soichi Sakamoto knew. Something else. Entirely.

Chapter Two

HARDHEAD

Soichi Sakamoto was possessed of an audacity of spirit that spurred him on to an endeavor that in scope and ambition rivaled the exploits of other great men and women of his time. He was of Japanese ancestry; more clearly, he was Japanese-American, with an emphasis on the word following the hyphen. He was a man who was made of the distinctly hopeful stuff of which the poet Walt Whitman wrote, only Soichi Sakamoto was even more hopeful than the average man: in him flowed the most expansive visions.

He was a glorious amateur in the American style.

The type is found again and again in the nation's history, especially in earlier times when idealism and patriotism were the fuel for both the American and the individual project, when the seemingly impossible seemed possible by dint of labor, ingenuity, and immense patience for trial and error. Think: the Wright brothers. Think: Charles Lindbergh.

Like others' of his ilk, Soichi Sakamoto's path wasn't quite a straight one. It hadn't helped that he'd started out impatient; impatience carves rambling trails. In youth he was impulsive, and his pluck took the form of rebelliousness; in adulthood he at last discovered how to turn a reflex into reflection, and defiance into daring. But he also paid the price that genius will exact: by virtue of attending only to his dreams, he spent his lifetime disconnected from those who lived and breathed, those who loved him most and who might have served as comfort to him in times of desolation.

Even from birth he was extravagantly different from other Nisei children.

Such Stuff as Dreams

His parents were *Issei*, first-generation immigrants, and their firstborn son was everything a second-generation Japanese boy ought not to be: untethered to his heritage, irresponsible, a dreamer living amidst a world of air castles. He had been delivered to his mother, a picture bride, on Maui at a most inauspicious time: according to the zodiac, 1906 was a "Fire Horse" year, and babies born within its parentheses were not just equine—hard to bridle—they were blazes worth of trouble. Fire Horse children could suck down money, extinguish all familial joy, and drive their parents to an early grave. Soichi Sakamoto's parents tried to rein him in, but their efforts were useless, like spitting straight into a raging wind.

The elder Sakamotos presented their child with stellar role models. Soichi Sakamoto's mother had been abandoned to a Tokyo orphanage but had managed to immigrate to America and marry well. His father had fled from the lowlands of Yamaguchi prefecture at the age of eighteen, indistinguishable from thousands of other young men who boarded steamers at Yokohama harbor in 1899, lighting out for a better life in Hawaii, but he had risen quickly from a bottom rung to something nearer to the ladder's top.

The surname Sakamoto translates roughly from the Japanese as "one who lives at the lowest part of the slope," and it was right there that Tokuichi Sakamoto started out, arriving on Maui in the midst of an outbreak of the bubonic plague so virulent that authorities torched houses and stores to the ground in an effort to eradicate it, and finding his only work on a near-bankrupt plantation where diseased young men dropped dead beside him in the fields.

In short shrift, however, he became a clerk at a fancy dry goods store in the old whaling town of Lahaina. The shop was known as Hackfeld's—later it would become the renowned Liberty House—and it sold Turkish towels, parasols, and looking glasses to the cream of Maui's whites and became for Tokuichi Sakamoto his Harvard and his Yale. It was there he studied the habits and tastes of the *haole*, white, upper middle class, and sought, the best he could, to imitate them.

He grew an *en vogue* chevron mustache trimmed neatly to the corners of his mouth. He wore a Bollman homburg in the Edwardian style and a crisp white shirt, around the winged collar of which he looped a batwing bow tie;

he bought himself a sack jacket, from the lapel of which he attached a dainty pin, its little chain dangling down into his left breast pocket; and within a year or two, he opened up his own dry goods store in the dusty valley town of Waikapu, an outpost village, about which a turn-of-the-century guide-book advised travelers coming upon it not to bother to dismount from their horses, as there was nothing in the place to see.

What was there was a sugar plantation, and Tokuichi Sakamoto, whose store was rough-hewn and hand-built—little more, in fact, than a wooden barn on stilts—sold to workers and their families kerosene wicks, tinned ham, burlap sacks of rice, and pig feed. In his next store he served a slightly tonier clientele, plying paper, pens, soap, dried cuttlefish, seeds, and soda pop; and, in a demonstration of great savvy, he secured the exclusive licen-sure to peddle an expensive patent medicine popular among Asian immi-grants in Hawaii: Ninjin Homsuey was a rare Korean carrot ginseng that could—the label on its tiny brown bottle professed—cure every malady from itchy eyes to indigestion, madness, headaches, and diseases of the uterus. The sale of it made Tokuichi Sakamoto a wealthy man, and by the time his son was ten years old, he had a father who was solidly a member of the Issei bourgeoisie.

Soichi Sakamoto's parents wanted their children—there were six in all—to address the world as they had done: speaking Japanese and marrying within their own kind; but from early on their eldest son made it plainly clear to them that the rich stone soup they offered him was, while certainly nutritious, wholly tasteless to his tongue.

He was a wanderer in both mind and body, the sort of child who, stand-ing in what looked to others like the thick of the woods, appeared lost, but who insisted that he knew precisely where he was and the route by which he'd gotten there. He was never the kind to head straight home from school on the same road as others, and he was distracted by—he would have said *drawn to*—whatever near him served to intrigue him. He sat for long hours at hidden streams in observation of the locomotion of mosquito fish, the slithering of native snails in single file along a narrow riverbed, and how it took a whole afternoon for an 'Ōpae kala'ole, a freshwater crab, to ascend undauntedly a cascade.

25

Such Stuff as Dreams

His attendance to and interest in the natural world was something he wouldn't share with others. He liked hiking, but always solo, and even when his parents insisted that he join the Boy Scouts—something that most middle-class Japanese-American boys did—he far preferred earning the badges that required of him intense and solitary work.

Whatever he felt, he learned to keep such things inside, for fear of mockery and condemnation, and throughout his life he remained tight-lipped, rarely speaking of himself at all but only, when he was so moved to, of the ideas that felt as though they might otherwise burst out of him at the seams. He wanted to be an explorer, say, or an inventor, or the president, and his mother, in particular, found his ideas odious and scolded him for building an imaginary world of what she said were air castles.

Castles in the air: that is what indeed occupied his mind, although as he grew a little older he learned to share less and less of what they looked like to him. He became ever more intentionally inscrutable, protective of his interior life, and he was largely friendless; most people found him puzzling, others simply irksome.

His parents could attempt to part his hair neatly to one side and dress him in a shirt and tie for Christian church or Japanese school, but even then, he'd cant his loose-limbed body far away from them and wear a scowl, as if everything in his proximity disinterested or, even worse, sourly disappointed him.

Most things likely did. His ideas, he was sure, were too important to be contained on a dot of an island in the South Pacific, far from the excitement of a life he imagined he'd find elsewhere. He'd never traveled, though he read and traveled widely in the pages of his books.

He believed that he was destined for a more important life, one brimming with excitement and imbued with meaning, and he was solidly confirmed in this belief when at the age of twelve, he nearly died. He'd been riding his bicycle outside his father's shop on an ordinary day when a police truck struck him squarely from behind and felled him and his bike and tossed him in the dirt. He lay there, ribs shattered, lung punctured, bleeding, and the crowd that gathered round him took him for dead, until someone detected a faint pulse. He was as good as dead, though, and at first, at the hospital, the doctors couldn't stanch the bleeding, and then they did, and while his recovery felt endless—he missed months and months of school—the incident changed him positively—at least from his own unshared point of view—because he was certain he'd been saved from death by police truck to live a life of higher purpose. Just what that purpose was to be, he didn't know, but the journey was his own, his life's work ahead of him. He thrilled at the idea, and he became ever after a perspicuous lookout for his own particular destiny.

For some time, he thought that his destiny was music. He could pick up any instrument and teach himself to play it: wood or string, brass, the saxophone, the violin, the steel guitar. He had an ear for composition, perfect pitch, and his singing voice was lovely. After his accident, he started sneaking out at night to play music with a little band he'd formed.

His music drove his mother to distraction. She was a woman of pinched soul, her face enigmatically scarred, perhaps from abuse she'd suffered in childhood. She was orderly and strict, and she had a nose for misbehavior. Whenever Sakamoto thought he'd found the perfect hiding place for a new instrument, his mother always sniffed it out, smashed it into shards, and burned it to ashes right in front of him.

In school Sakamoto's grades were lackluster; in athletics he excelled in nothing, running only once a forgettable mile. His next youngest brother, named Takeo, was, by comparison, a model citizen. Give Takeo—also fondly known as "Bill"—a bit of balsa wood, and he could build a model airplane that could float in breezeless weather. Put a camera in Bill's hands, and he would take pictures with it that won cash prizes from the Eastman Kodak Company in New York. Bill had been born in the year of the Rooster, after all, and roosters were reliable: without fail, they showed up and crowed at every dawn, announcing morning and driving evil spirits off each day.

The spirits Bill could not ward off were those that inhabited the souls of his older and his younger brothers. Benzo Sakamoto showed early on the signs of dissipation that Soichi did; he preferred billiards and bowling to just about anything else, and the motto by which he lived, and which he quoted often, was the one that starts: "Eat, drink, and be merry, for…" Only time would tell.

As for Soichi Sakamoto, though, time was up. In his senior year at Maui High, he took ill—he never revealed later what it had been, but he was bedridden once again, just as he'd been at the age of twelve, only this time he didn't arise from his sickbed feeling so exceptional. When he returned at last to classes, he nearly failed each one, and he terrified his parents when he nearly didn't graduate.

He had slipped into a slough, they thought, of moral turpitude, and the situation was untenable. The only solution remaining was to pack the boy's trunk and send him off to the Territorial Normal School. He would become, they had decided, if nothing better, then at least a teacher.

Unsurprisingly, however, far away from his parents on Oahu, Sakamoto only continued to go astray. He loathed the idea of teaching just as much as his parents believed it the perfect way to bind him to the ordinary. He bristled at becoming a Normal School "cadet," as students there were called, and he loathed the idea of going back to Maui, where he was to be sent eventually to teach children how to spend their cheerless lives forever on that island, too.

In truth, the curriculum at the school was advanced, even radical for its time: its philosophy was shaped by the ideas of the progressive age, but Sakamoto paid little attention to what was taught, salting away only this bit and that bit, but sure that nothing would prove useful. He despised anything that smacked of usefulness.

Instead, he played his music, and he taught himself to speak Hawaiian. He grew his dark hair long, greasing it off his forehead and slicking it behind his ears in the manner of a movie star. He endeavored to grow a mustache, achieving, alas, only a wispy approximation of the film star Errol Flynn's, and he took to dressing in a dark suit and a polka-dotted bow tie. The total effect of this was that by the time he finished his studies, he little resembled a teacher but looked more like the bandleader of a hotel orchestra.

Hardhead

As often as he could he ran off to Honolulu for the thrill of it. It was the Jazz Age, after all, and Waikiki was roaring.

Sophisticated men and women who'd grown tired of Newport or Palm Beach were spending "a season" in Waikiki. There, visitors could "go native" and still enjoy the comforts of home: white-gloved bellboys, ice sculptures in the shape of swans, caviar, and telephones in every room. During the day they could bake in the sun and marvel at the antics and impromptu performances of the local beachboys—men like John "Hawkshaw" Paia, who rode his giant redwood surfboard into shore while sitting in a chair and strumming on a ukulele—while in the evening, they could dance to big band sounds and do the jitterbug and Lindy.

Sakamoto was drawn to the place where all things glittering and of the Mainland met all things Hawaiian.

He loved the *hapa haole* sound of that period—a mix of ukulele, jazz, and ragtime played by beachboys on the piers of Waikiki—and he played it in juke joints and on the radio, becoming, according to those who knew him, the most Hawaiian-American Japanese anyone had ever encountered.

In the formal photograph of him at his college graduation in the year of 1927—the picture grimly taken in a gaping field of weeds—Soichi Sakamoto appears, perhaps as he intended, perfectly out of place. While the other young men of his class are dressed in tweed and wearing wire spectacles, and the young women stand in dusty Mary Janes and in dresses with decidedly un-flapper-like hemlines, Sakamoto sits at the far end of the group. He is slumped forward, his legs spread wide, with one shiny shoe pointed like a compass needle toward something clearly beyond the boundaries of the place and of the picture frame, and on his face an expression suggesting that he alone is in possession of a cosmic joke.

At home again, living under his parents' watchful supervision and their roof, Soichi Sakamoto discovered, however, that the joke was at his own expense. During his years on Oahu, he had become a spirit too expansive to live in such confinement, and, worse, there looked to be no escape at all. Upon graduation he was assigned to teach precisely where he dreaded most being posted: in the rural town of Haiku, on Maui, where the conditions were the dreariest he'd ever seen. The school was thatch-roofed, the half-clothed children barely able to speak or write in English, and instead of inspiring him to help them, the children's situation served only to depress Sakamoto even more. After a year, he managed to wrangle a reassignment to another rural school, although it was better only by degrees. It was situated in the very heart of Maui's largest and most modern plantation, Hawaii Commercial & Sugar, and the children who attended the school lived inescapable lives there. This was Pu'unene Plantation.

The plantation was a closed circuit. To get in or out one had to sign one's name, and if one lived there, one had always to return. Children lived with their families in segregated work camps adjacent to the fields of cane; their parents were supervised by *lunas*, or bosses, well-equipped with tempers and with whips; and the wages that the fieldworkers earned were never enough for even the most enterprising person to grow a nest egg in a bank account; just feeding one's family put most men deeper and deeper in debt each month: in time a family of four could owe the plantation as much as $5,000, a fortune and a noose around the neck.

The conditions were as close as one could get to slavery, worse than sharecropping: workers, who wore heavy denim from head to toe or plaid cotton shirts to protect themselves from the sun, the slash of cane, and the bite of centipedes, hoed the soil and cut the seedlings, did all the work there was to do by hand. There were jobs like driving trucks, oiling the machinery, or cleaning out the green waste after cane had been spun out at the mill, but no matter what kind of work one did, if a person was too ill to go to work in the morning, the camp police stomped into his house unceremoniously, across the clean tatami mats, with horse manure stuck in thick clots on their boots, and hauled the sick man back to the gang, convinced that he was faking.

Hardhead

Every camp kid had a nickname: A speedy runner was "Cyclone." A kid with long pins was "Legs." One with any meat on him was "Fat," "Fats," or "Lardy." A boy who couldn't keep his eyes off girls was "Romeo." There was "Poison," "Pepper," "Leech," "Johnny-Suka-Thumb," "Moocha," "Gandhi," "Hippo," "Whitey," "Zuke," and "Futbag." "Chow" Shibuya ate like crazy. "Dynamite" Nakasone was an eccentric personality.

Some kids got their names from picture shows: "Iron" Maehara got his from *The Iron Claw*; "Alfalfa" came straight out of *Our Gang*. There was a "Tonto," a "Dillinger," a "Happy," a "Slumpy," and a "Snuff." Serious-minded kids took English names like Warren or Fred. A nickname arose from a child's character, and sometimes it served to determine his fate.

The camps had nicknames, too: Pump Camp, Stable Camp, Dairy, Green, and Hospital. Some names came from the camp's function and from the immigrants who had once lived there. Workers had come to Puʻunene in waves, first the Portuguese, next the Spanish, then the Chinese, so the names were Portuguese Camp, Sam Sing, Ah Fong, and Pake Camp; another, Alabama, had been named for the freed slaves who'd come to Maui from the Southern United States after emancipation—men who had the life experience and good sense to figure out in little time that that plantation work on Maui was more onerous and unjust than sharecropping they had known at home, and who'd up and left for better pastures.

By the late 1920s and '30s the plantations were peopled with the workers who had most recently arrived—the Japanese and Filipinos—who lived in camps that hadn't been changed for them, in rows and clusters of ticky-tacky houses that sat no more than five or ten feet apart from another and that faced each other precisely across a dusty road and whose front doors were always open to the weather and to one another.

The shacks were squat and squarish and each was built on skinny stilts atop a grassless footprint, each painted in earth tones, mostly green and brown, and constructed of one panel of clapboard, with no flashing, no butt joints, and no insulation, so that the humidity warped each shack so it bulged here and there, opening at the seams.

Shacks brimmed over with mothers and fathers and grandfathers and six or ten or twelve children, and maybe a nephew or two who'd just come from Japan looking for work. Three or four skinny sisters shared a tatami mat. Boys, more precious in Asian families, slept in beds. For better or for worse, all the life in one cramped house spilled over into the next.

Camp people said that in the camp, you're so close to each other in the shacks that "you nevah alone." Not ever. Neighbors sensed the moment when a heart next door was on the verge of breaking or a marriage down the row was on the road to spoil. They smelled each other's canned sardines and corned beef cabbage, their *nawa fu*—dough baked on a rope—and their pickled turnips and long white radishes at the beginning of each month, and at the end of the month, when they smelled nothing, they had nothing, too.

Chicken pox and fevers ran through house after house and then traveled row by row. This man had blisters on his lips? That man over there had blisters, too. This kid had lice? That kid and that kid and that other one would have to shave his head.

Break a bone? The next-door carpenter will set it.

A man was sick from sex he paid for? Camp people knew the cure for it was to boil up sweet potato leaves and have him drink the broth until his *shishi* turned to *green*. To calm that bad man's crying wife, you brought her soup and sat with her and made her eat it.

Almost every family kept a chicken coop, birds caged beneath the floor, or a goat tied up for milk. Inside, everybody had the larder built of hand-hewn shelves encased in chicken wire, the whole thing on high legs, the foot of each immersed in a tin can filled with water: it kept the bugs from climbing up. And every four houses shared a *furo*—a bath—and an outhouse with two *pukas*—holes, at the bottom of which rats skittered.

Camp families shared a common hose bib that gummed up with guppies that they strained through burlap Bull Durham bags. There were fish bones, sticks, and rocks, as well, and refuse, because the families also used the ditches for their garbage, and on some days, when they were lucky, the tap ran clear, though on others it was dirty *pilau* water or cat or dog or garbage soup.

Camp was loud; with the houses so close to one another, everyone heard everybody's grandfather's midnight raving and everybody's auntie's sneeze and then her blow and sniff. Outside, on the road that Soichi Sakamoto took to work each day from Waikapu, missing babies, crying, wandered barefoot in their diapers. Mothers were up late at night doing single men's laundry for extra cash, stirring a giant pot called a *tirau*. Day and night the sugar mill never stopped grinding, rolling, boiling cane, spinning cane: the sounds invaded even sleep. Cane chugged in loudly from the fields on nine different sets of tracks; "The Mighty #8" train, with its hundred cars or more, took forever to chug in. The wake-up-the-workers whistle was at 5 a.m. At noon, order-takers from the shops rolled in on bikes and rang their bells, *chirin-chirin, karan-karan-karan*. They were slick and handed out cigars and joked too loud and thumped around the camp with tubs of soy and oil. From the porch of the plantation store, a radio blared news and music all the time, so there was nothing anyone could do but shrug when a poor guy who worked the night shift flung his window open wide and cried during the day: "Hey, quiet! This man no can sleep!"

But that's how it was, the children said. Because in camp, "you nevah alone."

People who were trying to get to sleep in one house were no different, really, than the people awake in the next one. People steaming in the furo and washing off the day's dirt were no different than the family up the row fighting over the last one of the Vienna sausages left in a tin. On Tencho-setsu, the emperor's birthday, every grandfather and grandmother lined up and handed every child an apple, an orange, or a little bag of candy. When there was sumo wrestling or Bon drumming, everyone came to watch, and when anybody had an extra coin, they got some of Mr. Kobayashi's Kitch'n Cooked potato chips, fresh from the vat. If someone died, the whole camp mourned. If someone married, the whole camp pooled its change to buy a hundred-pound sack of rice for the bride and groom and deliver it to their door with ceremony.

Every road in Pu'unene was red dirt, and during every rainstorm those roads were muddy rivers full of potholes that people had to cross again and again to get wherever they were—or weren't—going.

In camp, the kids did "all kine tings." All kinds of things. And when they played they spoke pidgin. "Peepo" was "people." "Dat" was "that." "Tink" was "think." "Ting" was "thing." *Dat kine ting.*

From the road the children gathered gravel and played pebble marbles in the dirt. From the elephant pod trees, they took seeds and made them into gambling money. They sawed old broomsticks into thirds and played Piowee: the first third of the stick they stuck into the ground, the second they stuck into a hole carved in the first one, and the last part they used to whack the first two, so stick #1 went flying into the air as far as they could make it go.

Every day, they made something out of nothing. From the branches of the monkeypod trees, they made slingshots and shot at birds. From bamboo and cane they built stilts and stumbled all around. From empty thread spools, string, and some rubber and a chopstick, they made yo-yos that wound up and down just fine. There was hide-and-seek and Indians and cowboys to play. There was filching guavas from the bosses' orchards, and jumping on the trains to steal burnt cane. When they got some cane, they broke the stalks in half, sucked the juice right out, and jawed the splintery chaw. Girls played "hopscotches," as they called it, and toss-the-beanbag.

And the boys, when bored, took up a game that they called Hardhead.

Hardhead was like cock fighting, only there were no razors and there was no blood and no one died, although it hurt like hell. They gathered in a circle somewhere out of sight of all their mothers, and two at a time they came to the center and knocked their heads together, hard, until one kid gave up or got conked out cold.

It went on like that for hours, noggin hitting noggin, until there was just one kid—the best—left standing. Concussed and bruised and seeing stars, he was the one and only Hardhead. And in the camps, being Hardhead was almost as good as being king.

New England missionaries had come to the Valley Isle a century earlier to convert souls to Christianity, but their children and their children's children—with family names like Castle, Cooke, Alexander, and Baldwin—converted something else: they turned the island's soil into a fortune by growing sugarcane on it.

On Maui sugar was king, and it was a hungry and thirsty crop: it took an entire year of labor on one acre and a thousand gallons of water for that acre to produce a single pound of it, but the only place to grow fields of cane on Maui was in the arid valley flatland, where the rainfall was just six inches each year. Families like the Castles and the Cookes and the Alexanders and the Baldwins dreamed up an ingenious way to bring the water down from the mountains: a network of irrigation canals, called ditches, ran from the rain forests and traveled, with the aid of flumes and pipes and tunnels, hundreds of feet downstream to reservoirs with gates and valves.

In Pu'unene, the ditches—hundreds of branches of them, some lined with concrete, some with mud bottoms—were everywhere, snaking around and through the workers' camps, sometimes right by the family shacks. Pu'unene was nowhere near the ocean—a good day's walk and back—there was no pool in Pu'unene but the haoles' pool; and the ditches were the domain of the sugar and the mill. They were strictly forbidden for camp kids; they were, in fact, ridiculously dangerous; their current swift, they could carry dead cows and pigs and chickens, dogs and rats, red soil, sticks, branches, cane leaves, a worker's spade, a scythe, a bolo knife all the way downstream; and camp bosses all too often found the lifeless bodies of children near the intake of the sugar mill.

Still, they were impossible to resist. The children snuck beyond the barbed-wire fence around the trenches, threw off all their clothes, and played until the luna, whip in hand, would chase them out and lash the ones he caught and deliver brutal punishment, but then, when the punishment was over and the luna disappeared, the best place to go was still back into the ditch again.

After teaching at Pu'unene for several months, Soichi Sakamoto was still wretched. His colleagues found him sullen, difficult. He lived at home, under his parents' roof and watchful eye. By Christmas of 1928 he felt himself adrift, desperate for anything to come along to give him meaning. School was out; one night during the holidays he had a job to play music at a wedding. His parents were away in Japan on a business trip, and both their absence and the chance to play some music were welcome things, but the night turned out to be disastrous. The band was supposed to be a quartet, but only Sakamoto and one other musician showed, and though the two of them tried their best to liven up the party, the night was over early, and Sakamoto drove, miserable, toward home.

In Kahului, a harbor town not far from Wailuku, a building was lit up and, instinctually, he drove toward it. From outside he heard music, and when he peered in the door, he found a hall of revelers. Shy with girls and a dead-hoofer dancer, he thought to leave, but across the room, he saw one he had seen years before, when his parents had made him work a summer in a pineapple cannery, sticking label after label onto tin cans; another time he saw her walking on the roadside with a group of friends.

She was Hawaiian through and through, her hair a mass of dark, shining ringlets. Her name was Mary Kalaaupa Po'o pa'a, and she was thin but ample-hipped and had a soft face, full violin-shaped lips, and dark onyx eyes that appeared impenetrable and that suggested to him a toughness in the girl, a fortitude and self-reliance that he was certain made her admirable. Indeed, she worked and earned a living wage and at something rather technical: she was an operator at the newfangled Wailuku telephone exchange.

Her job suggested that she had at least a technical education. And her family, for a Hawaiian one, was successful: her father was an overseer at a plantation. Her large family of brothers made her comfortable with men, but not too much so. She saw them, it was clear, in a brotherly way.

They waltzed. He wasn't good at it, but she danced beautifully.

Yes, she told him, she *did* love music; yes, she loved to sing, she said, and she played the ukulele.

He played as well, and the steel guitar, he offered.

And *he* spoke Hawaiian? How unusual. She spoke Japanese. How funny.

As much as he had been searching the world for a sign of his life's purpose, he realized he had been as much in search of someone who would help him to find it. He knew instantly now that this girl, Mary Kalaaupa Poʻo paʻa, was the one to help guide him, and in spite of the fact that she demurred when he asked to drive her home that evening, saying that she couldn't possibly allow it—she had come down from Paia with someone else—Soichi Sakamoto told her with a firmness of mind he had never before experienced that only he would be taking her home that evening. He felt certain that his insistence wasn't born of a child's tantrum or an instance of adolescent entitlement—behaviors of which, before now, he honestly would have been accused. Instead, he knew that his brazenness was because now, something greater than he—it might be god; it might be fate—spoke through him, and he stood at the start of a road on which he knew he'd find his life's path.

Soichi Sakamoto drove Mary Kalaaupa Poʻo paʻa home to Paia that night, and just three days later they were married.

In their wedding picture, taken in a local photographer's studio, they look drunk with love, their eyes glazed. Perhaps sensing the modernity of their union—Japanese with Hawaiian—the photographer posed them most unconventionally. Sakamoto, the dreamy-looking groom, is just a few inches behind Mary's right shoulder. He's dressed in his bandleader's suit, his white shirt, and his crisp bow tie. Mary is in white as well, a modestly ruffled but in no way old-fashioned blouse that is sleeveless and that reveals the smoothness and darkness of the skin of her arms.

There is something odd, though, about the pose: their heads are touching, and they are leaning slightly inward toward each other, but when the camera flashed and puffed, it caught Sakamoto looking toward the right, as if to some mesmerizing vanishing point far beyond the room; in turn Mary faces outward, but toward the left, the gaze of her onyx eyes strangely flat. While her husband looks contented, the way one might after lovemaking, Mary appears to slump ever so slightly, her shoulders forward, her face, though almost imperceptibly so, remarkable for its suggestion of her disappointment.

Outside the photograph, in life, Sakamoto and Mary seemed an aberrant—but exuberant—couple. In the few weeks they had together before Sakamoto's parents returned from their business trip to Japan, the differences in the couple's origins, the clash of their cultures and the boldness of their union, drew stares and raised eyebrows, but they seemed not at all to mind.

They had taken up residence in his parents' house, in Sakamoto's own room, and on the night of his parents' arrival they hid there silently and waited, saying nothing even when his parents entered the house. Maybe morning would be better to deliver news of the sort he had to tell. Only when his parents had retired to bed did Sakamoto, with Mary in tow, knock upon their closed door, waking them.

He introduced his parents to his bride, on whose finger was a $14 wedding ring he'd bought for her. His parents, aghast, said literally nothing. A Hawaiian girl; it was unthinkable. Their Fire Horse son might as well have drowned himself; at least he would have snuffed out the flames that he now fanned around the family, a conflagration they were certain would ruin the Sakamoto name at last.

Days passed, months, and still they remained mostly silent, but by the fall of 1929, when Mary gave birth to a baby, Raymond, Sakamoto's parents made one last attempt to turn their son around. If he would like, they would pay for Soichi—without his wife and son—to spend the summer in Japan.

Sakamoto thought of himself as a proper husband now; he and Mary and the baby moved to their own rented house in Wailuku, a declaration of their independence, but the offer of the trip was too good for Soichi Sakamoto to refuse. The journey was sponsored by the Maui Boy Scouts; his brothers, Bill and Benzo, both Scouts—and some twenty-eight other young men— would go, but in order to qualify, Sakamoto, now twenty-four, would have to earn the rank of Eagle Scout, and he would have to do so in just a few months' time. Earlier in life, he would have balked at the requirement, but now, buoyed by his confidence since his marriage to Mary, took on the challenge with the certainty he'd master all of it.

The Edgar Guest poem "Equipment" appeared in the first pages of the 1927 *Revised Handbook for Boys*. "Figure it out yourself, my lad," and the reassurance that one only needed arms and legs to achieve one's goal, must have spoken to Sakamoto's independent spirit, and with gusto he completed nearly all of the badges: tying knots like the sheet bend, the reef, and the fisherman; learning Morse code, semaphore, and Indian signs; blacksmithing; and studying animals in their natural habitats.

One badge, though, eluded him; it was in swimming, and by spring of 1930 he had yet to earn it. He took Mary and the baby up into the hills to Iao Valley, where there was a stream that fed a muddy Boy Scout pool; he had Mary draw a furo for him every night, but even in it, trying to float, he merely flailed and floundered, and then he sank. Water simply wasn't his element. The exam involved both swimming *and* lifesaving, the latter itself a challenge since he could barely save his own. He was required to jump into the water in his uniform, remove his clothes and shoes and hat, and then swim a competent 100 yards, roughly four laps, to show that he had in him a Scout's endurance.

Not long before the ship was set to sail for Nippon, Sakamoto ventured at last to take the dreaded test, diving into the pool, struggling with his shirt and pants, and managing barely with a sidestroke to make it across. When the examiner congratulated Sakamoto for passing, if barely, he thanked him for the most tragic and pathetic performance he had ever seen.

Chapter Three

A WIDE AWAKENING

On July 5, 1930, Hidejiro Nagata stood in Hibaya Park, in sight of the Imperial Palace and on the grounds of the feudal shoguns. He was, as he had been since May, overjoyed. He always felt as buoyant whenever he prepared for the arrival of guests from far away, and in his second term in office as mayor of Tokyo, when he'd seen his city rise again, he loved any opportunity to celebrate it and promote it. He had also lately become inspired by ideas of the city's future.

Hidejiro Nagata was tall and lean, with the physique of an athlete, and though he wasn't made for sport, he adored it almost as much as he loved his city. A photo taken for *Time* magazine revealed him in the act of sending the first ceremonial toss in a baseball game from a pitcher's mound. In the picture he is dressed in a black silk top hat, and he is leaning forward, having just released the ball, his arm in the midst of a follow-through, his pleasure at the act most unmistakable in his wide smile. In the summer of 1930, he was fifty-nine. He wasn't quite a handsome man—he was nearsighted and his smile jutted out into a prodigious overbite, but it was the latter that made him most appealing to anyone he met.

In past years, he'd had few occasions during which to show his teeth. He'd endured, along with his country, the worst of times, and he'd had too many occasions for grief and mournfulness. His first term as mayor had been defined by tragedy: he had barely been sworn in when, on a Saturday at noon, September 1, 1923, the worst earthquake in the history of the Empire had leveled Tokyo, Yokohama, and every village and community within thousands of miles of each. The quake had been forceful enough to toss a grown man into the air, but somehow Nagata had escaped injury.

In all, though, 140,000 people died, the first in buildings that pancaked immediately on top of them; the second swept away by a tsunami that had followed hard upon the great tremor, and the third in a pillar of fire that consumed everything it found in its freakish path.

Tokyo was gone. A pile of rubble, ash, the smoke of fires, even after months, still rising from the ruins. Mobs had taken over the city, gangs in the streets torched what little there was left of shops and homes, sowing even more fear among the people, who worried that the government, too, might fall.

Hidejiro Nagata had looked around at the devastation. All of the city's infrastructure was gone, every bit of railroad track twisted, tumbled, wrenched from the earth; every office building, every bank, every water tank and electric plant fallen to the ground; every telephone line severed; and fields that once had fed the city were covered now in rotted fruits and vegetables the once-good earth had spat up from a place even deeper than the roots. For weeks there was no silence in the night, just the sobbing and the shrieking of the injured and grieving.

Nagata traveled where he could, finding most roads impassable, but offering condolences in every corner of the city and the villages nearby. The city was unfixable, and he found himself confounded by the idea that it would ever rise again. The thought was merely unimaginable. He was, however, a career civil servant, and he'd always been proud to do whatever was required of him in whatever position he had held, low or high: he had been a high school principal; he had headed the Kyoto Prefectural Department of Police; and once, for a seven-month term, he had served as governor of Mie Prefecture. In the winter of 1923, he set out to learn what must be done and how, if ever, it could be accomplished.

He'd met with engineers and architects; he'd become familiar with blue-prints and with the qualities and relative merits of different kinds of mortar and stone and how to rebuild the city to withstand such disasters. He'd become aware of the challenges of delivering water to the people, of laying pipes again, of laying track, of building streets. Inspired, Nagata wrote a book called *Return to the Spirit of the Founding of the Japanese State*, and in it was a history of the Empire and Nagata's hopes for the role that Tokyo would play in the glorious nation's future.

Hidejiro Nagata was too humble a man ever to admit his role in the restoration of the city, but standing in Hibaya Park in July of 1930, one needn't cast one's eyes far to see his handiwork. The entire city had had to be remapped, and the effort, just to rebuild public services and spaces, had cost 700,000,000 yen—the equivalent of 350,000,000 American dollars. That amount had paid for the renovated Meiji pools and the rebuilt shrines, and a city even better than it used to be: with highways, canals, efficient power plants, bridges, brand-new schools, a railway system that functioned to perfection, and in the newly asphalted streets of Tokyo, a charming set of trolleys that ran all hours of the day and night. It had cost billions more to construct new office buildings, shops, and homes, and it would cost another 15,000,000 yen to rebuild the still-fallen parliament building.

In May, just two months before, Nagata had hailed the city's rebirth with a magnificent celebration called the Reconstruction Festival, a fete the likes of which the people of Japan had never witnessed. For three days, all of Tokyo cheered the city's rise from ruin. Through the streets rolled the bright new trolleys, covered in origami flowers and filled with revelers who flocked in the day to rallies and other gatherings, and who, in the night, paraded down the wide new sidewalks and thoroughfares in happy groups to attend musical recitals, plays, and festive, bounteous banquets. Everywhere one looked during the festival, lanterns lit the city's freshly paved walking paths, and in the air when one stopped to listen was the refrain from the lilting song Hidejiro Nagata had commissioned to be composed to mark the august occasion.

It was a breathtaking festival, but more astounding than any part of the celebration was the presence in public of the new Showa emperor, Hirohito, who swept through Tokyo in an entourage of sleek black limousines, stopping here and there at appointed sites throughout the city, emerging from the automobile with the ease, it seemed, of an ordinary man on daily errands. No emperor had ever appeared so broadly before the public, if at all; none had ever come out of the sovereign's religious and physical seclusion. It was unheard of, in fact: until now, the emperor was a heavenly being whose feet ought not touch the earth, whose voice commoners ought not hear, and whose face ought never be seen.

In May, however, the emperor inspected the changes to the Imperial capital, his route totaling more than thirty miles, and everywhere he stopped, he spoke not with, but to, the common people in formal and stirring speeches, praised the reconstruction effort, congratulating those behind it and offering to the entire endeavor his worship and his blessing. It was, in fact, the emperor's appearance, his speech, his face, his goodwill at the festival that had put Hidejiro Nagata in mind of something else—and far more extraordinary, perhaps—that he could do for both Tokyo and the Empire itself. If the city was capable of bringing the emperor to the people, then there was nothing that Tokyo couldn't do for all of Japan.

In 1930, Japan was an isolated and distant country from the West. It also bore the weight of great mistrust and had failed to attend to careful diplomacy in years. Nineteen thirty marked a treaty-less period between it and other nations, and the world, including President Roosevelt in Washington, had become jittery and certain of conflicts to come. Hidejiro Nagata was among those in the government who felt Japan was misunderstood, unknown; the Empire of the Sun was still far too exotic to Westerners, too far for tourists to visit; each year fewer than fifteen thousand made the trip, and if that could change, then the perception of the country would change as well.

Not long before the reconstruction, Japanese necromancers had, through consulting calendars and performing magic, determined that the year 1940 would mark the 2,600th anniversary of the founding of the Japanese Empire, and the rise of the first emperor, Jiju. With the success of the May festival, it became ever clear that the city of Tokyo could host in 1940 an even grander celebration of the *kigen*, anniversary. It would be an occasion to celebrate the glorious past and speak loudly of the Empire's strength, but Hidejiro Nagata's idea was to take the 1940 celebration even further: simultaneous with the anniversary, Tokyo could host the Twelfth Olympiad, and demonstrate not just to itself but to the world the millions of miles it had traveled into modernity. To this idea Nagata had awakened, and it was this idea that was very much on his mind in the summer of 1930.

To some, ten years hence might have seemed far away, but Nagata had read about the Games and learned how far in advance a nation must plan and make its bid, and he'd quietly begun the work at once. Japan had never hosted an Olympiad; neither had it ever been a great part of the Games. It had come later than most countries to the movement of the modern Games begun by Pierre de Frédy, Baron de Coubertin.

Until 1912, only Europeans, Australians, and athletes from the Americas had participated, but in that year, to Stockholm Japan had sent two athletes, one a runner, the other a swimmer, and though those athletes' performances had been lackluster, it had been, if not a great one, then at least a start. Japan had yet to begin a thorough national program for physical education; the nation was eons behind others in all sports but the martial arts. At Stockholm the Japanese swimmer had been received with arrogance, as snarky commentators described him as employing a ridiculous and out-of-fashion sidestroke.

By Antwerp in 1920, though, before Hidejiro Nagata had taken office, the Japanese delegation grew to 15 athletes, and in spite of the devastation at home in the earthquake of 1923, in 1924 Japan had been able to send 4 more delegates and athletes to Paris, for a total of 19. In 1928, there were 43 athletes and coaches, and it was there, in Amsterdam, that Western nations began to notice the presence of the Japanese Empire and its growing strength in athletics, especially in the sport of swimming.

The next Olympiad was a mere two years hence, in Los Angeles in 1932, and it was Nagata's hope in the meantime to create enthusiasm for Tokyo's 1940 bid. It would likely take until just before the 1936 Games for the candidature, as it was called, to be secured. Tokyo would be competing with the likes of Alexandria, Barcelona, Helsinki, and Rome.

He had traveled abroad before but had no plans to do so in the immediate future, so he discreetly approached a friend of some political standing and asked him to sound out popular opinion of Nagata's proposal. The man left in June and was to return sometime in December, during which time Nagata sent him to take the temperature of every possible Japanese consul as well as the mayors of major European cities.

It was that man's return that Nagata awaited in July of 1930, and it was the hope of hosting such a grand event for foreigners in which Hidejiro Nagata was most invested; he had come to make it a habit to personally greet every delegation of foreigners arriving in his city, and in so doing to show them both the warmth of his and others' welcome and the grandeur of which the new Tokyo was capable.

The day's visitors were Scouts from the American Territory of Hawaii. Most were from the island of Maui, a rather small and backward place, but Nagata had determined ever since he knew that the group was coming to treat them like the finest ambassadors from any other place.

In advance of the visit, he had made sure that someone high in the government wrote to the group, to ask personally about each lad, to offer them all special rates on Japan's newest trains and rooms in its gleaming and most comfortable hotels. He had ensured that, everywhere they were to visit, they would be entertained and feted at banquets, and he had even bent a rule for one of the boys who asked if he could bring his gun with him and do some hunting for some specimens to take back home. *Anything*, Nagata thought. Anything that helped. He had awoken to Tokyo's great possibilities, and whatever he could do to more widely awaken the world to the same, he would endeavor to do.

He was now dressed in khaki knee pants, kneesocks, and a felt Stetson, in the habit of the Scouts, and beside him stood counts and viscounts and other dignitaries he had commandeered to greet the group with him and an enthusiastic crowd of hundreds of others, including troop after troop of Scouts as well, Japanese Scouts, awaiting the arrival of their American counterparts. All stood on the grassy grounds that, before the Showa Empire had begun, had served as the ground of the feudal lords of the former shogunate.

When the visitors arrived, young boys and young men and an older chaperone or two, the American Scouts marched in two neat lines toward

Hidejiro Nagata, the Japanese Scouts, and the horde of dignitaries. As they came forward, Nagata signaled for a band to play, and as the group drew even nearer, he raised two fingers to his forehead in the traditional Boy Scout salute.

There was much more fanfare: the ceremonial raising of both the American and the Japanese standards, side by side, on specially erected poles. There was the ceremonial exchange of gifts and speeches. Nagata held forth with a speech about the international brotherhood between the two nations represented in the park that day. And that afternoon, although neither one would know, the mayor of Tokyo, who desired nothing more than to host the 1940 Olympics in Tokyo and who, waiting on word of his chances in that venture, would experience a moment in time directly with a young man from Maui named Soichi Sakamoto whose ideas about the Games of 1940 hadn't even begun to form.

Still, it was a connection worth noting, at least for the way that sometimes lives, by accident, can align, when each man reached out with his left arm, the one closer to his heart—in the gesture known as the "international handshake"—and warmly clasped with his hand the other's, exchanging as well the expression on his face, a smile—a sign, it's said, of brotherly love, fidelity, and great promise.

The event in Hibaya Park was one moment among many that Soichi Sakamoto experienced during his trip to Japan that summer; he had captured it in a photograph—which, like others from that summer, he pasted into a scrapbook when he returned to Maui. Likely, he didn't forget the moment, but he couldn't have foreseen its significance. Neither could he have foreseen the role that Tokyo would play in his life in just a few years' time.

He had been duly impressed by Japan, though it was not what Sakamoto thought it would be. He had expected a whirlwind of ancient teahouses and temples, Kabuki dramas, hot springs and shrines, hikes in the jade-green countryside and up the snowcapped peak of Mount Fuji, and there had been all of those things, and sleeping, too, under the stars at night in a world so different from his own he could hardly imagine it. But what he found and enjoyed most on his trip was not the Japan of the past but a country in the midst of embracing its modernity. Like everyone, he had heard much about the destruction of Yokohama and Tokyo—the quake had occurred during the year in high school he'd been ill—and so when he found that both cities had risen from the rubble and the conflagration, it was among the sights that stunned him. Gone were the scars of 1923, and everywhere he looked were new factories on a scale he could never have imagined; new buildings that rose up tall and clean; elegant bridges and freshly paved roads and streets and new schoolhouses, and people nattily dressed and the children in the schools as fresh-faced as their city. Well-fed, disciplined, and dressed in starched, clean uniforms, the schoolboys and schoolgirls performed songs and demonstrated calisthenics and precision military drills to show that theirs was a nation and a people, just like Tokyo, also strengthening, also rising.

Sakamoto had found the new generation of Japanese people warm and gracious and promising. Somewhere in the recesses of his mind, he must have thought he would return someday, not to the world of his ancestors but to a Japan even more advanced, but in the summer of 1930, he could have had no idea of what would ever bring him there again.

There had been much fanfare in Waikapu the night the Scouts departed back in June, a great Aloha celebration with saimin and Portuguese sausage and a harmonica band playing and photo after photo taken in front of Sakamoto's father's store; and at Kahului Harbor at night, Sakamoto said farewell to the baby and to Mary—if she looked forlorn, he wouldn't have seen it—and he sailed first for Honolulu and onward, bound, with twenty-eight other young men, for the port of Yokohama.

On the liner called the *Empress of Canada*, he lived simply, as the others in his group had: he slept in steerage and he ate food from *kau kau* tins, but Sakamoto loved everything about the passage. The world was far wider to him now, promising, and what was more, he and the other Scouts had the run of the vessel, parading along the promenade like children and singing songs and crying Indian war cries. They played the ukulele and sang Hawaiian songs for the first-class travelers—something Sakamoto would find useful to do later in life—and he was thrilled when the captain invited him and the others to his cabin for tea and cakes, where he told them sea yarns, took them on a tour of the bridge, and at the ship's wheel explained intricate nautical charts and allowed each Scout to blow the boatswain's whistle.

When he returned home, he found Mary and the baby in good stead. Mary was becoming the godsend he had hoped for. She was generous and uncomplaining; she'd said nothing untoward at all about his leaving her for the summer, and when he came home, she welcomed him as if he'd never been away. She was wonderful with Raymond, who was now over a year old, and another child was on its way: she did all that, and uncomplainingly, a character trait he attributed to her having been raised in a crowded home and having herself been ill as a child. She appreciated life, it seemed, appreciated being alive, as if it were some extra gift she hadn't ever expected to receive, as if, perhaps, she wasn't quite worthy of the magnitude of it; and because she appreciated life, he began to do so, too.

He had been still a boy while in Japan, but upon seeing Mary again, he became ever more certain that it was time to give up boyish ways, and in the mirror, he began to see a pointy chin that was growing round and his hollow cheeks were filling in. There was stubble on his face; he had to shave it, and he cut his hair and kept it neat, with no rogue's swoop across the eyes. Another son, Donald, was born to them, and then a daughter they named Janice. And with the exception of his dark bow tie, Soichi Sakamoto no longer dressed like a bandleader, replacing his dark pants with light trousers and buying a pair of practical shoes for teaching and not for dancing, and in those shoes he began to stand more firmly on the ground—a man—and from where he stood, he looked around.

A Wide Awakening

From his childhood in his father's dry goods store, Soichi Sakamoto had learned something about plantation life, but never so up close. He'd understood the firm division between the Issei who *had* and the Issei who *had not* and the effect that having and not having had on their Nisei children. He understood how on one side of the counter stood an Issei who owned his own business and whose name was writ large—T. Sakamoto Store—upon a sign outside for all to see; and he understood how on the other side of the counter stood plantation workers, who wore around their necks chains from which their wafer-thin *bangos* hung, those round tags bearing not their names at all but mere numbers by which the plantation could keep track of them. He had thought of the plantation parents, but he had rarely thought of their children. When he thought of who a Nisei was, it had always been his own image that had come to mind.

For the Nisei at Pu'unene School, the life that awaited them was nothing to which they could or should look forward. For those whose parents had the extra $10 it took to send a child to high school, upon graduation, the fields would still be waiting. In his civics lessons, the children learned about democracy and the freedoms afforded to American citizens; but Sakamoto saw, all too clearly, that those freedoms existed only on the Mainland and that camp kids would never partake of them.

Pu'unene Elementary School was modern, two stories tall, and painted a fresh, pale king's blue. Its front doors were glass and wood and wide and had an overhang and Doric columns on each side. Dozens of tall windows lit up the classrooms that were large enough to fit hordes of children, grades one through eight, who came each day from the workers' camps. The school had a library, a kitchen in which to teach domestic science to the girls, a woodworking shop in which to teach carpentry to the boys, and the building was fitted with indoor plumbing and electricity, which most of the children didn't even have at home.

Soon, he found himself taking up tasks he never thought he would, and as the year turned, he volunteered for more. He became the master of Scout Troop 27 back in his hometown of Waikapu; with no experience at all in sports, he began a Little Tots barefoot basketball squad and then a track team, and soon was everywhere else becoming a right Johnny-on-the-spot, as he called himself. The children on his teams were as poor as sin and some were ruffians. In the classroom, he taught them science, but he knew now it was largely useless to them. Their future was to learn of planting and harvesting in the nearby fields or spinning molasses in the chugging mill. "Cane College" was soon to be their higher education. That was the highest they would go.

In late 1932, Soichi Sakamoto emerged from Puʻunene Elementary and came upon a scene of chaos. Just across the Camp 5 road, in the irrigation ditch, was a riot of turmoil. Naked, wet, and screeching, more than a hundred camp children scrambled out of the trench, clawing their way up the slick embankment, and, as soon as they could make their way past the barbed-wire fence that surrounded the ditch, they escaped into the cane, or ran barefoot and balls-out through the hot grass to the camps or across the field to the Japanese school, in search of shelter.

In hot pursuit of them was the dreaded luna. He sat astride an enormous horse, his face frozen in determination, and in his hand he held tightly his leather whip.

The children knew to drop the upstream gate, turn tight the valve to shut the current off. And the luna—his name was Albert DeLima—knew, when the water built up in the reservoir above the Camp 5 ditch, just where he'd find the children and what to do with them: he whipped them, grabbed them by the neck, and put them in the horse stable, naked, where it was dark and malodorous, and for hours, until he was satisfied. DeLima left them alone in there to contemplate the gravity of their trespass. When they came out, they were dirty everywhere, smelly, and still naked, too.

Soichi Sakamoto watched as, from time to time, DeLima gained advantage on the fleeing horde. His horse was swift, but then the children bolted away, the boys running with loose, long strides, the girls covering their privates but skittering fast.

A Wide Awakening

DeLima focused on one child, then another. His horse kicked up red soil behind him. DeLima aimed to corner a group of little ones, but they managed to elude him. Then he sped up and zeroed in on the teenage boys, but as he approached a pair of them, one boy would peel off suddenly left and the other would peel right, and over and again DeLima was forced to pull up on his reins until at last he sat, defeated, in a cloud of useless dust. Somehow his hat was still atop his head, but he was fuming so much it ought to have been propelled by steam straight up into the sky. Nothing was left behind of the children but their raggedy clothes hanging on a barbed-wire fence, their shirts and shorts flapping in the breeze like rebels' flags.

Across the way stood Mrs. Maehara. When DeLima approached, she shook her head, pretending not to know where any children were, although they were hiding behind anything they could find—wash bins, a bush, or beneath the floorboards of the school.

From Sakamoto, Mr. DeLima demanded the children's names. Surely their teacher knew who they were. But Sakamoto just shrugged and shook his head. He knew them, certainly, but he wouldn't say. He knew all too well what it was like to be young and kept from the simple things that gave a child even an ounce of pleasure.

Days later he was surprised to find himself standing upon the little bridge that crossed the Camp 5 ditch from which the children had been fleeing. Somehow he'd wrung permission from Mr. Priest, a kindly man in charge of Pu'unene camp activities, to let the children play in the ditch an hour each day as long as Mr. Sakamoto promised to watch over them. He was surprised in part because he hadn't time in his schedule for one more thing. So much of what he did for the school and outside of it took him away from Mary and the children, but what was more surprising was that, as a man who couldn't really swim, he'd asked permission to oversee a hundred children doing so.

But that's what he was doing now; he was on the bridge above the ditch and watching. The ditch in front of the school was perfect for the children—8 feet at its widest, only 4 feet deep—lined on its sides and bottom with

51

concrete, and safer when the current wasn't rushing through. Each day he turned the valve round tight and cut the current off, creating a peaceful stretch of ditch in which the children could splash and tadpole all around. There wasn't much more for Sakamoto to do than count their little heads and let them play. It was the first, if ad hoc, pool the children had ever been in. It wasn't a true pool, by far; it was too narrow for more than three swimmers, however young and skinny, to go up and down it at any time; it had no ends or walls to touch and from which to turn, just an open place where each bridge crossed the canal. It was filled with debris, so that made it hard to swim without remembering to close one's mouth but not one's eyes.

Quietly, Soichi Sakamoto watched the children splash and play, dunk and dive. Babysitting, he called it.

It had, though, elsewhere in the world, been a summer of possibility. Like so many other Nisei, he had kept his eyes on the cheering headlines from distant Los Angeles. There, something remarkable had happened that had renewed the spirits of the Japanese-American community on the Mainland and had stirred up hope on Maui, too.

For the first time in history, Japan sent an enormous delegation of athletes, coaches, and dignitaries to the 1932 Olympics—200 in all—including 131 athletes, second largest of all the countries in attendance in LA. The Games also marked the first time in history that any Asian country had prevailed in Olympic sport over Western nations.

In the sport in which Japan once had been belittled in Stockholm, the nation had established a *suiei okukku*, or "swimming kingdom." Now the Japanese were the finest swimmers in the world. In sprints, in middle distance, and in long, the Japanese had drained the pool of their competitors. In the 100- and 200-meter freestyles, some took gold and silver. In the 100-meter backstroke, some took gold, silver, and bronze. Women and men alike showed themselves to be competitive, some placing third, fourth, and fifth in middle-distance freestyle at 400, and, most astonishing of all, copping the men's 800-meter freestyle relay—a win that made it clear they were unstoppable. More, it was said that Japan wished to host an

A Wide Awakening

Olympiad as well, and the news from Los Angeles suggested that the wish might just come true in 1940. The events of Los Angeles that summer had changed so much for Japanese-Americans. Both Issei and Nisei in California had spent more than $100,000 on tickets to watch events, and again and again they saw the Japanese flag rise over the stadiums, an image filled with symbolism. The Japanese sports commentators had even ventured to say that the sporting world of the West was now firmly at the feet of the Empire.

After years of being second-class citizens, experiencing prejudice, alienation, and racism, those of Japanese ancestry in California and across the United States were buoyed with pride. Suddenly, too, other Americans had a new vision of Japan as both friendly and competent, and it seemed as though the tide might turn on the Mainland and a wave of acceptance might come. Famously, one Nisei in Los Angeles told the story that since the Games, white men no longer literally stoned him in the street, and he could look, he said, into his reflection in a shop window and feel, for the first time, respect even for himself.

Swept up in the same spirit and hope, Issei and Nisei on Hawaii and even Maui had been buzzing with hope as well. It's not known what Sakamoto knew about the Olympics but, like everyone else, he must have been impressed by what Japan and its young people had been able to accomplish. So it was perhaps that impression that gave rise to a moment when Soichi Sakamoto looked out at the children in the ditch and saw them suddenly not just as camp kids. They were Japanese-American kids, and he thought he saw something in their antics in the ditch—Sakamoto wasn't sure what, maybe talent, potential, but they appeared—and he would recall that moment for the rest of his life—like bright gems bobbing before him in the water. They were something, he saw, of value.

At first Sakamoto said nothing. He continued to watch the children play for weeks on end. He was at a loss for words. He held his tongue longer, for months, and then he couldn't keep himself from letting an idea spill out of him. At the very end of 1932, Soichi Sakamoto called out above the laughing and the noise of the children and asked them to listen to what he had to say. Their splashing ceased. The ditch grew silent. But still the children stood there shining, gleaming.

Soichi Sakamoto had no good reason to do it, no right to, no knowledge of how to, but he called out to the children, nonetheless, "How 'bout I teach you something about swimming, eh?"

Chapter Four

THE PURSUIT OF
GREATER VENTURES

SHORTLY THEREAFTER, on September 3, 1932, Hidejiro Nagata was once again greeting a crowd in the park, only this time it wasn't a crowd of American visitors but citizens of the Japanese Empire. Along the parade route between Marunouchi and Hibaya Park, five million people turned out to greet the returning athletes. Cries of "Banzai!" filled the morning air. Above the throng that gathered now before Nagata in the park flew a flock of thousands and thousands of brightly colored flags—the Japanese and the Olympic standards both, as if the city had managed to become even more than Hidejiro Nagata could have dared to hope: not the capital of one country alone but of the larger world as well. In the park, the army band, the musicians resplendent in their crisp uniforms, played the national anthem.

As Nagata stood on the dais, the anthem swelled. That day was most fine; the Japanese Amateur Athletic Association, relatively newly formed, had hosted the homecoming celebration for the athletes at the Tokyo Meeting Hall. Groups as large as those during the Reconstruction Festival paraded throughout the city, past the Imperial Palace and the Meiji Shrine.

Nagata looked out upon his handiwork. It had, thus far, been a difficult road, and he had traveled it with little support and little funding. He had worked obsessively and constantly. Back in December of 1930, when his emissary had returned from abroad, the emissary reported that from the leaders of America and Europe, the response had been overwhelmingly positive.

Such Stuff as Dreams

Nagata had then proceeded enthusiastically—if alone—forward. On December 4, 1930, he had held his own press conference to announce his city's campaign for the Olympic bid in 1940. The Games, he pointed out, would be the first ever held in Asia. And while no official showed, and only two Japanese newspapers ran minuscule notices of the announcement, Nagata was not deterred.

He approached members in the national government; few showed any interest. One even told him that it was one thing to send two hundred people to the Olympics, but it was a separate issue entirely to host them. The first government official to sit up and take notice, however, was the nation's minister of railways. He saw the great potential for revenue in the arrival of hundreds of thousands of visitors to Tokyo, but the minister stood alone with Nagata for some time before any others of influence could be persuaded to come aboard.

At first, Nagata's strategy had been to appeal merely to Japan's sense of nationalism, to pair the Olympiad with the anniversary of the Empire, with the intention of showing the rest of the world the nation's greatness; but in a brief time, he had to change his strategy. In 1931, Japan had made a move considered by the rest of the world most warlike; the incursion into Manchuria proved to be most unpopular worldwide. Even as early as 1930, Japan had become increasingly isolated from other countries, having withdrawn from the League of Nations, and having made no effort to reestablish with Britain a treaty governing the seas.

The Manchurian incident, as it was known, became the fuel that kept Nagata's Olympic idea alive for yet another year until he could persuade others that the 1932 Games were also an opportunity for positive public relations. By sending a large delegation of athletes and diplomats to Los Angeles, and by performing well there, Japan could demonstrate its increasing commitment to athletics, its friendliness and warmth, and its rising competitiveness in sport of all kinds. With the help of some new allies in the government, Nagata had been able to secure both the emperor's assent and his financial support.

In preparation, Nagata had read much about how one proceeded to bid to host the Olympics, how one had to obtain consensus and then what was called candidature—official recognition from the International Olympic Committee, or IOC—even to be considered a contender. What he understood was that behind the scenes, at every occasion when the IOC met, and it met often, it would be important to politic wisely; and that in advance of those meetings a quiet, if persuasive, diplomacy with the leaders of the most influential nations needed to be part of Japan's overall strategy.

In addition to its other meetings, the IOC always convened before each Olympiad, just before the events were to begin. It would be at Los Angeles, Nagata knew, that Japan would have to make its best and first impression, and he must send there his greatest and most skilled ambassador.

Nagata now leaned down toward the microphone. "I am extremely grateful," he said, his voice echoing back to him from the giant loudspeakers arranged along the perimeter of the famous park, "for the national awareness that you have clarified," he continued, "in the hearts of the Japanese."

During the Games, Nagata had made sure that all of the proceedings had been recorded and then broadcast on national radio in Japan, thus influencing millions. And there was more; he emphasized what, for two years, had become a cri de coeur: that nothing could bring the Empire more glory than sport itself and that athletes were among the nation's greatest ambassadors. "Without being formal diplomats," he continued, the athletes had greatly improved the image and understanding of Nippon not just in California or in America but across the entire world.

It was that very policy of which some in the Japanese Diet and formal diplomatic corps had also become persuaded; in their efforts to ease relations with the West they had been less than successful. Upon leaving America's shores, however, the athletes carried with them, along with their medals, a singular but decisive victory: as they had departed from the pier, Americans had called out to them, "Banzai," and in return they had been able to cry out, at least hopefully, "See you in 1940."

Nagata then turned to those delegates from Japan in their silk sashes with their medals and their badges, who had, behind the scenes, performed at least as well, if not more than, the athletes had in public. Nagata had himself thought it better not to make the trip. It was he who notified the IOC of Japan's intention for Tokyo to host in 1940, and it was he who assured them and others that while he was not to be present, Japan was ready to take on the '40 Games. In his stead, his diplomats continued on. They had engaged in a concerted, ardent campaign to deliver Nagata's message about Japan's fitness and readiness to host its first Olympiad.

While some in the Japanese government had said that the best way for Americans to understand the real Japan was to demonstrate to them the nation's power in both athletics and politics, the delegates had been tasked with showing instead the nation's generosity and friendliness, its courtesy, and its civility. They filled their own social calendars with teas and other events, and they hosted fetes of elaborate proportion and expense to which they invited droves to attend.

At the most elaborate of all the parties, held at the Biltmore hotel on the last day of the Games, Nagata had made sure that one man in particular gave the keynote address. That man was Baron Jigoro Kano, and Nagata had recently been able to persuade the man to become a formal and central part of the effort to secure the Tokyo candidature. Kano was uniquely qualified and perfectly positioned to take up Nagata's mission.

Jigoro Kano was seventy-seven years old, and in spite of his advanced age, he was spry and clear of mind and respected in his position. He had risen in life from relatively modest beginnings, but he was well-educated, a polymath with mastery in calligraphy, the Japanese classics, mathematics, English, German, and Chinese. It was said that as a child, Kano had been a weakling, the butt of jokes, and to compensate, he had then taken up the martial art of jujitsu. That alone might have made him formidable, at least in situations requiring hand-to-hand finesse. He was also, however, a famous baron and a member of the House of Peers, regarded with great respect for, among other gifts, his power of passionate, effective, rhetorical persuasion. In appearance he was unthreatening: tiny—as he'd always been—at least a head shorter than any Westerner and so light of frame that one might think, if one didn't know better, that his body weight might have been less than the weight of the white, bushy mustache that flourished above his upper lip and below a pair of twinkling eyes.

Small as he was, he was the master of everyone he met. Years before, he had found the practice of jujitsu both unappealing in its bone-cracking brutality and also to some degree insufficiently challenging mentally. After, as a young man, he succeeded all too easily in besting his own jujitsu teacher, he departed from the dojo and set out to form his own.

There, he developed his own practice, which he called judo; he became father of that most famous martial art, and in so doing, had thousands of followers at the time, and millions who practice judo today. His dojo was a magnet for those who agreed that jujitsu, a tool of the ancient bygone samurai, was not meant for a modern age.

That it was well known, and often demonstrated, that Kano could level with perfect ease men twice his size in four seconds flat was to his great advantage and contributed much to his reputation. Judo involved the careful and subtle leverage of one's force and a fine balance in one's strategy of when to use force at all and when to yield in order to conquer.

That he was patient and not easily ruffled, too, as Kano had demonstrated many times, was of great help. The most notable of the situations in which he had shown his unflappability, an incident that had in his time become legend, was this: Once, he had been a passenger, along with many others, in an overcrowded automobile. The auto skidded off the road and came to the edge of a precipice where its front half hung precariously off the edge of a deep ravine. While the other passengers grew hysterical and fussed and moved about and exited the vehicle in the most dangerous of ways, Kano remained calmly in the car, completely alone, until all of the frazzled others had abandoned it and stood at last on solid ground. Only then, calmly, did he exit the car.

Nagata had reached out to Kano also because of Kano's longstanding, significant relationship to the Olympic movement. It was Jigoro Kano whom the government appointed as emissary to the movement as early as 1909, when Pierre de Coubertin had reached out to Nippon to assay its desire for involvement in the Games. In July 1911, Kano went on to found the most important athletic association in Japan—the Japanese Amateur Athletic Association—the equivalent of the US AAU. And when in 1912 the two Japanese athletes traveled to Stockholm, it was Baron Jigoro Kano who accompanied them on their long journey. He was greatly used to traveling long distance, and he was familiar with the West. Having studied abroad, he spoke perfectly inflected English. He had continued through the years to travel with the Japanese Olympic team whenever he was able: to Antwerp, Paris, Amsterdam, and now, most recently at the request of his countryman Nagata, to Los Angeles, where he took on an even greater role.

Everywhere he went in California, he was found charming by American hosts, Europeans, and the press. One newspaper article reported that Kano was as much a playful man as he was sensitive and charming at a party. He was described as taking delight from time to time at raising up the hem of his robes to reveal a pair of legs he considered, and told others, were particularly attractive, even at his advanced age. And at one of the events of the LA Games, he was spotted in the gallery to be gently weeping, his tears suggesting a depth of character often hidden from Westerners by the Japanese. Those things endeared him to all who encountered him.

And at the grand fete at the Biltmore hotel, his keynote speech had roused the entire room, and in particular the delegates from all nations to the IOC, including its president and heir to Baron Pierre de Coubertin, the Belgian aristocrat Count Henri de Baillet-Latour. Latour was known, in part, for his ardent defense of amateurism in sport, but he was even better regarded for having organized the first Olympiad to follow World War I, the Antwerp Olympiad of 1920. Baillet-Latour, rarely seen not puffing on a cigar, was a deceptively dour-looking idealist buoyed inside by the same beliefs in the power of internationalism that had driven his predecessor.

Jigoro Kano's remarks at the Biltmore were directed as much at the Belgian baron as at anyone: Kano spoke of the fear that it was too easy for the world to have of other countries. "People," Kano intoned, "are prone to think that what they are accustomed to is good and right," and that "whatever is foreign to them is mistaken and harmful," and he pointed out that the Olympics, if held in Tokyo in 1940, would serve to echo and reinforce the beliefs and values that served as the foundation set down by the movement's founder. To hold the games in Japan was to extend Coubertin's vision and to bridge the global gap that existed between West and East and bring together all nations in pursuit, Kano said, of "a common purpose." And while Kano hadn't returned home in 1932 with the candidature yet in hand, he had succeeded in appealing to Baillet-Latour and others like him, who were open to a wider vision of the world.

It was on Kano that Hidejiro Nagata, mayor of Tokyo, civil servant of much lesser influence, now pinned his plans; to Kano he was handing the solemn responsibility of making the Tokyo Olympiad a reality. And it was to Baron Jigoro Kano that others, in both Japan and the world, would now turn their greater attention in all matters Japanese and Olympian.

In going forward with the Olympic bid, Jigoro Kano would make use of all his talents, not just his elocution, but his skills from years of judo practice. He would have to decide when to yield and when to apply force. And he would have to keep his head about him while others lost theirs when they found themselves balanced upon a precipice.

At the same time, thousands of miles from Tokyo and the machinations of the Japanese in securing the bid for the Twelfth Olympiad, at a ditch in Pu'unene, Maui, Soichi Sakamoto, nonswimmer but enthusiastic amateur, was flying by the seat of his practical pants.

In the fall of 1932, he merely told the children to dunk their heads, to go under the surface, and to look around; he told them to do it until they were no longer afraid. He told them next to wade into water until they stood waist-deep in it, and when they'd gained their footing to squat down until their shoulders were submerged.

He told them to put their arms above their heads, then to lean back and let the ditch water be their bed, their pillow. "Let your feet rise up," he told them. "See?" he said.

They were floating now on their backs. When they were ready, he had them reverse the process, lean forward, and float upon their stomachs. And throughout the spring of the following year, 1933, that was all he could manage to teach them. When they were bored, he began in spring to have them practice swinging their arms like wheels and kicking their legs against the surface of the water, one, two, three four, splashing, splashing, unafraid of the commotion, until at last they moved, even just inches or feet, forward in the irrigation ditch.

Soichi Sakamoto counted himself successful, at least in the basics.

After the children had begun to be able to move themselves in the water, he cried out to them: See? That's all swimming is. It was floating, he said, but faster. He called it "speed-floating," and for the rest of 1933 that's what he had the ditch kids practice.

By the fall of 1933, Sakamoto's life was full to brimming over. He was ever more a schoolteacher, but he took on more responsibilities outside of school, and by the spring of 1934, he taught all day at Puʻunene Elementary, all of the fifth and sixth grades, not only in science but also in physical education and health. In the afternoons he was always at the ditch. In the evenings and on the weekends, he now had Little Tots barefoot basketball teams galore. He managed "The Kapus" (short for "Waikapu"), "The Beginners," "The Kapu C quintet," and a squad called "The Mix." In those groups he had subteams of kids: "Kapu C," "B," "Kapu 85 lb. team," and the Kapu 120-pounders. He also had encouraged others to form a bigger league of Little Tots teams, so his kids had someone to play against. On the weekends, he was also scoutmaster of Maui's Troop 27, a big lot to wrangle. During summer vacation he led two four-week Boy Scout jamborees way up in the mountains of Iao Valley, where, in addition to the old pool, there was a camp by the name of PenCarPo. And the track team he had begun to coach at Puʻunene Elementary was getting better and better.

The Pursuit of Greater Ventures

Although Sakamoto never intended to court attention, the local newspaper noticed him. In January of that year, the sports editor of the *Maui News* featured him in an inaugural column called "Men You Know in Sports." Urban Allen, who had come to Maui from a Honolulu paper, held much sway in town. "Ask the youngsters in Waikapu who, in their opinion, is just about the grandest chap...in those hinterlands," Allen wrote, and "invariably they will answer in one voice the name of 'Soichi Sakamoto.'" In the world of Maui sports, Soichi Sakamoto had become "a potent leader in his bailiwick," serving, Allen said, as a role model to young boys.

At home, Mary seemed as busy as her husband was. He had convinced her to give up her job at the telephone exchange, and she had done what he had said; he'd wanted a proper wife, he told her, and now with the children, her hands were full. She seemed cheerful and happy to see him when he was able to come home. She drew the furo for him when he arrived; she always sensed the hour he would come, and she had a warm meal waiting for him as well.

As modern as they'd thought themselves to be, and as Hawaiian as Mary was and as Hawaiian as Sakamoto had always behaved, now it was as if Mary were a Japanese wife and he a traditional and Bushido—strict and traditional—Japanese husband. Mary was, to his satisfaction, becoming the backbone of the family. She bore the weight of everything, waking up before anyone else, even the babies, or with a baby on her hip, cooking breakfast and doing the family's laundry. She never sat down at the table to eat with her husband or her sons—a typical Japanese tradition—and during the day, she managed every aspect of the household.

She repaired leaky pipes and patched the roof herself, sewed window screens back together, cut the grass in the yard like clockwork so that it was trim and tidy all the time. She grew vegetables in a garden and had planted guava and avocado trees. In the morning, she fed the chickens in her coop and gathered their eggs, and she took the babies with her whenever she walked to the store to buy provisions. She came home with cooking chickens, wrung their necks with her own hands, plucked them, and fried them up for dinner.

Such Stuff as Dreams

And though she looked joed, her eyes often droopy with sleep, and she no longer had dancing ringlets of dark hair but pulled her hair straight back for practicality, she seemed satisfied. She was full of cheerful sayings. They were adages that might have sounded stale and cliché, but Sakamoto listened carefully to them; he was fond of any wisdom of that kind. She always said, whenever he found it difficult to understand something or someone, that he needed to put himself in another person's shoes. And she told him also of how dangerous it was, in persisting in keeping control or winning an argument, how dangerously one could risk, if one were not careful, losing a friend.

In his article in the *Maui News* in January, sports editor Urban Allen hadn't even mentioned the babysitting and rudimentary hour-long lessons Soichi Sakamoto was doing in Puʻunene; it's likely that he didn't even know about it. No one beyond the camp did; it was a local thing only, and there weren't any competitions. The kids had no pool for it, and Sakamoto had just focused on "speed-floating," with an emphasis on moving in the water but not really at any "speed" that mattered.

That spring of 1934, however, a group of ditch kids, most of them from Camp 5, approached him and said they were tired of speed-floating. Sakamoto brought a yardstick and a piece of chalk down from his classroom and marked up the edges of the ditch: 25 yards, 50, 100, 150. He had the children practice speed-floating to those distances, and then, once a week, he let them race. The races pleased the kids, but they were nothing formal. Sakamoto named a couple of captains and had them pick teams; the kids already knew who the strongest and fastest swimmers were, so they loaded their small squads up with as many of them as they could. Most of the standouts were from the "Camp 5 Gang," as they liked to be called. There was Kiyoshi Nakama; his nickname was Keo. There was another named Takashi Hirose, and bunches of others like the three Tsukano brothers—Pachi, Shangy, and John, who used to spend their off-time playing Hardhead for fun.

Everybody called the races the "kid races," and anyone in proximity to the ditch knew about them because the event was so uproarious. On "kid race" days, usually at the end of the school week, hundreds of Sakamoto's beginning swimmers and lookers-on lined the 50 meters between the two ditch bridges, and they screamed and screeched and applauded and cheered on their favorites, and sometimes camp families complained that the noise was worse than the Mighty #8 train or the whistle at the mill. Still, Soichi Sakamoto hadn't the heart to quiet the kids or stop the races. There was just too much happiness; there was just too much fun.

He kept up with chalk-practice and the races all spring of 1934; and by the end of March he saw that some of the kids were fast enough that maybe they ought to give it a try, for fun, and enter themselves officially, either as Scouts or as members of a church or school team, in the annual Maui Public School meet that took place every May.

The MPSAL (Maui Public School Association League) was run by the director of all island sports, and the meet took place at the one pool in camp. That pool was the haole pool; its formal name was the Puʻunene Club pool, and after the annual meet when they let the camp kids in, the haoles always drained the tank to clean it.

The best Puʻunene camp kids took Sakamoto up on his idea, and when May came along, Soichi Sakamoto stood for the first time on the deck of the Puʻunene Club pool, not even as a coach but as a bystander, watching some of the kids he gave lessons to take part in the big races. Keo Nakama and Takashi "Halo" Hirose and the other boys—wearing their cutoffs or the knee pants they had for school—took their chances against kids whose last names were Castle, Cooke, Alexander, and Baldwin, kids who'd been swimming in that pool for years, had proper bathing suits, and who knew how to do a push-off turn at the wall, because they *had* a wall.

There were plenty of weak points in the ditch swimmers, and while they acquitted themselves admirably, none of them won, even in the single event they knew: the freestyle. The other problem was that the children just weren't strong enough. What he would do next would change not only the swimmers in the ditch but swimmers across the world for years to come.

One day, he walked upstream to where the gate and the valve for the irrigation ditch was, at the reservoir, or *punawai*, and he opened the gate high and wide and turned the wheel of the valve all the way to the left.

Swim like salmon, he told the big kids, but none of them knew what in the world a salmon was; Sakamoto explained. Swim upstream, he said. He had them swim against the current—it was no more than 3 miles per hour at its fastest, but it was strong enough to suit—all the way up to the far bridge and then turn back around and swim back to him on the footbridge where he always stood. Up was like hell, speed-floating against the current, hard, some 50 meters, but the reward was in the lap downstream toward Sakamoto. They still had to wheel their arms around and kick, too, but now they had the sweet assistance of the current beneath them, and this lap was all pleasure. Unknowingly, but intuitively, Sakamoto had invented a kind of interval training we still use today.

Up and down he had the children swim. Up and down every day, their mouths closed to keep out any detritus that flew at them when they were trying to go up against the current. And in April, just before the MPSAL meet in May, Sakamoto started teaching the kids how to do the wall turns. To do so, though, he had to scrounge up his savings and buy a car: the only place to practice was miles and miles away. He got the swimmers out of school a half hour early and hauled about twenty kids up to the muddy and frigid Iao Valley pool, which, in spite of its shortcomings, actually had sides, so the ditch kids could practice their turns. It was hard to fit all twenty of the children at a time in his auto, so sometimes Sakamoto had to make two long trips up and back again just to get everyone there, and other times he risked it and he just piled as many skinny kids as he could in the front and the back and the rumble seat, and on the hood and fender, and he made others try to balance on the running board. Still others would jog alongside the packed car until they ran out of steam, and then they took their turn in the car, sitting or standing. Whenever the Wailuku police car went by, which wasn't often but was often sudden, Sakamoto shooed all but about four kids out of the car entirely, and he crawled along the dirt road and had the rest walk dutifully beside him as he climbed the hill.

This time, when the MPSAL meet came up, the best of his ditch kids— about ten boys, including Keo Nakama and Halo Hirose—beat the fleshy haoles in the Puʻunene Athletic Club tank, coming in 1-2-3, first, second, and third place, in every freestyle event from 25 yards on up. And Keo Nakama, to the surprise of everyone watching, swam the 100-yard freestyle to win at 1 minute and 3.6 seconds—a new island record.

The date was May 25, 1935, and even though once Keo Nakama and the other ditch kids got out of the tank the haoles did their annual drain and clean of the pool, it was the ditch kids who, in fact, cleaned up that day.

A flurry of editorials in the newspaper followed hard upon those races. Now local citizens held forth, asking how could it be that the Valley Isle's best swimmers were training in a ditch? "It is not an exaggeration to say," wrote one, "that at least one third," meaning camp kids, in the meets in '34 had learned everything they knew about swimming in a ditch. By '35, there were more camp swimmers still in the ditches, and those kids were winners.

Way in town in Wailuku, people wrote, was a pool run by the local philanthropic organization that oversaw all island sports; the organization was called Alexander House, but its tank was miles from the plantation, and it was not just inadequate but "pint sized." Critics also derided the up-valley Iao Pool as "unsuitable."

What was most unacceptable, most unfair, unjust, and even unchristian, was this: that the nearby Puʻunene Athletic Club tank was first class, but it wasn't open to camp kids. It was for members only. One editorial put it this way: "Participants in the meets who do not belong to the Puʻunene Club are unable to practice in the pool in which the[ir] meets are to be swum." Their exclusion was an embarrassment to and the shame of the people of Maui, the island's athletic director, and the owners of the plantation. There had to be a solution.

Such Stuff as Dreams

In May of 1936, Hawaii Commercial & Sugar christened the sparkling new Baldwin Park, a recreational complex built at an expense to the company of some $65,000, even more than the plantation had spent on the elementary school. It was a full eleven acres of plowed-up cane fields—the opportunity for cane production nearly as exorbitant a loss—with a giant playground, a new baseball diamond, a cinder running track with a 100-yard straight-away, a basketball court, a field for soccer and barefoot football, and a large picnic area with a grassy lawn. And the jewel in the crown of it all—and a solution to the island's problems of where camp kids could swim—was the new Baldwin Pool.

It was more than a solution, though; it was a miracle. It was glorious, and it seemed too good to be true. Soichi Sakamoto and the ditch swimmers had to blink their eyes, the way that Duke Kahanamoku once had to in 1927, when he'd declared that Waikiki Natatorium must not be real but only a dream.

The tank was a full 25 yards long and 8 lanes wide. The smooth bottom—at both the shallow and the angled deep ends—was painted the same king's blue as the outside of the elementary school, and along the length of the pool ran dark T-lines, professional and perfect, straight as they could be. There were ropes and cork and hooks to divide the pool into lanes, and the water that the ropes crossed was pure and cold and thoroughly transparent; it was from a separate water source than the irrigation ditch, and when rays of the sun hit it just right, the light split off it into colored prisms that seemed perfect and impossible and also always to be fleeting.

Around the perimeter of the pool area there was a bamboo fence to keep the wind out and a riot of flowery bushes that were going to bloom all year long and newly planted trees. On one side of the pool were rows and rows of permanent bleachers, enough room for twenty-five hundred spectators. Mounted up on high wooden beams, all around, were spotlights you could keep on at night for swim meets *after* dark.

There were two clubhouses at each end of the pool, one for offices for the plantation athletic director, the other for lockers and showers and dressing rooms for girls and boys. There were real sinks and toilets, and everything was spit-spot clean. The deck around the pool was brick—ochre colored—freshly laid into a pretty zigzag pattern into which a mass of masons had to have put in days of labor.

At the opening of the complex that late May of 1936, the Baldwin family, owners of HC&S, held a gala celebration that included round after round of congratulatory speeches. Before a crowd of five thousand workers and their families, the patriarch of the great Baldwin family, Frank Baldwin, held forth.

Frank Fowler Baldwin was the product of two of the most powerful kamaaina families on Maui. On his mother's side were the Alexanders; and the Baldwins, going back to his grandfather, had been among the island's earliest and most influential New England missionaries. Some called them "pioneers." As the scion to a great fortune, in youth young Frank, though born on the island, was sent off to the Mainland for schooling at Hotchkiss and then Yale, following in the footsteps of the men in his family.

In youth he had been a bit of a troublemaker. Once, in 1896 at Yale, the *Washington Post* made note of an instance of uncivil misbehavior when Baldwin came to the aid of another Eli who had been arrested on some minor infraction. The friend was locked up in the New Haven police station, and Frank Baldwin and a small gang of others rushed the police, demanding the release of their classmate, and in so doing, also physically attacked a sergeant, resulting in a long night in jail themselves.

At Yale, he was better known as a crack polo player, one of the absolute best in the country, and when he returned to Maui and to his ancestral home, it was to begin to learn the family sugar business, but he also established a stable of the finest polo ponies in the world. He was ever so fond of sports, and a good portion of his charitable donations went to running the island-wide sports system through Alexander House Settlement. Baldwin had inherited from his father, Henry—one-armed because of a famous mishap with a cane mangler—the presidency of HC&S plantation and was also president of its related "factor," or organization, Alexander and Baldwin Company, one of the famous Big Five on Hawaii, an enormous conglomerate controlling every industry in Hawaii, from shipping and banking to hotels, the railway, and the telephone company.

He was still about a decade away from the apex of power as a sugar magnate in May of 1936, but he was the greatest and most admired philanthropist in the island Territories. He was fifty-seven years old, short, balding, a man with a thick waist, thick hands, and a thick lower lip, and ears as big and round and flat as Sunday pancakes. His international reputation had earned him the nickname "King of the Canebrakes," and locally he was called, quite simply, "the General." He had in his heart a soft spot for the ditch swimmers; it was said that once, on a Sunday in his youth, he and his father, Henry, had, when the roads had flooded out in a storm, to swim in a ditch in order to make it to church on time.

Baldwin stood at the podium. The complex was but a small gesture, he told the crowd of workers, in order to demonstrate how paramount, he said, his workers' happiness was to him, to his family, and to his company. He wanted to let his workers know that HC&S was "in tune with the times," and that because camp residents had become in recent years increasingly "athletic minded," they required more from their employers. Baldwin Park would be a "garden spot," he said, open each day to the plantation's employees, their spouses, and their children, all of whom, he said, "deserved a proper place to recreate."

A band played, and even though a slight rain fell and the skies were gray, Sakamoto's ditch kids swam and beat the pants off every other kid in the water, including the haoles, and it was blue ribbons all around. Sakamoto stood back and watched the camp children in the water. In their faces he saw, for the first time, true joy and celebration.

That summer when one traveled down the Camp 5 road, past Stable Camp and the Japanese Christian Church, across Puʻunene Avenue and down toward the Catholic boneyard, there was the distinct sound of the crack of a bat connecting and the *chrinch-chrinch-chrinching* of bare feet racing toward the finish, but the loudest noise came from what the kids and

The Pursuit of Greater Ventures

Sakamoto didn't call the Baldwin Pool, but the Camp 5 pool, because that was where most of the ditch kids came from.

The pool was for all the camps, though, and Soichi Sakamoto divided the tank into a recreational side and a swimming side. One side was teeming with children of all ages, *thwinging* themselves off the glistening diving board and turning into missiles in the air, while other children waited their turns impatiently at the bottom of the slick waterslide, the ladder of which they finally, with great joy, ascended and then the angle of which they flew down and landed in the clear water with a great big splash.

On the other side, Sakamoto watched over his swimmers. There were more than a hundred children, and he had them in three groups: the first were those who attended Puʻunene school and whom he would now coach on the school swim team; the second were those who were older and in high school and who would swim for Maui High; the third was made up of everybody else—ditch kids who were somehow in between schools; older kids who had dropped out of school and had jobs in the fields or the mill. They weren't a team, that third group, but Sakamoto trained them just as hard as he trained the other two. All summer they worked, and into the fall, and all that same summer Soichi Sakamoto made the best possible use of his time to produce the best swimmers that he could. In whatever spare time he had—there was so little, and he rarely saw Mary and the children except when she stopped by to bring him his lunch or dinner—he went hunting for training equipment. He'd read a bunch of books about swimming, and all of them said that swimmers weren't supposed to train hard at all, but Soichi Sakamoto didn't believe what the books said. In his own experience, swimming upstream or running miles up to Iao Valley had strengthened his swimmers; in track and field, he knew, more vigorous training—mostly long runs through the woods with intermittent stops and starts—was recommended by Nordic coaches for their runners. He had his swimmers run, too, and he continued to strengthen them in the ditch, but he wanted more.

He scavenged whatever he could find in the trash heaps at the edges of the fields and near the piles of green *bagasse*—or cane pulp—by the sugar

71

mill, and from the ditches he fished out anything that might look useful: a broom that came downstream, a pair of trousers he could turn perhaps into a pair of swim trunks. With a homemade net for the water and a bamboo pole for the trash heaps, he poked around, searching like a treasure hunter for anything broken that could be made whole, any piece of junk that others had abandoned or discarded that somehow he imagined might be treasure: thick planks of redwood, uneven lengths of lanyard rope, rusty buckets, bamboo branches thick enough to have some purpose, slashed inner tubes, old railcar wheels, a pair of rusted pulleys. He'd had nothing, and soon he had, at least, something, even if it was a heap of rusty, dusty junk.

Perspiring in the sun, he split the lumber into chunks of equal length and width and thickness—about 2 feet by 3 feet, 3 inches high, and he sanded them smooth until they were good enough for kickboards—about 5 pounds each. He took two rusty buckets, filled them up with sand and rocks, and strung the buckets off of the bamboo poles or off of pipes, tying the ropes tight and fashioning a simple set of he-man dumbbells. He shaved the rust off of the pulleys, oiled the rigging, nailed the housing to a hook on the club-house wall. He ran ropes through the pulleys' sheaves and tied heavy railcar wheels onto one end of the lanyards, and on the other built handles out of rubber or lengths of hard cane or bamboo: a resistance arm-weight gadget.

But even as Soichi Sakamoto did all these things, as the summer went on he kept his eyes on the newspaper headlines, and not just the local ones, but also the Honolulu papers, and he listened intently to the radio about what was going on in Germany. He had no interest in Mr. Adolf Hitler; what he wanted to hear about was the 1936 Summer Olympic Games. And without telling any other soul what it was he was thinking, even Mary, Soichi Sakamoto paid particular attention to everything that was happening in the enormous competition swimming pool in the heart of Berlin between August 5 and August 15.

In Berlin, the Japanese swimmers were still stars, walking away from the pool with four gold medals to America's two. Hungarian Ferenc Csik won gold in the 100-meter freestyle with a time of 57.6 seconds. American Jack Medica won gold and broke an Olympic record in the 400-meter at 4:44.5 (4 minutes 44.5 seconds).

The Pursuit of Greater Ventures

Driven with those numbers in his head, all through the summer and fall, Sakamoto kept up with the kids' training. He worked them through the winter, in the ditch and the pool and on his resistance machines and boards, and he tried to lower their times in as many events as they could. By spring, his rough-hewn, dirty-faced Puʻunene Elementary School division swimmers weren't exactly pacesetters or record breakers, but they nabbed the school division championships with ease.

He had on a clipboard a set of numbers, too, that included Maui island records; interisland meet records; the standing records in the Hawaiian Amateur Athletic Union (AAU) meets held every year; he kept the figures for the American and world records in events and any collegiate records in yards.

Sakamoto's two best swimmers were Keo Nakama and Halo Hirose. Each was both a different kind of boy and a different kind of swimmer, and all sorts of things went into determining who was a better natural sprinter and who might be a middle- or long-distance fellow. That hadn't shaken out yet. Both boys were growing, though, and while they alternated between sprints and middle distances, soon, Sakamoto felt, time would reveal where they best performed.

In 1935, Keo Nakama had swum the 100-yard freestyle in a time of 1 minute 3.6 seconds, and by the spring of 1937, his freshman year at Maui High, just two years later, he blazed the 100-yarder in 57.8. He had shorn 5.8 seconds off the clock in two short years. Meanwhile, the American record for the 100 in '37 was 56.4 seconds; Halo was only 1.4 seconds off of that. It was unbelievable.

Hirose wasn't doing quite as well at the 200-yard freestyle, but in the spring of '37 he was negotiating the time at 2:34.4. The standing American record was 2:09.7. That was a gap of 24.7 seconds. Sakamoto looked at the kids' numbers, watched them all season, never took his eyes off them except to train the children, look at his own stopwatch. He saw nothing but those numbers, and he even saw them in his head, and all spring of 1937, he kept doing calculations.

All spring long, he worked with the children, and their improvement was steady, and as he tracked it, he saw that it was nothing less than exponential.

Such Stuff as Dreams

His ragtag Pu'unene School team was Maui's public school champs. And on Memorial Day weekend in Honolulu, Keo and Halo beat swimmers from the university in a meet on Oahu in the men's division. Nakama broke the Hawaiian record in the 400-yard free, and Hirose swam faster than big guys in the sprints. The papers on Maui and on Oahu both said the boys were more than promising. The two came home carrying enormous trophies. They had a future. Maybe a big one. That weekend, the wheels in Soichi Sakamoto's head were spinning like crazy. In Sakamoto's mind, the next test for Halo and Keo would be at the Duke Kahanamoku Outdoor Meets in August. It was a new invitational; swimmers were coming from the Mainland, a group of mermen from a San Francisco club, big college boys, and even one Olympian by the name of Ralph Gilman. It would be the first time that Sakamoto would be able to put his fish in an "outdoor," or meter-measured, race. Meters were the measures for the Olympics.

Sakamoto became giddy, sleepless. Much to Mary's consternation, for days he stayed inside his room, keeping company with no one and nothing but his own ideas. When he emerged he was rumpled, unwashed, and squinting in the sun. He carried with him two enormous signs on which he'd spent the weekend working, a notebook, and a pen.

It was June, one of the last days of the school year.

He hardly noticed what else was happening around him. Ash should have filled the air, spinning upward in black storms, where blazes at this time of year roared and snapped even in daylight; it was a world when, at night, the smell of smoke ought to have been strong enough to wake children from their dreams.

It was burn and harvest season, but there was no fire anywhere; a strike at the plantation was two months old. No front loaders crawled across the fields; no men with torches came to torch the crops; and on every tongue was the taste of bitterness and brutality.

He came closer to the village of Pu'unene. In the camps around the ele-

74

mentary school, the Filipino bachelor barracks, in particular, stood empty, the screen doors slapping open in the wind. There had been a walkout—forty-five hundred men in all—the largest ever to hit HC&S. Workers had literally dropped their spades and hoes in front of the plantation office, after which the bosses forcibly removed them from camp housing. The men now waited in a gypsy camp down by the harbor, sleeping in rusty iron cots beneath tarps stretched from tree to tree, fishing and cooking their meals over open fires. They vowed they would eat dirt before they would crawl back to the conditions they had left behind.

The strike had started, Sakamoto learned, when a field hand, furious because he was demoted from driving a loader to having to load by hand, wanted his job back. At dawn one morning before the shift whistle, he made his way to where his field boss lived; he waited outside the door, arms crossed, ready to make his case, but when the boss emerged, the two men had words, and when the boss was halfway up in his saddle, the worker came at him from behind and struck him in the neck with his machete.

Thanks to a thick sweater, the collar of which the boss had by chance turned up that morning, the man survived with only flesh wounds and some broken teeth; but the police arrested the worker for attempted murder, and the strike spread from camp to camp until the cane stood, as it did now, desiccated, waiting.

The first to strike were the workers who did *kachi kane*—cut the cane—and then the *hapai ko* men—those who *carried it*. The former cutters earned their pay by the number of feet of cane they hacked, and the latter earned theirs by the tons they could hoist on their shoulders, carry up a twelve-inch-wide wooden ramp, and heave into the railcars.

The plantation owners had rounded up the local strike leaders; they'd called in the scabs, and just outside of Pu'unene, police had set up two operation centers wired with telephones and stocked with guns. All over the island men from one walk of life met secretly in copses of trees or by the sides of streams to discuss their demands while men from another walk of life entirely met in wood-paneled boardrooms to discuss how not to give in to them.

Such Stuff as Dreams

By noon on that June day, Soichi Sakamoto was poised to begin to organize a labor union of his own. His classroom overflowed with children; some couldn't fit in at all and were stuck outside the door, necks craning to see in from the long, dark hallway. Sakamoto hazarded to guess that more than 120 had decided to come.

Each was shirtless, shoeless, tanned. Some already sported the jagged haircuts and buzz cuts that they gave one another every summer. Some were broad-shouldered from extra fieldwork; others were so small and weak that they could barely manage to carry a single schoolbook in their arms; and some were so black and blue with welts from their parents' beatings that, even in daylight, parts of them looked cast in shadow.

Some of their mothers were crazy; some of their fathers gambled on cockfights. Some of their parents were like saints and worshipped at the Hongwanji, the Buddhist church; others' parents prayed to a Christian god or not at all, but all the parents, good at heart or bad, wanted better for their children than the lives that they had been consigned to lead, a life of virtual slavery, in the fields or in the mill.

Up in front were the kids from the Camp 5 gang: Hirose with his dark thick hair and chiseled teeth, so white. Nakama, skinny as a scarecrow, bowlegged, too. The Tsukano brothers from Mill Camp were up there, too. Pachi, the eldest, tallest, and least serious of the three; Shangy, who, even at a tender age, thought one day he'd be a boxer; and serious-minded Toshio, who had no objection when Mr. Sakamoto had started calling him "John." In the mix were a Shibuya and a Ginoza, a Yamashita and a Castor—most Japanese, and here or there a Filipino.

Soichi Sakamoto knew them all. Some had started with him in the ditch in 1932. Some he'd coached in Little Tots basketball or track; he'd taught each one science and health in the fifth or sixth grade, but no matter how he had come to know them, over the years they had become more familiar to him than his own children. Some had been in his Scout troop, or during some weeks in the previous summers he'd overseen them at a Scout camp up in PenCarPo.

The Pursuit of Greater Ventures

Now the children looked beyond him at the signs he'd hung upon his classroom walls. One read: "Join Now! Sign Here!" And on both Sakamoto had drawn a crest of his own designing, an image that had turned out imperfect and inelegant but for which he'd borrowed the calligraphic style of merit badges in the Boy Scout handbook. Into the crest he tried to put too much—both significance and style in the various characters. He'd tried to make the letters and the numbers stay inside the boundaries and form a kind of whole, but everything had bunched together and angled up, and the end result was jagged and unreadable like a cattle brand in ancient Greek.

Sakamoto watched the children try to make meaning of the signs. He looked out at them, and they stared back. They could have no idea what it was that he was going to say.

At last he cleared his throat and began.

"The 3YSC," he said, pointing out the single number and the letters on the crest. "The Three-Year Swim Club," he explained. Nearby, he placed signup sheets and little cards. The club was like nothing else, he said, unlike anything the children in the room had ever known. If they joined, they signed the notebook and the cards and took an oath. It was a solemn oath, a commitment of three years. Three years of hard work and submission to unbendable rules: no smoking, drinking, gambling, cursing, spitting. No eating candy or drinking soda pop, no late hours, no social functions, movies, or romance. No other sports.

They would be a team. And he, Sakamoto told them, would be their coach.

If they signed on, they'd obey him and be loyal to the club. They'd show up to practice right on time and follow the routine.

At home, they had to respect their parents, too.

Three years of discipline. Three years of sacrifice. Three years of nothing except swimming. Only swimming.

Three hundred and sixty-five times three days.

Did they see what he was getting at?

They looked blankly back at him.

"In three years' time," Coach Sakamoto said, "if we all do our share," he continued, and looked around the room. "If we train hard and never surrender, I promise, we will meet our goal," which, he said, was nothing less than, in three years' time, to become members of the men's swim team of the United States of America at the Olympic Games in their parents' Tokyo.

No one said anything. A few children in the back giggled and then fell silent. Soichi Sakamoto could see that behind the children, beyond the glass windows of his classroom, the Kona winds were up that afternoon, blowing stalks and golden tassels forward and then back, as if the cane itself were wavering with indecision. Soon, the strike would end—it always did; the workers never got ahead—and life in Pu'unene would return to normal. The sugarcane would blaze, flames would light the night and lick familiarly at the morning haze, and the world would smell again as it always did—of money and molasses.

By Sakamoto's calculation, there were just 179 more days in the calendar year of 1937. Then there were two years more—'38 and '39, but then only half of 1940 for them to prepare for the challenge he'd put before them: to qualify for the Games at the summer trials that took place before the start of the Twelfth Olympiad. Soichi Sakamoto wasn't asking the children in the room merely to swim their hardest; he was asking them to do so with the knowledge that perhaps only one or two of them might even make it in the end. Still, the children came up one by one.

The first happened to be the eldest; his name was Chow Shibuya, and he was even married and drove a truck on the plantation; he had his children now, but he had told his former teacher that he'd always wanted to join a real swim team. The younger boys followed him. There was Hirose; Nakama; two Filipino kids, one named Jose Balmores and the other Benny Castor. The three Tsukano brothers, a boy named Shiro Mukai, one called Dynamite Nakasone, a kid named Tommy Yamashita, Tsugio Yamada, a Suzuki, a Yoshizawa, a Nakamura, and a hundred more.

Sakamoto gave each one a membership card and then he led them in the Pledge of Allegiance and the singing of "The Star-Spangled Banner," and he had them shout the club's motto at the tops of their lungs: "Olympics First, Olympics Always!" they cried in unison.

The Pursuit of Greater Ventures

For good measure, Soichi Sakamoto offered up a prayer. He liked the Lord's Prayer best. After all, if it took a thousand gallons of water to turn an acre of cane into a pound of sugar, then it was going to take a whole lot more than that—on earth and in heaven, Sakamoto knew—to take his swimmers, his sugar ditch kids, and turn them into Olympians.

PART TWO

ON SUCH A SEA

1938

The man who is swimming against the stream knows the strength of it.

—Woodrow T. Wilson

Give me six hours to chop down a tree and I will spend the first four sharpening the axe.

—Abraham Lincoln

Chapter Five

AN EXERCISE OF WILL

Bᴀᴄᴋ ɪɴ the days of Hawaii's Golden Age of Duke Kahanamoku, Buster Crabbe, Johnny Weissmuller, the Kealohas, and the Kalilis, Waikiki was the center of the universe. The great white fleet of the Matson line, luxury liners traveling between Los Angeles and Honolulu, Honolulu to Australia and New Zealand, and the greater speed and comfort of Japanese steamer travel, too—made Waikiki a veritable mecca for swimmers who wanted to get a good gander at one another. In the name of international friendships and cultural exchange—athletes, bearing gifts, plied the seas in large and cheerful groups to Honolulu, with its newly dredged harbor and modern pier, its fine tourist hotels and its newly built modern pools. The swim meets at that time were grand; the earliest, before the Nat went up, took place in Honolulu's two smaller pools. There was one at Palama Settlement House and one at the University of Hawaii, both of which were perfectly serviceable; but Punahou's Waterhouse Pool, named after a Punahou alumna who had died in a tragic car accident, was a sleek venue, modeled on the competitive pool at Yale, with perfect depth that cut down on drag, side gutters that absorbed water waves, and clean lanes, and it was considered the fastest pool in the islands.

Duke Kahanamoku had had long sojourns in Australia in the teens, during which time he helped to invigorate and transform swimming there, and in 1916 a Punahou girl was the first in Hawaii history to travel to San Francisco for a competitive meet; by the 1920s, swimmers from Yale, headed by their indomitable coach, Robert J. H. Kiphuth, came to town often, as did the Japanese, who competed in a meet when the Nat opened in August of 1927, and who, in a gesture of friendship, brought with them a bowl of water from the Meiji Shrine Pool to mix with the waters of the new tank in Waikiki. There were few weeks in the summer when an exhibition meet wasn't on, and tourists flocked to see the matchups. When the Golden Age was over, those passing through most often were American collegiate swimmers under the leadership of Kiphuth, who, in addition to his responsibilities to his Elis, had also been coach to the American Olympic team for more than a decade.

After the lull, the San Francisco O's came to Waikiki in August of 1937, during a booming year for swimming. The effort to jump-start a second golden age in Hawaii also brought to town another group of visitors—Americans under another Mainland coach, Stanley Brauninger, of Chicago's Lakeshore Athletic Club—who were on their way back from an All-Japan Championship in Tokyo.

In the wake of Keo Nakama's scintillating performance against Ralph Gilman on the twentieth of August, the Junior Chamber of Commerce asked Soichi Sakamoto and the Three-Year Swim Club to stay on in Waikiki for a second big meet between the "Americans" and the "Hawaiians."

On the night of Keo Nakama's win over Olympian Ralph Gilman in the Waikiki Natatorium, Honolulu's sports reporters had stayed up way past their bedtimes swatting away at the keys of their typewriters, and the next day's headlines were as bold as the letters on a movie marquee: "Youngster Defeats Olympic Star," "Hawaii Still Has Possibilities," "Maui Lad Steals Thunder in Duke Meet."

The *Honolulu Advertiser* pronounced the meet one of the most exciting in the history of Hawaii, and in the Japanese- and English-language newspaper, *Hawaii Hochi*, Ralph Gilman gushed about Nakama: the boy was unbeatable, carried on by fight that night, and in a year or two he was headed somewhere; Nakama's performance was of national and perhaps even international caliber. Only one week later, Nakama would have the chance to prove that he was well on his way to becoming a pro.

With the second group of Americans, the expectations of Nakama were higher and so were the stakes. This time, the group was led by Coach Stanley Brauninger, and his team had on it *only* Olympians: among them were blond-haired blue-eyed Olympic backstroker Adolph Kiefer, whom Brauninger had discovered at the age of eight or nine swimming in a Chicago canal; sprinters Otto Jaretz and Paul Wolf; and the famed king of the 400-meter freestyle, Jack Medica, the only swimmer to have won gold at Berlin. There, Medica had smashed Johnny Weissmuller's Olympic record to bits with a time of 4:44.5.

Stan Brauninger was older by some twenty years than Soichi Sakamoto, but similar to Sakamoto, he had a soft spot for poor kids; he'd do anything to help them. Not only had Brauninger discovered Adolph Kiefer, but he had also coached him to stardom and Olympic glory; and he had taken him under his wing both in sport and in life: he was the kid's legal adoptive father.

This time, Soichi Sakamoto brought with him two of his virtually adopted children, not just Keo Nakama but Takashi "Halo" Hirose, as well. Sakamoto knew that Keo had Adolph Kiefer's drive, but he wanted to test Hirose out against the big boys now: Hirose had shown much promise as a swimmer, but he had yet to prove whether he had the strength of character to become a true champ.

Hirose had the potential to be as big a star as Nakama; his trophy-winning performance against University of Hawaii collegiate swimmers in the men's division on Memorial Day weekend at Punahou School in '37 suggested a bright future and had won him a big trophy, but Hirose wasn't cut from the same cloth as Keo Nakama. And even though the two boys lived in houses that sat directly across from each other in camp—their front screen doors even aligned—their families couldn't have been more different from each other. Everyone, including Soichi Sakamoto, saw that Nakama was a survivor, a child in a relentlessly physically abusive home; whereas Hirose was the prized youngest male in a family with a high opinion of itself. Nakama, even bruised all over, *could* have complained about his life but never did; instead, he always stepped up, was solid, reliable, and driven, and he'd earned his nickname by being the "key," the go-to kid in the Camp 5 gang.

Hirose was another story. He had little about which to complain, but he was a whiner. He had been nursed until the age of five, and he was chubby, entitled, and greedy beyond need. He'd be fed dinner at home—first, of course—and then he'd wander upstream to a relative's house, complain he had an empty belly, and mooch a second meal. Once, he stole a watermelon from the Camp 5 store, and though his punishment—having to eat the whole thing in one sitting—was intended to ruin his taste for theft, he'd relished every bite.

In school, Hirose thinned out in the belly, and he became muscular, and brazen in personality. He had a high cowlick at the front of his forehead— anywhere farther back would have been unfortunate, but where it was it gave him a handsome hairline and his spectacularly thick black hair made him look like a star of the silver screen. In the days before good dentistry and orthodontics, he had improbably white and straight teeth and a wide smile, on either side of which were dimples deep enough to hide secrets in.

In fact, he had secrets, or he pretended he did. He cultivated for himself an air of mystery and a life of excitement, and if he wasn't an outright liar, everyone knew him to habitually mix fact and fiction, always leaving out of any story details that might have been unflattering to him. The older he grew, the more smug, self-important, and lazy he became. By fifteen there remained little hope of resetting his self-regard and moral compass. He had grown far too handsome for his own good; he adored girls and they adored him. He was pie-eyed and distracted almost all the time. He'd earned his camp nickname when, in a sandlot baseball game, he missed a cinch of a pop fly and the ball dropped right at his bare toes and lay there while he considered it. He took his time picking it up and tossing it in, after which the Camp 5 gang called him hollow-headed. He was "Halo." The name fit him perfectly, and it stuck.

The problem was, though: the kid could swim, and Sakamoto couldn't risk losing him. In practice, he always had to push him; Halo liked short distances, sprints, because they required less of his time and energy. He preferred short pools to longer ones, and he used push-offs from the wall as his crutch. But he was also like lightning in the water, likely a future sprinter.

An Exercise of Will

Sakamoto wanted to see how Hirose would fare, without his crutch, in a 100-meter pool. He put both Nakama and Hirose in the pool with Jack Medica.

Nakama's performance was no surprise. He proved that his win over Gilman was no fluke by pressing his second Olympian contender in a week throughout the 400-meter race, even overtaking him in the last lap, although Medica managed to pull ahead in the end—but by only one stroke. The Olympian came in at a time of 5:02.3, and Nakama was right behind him.

In the 220-yard freestyle, Halo Hirose surprised everyone, coming in, as Nakama had, just one second behind Medica's 2:18.3. He could have done even better, Sakamoto knew. Hirose had gotten caught up in the ropes and gone crooked and that had put him just a tad off course.

In the locker room postrace, Medica yelled out to Hirose, "Keep it up, young man!" and he told him that if he was ever in the Big Apple, he and his friends ought to drop by the New York Athletic Club and see him, an offer of which Halo, who was impressed by such things, made much talk.

At the start of the school year in the fall of 1938, both Hirose's and Nakama's successes brought droves more plantation kids to the Camp 5 pool, so many, in fact, that a joke went around that Soichi Sakamoto might have to hire a couple of junior police officers to control the flow of traffic. A few of the originals had moved on: a kid named Kotoro "Emerick" Ishikawa was more interested in weight lifting; and some, like Rikio Ebisu, who was one of Sakamoto's younger brother Benzo's friends, just didn't have that much interest in the water.

However, through the fall and the spring, the pool teemed with new members who showed up every day despite what Coach Soichi Sakamoto demanded of them. Practice was twice a day, every day, Saturdays, Sundays, holidays, birthdays, no exceptions. Morning practice began at 6 a.m. and ended just before the first school bell. If a swimmer was late, he was off the team. Afternoon practice began at 3 p.m., and it carried on until dinnertime, usually until after dark when the children watched the workers leave the fields long before they left the pool.

On Such a Sea

Every practice session was lockstep: a swimmer signed in, showered, checked the boards—there were two, a blackboard for special announcements and a wooden-framed board with interchangeable painted slats that spelled out the day's regimen: calisthenics, arm machine, board-kicking, tire-pulling, land-stroking, loosening up. One exercise was called slow swimming for distance, another was speed-swimming. For distance and endurance Sakamoto wanted every swimmer to work up to a mile per day. Hardworking old-time ditch kids like Nakama hit the mark early, as did eleven-year-old Johnny Tsukano, the youngest and most serious of the three Tsukano brothers; he'd hit 72 laps in just a few practices.

Other kids struggled, but nobly. Charlie Oda was a new kid out of Kahului, rail-thin, sweet-natured, with a pair of Tom and Jerry eyes dark as ink. He was so poor that for breakfast he had one hardtack cracker and for lunch he had nothing; he spent his lunch money to get to the Camp 5 pool by bus. He and Yoshio Shibuya, a pointy-chinned mite of a kid so weak he didn't have the strength to lug his books to school, struggled to do just one 25-yard lap across the tank.

But Charlie Oda, Shibuya, and other children like Jose Balmores, out of Camp 5, were spunky kids, and spirits ran high throughout the club's ranks. Sakamoto's message to the children was that any one of them could be an Olympian; it was a matter of sticking to the program, and Sakamoto built in incentives for them to stay.

Saturday practices were all day long, two sessions, but Mary came by with lunch for everyone. With the two boys in tow, she rolled in a cart, handing out rice and fish. The hungriest kids were the most grateful, but all the children started calling her "Missus." Sundays were all day long, too, but they started with time trials. The kids loved to race and to keep track of their improvement in their own notebooks, and after another lunch from "Missus," Sakamoto let them rest in the shade while he held forth on all manner of topics from healthy eating to cultivating a champion's mind-set. The kids joked and called the lectures "Coach Church" or "Sakamoto's Sermons."

Sakamoto took a page from Mary's playbook, and from *The Revised Handbook for Boys* and Norman Vincent Peale's weekly radio show, encouraging the swimmers with positive thinking and adages that he posted on big sheets of paper or wrote out on the blackboard.

"Set your goal high." "Be ashamed of yourself when you are giving up." "Constantly correct your mistakes and weaknesses and strengthen your character!" "Be greater than ever and you will tower above the others." "By doing your very best always you form a splendid habit and virtue."

Every day at practice, he told the kids that they were one day closer to the Olympics. He asked each one, "You want to be a champion?" and he told them that, if they did want to be one—in the pool *or* in life—they had a choice. Signing up for the Three-Year Swim Club was a commitment, but to keep a commitment over time one had to exercise one's will. Will was the application of that original commitment. Will was a choice. And the choice was in the children's hands. "Make no bones about it," Sakamoto said. If they wanted to meet their goal, they had to make conscious choices, every day.

In the spring of 1938, Soichi Sakamoto's goal was to prepare as many of his swimmers as possible to be competitive in the Hawaiian AAU championships in June. Those who hit fast enough times would qualify for the Men's AAU Nationals in Louisville, Kentucky, in July. An added bonus was that the AAU was putting up the cash for other Hawaiian swimmers to travel to the West Coast before the Nationals in order to participate in an invitational that would take place throughout California. The Pacific Coast Association billed the meets as a preview to the 1940 Games, and the best collegiate and club swimmers on the Mainland would be there.

In order to calculate how the swimmers could qualify for Louisville, Sakamoto worked backward. He consulted his charts: At the end of 1937, the 100-yard freestyle collegiate mark stood at 51.4 seconds. Halo Hirose and Keo Nakama could negotiate that event at 57.4 and 57.8, respectively. In the 220-yard freestyle, the collegiate mark was 2:09.7, and Nakama was negotiating it at about 2:20 even.

The answers were hard to swallow. To be competitive, Hirose and Nakama would have to shave between 5 and 10 seconds off times in their events. It was a staggering gap to close; it was the equivalent of asking a runner who ran a 4 minute 10 second mile in March to get his time down by June to 4 minutes flat.

Sakamoto's training regimen grew out of the belief that if the children's parents were capable of working as hard in the fields as they did, then the children could do the same in the pool. He sought out the best fieldworkers, the ones who earned bonuses; he stopped them in the roads as they were headed home after a long day in the fields. They were covered in mud and tired, but they were kind and polite enough to answer what might have seemed to them odd questions.

"How," Sakamoto asked them, "do you manage maintaining your job all day long with your back bent and your cutting…without getting overtired?" And they told him: "Steady, steady, steady." Work at the same rate all day and every day, they said.

And how did the workers get faster, better and better at what they did? he asked.

"Keep your tool sharp," they answered, pointing to their bolo knives.

The first he understood completely, but it would take him a little longer to sort out what tool in the pool had to be as sharp as a machete in the cane field.

As the official swim season approached, Sakamoto increased practice time, with the second practice of each day extending well into the night, sometimes as late as 1 a.m. On Sundays, the lectures got longer and more intense. The children, Sakamoto told them, would have to do their best, not just in Maui, not just in the Territory of Hawaii, but also on the Mainland and beyond. They would have to be the best wherever they were. In their homes. In the entire world. He reminded them of their promise to themselves: "Olympics First, Olympics Always!" Success, he told them, led to success. And "steady" was more than just swimming. Sakamoto meant it to be a way of life. But not everyone agreed with Soichi Sakamoto's philosophy or had faith in his methods, and in the early spring of 1938, Sakamoto found himself summoned abruptly to an urgent meeting in downtown Wailuku to discuss those very methods with E. L. Damkroger.

Ernest Leaphart Damkroger had reigned for fourteen years over a peaceable kingdom of his own making. As director of athletics on the Valley Isle, he had created and now supervised a sports and recreation program par excellence. Each year, thousands of Maui's young people, most but not all of them plantation children, delighted in the opportunities afforded to them. Boys and girls played barefoot basketball and barefoot football, tennis, soccer, and golf, wrestled and ran track on hundreds of island teams in more than sixty distinct athletic leagues. Damkroger's system was founded on logic and practicality; there was a season for each sport, sign-up sheets, regulations and rules for play, schedules for games and matches, annual island and interisland competitions to which the children could look forward, and of course, culminating each season were championship meets from which hundreds of children with little else to their names walked proudly away with troves of ribbons, trophies, and certificates that bore their names. Each island team had a coach, uniforms, and, depending on the sport, caps, helmets, rackets, bats, balls, and the like.

Damkroger was perfectly suited to his employment. A transplant to Maui, he was a Mainlander who via various employments had migrated farther and farther west in his twenties, ending up teaching physical education in California, then living on Kauai and finally moving to the Valley Isle, where he had put down roots. He was born in the Midwest and was of solid German stock, his own parents first-generation immigrants who had farmed on the outskirts of St. Paul, Minnesota, and he brought to all of his endeavors a kind of precision and a no-nonsense, corn-fed way of thinking. He had gone to Springfield College in the East, an institution from which he had not graduated, but from which he had still received a diploma: his studies had been interrupted by World War I, and after having served as a doughboy and returning home, he received a certificate in the mail from Springfield.

Damkroger, who had played football in high school and college, dressed, intentionally it seemed, more egghead than athlete, in neatly pressed clothing and a pair of tortoiseshell glasses with frames as small as mercury dimes and through which he cast his gimlet gaze down upon anyone with whom he was keeping company.

He was a tall man, 6 feet 2, so looking down on others suited his size, and some described him as rangy, though he was more gangly than rangy, awkward, with long, useless-looking arms and a moon face, a countenance suggesting softness, for which he compensated by wearing his trousers tightly belted and high above his waist, just below his lungs, as if to demonstrate his fortitude in needing less air to breathe than others. Damkroger came directly from the business world to Maui in '24, having previously been in the employ of a sugar plantation on Kauai, where he worked in "industrial relations." Union agitators unsettled Kauai, and E. L. Damkroger's win over the workers was achieved by painting management in a good light.

Successful there, Damkroger was soon recruited for a similar challenge on Maui: sugar planters hired him to bring order to the chaos in their island-wide athletics program.

In the words of one of the island's historians, Maui was, from its early days, "sports crazy." Missionary children had taken to Maui's gnarly waves and carved curls on homemade redwood surfboards. They'd played America's favorite pastime as well, and when a fellow by the name of Alexander Cartwright—who, with US Union Army general Abner Doubleday, was one of the fathers of baseball—visited the islands in 1849, hoping to introduce baseball, he found that missionaries had already laid out regulation diamonds and played the game every day save the Lord's. Brits introduced lawn tennis and tea parties in the 1880s, and by the '90s, sugar barons played volleyball, basketball, and football. For shoulder pads in the latter game, they used leaves and twigs.

The most popular pastime on Maui was the Sport of Kings. In polo, the Baldwin family enjoyed island-wide, national, and international fame. In 1915, it was said that the colt named "Carry the News," belonging to

An Exercise of Will

Dr. William Dwight Baldwin, Frank Baldwin's grandfather, was the best polo pony in the world. Edwin Baldwin, all of twelve years old, was called the game's rising star. *Polo* magazine named Lawrence "Chu" Baldwin the number-one-ranked player in the nation; and when the Eli cracked his collarbone in a match against Harvard, the *New York Times* ran a front-page article. Once, George Patton, the general himself, traveled to the Baldwins' grounds to play a match, after which it was said that he celebrated by standing on his head and drinking a glass of whiskey upside down. Frank Baldwin sent his ponies as far away as England to compete, and when the Baldwin stables went up in flames in 1925 and all its mounts were lost, the *Washington Post* carried news of the tragedy.

The Baldwins, Alexanders, Castles, and Cookes played and worked together; sport went well with cocktails and contract and merger negotiations, and sugar. Sport was a civilizing force in all men's lives, and, the sugar barons knew, it was an effective way not only to keep their fieldworkers healthy but to organize them into groups more pleasing than those into which the workers might have "organized" themselves.

When E. L. Damkroger arrived on Maui in 1924, he found the sports program broken beyond repair. The churches that had once provided both financial support and a moral compass for sport had abandoned their role, and what remained was chaos: a handful of raggedy teams that had devolved into brutal self-rule and moral depravity, and whose players resorted to violence, even on the field. Most of the players on Maui's sports teams were thuggish adolescents and degenerate grown men. Maui County's sheriff put it best: all games on the Valley Isle were played at that time in three halves, two on the field and a third on Main Street, afterward.

In E. L. Damkroger's first attempt to bring about order, he officiated at a football game, during which he experienced all of the following: a rowdy *paniolo*—upcountry cowboy—equipped with a lariat, who made it perfectly clear that he didn't like to hear referees make calls with which he didn't agree; a burly wide receiver who took a swing at his opponent tackler, which led to fisticuffs, which led to cursing the likes of which E. L. Damkroger had never heard before. And finally, in the last quarter of the game the players on both teams announced they would like to "see" Damkroger after the last blow of the whistle, after which E. L. Damkroger ran for his life, barricading himself in a nearby house until the mob scattered.

Damkroger girded his loins. He summarily disbanded all the island's teams and forbade all thugs from participating; he recruited Japanese youths from the plantations, and he reset the moral compass behind the rules and regulations. He began to eject miscreant fans so freely that by the end of games, there were often more players on the field than spectators in the bleachers, and as a means of educating the rabble, he handed out quizzes on game rules and etiquette and awarded the fan who had the most correct answers a cash prize.

Within a year, the *Maui News* lauded E. L. Damkroger for his achievements. No one, it was said, had ever "conducted...affairs so systematically." But as successful and as well-intentioned as Damkroger was, he continued to be disliked and proved unpopular not only with teams but also coaches, who found him tyrannical and zealous and who accused him of being an Abercrombie with a "superiority complex." Even those who'd hired him took pleasure in calling him behind his back "that *Damn*-kroger": their emphasis on the letter *m*, turning his surname into a profanity.

Sakamoto had been a mere flea in Damkroger's ear until January of 1934, when, with the publication of Urban Allen's inaugural column, "Men You Know in Sports," he came to public attention (Allen didn't acknowledge Damkroger until four months later); and then, in 1935, when Sakamoto's ditch kids won the island's annual swim meet, drawing attention to the fact that Damkroger hadn't arranged for a pool in which they could practice, Sakamoto's name rumbled in the man's ear like thunder. And the Three-Year Swim Club blasted Damkroger's ego like a cannon shot. Sakamoto's club was completely separate and financially independent from E. L. Damkroger's control, as Sakamoto had intended it to be. Damkroger endeavored to get control over the 3YSC, going so far as to get himself elected proxy of the Hawaiian Amateur Athletic Union, but even that had failed to keep the Three-Year Swim Club down.

In the spring of 1938, Damkroger had been distracted by minute details. One of his employees had submitted her resignation, and the recruit who was to replace her had no expertise in the hula; a group of kamaainas, unnerved by the Japanese invasion of Nanjing, complained about the sight of squads of Boy Scouts marching about Wailuku town in uniform. Mrs. Mabel Brown, in charge of the annual girls' water pageant, had a tendency to overspend her budget, and she said this year's program, "Nature at Play," would depict the tranquil home life of a Hawaiian family living on the edge of a secluded pool, and it would feature King Neptune—costumed far too expensively, in Damkroger's mind—who would perform the marriage of characters named Mr. H-2 and Miss O. An earthquake had rattled Maui, but it seemed as though the only one it bothered was E. L. Damkroger, although what really rattled him was the 3YSC, and soon Soichi Sakamoto found himself called into Damkroger's office for a meeting.

Sakamoto knew that he and E. L. Damkroger were bound to clash someday, but when he arrived at his office at Alexander House Settlement, Sakamoto was surprised to see that Damkroger wasn't alone. Among those gathered was Robert E. Hughes, a powerful executive at HC&S and longtime member of the island's swimming committee. Another was "Bud" Crabbe, brother to the famous "Flash Gordon," Buster Crabbe.

Hughes had a rather high opinion of himself and about what he thought of as Maui's own golden age of swimming. Though Hughes was originally from Honolulu, he'd been central to boosting swimming on Maui through Damkroger's program, and he all too fondly remembered the good old days: the days without newfangled bathing suits or lane lines or even pools. When he'd been in the tank, Crabbe had acquitted himself reasonably, but he had never reached the height of his brother's fame.

Bud Crabbe took the first shot. He leaned in and said, "Sakamoto, don't you think you're burning the kids out?" and he pointed to what he said were outrageous practice times. Why, the Maui High swim team did an hour per day, and not on the weekends.

Hughes's son, Donald, had swum for Maui High. In the previous year, Donald Hughes had been named one of the top up-and-coming Maui swimmers, but he'd been eclipsed entirely by Nakama and Hirose.

And why, Hughes asked, were the children made to swim a mile each day? And why was Sakamoto putting them into competitions with adults? That simply wasn't done.

When it was his turn, Sakamoto tried his best to explain: swimming against the current; steady-steady; the great success he was having with resistance training and fast-slow work in the water. The inner tubes, the kickboards, the machines. "Nobody who starts with me," he began, "is swimming a mile on the first day."

Did they see? he asked.

They didn't. They couldn't.

Conventional wisdom on Maui and almost everywhere in the world was that athletes were at their best when babied. In the Ivy Leagues, a difficult workout had long been thought to be a couple of laps in the pool followed by a vigorous rubdown and a fine cigar. In Japan, while everybody knew the Japanese had ramped up their training programs to the highest degree—with practices equally as challenging as Sakamoto's, the inhaling of oxygen, and the eating of special diets said to consist only of soybeans—at least in writing, the Japanese advice was that whenever a swimmer might find himself exhausted, the best thing was to stop practicing entirely and take a little trip.

Damkroger had said little, but Sakamoto knew what he thought. Not long before, Damkroger had told the papers how impressed he was by Soichi Sakamoto. Here, he said, was a man—even so untrained, so unprepared—and elementary school teacher who hadn't let his own shortcomings hold him back from developing excellent swimmers. The man had worked hard. As hard as he possibly could, Damkroger had said.

And this day, Hughes and Crabbe had made Sakamoto out to be a sadist. When he left the meeting, he felt as if he had been hung up by his thumbs.

On a March day, at a time when none of the children happened to be around, Sakamoto looked up from his work to see the figure of Ralph Gilman come through the gate of the Camp 5 pool. He hadn't seen Gilman since the night that Keo Nakama had beaten the Olympian at the Natatorium in August, and Gilman might as easily have been a ghost or a premonition of something, but there he was, standing on the zigzag deck, tall and smiling, and dressed in a short-sleeved shirt that showed off his drumstick arms. His blond hair waved in the Kona breeze.

Sakamoto shook the giant's hands.

Gilman explained that he had returned to the Mainland after the Duke meet, and after having toured around and visited Maui, he had fallen in love with the place. Back home, he'd married a sweet girl named Maureen and convinced her that she'd love Maui as much as he did, and here he was. He'd hung up his amateur status and swim trunks, had found a good job at Maui Soda & Ice Works, and he was here to stay. How happy he was, he said, to see Sakamoto, and then, unbelievably, Ralph Gilman asked, "So, Coach, how can I help you out?"

Sportswriters had spent time in the bleachers in the preseason mesmerized by the improvement of the kids in the 3YSC since '37. Nakama and Hirose had been churning faster and faster times in workouts; Keo took over the middle and long distances, and he hit the 500-yard swim, 20 laps in the Baldwin Pool, at under 6 minutes. Now, with Ralph Gilman's help, it was assumed that both boys would speed ahead.

Halo Hirose did. Like a greyhound with a rabbit to chase, he began negotiating the 100-yard freestyle below the minute mark, at 55 seconds even, and his 50-yard "split" was 25.6 seconds. By the time the spring island season was over he had sliced almost 3 seconds off his time, and he hovered not far away from the collegiate mark of 51.4.

Disturbingly, though, Nakama plateaued. He was late to practices and meets and his mind just didn't seem to be at the pool. In fact, it wasn't. Ralph Gilman solved the mystery; he spied Keo out on the Baldwin Park baseball diamond, fielding balls and pretending to be Casey at the Bat. When Gilman brought the boy to Sakamoto, Sakamoto wasn't angry, but he sat Keo down.

Sakamoto told Nakama the sad truth: there wasn't any future in base-ball; did Keo see any Japanese people playing in the major leagues? Keo shook his head. Japanese were too small, Sakamoto said, and he reminded Keo how small, in particular, he was. Keo could languish on the plantation baseball diamond on Maui or he could swim competitively across the world and even get a college scholarship on the Mainland. Nakama was crest-fallen, but he knew what Sakamoto was saying was true, and the next day he was back in the pool, literally making up for lost time.

Gilman was helpful to the cause of the Three-Year Swim Club in other ways as well. As an Olympian, he served as a walking, talking public rela-tions machine. Nakama and Hirose were "ripe," he told reporters, not only to take an interisland cattle boat to the Hawaiian AAUs but also to take a steamer to the Mainland.

The trip to the Mainland was expensive; the steamer alone cost nearly $100 per round-trip ticket, and there was the cross-country train trip, meals, accommodations, uniforms, and more. He didn't want to burden the chil-dren's families—they had already dug deep into their pockets, so Sakamoto had led a grassroots fund-raising campaign. He washed their faces and neatened them up and sent the children out into the larger community. He taught them how to knock on doors politely, to sell bread and candy; and he arranged with the owner of the movie theater for the club to show Japanese-language movies on Samurai Saturdays. But the biggest moneymakers were the club's water carnivals, including one featuring Olympian Ralph Gilman as the star. Crowds came out by the thousands to watch Gilman swim and to see their local heroes, Keo Nakama and Halo Hirose, speed up and down the length of the Camp 5 pool.

Gate receipts were generous enough that when Nakama and Hirose did, in fact, qualify for the Men's Nationals, there was enough money in the 3YSC kitty to send the two boys and their coach to California and on to Louisville.

That same spring, in faraway Tokyo, Jigoro Kano was packing his trunk for a journey of his own, preparing for another voyage at sea. He'd been abroad twelve times before, most of his trips on behalf of the modern Olympics. Now he was headed to the International Olympic Committee congress in Cairo, Egypt, almost ten thousand miles from home.

He was nearly seventy-nine. The past five years hadn't been particularly kind to him. Since 1932, the path to the Tokyo Games had been littered with every possible obstacle one could imagine encountering and then more that could never have been anticipated. It had taken all his moral strength and courage to carry on, and now, although he hated to admit it, his body was failing him. He had begun to use a walking stick, and he had acquiesced, but not easily, when his wife insisted he take a companion along with him to Egypt, a caregiver, in fact. He looked frail to friends, tired, but he was far from ready to give up the fight.

It had taken until late 1936 for Kano finally to secure the 1940 Games for Tokyo, and the process had been most unpleasant. Kano was a spectacularly talented diplomat, but some of his colleagues on the Japanese Olympic Committee weren't as gifted, nor did they understand Western ways as well as he did. There was a protocol for things in the West, and there were particular protocols for how the IOC conducted business. Kano's colleagues fumbled repeatedly.

In Los Angeles in '32, Kano had politicked meticulously. His speeches, the parties he'd thrown, his appearances at events, and his warm and cheerful character had endeared him to members of the IOC and had won over the infamously prickly Avery Brundage and the IOC president, Count Henri de Baillet-Latour. But between 1932 and 1936, some of Kano's colleagues, fearful that Tokyo might not be chosen, engaged in backroom dealings that served only to offend Baillet-Latour and the committee. The Japanese weren't being underhanded; cultural differences between Asia and the West abounded; in that gap, there was plenty of room for misunderstanding.

Tokyo's competitors for the candidature had originally been Alexandria, Barcelona, Helsinki, and Rome. At the 1932 Games, the Italians had set a poor precedent by sending telegrams to the IOC every day urging it to keep the heart and soul of the Games in Europe. In the ensuing years, Jigoro Kano had done much to persuade the committee otherwise. He had successfully convinced many that Tokyo was no different from London, Paris, Los

Angeles, or any other city, and he had won hearts when he asked that "the Olympic torch light the way to the Orient."

Prior to the 1936 IOC meeting in Berlin, however, one of the other Japanese delegates visited personally with Mussolini, negotiating with him to withdraw Rome's bid. The deal was not only questionable in terms of protocol; it was also alarming to many that Japan, Italy, and by extension Germany, which was also involved in the agreement, were politically aligned. Specifically, Japan had brokered Italy's withdrawal of its own Olympic bid by agreeing to cease selling arms to Ethiopia—a region in which both Italy and Germany had military interests. In addition, Italy and Germany had agreed publicly to support Japan's candidature. Japan was now favored to host the Games, but when word reached Count Baillet-Latour of the nation's secret dealings, he made it amply clear that he would put a hold on a decision about Tokyo until *after* the Berlin Olympiad.

Kano had succeeded, somehow, in winning back Baillet-Latour's favor, and at the beginning of 1937, the Tokyo Games appeared to be on track. What the world saw from the outside was a nation readying itself to play host to the biggest sporting event in the world.

It was reported that the OOC—the Japanese Olympic Committee—was flush with cash, including some 9 million yen from the emperor himself. The OOC had organized itself at last and had formed its committees and its subcommittees to attend to questions large and small. Would Tokyo's infrastructure, put in place by Hidejiro Nagata in 1930, support the weight of the Games ten years later? Would there need to be an Olympic Village? Would the hotels properly accommodate tourists? Would the city need to build additional hotels? Were the railways ready? The banks?

Questions arose about the appropriate venues for sports like yachting—a Western event with which Japan had no tradition or experience. And in other places where East was to meet West in '40, was Japan culturally prepared? The government embarked on an energetic campaign to improve moral behavior and public etiquette, and to develop a more "genteel" populace. The Japanese people must learn what in Britain it meant to take one's tea; they must refrain from habits such as tossing litter in the streets and "promiscuous" public spitting. Tour guides must be fluent in English—mastering all the foreign idioms. When William May Garland, head American delegate to the IOC and former president of the Los Angeles Games, returned from Japan after visiting there with his wife, he announced that he was most certain that the 1940 Tokyo Games would be the best ever held.

But all was not well. In June of 1937, the same month in which Soichi Sakamoto formed the Three-Year Swim Club, Japan invaded China, setting off alarms across the world. By December, the Japanese had taken Nanking; the death toll and reports of atrocities on the part of the Japanese were shocking. Western countries began to question not only whether Tokyo would be capable of holding the Games in 1940—but whether the Empire of Japan was even civilized enough a nation. How could the Chinese and the Japanese participate in an Olympiad while they were at war with each other?

One newspaper reporter asked how two countries, which had just one summer before so politely competed against each other on playing fields, could come to be such enemies on the battlefield. Athletes who had thrown discuses in the 1936 Games now tossed grenades at one another in war. How could the Olympics be held in that situation? Governing rules of the IOC held that nations at war could not host an Olympiad; however, Japan had refused to formally declare the hostilities a war.

Count Baillet-Latour set the agenda for the upcoming spring 1938 IOC meeting to include primarily a discussion of whether Japan was fit to keep the Games for 1940. There, the committee as a whole would hear from Jigoro Kano himself, as he defended why the IOC oughtn't to rescind and reassign the Games.

Jigoro Kano prepared now to leave. It was early spring of 1938. He would travel to Cairo and give it his best effort. After all, he joked with one reporter, even at his advanced age, he still had the ability to fell an opponent twice his size. If his verbal persuasions didn't work on the IOC, "as a last resort," he said, he "could always use some judo on them."

Chapter Six

OWING TO THE
PROTRACTED HOSTILITIES

On Friday, June 24, 1938, the SS *Matsonia* steamed out of Honolulu Harbor bound for the city of Los Angeles, and among the eight hundred souls aboard were a man and two boys whose first-class tickets were evidence of the measure of their hard work over the past year. The *Matsonia* was a floating palace, rising six towering decks high to its double-funnels bearing the signature, navy blue *M* of the Matson luxury line.

Inside, wood-paneled lifts carried guests from floor to floor, where Sakamoto and the boys found a ballroom, a barbershop, a smoking room, and a glassed-in promenade deck. On another deck was a library with real leather-bound classics, a playroom equipped with pick-up sticks and puzzles, a lounge with a grand piano, and two movie theaters. And should any of them run out of necessities, there was a little novelty shop stocked with smelling salts and handkerchiefs and notecards.

The first evening aboard the ship, the ship's inaugural Aloha dinner took place, and Sakamoto had bought for himself and the boys matching white linen suits. The dining room was massive—a third of the length of the entire vessel; the ceiling rose two decks high to a balcony where an orchestra played strains of "Rose Marie." Along the walls of the room were arched murals, and every table, round or square, was covered in damask. The room was full of first-class passengers resplendent in their evening wear and drinking wine from goblets.

Owing to the Protracted Hostilities

At the table to which Sakamoto and the boys were assigned awaited the All-Hawaiian team, a group of Honolulu swimmers, youngsters the same age as Halo and Keo, girls and boys with whom they'd be traveling all the way to the coast and then through California for two weeks. At the head of the table, unbelievably, sat the group's official chaperone, Duke Paoa Kahanamoku, his silver hair combed back with perfection, his three-piece suit impeccably pressed.

Sakamoto and the boys took their seats, and what lay before them was an astonishing display: fat black olives, sticks of celery, salted pecans in crystal dishes, and before each person a tower of bone china, at the top of which lay the evening's menu—a four-page affair printed on cream-colored parchment.

Dinner was a dreamlike feast. From the bustling galley emerged waiters who bore each course on a silver tray. First came a cocktail of slices of pineapple and tangerines; next was turtle soup. Then Royal Hawaiian Frog Legs browned in butter. Sweetbreads were next, along with bright green baby peas and the tiniest potatoes. The entrée was a capon for each guest, with chestnut dressing inside the bird; and after dinner, there were French dainties and coffee and a dessert called Frozen Delight.

Neither Halo nor Keo knew how to eat with a fork and knife, and they struggled through the meal. Halo was particularly ashamed, his face red, his frustration visible, yet unwilling to take help from anyone, pushing Sakamoto away; but after dinner, the mood lightened when someone at the table suggested that the group pass around its menus and autograph them as keepsakes.

Duke Kahanamoku signed his name on the front of each one, his signature in curlicues—his full name, too—the *D* and *P* and *K* oversized. Some of the Hawaiian kids signed their full names—Barney Pung, Diamond Martin, Lulu Kea—others wrote "Aloha," or "Here's to good times," and signed with just initials. The group was so jolly that even members of the crew signed, too: "Bob Needhorn, Bellboy #4," and "Fred Svetz, Elec. Optr. #A." The latter underlined his name with a John Hancock swirl. For the other swimmers, Sakamoto left just his signature, but on Keo Nakama's and Halo

Hirose's menus—he hadn't taken Hirose's mood personally—he left a special message:

> A great moment for us 3—isn't it? By Jove!
> Let's make the most of it, and let's bring home the bacon!

And he signed his name familiarly, "Soichi."

His experiences with Damkroger, Crabbe, and Hughes had shaken Sakamoto's confidence, and as he'd gotten on the *Matsonia*, Sakamoto imagined that a trip with so many haoles would be bleak and humiliating and that he would continually be aware of his role as a second-class citizen with a first-class ticket.

To his surprise, though, everyone was warm and kind. The passengers, captain, crew, and stewards—all of them treated him and the children as honored guests, not as country bumpkins who didn't belong, from the moment they had walked up the gangplank. At home, it would have been unheard of for Sakamoto and the boys to socialize with, let alone dine in the company of, haoles, but here they were part of the stream of things.

It was comforting and refreshing to be treated well. It was something Sakamoto hadn't experienced in Hawaii, but now the ocean between Hawaii and the Mainland appeared to wash away prejudice. The people of Hawaii weren't Filipino, Chinese, Japanese, or Native Islanders—they were all Hawaiians, and haoles found Hawaiians charming to the highest degree.

Traveling as the All-Hawaiian team coach was current AAU president Bill Cox, and with Kahanamoku as official chaperone to the trip, Sakamoto had assumed that Cox and the Olympian would consider Sakamoto of lesser stature. That, too, turned out to be wrong. When Sakamoto, Cox, and Kahanamoku tried to begin training the swimmers aboard, they'd discovered that the ship's enormous indoor pool, the Pompeian, was reserved for recreation and not available to them at all. The temporary canvas pool up on the sundeck was inadequate for twelve swimmers. Cox and Kahanamoku turned to Sakamoto for advice in what sort of training regimen they might work out, and Sakamoto ran calisthenics sessions and rigged up leather swimming belts so that as many swimmers as possible could practice in the water, and brought the group to the weight room.

It was Kahanamoku's deference, in particular, that impressed Sakamoto, and it continued with the trip.

The days and nights at sea had a welcomed rhythm. When the team wasn't at practice or gorging on prime rib and lamb chops—they joked that Honolulu's Diamond Martin was developing a malady they called "steak-itis"—they made their way about the ship, engaging in new activities wherever they found them. On the sports deck there were potato sack races for couples and shaving races to watch; they played Ping-Pong and watched skeet shooting—discovering that it was nearly impossible to hit a clay pigeon at sea—and they looked on as other first-class guests filled out race cards, rolled dice, and bet on wooden horses that stewards moved around on a little track, mimicking the Derby. They took up checkers and played card games, responding politely when passengers interrupted them to strike up conversations.

Their favorite activity of all, though, was what Sakamoto called "deck-walking." Dressed in their white linen suits, they promenaded like a gaggle of geese in the sunshine, stopping now and then to serenade guests in deck chairs. Barney Pung played his ukulele, and Diamond Martin strummed the steel guitar. Sakamoto could have cursed himself for not having brought his own instrument along, but both boys lent their strings to him. And as if his voice were some siren out at sea, whenever Sakamoto began to sing, it seemed the whole ship came to a standstill. He had recently composed hapa haole songs of his own. "Aloha, Hawaii, aloha to you," went one. Another he called "Beneath the Hawaiian Skies." A crowd gathered, mesmerized by his voice, applauding for encores, and begging him—and the children—to return to the very same spot the following afternoon for a repeat performance.

People were so kind, so curious about their enterprise and their lives on Maui. The notion that Keo and Halo lived on a sugar plantation but had dreams of something greater seemed to cheer those they met. A wealthy

On Such a Sea

Californian was so taken by their Horatio Alger–like tale that he extended an invitation to Sakamoto and the boys to, upon arrival on the West Coast, come out to his ranch and practice in his private swimming pool. Everywhere they went, the group became known as the "Swimming Musicians."

At night, after every sumptuous dinner, there was always occasion to walk again on the deck in the inky dark, with the sky above chockablock with stars. One evening, at about ten thirty, distant lights appeared on the horizon—a boat advancing—and as it came closer and closer, it revealed itself to be the *Lurline*, the sister vessel of the SS *Matsonia*, traveling in the opposite direction, toward Hawaii, having made its way already to the Mainland coast. The two ships were like lighted castles upon the sea, and on the decks and in the windows of the cabins, passengers waved from across the way and the captain of each ship blew his horn in greeting and farewell, and then each vessel traveled onward.

Sakamoto wrote home to E. L. Damkroger that night about what a wonderful time he was having. He described the deck-walking and the Ping-Pong, the singing and the sumptuous meals. He wrote of the calm sea, Diamond Martin's steak-itis, the California rancher, and the passing of ships in the night. He said he had never in his life been treated so well.

But there was one thing about which Sakamoto told Damkroger nothing, and he decided that he never would. It was that one night, at the end of an after-dinner promenade, Duke Kahanamoku had gestured to Sakamoto to stay behind as the group went on to their cabins. He had something he wanted to share with him, Kahanamoku said.

Sakamoto thought that during the trip, from time to time, he saw not just deference from Kahanamoku but even, perhaps, respect, as Kahanamoku watched him lead practice, and he was satisfied merely to be in the champion's presence.

That night, Duke Kahanamoku led Sakamoto through the dark, and Sakamoto followed him, surprised as they ventured farther and farther into a most unfamiliar and dark part of the vessel, until at last Kahanamoku turned to speak.

"The secret is in the stroke," he said. "It's in the stroke. Everything is," he said. The power a swimmer had wasn't in the legs; it was in the arms, Kahanamoku told him.

Sakamoto nodded silently. He had suspected it for months but hadn't been sure; now he had it on authority that the stroke was the machete in the cane field, the tool he must sharpen and keep sharp in his swimmers.

Kahanamoku's own method was quite specific. For him, it wasn't enough to "pull straight back," he said, with a closed hand and no bend in the elbow. The straight pull was conventional wisdom, but Sakamoto had found that even cupping one's hand during a straight pull didn't do much. For himself Duke had employed for years an S-motion in the pull, taken at the hip: two smooth half-circles in the downstroke just before one raised the elbow. The movement was counterintuitive; almost a zigzag, he explained, and it should have created drag. Instead, he explained, it had increased his power and speed, and it had made him the successful swimmer he'd become. But whatever the motion, the secret to success was in the arms.

Just as on board the ship, where the passengers had been wild about the Hawaiian team, Los Angelinos were wild about them, too. LA hailed the return of its hero, Duke Kahanamoku. The swimmer had first come to their attention when he'd passed through in the aughts, teens, and early twenties as a young swimming god. He was celebrated for teaching Californians how to surf, and he'd hung around with Hollywood types and had roles in movies. One oft-told—apocryphal—story lent credence to his greatness. It was said that once, off the coast of Oahu, Kahanamoku had "battled to the death…a ten-foot eel," losing in the process his right index finger. Another well-told tale, though this one was true, recounted the time when Kahanamoku had rescued (though not single-handedly) eight drowning people from a shipwreck off Corona del Mar.

Upon his arrival in Los Angeles in the summer of 1938, the papers hailed Kahanamoku as "America's All-Time No. 1 swimmer." His picture and the news of his arrival at port took up all the space above the sports page fold in the Los Angeles *Herald Tribune*; any incidental business about a filly by the name of Seabiscuit was relegated to a few small column inches below. One photograph caught Kahanamoku standing at the edge of the Los Angeles Olympic pool in Exhibition Park, dressed, incongruous with the setting but in keeping with his royal stature, in a three-piece suit and a tie. He gave off the gravity of a world leader as he oversaw his swimmers' practices.

As celebrated as Kahanamoku was in Los Angeles, it might surprise some to learn what happened next. It didn't surprise Kahanamoku one bit, however. In addition to being Hawaii's greatest, he was described as America's most "colorful" swimmer, and as much as some Mainlanders embraced Hawaiian culture, Duke's dark skin sometimes made it impossible, for those who didn't recognize him, to see him as anything but "colored," in the sense of the word as it was used on the Mainland at the time.

The last night of the crossing to LA had been choppy, then violent, and when the Hawaiian group arrived at last, it was with "ugly sea legs," as Sakamoto called them. All agreed it was best to get a bit of rest and meet up later for practice at the pool at Exhibition Park. Sakamoto and the others repaired to the same downtown hotel where swimmers and divers and coaches from across the country were staying, but Duke Kahanamoku preferred fancier digs, the sort with which he had become familiar during his Hollywood days. He had chosen the famously expensive and exclusive Aztec, one popular with celebrities like him. Stars such as Bing Crosby and Mickey Rooney stayed there in part because other stars like them did, but also because of the eccentricity of the place: built in the 1920s, its architecture was the then-trendy "Mayan revival" style; its facade was wave after wave of terra-cotta-colored swirls meant to resemble the engravings on the ruins of Chiapas.

The interior of the Aztec was a cross between Art Deco glamor and tribal exotica—meticulous mosaics lined the floors and walls, and the lobby's high stained-glass windows were inlaid with likenesses of Mesoamerican glyphs.

It was Halo Hirose upon whom Kahanamoku's odd return to downtown Los Angeles, bags in hand, made the strongest impression. Instead of meeting the team at the pool, the team ran into Kahanamoku on the street, emerging from a hotel quite nearby them and quite like theirs. Kahanamoku offered an explanation that could have been plausible: no vacancy. But when he'd arrived at the Aztec, he had certainly been turned away.

Only Duke Kahanamoku knew the extent to which his life had been marked by incident after incident like the one at that hotel. Some instances of prejudice were well-known: in his very first swim competition in 1911, Mainland AAU officials examining the Hawaiian's record times—even relying on four separate timepieces—had argued that Kahanamoku's performance was humanly impossible. Only a freak of nature or a liar would claim to shave a full 4.6 seconds off the world 100-yard freestyle record, and "in a murky, flotsam-filled harbor? Between two ships' piers? I mean, really, folks," one critic wrote sourly. At best, sportswriters scrambled to say that the tide must surely have aided the native Hawaiian.

That incident was only the birth of others' suspicions of him; in one of his first races on the Mainland, a crowd in Pittsburgh had booed him when, in the last 25 yards of the event Kahanamoku cramped painfully in the calves, and pulled up short. He was likely suffering from exhaustion and dehydration that come with travel, but instead of according him the benefit of the doubt, the crowd concluded that the vaunted Hawaiian was a fraud. The next night, when he dipped his toe into the pool to check the temperature, the crowd soundly booed him once again.

Events like those were widely reported in newspapers, but there were others that Kahanamoku chose never to speak about publicly. Some he hid even from his closest friends. He had, wrote one of his biographers, an "infallible memory," and so wouldn't have forgotten a detail, but he parceled out bits and pieces of those incidents infrequently and never lingered on them with the bitterness one might reasonably have expected. Some encounters, his biographer wrote, were as "brutal as a street accident." As much as Americans had come to fantasize about Hawaii as a tourist destination, their images of Hawaiians hadn't yet caught up with reality. In his travels across Jim Crow America in the 1920s and 1930s—north, south, east, and west—Kahanamoku was refused service at restaurants and made fun of at the counters of department stores when he attempted to purchase clothes. He was mocked for his accent and often presumed to be a kind of primitive whose home was a hut and who spoke no English at all.

On Such a Sea

Once, when a friend inquired why Kahanamoku hadn't eaten at a certain restaurant, why he had chosen to leave before he had even sat down, Kahanamoku had replied that he had left the place because poi wasn't on the menu.

Yet another time, in Lake Arrowhead, California, seconds after being turned away by a waitress who had told him that the restaurant "didn't serve Negroes," a woman diner who happened to recognize him from a social event in the past intervened before Duke could leave, and she invited him to join her at her table, attempting to be helpful by explaining to the waitress and the maître d' that Duke Kahanamoku was not a "Negro. He is Hawaiian," she said. And that, she added, was "certainly not the same."

In public, though, Duke was beloved. And it so happened that being Hawaiian on the Mainland was, in fact, as Sakamoto was learning, a kind of magical thing—at least in public. The papers described the group of swimmers as the "lads and lassies from the land of hulu [sic] skirts and steel guitars." At every event the crowds went wild to see the zippy and exotic island talent, whom they described as their cousins and brothers from paradise.

In San Francisco the crowd stood on its toes, praising the Hawaiians' strokes and their speed, but they were equally as entranced by Kahanamoku's 50-yard exhibition swims—his demonstration of the Australian and Hawaiian crawls—and Sakamoto caught on quickly about the power of entertainment; it could be as effective on land as it had been at sea. Kahanamoku had, in his lifetime, adopted the strategy of donning a straw hat and playing the ukulele, and now Halo, Keo, and Sakamoto did the same, playing their instruments again and joining Kahanamoku in clownish hijinks that delighted the crowd between races. The meets' emcees stumbled again and again over the boys' Japanese-American names, misspelling Keo's name variously as "Kiyo," "Kiyashi," "Koshi," "Nakamura," and the like; and mangling Halo's given name again and again: He was "Takshi," "Takahashi," "Tokahashi," or "Hiroshima," among others.

The California meets were exhibition swims but of no less consequence;

they were an unprecedented opportunity to see how Halo and Keo would stand up against America's top-notch swimmers in US pools. A few swimmers were known quantities: Jim Werson of the San Francisco O's club had been among the visitors to Waikiki in 1937. And Paul Herron of Long Beach had come through Waikiki with Chicago's affable Stan Brauninger, Jack Medica, and Adolph Kiefer back in August of '37. But there were new competitors from the University of Michigan, Harvard, the Los Angeles Athletic Club, and Long Beach Junior College, and Keo and Halo would be in the water with the likes of national intercollegiate champs in the 50- and 100-yard freestyle, and the 220-yard and 440-yard freestyle events.

The most unanticipated challengers, however, weren't the swimmers. One of the real tests was in the weather, the water temperature, and the wide and wild variability in the shape and size of the pools in which Hirose and Nakama swam. Los Angeles was about as standard a pool as one could hope for: it was, after all, the site of the '32 Olympics, and on July 2–4, before a packed Independence Day crowd, both Keo and Halo performed well and consistently. While his time was slower than at home—1:07.2 (some reporters have him at 1 minute 2 seconds)—Halo took the 100-yard freestyle with ease against the college and club boys; he beat out Ed Kirar of the U of Michigan, who came in second.

In the 200-yard freestyle, Keo swam a tight, head-to-head race against Paul Herron, but Keo took first at 2:18.4. Halo swam well in the same race, but because he was in an outside lane, it was difficult for him to gauge the speed of the fastest. He'd taken third. Any lag, compared to their home-pool times or what Sakamoto thought the boys were truly capable of, he chalked up to their fatigue from traveling and their inability to have practiced as intensely on board ship as Sakamoto would have liked.

As the group moved onward through their tour, the conditions changed drastically and often. In San Francisco, on July 10 and 11, they were swimming against the Northern Californians, and they dove into the most infamously odd and coldest pool on the Mainland: the dreaded Fleishhacker. The pool, which had opened in 1925 and had been part of San Francisco's long recovery from the 1906 earthquake, was the nation's first "oceanside" pool (the Nat was technically the first "ocean-fed"). It was located in the southwestern part of the city, between Sloat Boulevard and across the Great Highway from the Pacific, and had water piped in and out from under the highway through an elaborate filtration and cleaning system.

Fleishhacker was not unlike the Nat in a variety of ways, including its quirks. It, too, was gargantuan, only ridiculously so, measuring 1,000 feet in length and 150 feet in width. It was constructed of reinforced concrete, and it could hold 6 million gallons of water and accommodate 10,000 swimmers at a time, although the safety of those swimmers was in question, and so from 12 to 25 lifeguards patrolled the vast tank in rowboats.

For Sakamoto's swimmers, the greatest challenge was the cold. The water was a supremely unwelcoming 68 degrees for the Hawaiians, and when they weren't in it, Sakamoto dressed each boy in a head-to-toe, red-and-green zippered suit that looked like a skier's outfit, and over that he wrapped each tightly in a giant white terry-cloth robe. As small as they were, Halo and Keo almost disappeared inside the robes, and they were uncomfortable in the zippered outfits, but Sakamoto gave it his best effort to ward off hypothermia.

In spite of the cold, though, Halo blew his competitors out of the frigid water in the 100-yard freestyle, clocking in at 55.4 seconds, a Pacific Coast Association record. He followed that performance, teeth chattering all the way, with a time of 2:18.2 in the 220-yard freestyle for another PCA mark; and Keo, in the 440-yard freestyle, came in first at 4:55.8, yet another PCA record, then racked up a fourth PCA record for the two Maui kids when he entered the 300-yard medley—an event that wasn't even his. Sakamoto watched Keo pace himself perfectly and come in ahead of the pack by 8 feet at a time of 3:14.2. To Sakamoto's great pride, he wrote to Damkroger, the boys would be carrying home Olympic-style medals. Quietly, he had to wonder if the kids had won the medals not in spite of Fleishhacker's cold, but because of it. Still, it became impossible to judge, since all the conditions changed as they traveled.

During a short meet in Fresno, they were blasted by the heat but did well. In Stockton, in a horridly small indoor bath of a pool of 20 yards, both Halo and Keo hit times far faster than they had in Fleishhacker. Keo swam the 440-yard for a second place, at 4:52; Halo nailed the 50-yard freestyle for a first place at 25.4 (a better split time than at home), and he lowered his 100-yard pace to 54 seconds. Sakamoto was pleased, but he also knew the times weren't realistic—too many push-offs; in Halo's case, the shorter the pool, the better were his times, and in Louisville the pools would be regulation-size for the AAUs. What lay ahead was unclear.

What was certain was the pace of the tour itself: it was outrageous. They'd finish up in San Diego or Santa Cruz in the afternoon, and then, breathless from racing, they boarded trains, arriving just in time to perform in an evening exhibition meet somewhere else before what they were told was "a galaxy of big shots," maybe even Hollywood stars.

The sightseeing was equally exhausting. Sakamoto had experienced nothing like it since his trip eight years before to Tokyo. AAU officials, friends of friends from Maui, and sometimes members of delegations of California Japanese-American groups made certain that the Hawaiians eye-balled everything from Alcatraz and the San Francisco Exposition to Southern California's famous orange groves, where the boys could pick ripe fruit right off the trees.

On the sets of 20th Century Fox, Jimmy Ritz was filming *Straight, Place and Show*; at MGM, the comic duo Robert Young and Florence Rice were rehearsing scenes for the upcoming film *Vacation from Love*; at Fisherman's Wharf they ate Italian seafood for the first time, visited the beaches, and were enjoined again to pull out their ukuleles and sing and play on a local radio program.

Sakamoto wasn't much for sightseeing. Perhaps he'd gotten his fill of it in Japan, but he never had a taste for it after, and in California, while the boys took in the sights, he paid attention to other things. He saw that the Japanese-American community in California was thriving, but he also continued to notice that whenever he, Halo, and Keo—the only Japanese-Americans in the touring group—donned aloha shirts, leis, and played the ukulele or the steel guitar, they were more warmly welcomed than other Japanese-Americans. Decked out so, they passed as Hawaiian, and it seemed that as long as their skin was lighter than someone like Duke Kahanamoku's, the Hawaiian brand just might be a bit of magic.

Wherever they went, the boys received compliments from strangers not only on their fine swimming but also on their impeccable manners; and they easily made friends with the "American" swimmers, becoming as close, Sakamoto noticed, as if they had been bosom buddies for years. They were also made welcome by those who knew exactly who they were: In LA, they ran into Manuela Kalili himself, who greeted them warmly; and when they'd arrived at one of their hotels, a Baldwin family relative named Mr. Harold Rice had a fresh box of local cherries waiting for them. In San Francisco a pair of brothers, the Vasconsuelos, who were originally from Kahului before they moved to California to try improve their station by working as mechanics, took time off from work to stop by and offer a friendly hello.

By the end of the California circuit, Sakamoto and the boys were well-loved, but they were also road-weary; on the other hand, after their long days, they found themselves in the finest hotels—like the Plaza in San Francisco, and the luxurious Del Monte, the latter at which they arrived in mid-July so blindly tired that they practically had to feel their way to their rooms.

As challenging as the trip had been so far, it had been thrilling for Soichi Sakamoto. Yes, there were times when he and the boys felt homesick for Maui Nei, but he could see that the boys were enjoying the expansiveness of the trip as much as he was. It gave them an open vista to their future, the nearest part of which would be Louisville and the ultimate destination, Tokyo. What he didn't know, however, was that since March, the very possibility of the Tokyo Games had been a source of vociferous international debate.

Meanwhile, months before—as early as March—Baron Jigoro Kano had traveled to Cairo to quell a debate and save the Games. There were many problems to address when he arrived. The biggest challenge was to affirm that Tokyo was indeed fit to hold the Games at all, but there was more. The Japanese government and Kano's other colleagues had managed to offend the IOC again. Because of the hostilities in China—which Japan still did not declare as war—there would be no torch relay from Greece. Furthermore, it had been decided that the Tokyo Games must be delayed from summer to fall, running from August 25 through September 8, 1940. The reason the Japanese offered was that the weather in Japan wasn't conducive to sport any earlier in the summer, and to support its claim, in Kano's absence the government produced a six-page report filled with rather ghastly statistics about Tokyo temperatures, pressure, humidity, and mean average rainfall.

Western nations found the date change perfectly unacceptable, as it would interrupt collegiate athletics in the fall of that year and even perhaps cause the cancellation of whole football seasons. And if America couldn't abide by the change, it might, officials threatened, have to withdraw many of its athletes and keep them in the States instead.

The greatest sticking point, though, was the undeclared war with China. In Britain, Lord Aberdare, delegate to the IOC, raised the specter of danger for athletes who would travel to Tokyo. If the war continued, what was there to stop either the Japanese or the Chinese troops from attacking the ships as they sailed? How could Western nations seriously consider sending athletes on boats through a war zone?

Shortly thereafter, Aberdare pulled his support from the Games. The Czechs pulled out next. A Norwegian who attended a separate meeting in Paris proclaimed to the press that he publicly regretted that the Games had been given to a nation at war, and William May Garland, head US delegate to the IOC, who one year before had declared that the Tokyo Games would be the finest ever, now told the press that he saw no good on the horizon and predicted the Games would likely be rescinded. As delegates from all countries headed toward Cairo, sportswriters worldwide made fun of the mess. The old "gag" about "international amity" was a gag after all, wrote a columnist in the *Baltimore Sun*.

The journey to Cairo had been more onerous than others, and when Jigoro Kano had arrived at last in Egypt, one of his colleagues commented that the baron looked run-down, a comment to which Kano quickly objected. "It's the younger people who get tired," he answered wearily.

The congress opened strangely. At the opening reception at the opera, a small but symbolic affair hosted by the Egyptian king, few delegates even showed up. Most of those in the hall were local Egyptians whose connection to the committee was loose if not nonexistent, and during the feeble party the small group milled about without purpose until King Farouk, looking down upon the tiny assembly from his royal box, uttered all of fifteen words by way of welcome.

After the king, though, Count Henri de Baillet-Latour took the floor for an hour-long, windy speech, the sentiments of which were so bizarrely out of touch as to suggest that he was either oblivious to the controversies awaiting the committee or had entirely lost his mind. It was Latour's job to remain high-minded; by succeeding the deceased Coubertin, Latour had the responsibility to keep Coubertin's project aloft.

At the reception, Latour's remarks seemed patently absurd; he sunnily declared to the few listening to him that a period of peace was dawning in the world, but from what evidence he had arrived at that conclusion was unclear. Perhaps the fact that the IOC had insisted that the 1940 Tokyo Games be as unadorned as possible—a nod to the unacceptable militarism and nationalism of Hitler's displays in Berlin—had given Latour the impression that peace was at hand. It was difficult to know the lens through which he saw events. The Tokyo Games, Latour went on, were symbolic of a real shift in the world from what he called "destruction and difficulties of all kinds," although precisely to what particular troubles he was referring he did not say. Instead, he offered again and again the image of the 1940 Olympiad as Baron de Coubertin had conceived of it: an international celebration that occurred entirely outside the realm and racket of politics.

Someone had made the interesting decision to hold the entire IOC congress—all nine days—aboard the steamer *Victoria* as it made its way slowly down the Nile from Aswan, its delegates more or less captives. Immediately the arguments among those aboard the boat became heated and unpleasant.

Chinese delegate Dr. C. T. Wang, particularly inflamed, said that Japan had invaded his country. Notwithstanding his disagreements with the Japanese government, there was an ethical and practical issue at hand. The Games were not to be held in a war zone.

Avery Brundage was one of Japan's most energetic supporters. He had not long before been a guest of the Japanese government, and he argued that whether or not the world approved of Japan's military policy was of no matter. All that one should be concerned about was whether Japan was *capable* of holding the Games. If it could provide visitors with a track, a field, a pool, some ushers, and some seats, that's all a host country did anyway. It was, of course, an echo of his Berlin argument.

When it was Baron Jigoro Kano's turn to speak, he slowly stood, leaning slightly upon his walking stick but attempting to appear firm and strong. "War in China is nothing to do with sports," Kano said, and "Tokyo was safe," he said, nodding to C. T. Wang, "as long as the Chinese warplanes did not bomb" it during the Games. Kano, still composed, held forth. "I know of no reason for anyone saying anything about abandoning the Games. The war in China? That's nothing," he maintained. The IOC would be committing suicide if it decided to remove the Games from Tokyo. "Nobody," Kano warned, "would ever trust the IOC again." And there he left it.

Miraculously, his argument held sway; by the end of the Cairo congress, not only did Japan still have the Tokyo Summer Games in its hands but now the Winter Games in Sapporo, as well. Kano was ever the model of humility, but secretly he was thrilled. He traveled a veritable victory lap home, first through Europe, visiting Berlin, then lingering for a bit in Paris. He took a steamer to New York, and stepping onto American soil, felt certain he was in friendly company. After all, Avery Brundage was in his corner.

In New York, Kano was positively ebullient. In his suite at the Plaza, he demonstrated judo techniques for a group of "scotch and soda drinking" reporters. He spoke optimistically about the Games, while also noting, wisely and presciently, that nothing and no one's future was ever absolutely clear. When he left the East Coast it was to travel cross-country by train, visiting old friends in Seattle, and at the beginning of May he had begun his voyage home, tired but still reasonably assured that Tokyo had the Games.

Aboard the Japanese liner *Hikawamaru*, Kano usually sat at the captain's table, but one evening when he didn't appear for dinner, the captain announced to the others that Kano must be seasick. When Kano made an attempt to come to dinner, he became feverish and cold, and the other guests watched aghast as the blood drained from the baron's face.

Kano returned to his cabin. When the captain and the ship's doctor checked on him later, he was gravely ill. He was unable to speak, although from time to time he mumbled something incoherent about the need to take photographs. Perhaps he meant photographs at his dojo at home, someone suggested. But nothing he said could be understood. The ship's doctor applied poultices, and the ship's steward remained on vigil outside his cabin overnight. By the morning of May 4, 1938, Baron Jigoro Kano was gone. The official cause of death was pneumonia.

When the captain of the *Hikawamaru* radioed ahead to Japan, the news spread quickly across the nation and then across the globe. Kano was lionized everywhere, and when the *Hikawamaru* docked at last in Yokohama harbor, some three thousand people awaited the ship's arrival, watching dolefully as the crew hoisted Kano's casket—covered in the official Olympic flag—and carried it solemnly down the gangplank.

Jigoro Kano had left Cairo and died not ever knowing that while he had secured the Summer and Winter Games while in Egypt, he had actually lost Avery Brundage's support, which was key. Moving the Summer Games to the fall had been the very last straw for Brundage, and as Brundage went, so did the rest of the world.

Bill Bingham, the well-respected coach of the Harvard team, who had previously sat on the 1936 American Olympic Committee, pulled out, and his departure also boded ill. And even though a Gallup poll indicated that only 39 percent of Americans wanted to boycott Tokyo, the future seemed ever more grim. All across the Western nations, sentiment against Tokyo's war in China was growing stronger.

Since Jigoro Kano had died, the situation both outside and inside Japan had fallen apart. Within Japan, support for hosting the Games had completely eroded. The government, divided, said that it was the cost of hostilities with China that made it essential for Japan to cancel; others said the expense was in and of itself too much, never mind the war. Some in Tokyo were even vehemently opposed to seemingly small issues, such as the renovations to the sacred Meiji pools. Such disputes seemed like quibbles, but they weren't. By mid-July, the Japanese Diet had declared at last the death of the 1940 Tokyo Olympics.

Owing to the Protracted Hostilities

On the morning of July 14, 1938, Sakamoto woke at the posh Del Monte Hotel in California to the nightmare of Japan's announcement. The headline in the *Los Angeles Times* was as concussive a blow as any of the ones Sakamoto's swimmers had once suffered in the vicious camp game of Hardhead: "Tokyo Orders Suspension of Olympics." In the lobby of the Del Monte, Sakamoto could barely make sense of it all. Dizzy, he read the words Count Michimasa Soyeshima of Japan had sent to Count Baillet-Latour in Belgium. The cable read: *We regret that, owing to the protracted hostilities with no prospect of immediate peace. The cancellation simply could not be helped.*

What now was to happen to the Games, and what now, Sakamoto wondered, was to happen to his plans for the Three-Year Swim Club?

Chapter Seven

KEEPING 1940 IN MIND
ALL THE TIME

THERE ARRIVED on the desks of sports reporters across the world on the fifteenth of July, just one day after the Japanese cancellation, a missive that Japan had sent out a day or two before by mail. Its message was meant to have preceded the wire from Japan about the cancellation, and now, in light of the previous day's news, was excruciatingly ironic. The press release announced cheerfully that the city of Tokyo had officially approved plans for the construction of a main stadium, a new swim stadium, and an Olympic Village, along with what would have been the imminent publication of an Olympic reader for children, and pretty calendars as well. Now none of that would happen. And when Soichi Sakamoto woke for one last time at the Del Monte Hotel, he read in the newspaper the confusing news from the IOC that it had indeed accepted the resignation of the Tokyo bid and was at the same time casting about for another place where the 1940 Games could be held. There was some talk of California, of London, but there was more serious talk of Helsinki, known then as Helsingfors, the Finland capital city that, everyone knew, had wanted to bid for the '40 Games as early as 1932.

Sakamoto didn't know what to believe, and on the seventeenth, when he said farewell to Duke Kahanamoku and the rest of the All-Hawaiian team, he was uneasy. He and Halo Hirose and Keo Nakama watched the rest of the group board the *Lurline* for home, and they prepared for their own journey eastward. In a few short weeks, he, Keo, and Halo had racked up more than two thousand miles of travel, first across the ocean and then in the crazy crisscross of cities and towns in California. Next up was another two-thousand-mile journey to the state of Kentucky, to the site of the true and ultimate purpose of their endeavors for a year: the Men's Nationals. But what of the Games?

The newspapers suggested that the IOC transfer the Games to Helsinki, but how could Sakamoto be certain? At Union Station he boarded a train for a three-night, two-day trip to Chicago, and on that journey he tried to redraw in his mind the map of the world that he and his swimmers were to travel from now on, not east to Tokyo, but west to Europe. It was hard to imagine that journey.

In the meantime, he and the boys traveled cross-country on the Californian, an unstreamlined heavyweight of the Southern Pacific. FDR had recently declared the US locomotive industry on the edge of collapse, but from inside the Californian, one would never have known it. Sakamoto had bought tickets in a comfortable tourist car, and at night, for an extra $6.80, he and each of the boys had Pullman upper berths. Each car had a private lavatory, refrigerated drinking water, and even electricity, and the berths were large enough for two men, with curtains and soft bedding.

Porters were like resident butlers, available night and day to collect dirty laundry and deliver it fresh in the morning or to fetch a pack of cigarettes, and the dining car was replete with real china and cloth napkins. Breakfast cost a quarter; lunch a quarter and a dime. Fifty cents bought a feast for dinner: a three-course meal consisting of a vegetable and entrée as fancy as a fillet of fish or Swiss steak, plus a side of scalloped potatoes. The cooks made all the food on board the train from scratch each day, and when fresh pies came out piping hot straight from the galley ovens, Sakamoto felt as though he were in heaven.

Their journey took them south on the Sunset route, passing through the desert landscapes of Phoenix, Arizona, and Tucumcari, New Mexico, across the plains of Kansas, and northward to Chicago.

Sakamoto saw that Keo couldn't keep himself from staring out at the landscape that sped by. It was as good as a college education, he told Sakamoto with great enthusiasm, to be able to see the whole country out the window of a moving train: all the cornfields; the herds of horses, sheep, and cows; and every once in a while a big city skyline like the one in Des Moines loomed up, and you could get out on the platform and stretch your legs.

But Halo seemed distracted. Since the news about the cancellation in Tokyo, he was either angry or quiet, and now he appeared to have retreated inside himself. He had in fact begun to feel cheated, and he blamed his unacceptable situation on Sakamoto. Had Coach Sakamoto put a noose around Halo's neck? If there were to be no Olympics, then what was the purpose of anything? He bristled whenever he heard Sakamoto's voice, and he felt trapped in his company and in the 3YSC's plans.

On the ship and in California, they had lacked neither company nor care, but upon arriving in Kentucky, they found themselves alone and more adrift than they had ever been at sea. When they alighted from their train at Louisville's Union Station, they stood on the platform to find they were greeted by precisely no one. Neither their transportation nor their accommodations had been arranged for them, nor did they have any idea of where they would be fed. They gathered up their bags and left the station's echoing, barrel-vaulted atrium, only to find themselves outdoors at the dinner hour, shadowed by an enormous clock tower.

Louisville was built like a wheel, with each of its spokes leading, it seemed, toward the downtown. Louisville was, even after one year, a city only beginning to rise from destruction. In January of 1937, floods and fires of biblical proportion had visited the city. Rain had swollen the Ohio River until it crested to more than 59 feet, submerging houses to their roofs and whooshing railcars off their tracks, displacing thousands and carrying corpses under the city bridges.

The flood disaster had darkened the downtown, leaving the light of only candles and lanterns and leading to looting and lawlessness of other kinds. Federal troops came in to enforce martial law and try to keep a tenuous peace. Even the downtown buildings on Broadway still bore cracks at their foundations, and here and there were signs of the enormous sinkholes that had yawned wide open in the streets. In July of 1938, you could still find a signature Hot Brown in a Louisville diner, but residents might have said that the sandwich didn't taste like it did before the flood. It might be a long time before things were back to anything resembling normal.

At about Broadway and Fourth Streets, near a cluster of the once-waterlogged hotels, Sakamoto and the boys encountered with relief a trio of familiar faces: Stockton swimmers Fred Van Dyke, Paul Herron, and Ralph Wright. Herron they knew, of course, from his 1937 visit to Honolulu under Stan Brauninger, and they'd vied with him and the others recently in the pools of California. It was good to be with chums. Van Dyke, Herron, Wright, and their coach helped Sakamoto and the boys settle into a nearby hotel, and theirs was the only kindness Sakamoto felt in a world in which they had suddenly but inexplicably become invisible.

The truth was, Louisville was the gateway to the American South—new territory, indeed, for the swimmers, who had seen prejudice in the West, but had not encountered it yet in full force on the Mainland. On their trip from Chicago due south, on a train called the Southland, they experienced America's indelible color line, the passengers separated according to race. While Kentucky had once been a slave state, it had become part of the Union during the Civil War, and ever since had prided itself on its progressiveness, claiming to have one foot in the North and the other in the South.

But what Sakamoto and the boys were to see was more of its Southern foot's heels. The only place in town where both blacks and whites were allowed in together—although segregated by bleachers—was the famous racetrack, Churchill Downs. After all, it was said, money was the same color green in anybody's pockets; it didn't matter what color the gambler's skin was.

Sakamoto found himself puzzled again when he arrived to find that he and the boys weren't welcome to practice at the pool where the meets were to be held. Rather, the club was by membership only; that might have been true in some of the California pools, but out West people had seemed to have much more comfort with Japanese-Americans swimming next to them than here in Kentucky. The problem of where to practice in Louisville was a big one. The Nationals were set to take place at the end of the week, Friday, July 29, in a whites-only neighborhood some miles south from downtown. The pool was whites-only, too, and its membership was restricted to a certain kind of whites—only those approved neighbors in the blocks around the club.

Officials made it amply clear to Sakamoto that he and his swimmers were welcome only on the actual days of the meet. How they were to practice in advance was up to them. However, their white friends from Stockton had gained admission, and, as they had helped with their hotel, they helped them now with the club, somehow managing to persuade the Lakeside Pool Association that the Hawaiians were worthy enough to enter its sacred waters.

The Stockton coach helped out by giving Sakamoto and the swimmers a ride, too. Otherwise, having had no help from the AAU or the club, they would have had to walk each day the four long miles to and from the neighborhood known as the Highlands.

The Highlands was what one might have expected it to be: rows of tidy limestone houses on tree-lined streets, with sidewalks largely deserted in the daytime except for the occasional sight of a black housemaid bringing in groceries or carrying out a white family's garbage. While the rest of the city—along with most of the Ohio Valley—had suffered greatly during the flood of 1937, the Highlands, as its name would suggest, was above-water and mostly spared. It was said the greatest suffering those in that neighborhood endured was having to put up with the sounds of sirens and the displaced persons—strangers not their kind—whom they had been forced to take in. The challenge had unnerved them.

At the Lakeside Pool, every face was white, from the women who sunned themselves on lawn chairs to the children diving in. That seemed less odd after a while. The club was the sort of place where white men in golf pants were pictured in photographs on the wall, and stuffed pheasants hung nearby.

"Lakeside" was a misnomer. The club wasn't situated on a lake at all but at the edge of a "cavernous...former limestone quarry" that, in the 1920s, had been converted into a "series of contiguous swimming holes," and "hole" was an accurate description. The quarry walls rose a majestic 40 feet above 3 million gallons of green, murky water that smelled like the *punawai*, or springwater, welling from the Maui earth at home. The pool was inconsistently lined with concrete, and it ranged in depth from 2 to 30 feet, depending on where one found oneself.

The part of the pool designated for the competition was a jagged circle, at the bottom of which lay rusty tools that had been left behind years before by the workers in the quarry. The AAU had done little to make the venue more attractive or even usable. They'd floated a pair of large pontoons at each end and had strung between them old ropes for lanes.

Even Sakamoto, who had never put on such a big event, could see how lax the preparations were. He thought the way he always did back home; he could see that the meet would likely fail to break even—a fate that he tried to prevent, and succeeded in doing so, at each meet he ran in Pu'unene.

He noted how little he saw of advertisements for the meets around town, and how downtrodden in general everyone seemed to be feeling in Kentucky. That spring, the Derby had been a disappointment, and for some reason that blow still seemed to hover in the air: the famed filly Seabiscuit had been out of the running, its jockey horribly injured, and the 8–1 surprise winner hadn't made too many folks in Louisville much of a kitty.

There was also bad blood in local politics. The state was in the midst of a Senate primary election that had turned first sour, then dirty, then criminal. Even the swim meet's honored guest, Governor Happy Chandler, whose likeness looked decent enough in the program for the competition, had recently been hospitalized for what he claimed was poisoning by his opponents. Cyanide, the governor claimed.

And then, hanging over the meet itself was the strangeness of the cancellation of the Tokyo Games, but by July 26, Sakamoto read in the paper that the Olympiad was slated for certain in Finland. Sakamoto and the boys now had some reason to rejoice and their spirits lifted—even Halo's.

As the week went on, they grew more accustomed to the Kentucky drawl and its extra syllable. *Wha-at ara youhoo doooin?* And in practice the boys did well. They were uncomfortable in the hot, brackish water of Lakeside and didn't like how slippery the push-off pads felt when they were trying to turn around on a lap, but they felt fine in both health and spirit, not as wrung out as they had been in California.

Halo and Keo now faced a number of new competitors from Ohio State and Michigan and Yale. Sakamoto also recognized the faces of some of the coaches, such as the cheerful Stanley Brauninger, who now was at the helm of the Chicago Towers Club; and Dr. Al de Ferrari, the vacation-minded San Francisco O's coach. New to him, though, were the best coaches in the collegiate world.

The two Midwestern powerhouses were Ohio State and Michigan. Mike Peppe helmed OSU, and the British-born Matt Mann helmed Michigan. Mann was of humble origins, born in Leeds where, as a youngster he'd learned to swim in the drainage of that city's woolen mills, and after going on to be a prodigy champ, he'd come to the United States and coached his way up in the NCAA. Peppe was the child of Italian immigrants and more middle class, a diver as a youngster, and then he took over the Columbus swim and diving squad and man by man built it into a national powerhouse.

There was Steve Forsyth, a coach out of the Miami Biltmore club whose claim to fame was having nurtured the unbeatable world champ Ralph Flanagan to freestyle glory in the thirties. Sakamoto stood in awe of those men, but there was no one more intimidating than the longtime coach of the Yale men's swim team and lifetime coach of the US Olympic Men's Swim Team. Soichi Sakamoto may have known little about the larger world beyond Maui, but he knew well enough that there was no one more powerful and perhaps more dicey to deal with in the world of swimming than Yale coach Robert J. H. Kiphuth.

Football had a long tradition of big-name charismatic coaches; the nation's gridiron had the eccentric presences of the famous Pop Warner, Fielding Yost at U of Michigan, John Heisman (Heisman trophy Heisman), Percy Haughton of Harvard, and Robert Zuppke of the University of Illinois. Each of those colorful characters had developed his own shtick. Haughton was an obsessive; he stayed up into the wee hours of the morning planning out the next day's practice to the minute, and he insisted that gridders never *walk* onto the field—the football field was hallowed ground, he maintained. The only way to show some respect for football was to come in from the locker room running like you meant it.

Bob Zuppke was an on-field orator who once announced to his players that they were his court and he was the Sun King, Louis XIV. Such nuttiness had become acceptable in football, but no swim coach had come close to those pigskin "zealots," as Rice called them, until Robert J. H. Kiphuth showed up on the deck of America's competitive swimming pools.

Kiphuth—his friends, the few who dared to, referred to him as "Bob"—was a swimming zealot, whose personality and accomplishments preceded him through any doorway: he'd been at Yale since the teens and for some 175 dual meets in a row, his natators had swum undefeated, and he also held unofficial tenure as head coach of the US Olympic Men's Swim Team. His athletes and Yale's loyalty to him was unbounded: in the midst of the Great Depression, and at a cost of $20 million, the Payne and Whitney families gave money to the college for the construction of a twelve-floor Gothic-style natatorium more elaborate than any other in the collegiate system. Some called it the Taj Mahal. Others called it Kiphuth's "Sweat Cathedral" because of the rumor that he worked his swimmers like no other coach had ever done.

Like Mann and Peppe, Kiphuth had modest beginnings. His was a blue-collar German family from Tonawanda, an upstate New York hamlet, where, prior to coming to New Haven, Kiphuth's sole coaching experience had been as a physical education instructor and director at a local "Y." He became, though, an object lesson in the transformative power of the Ivy League; with seemingly little to recommend him and only a high school diploma under his belt, he started off as an assistant instructor, but by the power of his personality and his work ethic, he'd risen to the rank of head coach in merely a handful of years.

In the 1920s, Kiphuth rapidly became a familiar and quirky figure on campus, bicycling each day through the leaf-strewn quadrangles of the college, dressed in an outfit of herringbone tweed, a larger-than-average bow tie, and upon his head a fedora in a shade of blue and accented at the brim with a dapper orange pheasant feather—in colors of the Connecticut school—appearing to passersby as the mixture of an Oxford don and a stevedore, a look that earned him the half ironic nickname "Mr. Yale." It was the rough-hewn dockworker in Kiphuth that made him a good and exacting mentor to the privileged young men of Yale, but it was the dandy in him that made him just suitable enough to be accepted to the faculty and administration who chose to name him a fellow in one of the university's colleges, a position unheard of for an athletic coach.

Kiphuth's metamorphosis had come about through a marriage that had brought him into the moneyed company of the New York elite; his wife, Louise Delaney, was both older than he and connected to a social circle to which Kiphuth would otherwise have gained no entry, and she taught him how to read the daily *New York Times* and then to read the books that paper recommended and to speak of them at parties. She taught him how to mix with alumni and what sort of automobile to drive—something sleek and fancy into which he could jump whenever he was required to speed up to "the city" to speak with an alumni: his color choice was often red.

It was Kiphuth's wife who also turned the man into the quirky coat-and-shirt-and-tie figure pedaling around New Haven on the bike, and it was the outfit—or the failure to wear it—that began to signal to Kiphuth the mark of culture in other men. His winning record, his seemingly easy access to unrestricted wealth and power, made him, among other coaches, an object of admiration, jealousy, and downright enmity.

He was a true Yale bulldog and a bulldog of a man; he was no taller than 5 feet 5, a square chunk with a bullet-shaped head, inside of which was a bull's-eye brain with an aim as sure as an arrow. His steel-colored eyes regarded the world and those around him with derision; he could look a man up and down in seconds and decide whether he was worth his time, and he was stubborn, arrogant, and loud, his opinions issuing not only from his mouth but appearing in *Amateur Athlete* magazine and quoted in the *New York Times*. He was everywhere and involved in everything, like a god at the creation of the world who'd decided to stick around and have a hand in everything directly and long afterward.

Not everyone was happy about it. In one way or another, Bob Kiphuth had offended most of the coaches in the nation with his gruff attitude and superior ways, and though Soichi Sakamoto was a newcomer to the coaching scene, he saw immediately that around Robert J. H. Kiphuth, he ought to step most carefully.

Sakamoto had had enough of a taste of internecine politics in sports at home on Maui to know he didn't want a bit of it in Louisville. While he had been reasonably friendly with other coaches while in California, in truth he'd been coming already to the conclusion that he was better off—and so were his swimmers—if he stayed close to his own and stayed quiet in the company of others. The advantage of his quietude was that it gave him opportunities to listen and absorb a great deal; it bonded him to the kids; and it prevented him, as such a beginner, from embarrassing himself.

As at home, in Louisville, too, he stuck to rigid rules he had set for himself. At Lakeside, he spoke to no visitor and no member of the press while in the company of the two boys. He had to keep his focus singular and never for once, he believed, give the boys the impression that anyone or anything was more important in their coach's mind.

He also never sat down when the boys were in the water. To do so, he'd decided, was to appear lazy and to separate himself from the swimmers' efforts. Neither would he separate himself from conditions the swimmers themselves had to endure. No matter what the weather, no matter how cold the wind might blow, no matter if it rained torrentially, Sakamoto vowed never to don a jacket or a sweater if his swimmers couldn't.

At Louisville his goal was to keep his swimmers, and their progress, and his swimming program always in his mind. One of his aims while in Kentucky was to keep his eyes open as fully as possible, looking out for other swimmers' successful techniques, not only in the freestyle events but also in the backstroke, where "speed-floating" hadn't easily translated into success for him in that event and where he'd not yet acquired the coaching skills to grow the 3YSC team.

In his travels, he'd splurged on a movie camera: a Cine-Kodak 16-millimeter job, the "M" model, with which for the first time he could zero in on other swimmers and take the moving pictures home to study. Home movie cameras in those days were exciting to own but clunky to operate. The Cine-Kodak Model M, the height of Rochester technology, required Sakamoto to be heroic in operating it; if he'd had six hands, he would have been well-served. In order just to set up, he had to drop a reel of film precisely into the camera's magazine, then thread it perfectly and wind the camera's clockwork motor up with the little temperamental lever on the side. Then, without letting go of the cocked lever, he had to find his vantage point for filming, his eye on the lens and nothing else such that he stepped on spectators, who issued imprecations and cursed his rudeness. Then, standing in place, he had to wait for the start of a race and then, just as a swimmer came close enough, he had to set the lens for distance, after which he'd let the lever revolve about twelve seconds before he'd stop it; twelve was just enough to capture a swimmer's stroke cycle before the lever spun wildly in uncontrolled revolution. Out of every windup he got about six good takes, and then he had to start again.

He focused on two swimmers in particular. The first was Steve Forsyth's freestyle ace, Ralph Flanagan. Through his narrow camera lens, Sakamoto watched intently as Flanagan, a thing of beauty in the water, taught him more about technique than any book Sakamoto could have read. Flanagan was among the oldest and most experienced competitors at Lakeside. He was twenty-one years old and a registered undergrad at the University of Texas at Austin, but he'd come from Miami and had trained under Forsyth forever. Flanagan had been a prodigy, though. He'd swum at Los Angeles in 1932 at the ripe old age of thirteen, and while he hadn't made it past the semifinals there, by the 1936 Berlin Games, at seventeen, Flanagan, a thick-backed Floridian with the longest feet and toes in the business, shared the silver medal in the 4x200 relay with Ralph Gilman. He was storied, experienced, and time-tested with lots of movement for Sakamoto to study.

That very March, an article ran in *Popular Science Monthly* that purported to describe Ralph Flanagan's stroke as a modified American crawl that Forsyth had invented. The way the magazine told it, Flanagan's secret involved lying low in the water, his head and shoulders level with the surface, a position, it claimed, that reduced the swimmer's arm movements by a whopping third.

But that's the opposite of what Sakamoto saw in Louisville. Flanagan kept his shoulders and head high in the water, almost as high as it was said Johnny

Keeping 1940 in Mind All the Time

Weissmuller used to do. Flanagan looked just like a hydroplane, his upper body rising like the hull of a boat and then moving faster and higher and gaining momentum until his body skimmed over the obstacles of the waves he himself created as he moved and over the bow wave in front of him, seemingly without effort. In fact, Flanagan was so high in the water, it appeared as though he might take off in air, although he never did. And in his limbs was zero jerkiness, no wasted energy that Soichi Sakamoto could detect.

Flanagan was efficient, yes, but the magazine writer had gotten it all wrong. What Sakamoto saw in Flanagan was a reduction of movement not because of Flanagan's flat placement on the water but because of the relaxation in the swimmer's entire body; even in the twelve-second takes that Sakamoto grabbed of Flanagan with his movie camera, he could not detect a single ripple in the swimmer's arms.

Tension, Sakamoto now could understand, was fatal to a swimmer's smooth movement. He had seen relaxation in the wild, in animals he had observed as a child: in the quiet, restful way in which a mongoose prepared, but seemed not to prepare, to pounce upon a rat or in the smoothness of a cat in mid-run. Tight muscles were a swimmer's downfall; they did no good. So were quick breaths; tight breathing formed tension in the torso. A tensed leg seemed to sink and a loose one seemed more easily to float.

When he filmed backstroker Adolph Kiefer, he found in him the same relaxation—in Kiefer's legs, his rolling arms, his outstretched but loosened palms and fingers, a catch that seemed effortless, a recovery that took no time at all. For too long Sakamoto had believed that Kiefer had merely been a talented natural whom Stan Brauninger had discovered in a concrete culvert in Chicago; Kiefer was talented, all right, but he hadn't become the world record holder in the backstroke without a technique that was, to Sakamoto, nothing less than genius.

What Sakamoto had learned from Duke Kahanamoku was that stroke was the tool that gave a swimmer the most propulsion in the water, but now Sakamoto saw there was no speed without relaxation in the stroke and in everything else a swimmer did, and that knowledge was something he could also take to the bank when he got home to Maui.

Unlike the California pools, Lakeside, even with its murky water, irregular shape, its bizarre configuration of floating docks where the blocks were set, and no lane lines at all, was strangely more hospitable to Sakamoto's swimmers. It was warm, slimy in places, but the sight lines from dock to dock weren't bad. Others of the coaches, namely Steve Forsyth of Miami, had much to say about Lakeside's faults, but Sakamoto was beginning to suspect that Forsyth had much to say about any fault he might notice anywhere.

Thursday began the prelims in the mile. In the first two heats, Flanagan came in an easy 12:30 above his competitors, then Steve Wozniak, a stocky blond twenty-one-year-old from Buffalo who was swimming unattached and who was no less than the reigning mile champ in the event, was more than a minute behind in the second at 22:54.8. In heat three, Keo stood on the dock, ready for the longest race he'd ever had, and though he struggled with the distance, he bested Wozniak's time by more than thirty significant seconds. Going into the final on the following night, it would likely be a contest between Flanagan and Keo, who announced, upon getting out of the water, that he indeed preferred the temperature of Lakeside to any other Mainland pool he'd been in so far.

On Friday night at 7:30 p.m., Sakamoto watched as Keo warmed up for the finals. In addition to Flanagan and Wozniak, there were three more collegiate swimmers, but Sakamoto estimated them as negligible. The night was humid, the air thicker than it had been, and oppressive, and when the starting gun went off it sounded muted, as if the puff coming out of it had been muffled by the weather.

Squinting in the dusk, Sakamoto looked on while Flanagan sped immediately ahead of Keo and Wozniak, who, for 10 minutes to the halfway mark, chased the Miami Biltmore freestyle king valiantly, but Keo was behind by a full two lengths. At the turn, Flanagan bolted. Even though his time was even clocking slow for him—his record in the event was 20:42.6—in the now dark green water, he expanded his lead on Keo to four full lengths by the three-quarter mark, then moved up until he had six full lengths as

Halo Hirose, age five, Camp 5 ditch, Pu'unene, Maui, circa 1927. *Courtesy Janet Ogawa*

Maui Boy Scouts prepare to leave for Japan, June 17, 1930, next to Sakamoto Store, Waikapu, Maui. Pictured: Soichi Sakamoto (third man from center, wearing lei), Mary Sakamoto (woman to the right), holding baby Raymond. *Courtesy Barbara Kikuchi*

Hidejiro Nagata, mayor of Tokyo 1923–24, 1930–33. *Courtesy National Diet Library*

Original Three-Year Swim Club badge. *Courtesy Sono Hirose Hulbert*

Keo Nakama, Camp 5 pool, Pu'unene, Maui, 1937. *Courtesy Sono Hirose Hulbert*

Diving in, Camp 5 pool, early club years. Pictured: Halo Hirose (Block 3), Keo Nakama (Block 4). *Courtesy of the Alexander and Baldwin Sugar Museum*

"Puʻunene School Swimming Champs, Div. 1–2, 1936, T. Hirose, Capt." Taken at Camp 5 pool; team that inspired Sakamoto to start the Three-Year Swim Club. Pictured: Halo Hirose (third from left, top row), Keo Nakama (fourth from left, top row), Pachi Tsukano (eighth from left, second row from top). *Courtesy of the Alexander and Baldwin Sugar Museum*

Jigoro Kano, founder of the Japan Amateur Athletic Association, father of judo, member of the International Olympic Committee. *Courtesy National Diet Library*

Congratulatory telegram from Wailuku to Keo Nakama, Soichi Sakamoto, and Halo Hirose in Louisville, Kentucky, July 31, 1938. *Courtesy of the Alexander and Baldwin Sugar Museum*

All-American swimming team aboard the SS *Bremen*, New York Harbor, August 5, 1938. Pictured: (standing, l–r) Elbert Root, Jim Werson, Bill Neunzig, Peter Fick, Paul Wolf, Ralph Flanagan, Otto Jaretz, Halo Hirose, Al Patnik; (kneeling, l–r) John Miller (Mercersburg Academy), Bob Kiphuth (Yale University), Max Ritter (AAU representative of International Swimming Federation). *Courtesy Yale University Athletics*

Keo Nakama returns from Australia, April 12, 1939, Honolulu. Pictured: (l–r) Keo Nakama, Soichi Sakamoto, Halo Hirose. *Courtesy of Lee Matsui*

The 1939 Hawaiian AAU team prepares to depart for the Men's and Women's National Championships, July 20, 1939. Pictured: (standing, l–r) Soichi Sakamoto, Peter Powlison, Carlos Rivas, Bill Neunzig, James Tanaka, Keo Nakama, E. L. Damkroger; (kneeling, l–r) Barney Pung, Halo Hirose, Fujiko Katsutani, Jose Balmores, Benny Castor. *Courtesy of the Alexander and Baldwin Sugar Museum*

Keo Nakama and Halo Hirose, circa 1939. *Courtesy of the Alexander and Baldwin Sugar Museum*

Fujiko Katsutani on her way to the Women's National Championships, Des Moines, Iowa, July 26, 1939. *Courtesy of the Alexander and Baldwin Sugar Museum*

The Three-Year Swim Club in their new uniforms, Honolulu, April 12, 1939. Pictured: (back row, l–r) Bunny Nakama, unidentified, Tommy Yamashita, Jose Balmores, Charlie Oda, Yoshio Shibuya, Takashi Ono, Yoshiyo Kitayama, Chow Shibuya, Bill Neunzig, Benny Castor, Soichi Sakamoto, Mike Ginoza, Keo Nakama, Halo Hirose, Takashi Kitagawa, John Tsukano, Tsyano "Dynamite" Nakasone, Tsuneo (unidentified surname), Hiroshi Shigetani, Sibio Perez, Shangy Tsukano, Pundy Yokouichi, Seizen (unidentified surname), Tetsuo Hamada; (front row, l–r) unidentified, Doris Yoshino, Chic Miyamoto, Yoshie Higashida, Kay Sugino, Toyo Takeyama, Mitzi Higuchi, Bertha Ching, Charlotte Shigehara, Hiroko Abe, Teruko Nakagawa, unidentified, Fujiko Katsutani, Tamiyo Shiramatsu (or Shiramizu), Lulu Nakagawa. *Courtesy of the Alexander and Baldwin Sugar Museum*

The Three-Year Swim Club makes its way around Waikiki. Pictured: (l–r) Jose Balmores, unidentified, Mike Ginoza, Bunny Nakama, Chic Miyamoto, Charlie Oda, Mitzi Higuchi, Fujiko Katsutani, unidentified, unidentified. *Courtesy of the Alexander and Baldwin Sugar Museum*

BENZO SAKAMOTO
"Eat, drink and be merry for tomorrow you may die."

Benzo Sakamoto, Maui High School graduation photo, 1930. *Courtesy Friends of Old Maui High School*

Blossom Young Goon, Baldwin High School photograph, circa 1939. *Courtesy Blossom Young Tyau*

Soichi Sakamoto at the Camp 5 pool, circa 1939. *Courtesy of the Alexander and Baldwin Sugar Museum*

he came in easily at the wall at 21:06.3, his long feet waving good-bye to his competitors.

That was the bad news. But the good news was great: Keo touched the wall in second, well ahead of Steve Wozniak. It took a minute for it to sink in, but when it did, it was clear to Soichi Sakamoto that Keo's performance was a triumph. In the boy's first-ever national championship event, he had taken second place to none other than an Olympian, and he had beaten out the US men's champ at third. Second place in the Nationals was a whole lot to crow about for a boy who'd started out swimming in an irrigation ditch.

In Louisville that summer, Keo swam twice again against Flanagan. In the 440-yard freestyle he was behind the long-footed Olympian but he came in ahead of Stockton's Paul Herron, hence copping his *second* second place in the national meet. Then on Sunday, beneath a torrential rain and darkened skies that couldn't help but remind one of how vulnerable Louisville must have been to flooding, Keo swam his third race against Flanagan, only this time, in the 880-yard freestyle, Keo clung to the champ, matching him stroke for stroke for the first 500 yards of the battle, and although Flanagan pulled ahead after that to win at 10:11.1, it was a huge—and third—and unbelievable second-place victory for Keo Nakama.

Halo's sprinting performances were no less successful. In the 220-yard freestyle he swam against a field of six that included Detroit, Michigan's Tom Haynie, a competitor who was new to him; Paul Wolf of the University of Southern California, against whom Halo had swum in '37; and Otto Jaretz, too. Strangely, Adolph Kiefer was entered as well, and although Kiefer took off and even sprang ahead of all the others, Halo stayed on the Chicagoan's heels, and when the backstroker freestyled into the wall at 2:18.7, Halo Hirose was only 18 inches behind the smiling Olympian. He'd had Wolf and Jaretz on his heels, but Halo Hirose had now placed second, as well, in his first-ever national championship.

Three second places in the Nationals was more than Soichi Sakamoto could have hoped for in the first year of the 3YSC. Though torrents of rain still bore down on Louisville, the wins were all sunshine to the Mauiites, and Sakamoto wired home to Damkroger of the wins, to which Damkroger replied with a wire of his own, congratulating the three Hawaiians on their remarkable victories.

It was once written of Bob Kiphuth that only Eleanor Roosevelt and Secretary of State John Foster Dulles saw more of the world than he did. Kiphuth grew no moss beneath his feet. From the minute he became involved with the Olympics, he was on the move. And never was Bob Kiphuth a casual tourist. Even if some questioned his effectiveness in his role—and rightly so—he took the job seriously, often seeking out solutions to his coaching conundrums in places across the globe.

Travel was how he conducted reconnaissance, and under the banner of friendly international relations and warm invitational meets, Kiphuth was American swimming's foremost spy.

In the summer before the Antwerp Games in 1920, when Kiphuth was not yet even a full coach, he'd lit out for Europe early to get a gander at the competition, and there he'd seen the Hawaiians swim beautifully in the Stade Nautique. He continued to travel, and widely. In the summer of 1930, he'd headed a delegation of handpicked swimmers to Honolulu for a test before Los Angeles. The next summer, he'd decided that, unless the rest of the world developed, the Japanese were going to take over in swimming.

He was right, in part. What happened in 1932 was exactly what he'd predicted, and from then on Kiphuth had put all his attention on the Empire of the Rising Sun. He transformed himself into a Japanophile, becoming known for his ability to hold forth on topics like the history of the kimono and the conventions of Bunraku theater. The Japanese were fascinating, but Kiphuth knew they were also his—and America's—greatest athletic foe.

He took two more trips across the Pacific. On the last one, in 1935, he brought with him fifteen new American swim stars who, he claimed, were supposed to give the "sons of the Samurai a stiff dose of their own medicine," but who delivered to the Japanese very little of the sort. Then, in 1936 in Berlin, the Japanese and the Europeans more or less crushed the Yanks as a team once again. Kiphuth was headed out on one more reconnaissance mission, and his eyes were wide open.

Bob Kiphuth had come to Louisville with an agenda. Back in the spring, as soon as the writing had appeared on the wall about a coming cancellation of Tokyo, he and a small group of others had arranged for an upcoming trip to Europe in the summer of 1938, right after the Men's Nationals.

Kiphuth planned to take an eight-man team on the junket, which would primarily pit the American swimmers against the Germans, and all spring long Kiphuth had been mentally putting together his roster. He needed four freestyle swimmers, one backstroker, one breaststroker, and he might even have room for another to serve as anchor in the relays.

For freestylers, he had in mind, without a doubt, Ralph Flanagan. His next best freestyler was to be Peter Fick of the New York Athletic Club; Paul Wolf and Otto Jaretz were his two backstroke choices; Bill Neunzig, a tall, Aryan-looking former OSU swimmer, and James Werson—one of the San Francisco O's who'd come to Hawaii in 1937—were to cover the breaststroke. And now, after the drenching rain at the end of the Louisville competition, Kiphuth cast about his wide eyes for his alternate freestyler and made his announcement. He named Kiefer, Hirose, and Nakama as his alternates for the spot, and in that order, and when Kiefer dropped out—he couldn't make the trip—the spot went, unbelievably, to Halo.

Kiphuth's choice of Halo Hirose wasn't the source of the hullaballoo that followed hard upon the announcement. The battle arose from longtime bad blood between Steve Forsyth and Bob Kiphuth.

Kiphuth had his share of rivalries; one was with Mike Peppe. Peppe was a blue-collar Italian, a native New Yorker and a pint-sized ball of fire. He was a shirt, tie, and coat man, but his suit was cut from different cloth than Kiphuth's. Being Italian was the first strike against him; Kiphuth, of German heritage, had an automatic one-upsmanship on Peppe in the American immigrant competition. Kiphuth treated Peppe as if the OSU coach were nothing more than a swigger; Peppe, a lifelong bachelor, was indeed a bon vivant, and liked liquor and was drawn to parties, but Kiphuth made much of it and was the source of ugly rumors about the man. In turn, Peppe didn't respect Kiphuth because of what he felt was his superior Ivy League attitude, his self-righteousness, and the fact that no swimmer was ever good enough unless his skin was white as snow and his name in the New York Blue Book.

The rivalry between the two was always on a quiet simmer. It was as if each man had come to accept their rift as little more than an inconvenience to which they'd grown accustomed, something like a bunion one had to live with.

But Steve Forsyth's hatred of Kiphuth was always on high heat. He hated Kiphuth, and he wasn't quiet about it, and on that night of drenching rain in Louisville, Steve Forsyth boiled right over. He wasn't unhappy with the team that Kiphuth had picked; after all, Forsyth's own boy was on it. What bothered him most was that it was Kiphuth who had picked it, Kiphuth who had a monopoly on such things in US swimming, Kiphuth the tyrant, Kiphuth who, Forsyth maintained, had his hands on all the swimming money in the nation.

The two men couldn't have had different kinds of lives. While Forsyth eked out a living teaching swimming to kids for $30 or $40 a pop, Kiphuth made his bread and butter from coaching undergraduates at Yale—a full-time gig. And to Forsyth it seemed painfully obvious that Kiphuth's entire life was underwritten by the upper class and those in power in the AAU and the US Olympic Committee. Forsyth had no sugar daddy of his own.

Forsyth had become incensed when, in 1936, Ralph Flanagan had qualified for Kiphuth's Olympic squad and Kiphuth hadn't handed Forsyth any money to make the trip to Germany. That stung. Every meet, every competition, every bed in every hotel and every bite of food at every restaurant had always come out of Forsyth's own pocket and his hide, and when Kiphuth didn't ante up to help defray the costs of traveling to Berlin, that was the end of any patience Forsyth might have had in reserve.

Kiphuth had named Forsyth an assistant Olympic coach, which meant he had the right to be on deck and coach his boy but had to buy his own way to and pay for everything in Berlin. It was a fortune for Forsyth to produce, and after arriving in Berlin, and beat for money, he seethed and stormed about and took offense at anything that Kiphuth did, like breathing.

One of Forsyth's beefs with the Yale coach was that, though all of America seemed to consider the man the nation's brain trust in swimming, Kiphuth's brain was out of whack. Forsyth resented that Kiphuth privileged the Japanese whenever he spoke about them. The Japanese this, the Japanese that, was always Kiphuth's refrain, it seemed. In Berlin, during a Japanese practice session in the pool, Kiphuth grabbed Forsyth by the arm and, practically apoplectic, pointed out to Forsyth the miracle he saw at work there in the water.

"There it is, Steve! There it is," Kiphuth said. "That's the Japanese crawl," and he pointed to something that Forsyth thought looked just like a badly thought-through adaptation of the American crawl.

"And believe you me," Bob Kiphuth went on that day, the Japanese crawl "is the greatest stroke ever developed."

It made Steve Forsyth retch. After all, he'd been hailed as the inventor of a new modified American crawl, and he thought rather highly of it. And he believed quite firmly that the Japanese methods were nothing to write home about, although Bob Kiphuth seemed never to be able to stop himself from talking about how fine their methods were.

Forsyth couldn't stand that every time Bob Kiphuth came home from a trip abroad, he announced to the press, depressingly, that the Japanese were going to beat the life out of the Americans at the next Olympiad.

What kind of good could that attitude do to swimmers, Forsyth wanted to know. How could anyone with such a negative attitude motivate anyone to swim past their competitors? He hated that Kiphuth had the best swimmers in America under some kind of awful spell, their eyes glazed with the certainty of the failures Kiphuth told them they would be.

And what right, Steve Forsyth wanted to know, did Bob Kiphuth have anyway, in leading the US Men's Olympic swim team over and over again when, since 1932, there'd been little real improvement in the teams that Kiphuth took abroad?

The man was a Neanderthal. He didn't know a thing about technique;

he didn't teach it, didn't believe in it. The bulk of his coaching was to tell his kids to do some pulley weights and when he wanted them to go faster in the water, to call out "speed up," and wait to see if they did.

Not only did Forsyth give loud voice to these matters in front of Saka-moto and the other coaches, but he also told his tale to the *New York Times*, which reported it immediately and did the Forsyth/Kiphuth relationship not a terrible lot of good.

As for Bob Kiphuth, he just ignored the Miami coach. He could. He already had his ticket bought for Germany, and he had his handpicked team in tow.

On August 5, when Kiphuth's All-Americans, along with Kiphuth's usual travel companions in Europe—Max Ritter, the Amateur Athletic Union representative to the International Swimming Federation, and John Miller, athletic director and head swim coach of the private school Mercersburg Academy—boarded the *Bremen*, a German liner bound from New York to the Continent, Halo Hirose could not have known how storied that vessel was. Three years earlier, as the ship was docked in New York Harbor, anti-Nazi protesters boarded the ship, climbing the vessel's jack staff, tearing off the Nazi party flag and tossing it into the Hudson River. The incident gave rise to Hitler's decision to forever after use the flag as the symbol of the Reich. What's more, two years earlier the *Bremen* was the very ship that transported the American Olympic team to the 1936 Berlin Games. Now, above Halo Hirose's head that August of 1938, the same flag flew. All accounts of the journey suggest that he wasn't concerned with politics. He found the cross-ing cold. Unlike the *Matsonia*'s tropical crossing, on the *Bremen* fur-draped women sat in tufted loungers on globe-lit promenades, hunched against the wind. The food was unfamiliar, the language confusing, and Halo was ever more self-conscious, now that he was in the company exclusively of hao-les, about the fact that he was less sophisticated than everyone else aboard and still didn't know how to eat properly with a knife and fork or off a plate instead of out of a rice bowl.

Keeping 1940 in Mind All the Time

In those early days of August, as the group sailed toward Europe, peace on the Continent hung by a thread. Adolf Hitler retreated to his Alpine home in Berghof but not for the purpose of repose. Day after day he considered his invasion of Czechoslovakia; it was no secret to those observing him that the end of the Nuremberg Conference, to come in early September, would bring about decision—and action. It was said that in August the number of high officials and foreign visitors to Berghof was so great—and that guests were staying so long—that the führer had begun to build an adjacent hotel for them; in the meantime, he provided them with pajamas.

That Hitler was behind closed doors seemed to some a reprieve for strife in and outside of Germany. In truth, though, in places like Vienna, landlords ousted Jewish tenants. In Berlin, Jews were restricted access to their bank accounts.

On the first Sunday of the All-American tour, in a drenching rain in Berlin, Halo Hirose and his teammates joined a throng of some eighty-five thousand citizens gathered in the Olympic stadium—the same one that had held the '36 Games—to watch a different sporting event; it was a long-awaited German-American track-and-field competition, and in between events, the Reich provided entertainment of the nationalistic sort. Brave German pilots had, that very morning, completed an unprecedented, speedy round-trip transatlantic flight to New York City and back. The trip was lauded as an advance for the future of better airmail between America and Germany, but many watching in the United States had to have been concerned about the ease with which Germans could now reach the American coast.

The next day, Halo and his teammates performed in their first swim meet in front of adoring crowds, although Halo found the chorus of adoration for Hitler to drown out most of the applause for the visitors.

It was, of course, Halo Hirose's first time abroad, to a place where people spoke a different language, where culture must further have struck him as so very different than it had been even on the Mainland. He was a country boy from Maui. Now the world was becoming a map for Halo and his fellow swimmers; the globe transforming into a set of pinpoints they had visited, another set of pinpoints for the places that they wished to go. Their starting point had been Pu'unene, a speck of sand in the middle of the Pacific, and from there they had crossed the water to another, larger island. A leap over water was next, a foray of zigzags on the coast; a crossing, and now at least for Sakamoto and Nakama, a return. But it was Halo who extended the reach of the 3YSC and opened up the doors—for the rest of them—to yet another continent.

Before Halo now were thunderous parades of German power that would have been impossible for him to ignore, but it also would have been impossible to know how intimately his own life would later become caught up in the frenzy of what he currently witnessed. While he could not have seen it, everywhere he turned his future was reflected to him, although for now, it seemed a mere form of entertainment, a diversion at swim meets and banquets.

"It was Heil Hitler this, and Heil Hitler that," he found, all over Germany, and he was struck by the strangeness of all the goose-stepping. At dinner the same salutes occurred. Halo decided to let his new German friends Heil all they wanted, wherever and whenever they desired. It didn't really bother him. The focus, after all, was on swimming.

The trip was a whirlwind. Germans had arranged for the American delegation a more demanding schedule than the California one. The swimmers had no time to rest or to sightsee. Their dance card was filled with meets in every possible swim tank from Magdeburg to Munich.

As occupied as the swimmers were in those weeks, the führer was busier by far. The American delegation made its way from town to town, engaging in friendly meets with the French, the English, the Hungarians, and the Germans. While Halo swam at Bremen and Hamburg, defeating the German team in a 300-meter medley relay with Wolf and Jaretz, Hitler celebrated completed renovations and the expansion of Dachau. He hosted a dinner for the Hungarian regent, Horthy, to whom, in the course of the evening, he offered the territory of Czechoslovakia in exchange for Hungary's help in conquering it.

While Halo Hirose swam in Berlin, he could look out the windows of the bus and see the Brandenburg Gate, people riding motorcycles on the tree-lined streets, sidewalks perfectly cleared of litter, barges making slow progress down a river, women in cafés smoking long and tapered cigarettes, and clusters of brownshirts marching in the streets. He was unhappy at having no chance to see more of Germany itself—at the end there was a brief side trip to the Alps—having only one day of rest. He was unhappy, too, at having found the German pools freezing cold "and having a hard time picking up any German."

When, at last, Halo Hirose returned to Maui by way of the ship *Europa*, it was late September of 1938, close to his seventeenth birthday. He was happy to be back, happy to return to Maui High, where he was welcomed back as a conquering hero. He had completed a twenty-thousand-mile journey, traveling farther from home than anyone he ever knew had done. He had swum swiftly but not as well as he had at home or in California or Kentucky. In Hamburg, in the 100-meter freestyle, he'd taken a second place, 1:00.7. In Magdeburg, in the 200-meter freestyle, he had placed second again with a time of 2:18.2. Halo blamed it on the pools. On the cold. On his fatigue. On everything else but himself.

His one great triumph had been in the 4x200-meter relay in the group's second exhibition meet in Berlin that summer. The American team, with Halo on it, had outswum the Germans in their home pool and set a world record that would be remembered long after the war.

When Halo arrived home, he was in possession of an even larger sense of self. He was becoming bigger in his own mind than he was in real life. He had collected prized souvenirs, which he enjoyed showing off: a ten-inch bronze trophy of a nude figure; a full-color commemorative magazine from the '36 Games, entirely in German, and filled with swastikas and pictures of Hitler; and an etching of the Brandenburg Gate, signed on the back with affection by nearly every swimmer he had met along the way. Because he was the smallest person on the trip, the German swimmers in particular had taken to him as a kind of mascot, calling him their "little boy Takashi" and teasing him about his chances with white girls. Perhaps in compensation, he had lied to them. He told those he met that he was the son of the owner of the Maui plantation on which he lived.

The Hirose family weren't Samurai—they were from Shimaken—but they turned their noses up at everybody else in camp. Halo's father, Denkechi, was higher in stature than others in camp, a scholarly type who could read and write and who kept a tidy collection of bonsai. Word was that in Japan, he had been traded by his own family to another one in order to pay off a debt, and having traveled to Maui to do so, he was too delicate for fieldwork and so had been made a yard boy for the Baldwin family. Yard boys were a step above the rest. And as for Mrs. Hirose, Shina, she was known as clever, a loan shark who sold hooch at a premium during Prohibition, but she was no princess. Halo's older brother, Tatsuo, known as "Fat," was a disappointing, gruff grub of a fellow, an overweight former Sumo wrestler who'd ended up becoming nothing but a luna.

In camp, the Hiroses looked down upon other families, especially those like Keo Nakama's. The Nakamas were Okinawan, and Okinawans were said to be less than Japanese, hardly human, hairy; they even had tails. The Hiroses weren't lowlifes; they weren't bones by the side of the road. If they could have, the Hiroses would have separated Halo from Keo for life.

In Germany Halo told his friends that his father's plantation was a beautiful place; he told them to visit him. He would show them Maui. He had become particular friends with the German Olympian swimmer Helmut Fischer, one of the fellows Halo had beaten in the 4x200-meter relay, and it was to him that Halo extended the warmest of invitations. Whether he had convinced the Germans or not was in question, but he liked to think so, and while he knew he couldn't fool Bob Kiphuth, he felt certain Kiphuth had taken a liking to him and been impressed by him as a swimmer during the trip, and that's what mattered most. On the back of an etching of the Brandenburg, Kiphuth had written a most encouraging note to Halo: "Keep 1940 in Mind all the Time," he had said.

Halo took Kiphuth's words to be a sign that his future would be linked with Kiphuth's and the Olympics, and this was what he told others when he returned to Maui. He began to think how nice it would be to study at Yale, and to escape the bonds of his relationship to Sakamoto and his real life on the Valley Isle. After all, Coach Kiphuth had told the press that he had great hope for the Maui boy.

Keeping 1940 in Mind All the Time

Halo Hirose was not, however, at the forefront of Bob Kiphuth's mind that August, nor would he be at any time. Halo hadn't the academic chops to get into Yale to swim under Kiphuth, nor did Kiphuth see him as a candidate for Finland.

Kiphuth's reconnaissance mission to Germany had given him plenty else on which to ruminate. In the two years since his American Olympic squad's performance in Berlin, a great deal had changed, he saw. At least on this junket, Kiphuth's handpicked kids had triumphed over an all-European squad and had also dominated the races in the dual meet with the Germans, but Kiphuth, as was his habit, was loath to admit to any optimism in public. As Steve Forsyth always said, Kiphuth was prone to whining or at least playing down America's chances in the Games whenever the man had the opportunity to do so.

Kiphuth might have thought one thing while in Germany, but once he stepped foot back on American soil, he again told the press that, yes, Ralph Flanagan had set a new record, and, yes, the All-American relay team had won and beat the Germans, but what fun, he asked, would Finland be in '40 without the participation of the Japanese? And what about those Russians? They were an unknown quantity. If they were to come to Helsinki, Kiphuth wasn't sure what they'd bring as ammunition, and he was worried.

Then again, he said, he was always worried. It was one of the ways in which he hedged his bets if his Olympians did poorly: he could say afterward that he alone had predicted the outcome. But Bob Kiphuth's thoughts, good or bad, about the Olympics to come were about as useful as Halo Hirose's fantasies about Kiphuth himself. Hirose had hitched his wagon to Kiphuth's star, but it was looking ever less likely that the stars were in Kiphuth's—or the Olympics'—favor. Soon, even Bob Kiphuth's opinions about the Olympics wouldn't matter one whit.

Perhaps it was nothing, perhaps it was merely symbolic, but in the days after the Cairo congress in March of 1938 came to an end, and after Baron Jigoro Kano of Japan had died, a small group of the IOC set out on a

143

pilgrimage; theirs was the literally grave mission of conveying to Greece the last physical remnant of Baron de Coubertin, father of the modern Olympic movement. Faithful to the baron's wishes, Count Baillet-Latour carried the heart of Coubertin to Olympia, where, with much pomp and circumstance, he buried it. As tenuous as the 1940 Games in Tokyo were, it was hard to know if the act of laying a heart at the feet of the Greek gods was a hopeful offering or if it was a farewell to the very movement that had once quickened the hearts of both Baron Jigoro Kano and Baron Pierre de Coubertin.

PART THREE

TAKEN AT THE FLOOD

1939

We have always held to the hope, the belief, the conviction that there is a better life, a better world, beyond the horizon.

—Franklin D. Roosevelt

Chapter Eight

DOWN UNDER

Before Louisville and the Pacific Coast tour, Maui had never been anything other than a pin on a map in the South Pacific, but now it was a goose-shaped island in the middle of a blue sea, and on it was something of value that wasn't sugarcane or pineapple.

Keo Nakama and Halo Hirose had made international headlines in 1938, and in 1939, many in the world of swimming wanted to know what made them tick. The Japanese had always been mysterious about their swimming techniques and training methods. Now there were Japanese-American swimmers who were fast in the pool and also cheerful and willing to travel and share ideas.

Australians, in particular, had a long and robust history of water sports, and a hunger for knowledge about contemporary advances in technology and technique in both surfing and swimming. They also had a history of friendship and collaboration with Hawaii in the mid-teens, and in particular with the first Hawaiian swimming star, Duke Paoa Kahanamoku.

Two of Kahanamoku's biographers recount the process by which the relationship began at the Stockholm Games in 1912. Aussie swimmers were among Kahanamoku's greatest rivals, two of whom were Cecil Healy and Bill Longworth. In the very early days of the Games, Kahanamoku made an indelible impression on Healy and Longworth in the early 100-meter heats. Kahanamoku proved himself to the Australians to be both a supremely talented and an infinitely watchable swimmer. He led in all the prelims of the

100, his time an impressive and unprecedented 1:02.6. Coaches, swimmers, and sports reporters dissected Kahanamoku's technique. They decided that it was the champ's kick, not anything above the ankles, including the hips, that was the key source of his propulsion in the water, and they observed and marveled at his overall muscular relaxation during a race. The Australians also saw in Duke's stroke, and in the six-beat coordination of the feet with the stroke, an entirely new way of doing the traditional "Australian crawl."

Kahanamoku not only made an impression in the water, but he also did so on the deck, behaving modestly, gently, and thoughtfully in relationship to his competitors, which the Aussies appreciated as well. A mix-up in the program schedule led Kahanamoku to believe that the 100-meter semifinals were to take place a day later than they did, and because he was resting when the semifinals took place, he was at first disqualified. In his absence the Aussies had prevailed, but, with grace, Australian freestyler Cecil Healy went to bat for Kahanamoku with Swedish officials and made it possible for them to add an extra heat in which the American could participate. A day later, Kahanamoku was missing again from the finals; he was found by other swimmers to be catching some quick z's beneath a set of bleachers. Now awake, he competed in the 100-meter race, besting even Australia's Healy. After Kahanamoku won the event, Duke was so grateful for the thoughtful help of the Aussie that the two became fast friends and remained so for life.

After Stockholm, the Australians were eager to invite Kahanamoku to visit, and he did so in 1914 and 1915, making a strong impression with his kicking technique, his virtuosity on the surfboard, his ukulele playing, and his humility. He traveled across Australia and performed demonstrations of swimming and surfing, and was so popular that the nation erected a statue in his honor. When E. H. Sandell, of the New South Wales Amateur Swimming Association, heard of Keo Nakama in 1938, he remembered the pleasure and impact of Kahanamoku's visit years before, and he sent an invitation to both Kahanamoku and Nakama to visit Down Under in January of 1939. What Sandell had heard of Nakama made him certain that the Maui boy was the new Kahanamoku, and the double bill was a thrilling idea to organizers.

Down Under

Kahanamoku politely begged off the invitation, claiming onerous responsibilities in his office of sheriff of Waikiki, but in a cable to Sandell, he affirmed Keo Nakama's exceptional qualities both as a swimmer and as a human being. The message, along with sharing his secret stroke technique during the *Matsonia* crossing, was yet another nod to Sakamoto that Kahanamoku was a true supporter of the 3YSC. He wrote to Sandell that he had every expectation of Nakama's future greatness and called him a "swell kid."

Two obstacles stood in the way of Keo Nakama's traveling to Australia. Money wasn't an issue; his trip, including all his expenses, was covered by his hosts. The first problem was that Keo would miss three entire months of school; the second problem was that without Kahanamoku along, he would have no adult chaperone.

Sakamoto endeavored to send other swimmers along with Keo; he suggested Halo Hirose and Bill Neunzig—the latter had, like Gilman, decided to move to Maui—but the Australians were quite set on Nakama alone. Given Keo's age, Sakamoto had to go to bat for Keo with all of the island's authorities. Fortunately, he had a bit less trouble with Damkroger than he might have; Bob Hughes thought highly of the governing swimming body in New South Wales, and he felt certain that the organization was a solid and upright one that would take special care of Nakama. School personnel were more intractable, but after nearly a month of politicking, Nakama had a ticket in hand and a packed suitcase. He would leave in December, participate in the meet in January, then tour the country and the various islands around it.

Once the matter was settled and all parties reasonably happy, E. L. Damkroger insisted that he alone be allowed to make the travel arrangements. It wasn't clear why he wanted the responsibility. Perhaps it was because Bob Hughes was familiar with the leagues; perhaps it was because he wanted to spare Sakamoto the trouble of making complicated arrangements; perhaps he thought Sakamoto wasn't capable of doing so, but whatever the intention, Damkroger's involvement would later prove detrimental to Soichi Sakamoto.

On a previously scheduled trip to Honolulu for an AAU meeting, Damkroger would communicate with those in the Antipodes, secure Keo's passport, and take care of the requisite paperwork for the trip. He alone kept track of the schedule laid out for Nakama, and he approved every detail. He shared the itinerary at an Aloha dinner held in Keo Nakama's honor: Keo left on the SS *Monterey* on December 3, 1938. He would participate in the All-States Dominion Championships on January 6–8 in Sydney, tour the Continent for three months, and then return home, leaving Australia on March 30, 1939, on the *Mariposa*—in order to be in Honolulu by April 12 for the Duke Kahanamoku Indoor Championships at Punahou.

Keo Nakama had his return ticket in hand, and the dates were set in stone.

As wild about Duke Kahanamoku as the Aussies had been in 1914 and 1915, they were now positively over the moon about Keo Nakama. From the moment he arrived, Keo became the most famous and celebrated visitor in that country, and stories about him—editorials, cartoons, and more— appeared nearly every day in the papers. He was, for the duration of his visit, the object of a nation's fascination, its affection, and its tremendous curiosity and good humor.

When Keo arrived in Sydney on December 26, the Aussies met a young man who was a bit worse for the wear after the long voyage, but who was nevertheless cheerful, agreeable, and uncomplaining. Keo never told his hosts how difficult the crossing had been; he wrote home of it only to Sakamoto and the tone of his letters in no way approached the profoundly bitter and disappointed letters Halo Hirose had sent from Europe the previous summer.

The *Monterey* was another iteration of the Matsonian dynasty of white ships, luxurious for Keo even in cabin class. He found that the people traveling from Honolulu to Australia seemed a "much more...dignified society group," but he didn't feel cowed by them, just perhaps not as comfortable as he had during his crossing to California. He became better chums with the crew, in particular with a group of eight bellboys roughly his size and age, with whom he shared a number of adventures. Upon docking in Pago Pago in Samoa, the group took the day to sightsee on the gorgeously green and mountainous island. On Suva, in Fiji, the group of nine explored nearer the hotels, where Keo found the first pool he had seen since Maui.

The pool on the *Monterey* was the size of a bathtub, and perhaps because he was alone, or perhaps because Damkroger had not bothered to make arrangements, Keo found no canvas deck pool set up for him in which he could practice and keep in shape. For two weeks at sea he'd grown rusty. He was achy, he had slept poorly, he had been nauseous often enough that he had thinned out, and his muscles—the few he had—had begun to atrophy. When he jumped into a 50-meter saltwater tank on Suva, he was flabbergasted to discover how out of shape he was. When he attempted to practice sprints, he felt sick and breathless and perfectly awful, but after a brief rest, he gave a 100-meter swim a try and began to feel more human, eventually working himself up to an 880-yard, of which he was not particularly proud but still got his motor going. On the last night of the crossing, the seas were rough, the air cold, and he was more seasick than ever. It was a miserable Christmas Day, but arriving in Sydney to a warm welcome, he rose to the occasion the way he always did.

Waiting for him in Australia was a fine chaperone. Mr. Sandell of the association met him personally and escorted him to the St. James Hotel, and out the window of his room he could see Hyde Park and look upon Sydney Harbor. The latter reminded him of San Francisco Bay, which he had seen just months before, and he felt perfectly at home.

Thoughtfully, Sandell had arranged for Keo to practice in a fine nearby pool at the Tattersalls Club in Taronga Park, and even more thoughtfully, he had arranged for Keo to have the help of a handler by the name of Jack Plummer. Plummer wasn't a coach; he was a trainer in the old-time sense of the word, and during the trip, he would make sure that Keo was well-exercised, well-rested, and well-fed.

At the club, Keo jumped into the water and spent thirty-five minutes doing slow swimming and then forty more minutes using a kickboard, and when he asked to return for a second workout in the afternoon, Plummer was dumbstruck; he had never seen a swimmer complete as rigorous a workout (it was, in fact, pale in comparison to what Keo usually did at home) nor a swimmer with as much seriousness of purpose and solid work ethic. Plummer told others about the boy's workout, and he described Keo as a "human shark" in the water, speedy and unstoppable. The press began to swarm Keo, finding him a fun subject. He was deceptively small, sports reporters said, a thin child and short at 5 feet 4½ inches, who was nothing less than a superhuman "demon fish."

He wasn't used to giving interviews nor talking about himself, so when he did he spoke only about Coach Sakamoto and how wonderful he was, how giving, how talented. Keo gave all the credit for anything he knew to that man. "He is," Keo declared, "the best coach in the islands." The press was fascinated by Keo's backstory, not only his poverty but also where he got his start: it was positively unreal to think that the teenager and his friends had first learned to swim in a ditch, but when asked about it, Keo told them that swimming against the ditch's current was the very reason he was so strong.

They adored him for his quirks, of which there were many. For some reason, any time he saw a typewriter, Keo was so fascinated by it that he would sit down and play with the keys, and this became a story that was told about him over and over again. Similarly, he often ordered soup at meals, and cartoonists drew pictures of him slurping soup happily or even swimming in a bowl of soup. He cut some of the stories out and sent them home to Sakamoto.

At the meets, he immediately proved both his strength and his speed. On the first day of the competition at the gorgeous North Sydney pool, he was entered in no fewer than four widely different events, from the 110-yard swim to the 220, the 440, and the 880. He was one tiny swimmer in an enormous field of entrants—some eleven hundred in all, the highest number of participants ever in the championships, but on the Friday of the heats, the others looked on and realized they didn't stand a chance against him. He finished first in every heat he raced.

The famed Australian swimmer Robin Biddulph, a hefty 14 stone (196 pounds), had recently been sidelined by a rotten case of bronchitis, but even if he had not been ill, Biddulph told the press that he knew he was done for once he saw what the visitor could do. And he was.

On Saturday, January 7, competing in the 440-yard race against Noel Ryan, another Aussie swimmer, in lane one, and poor Biddulph in lane seven, Keo flew through the water in the second lane. In the stands young women waved Japanese flags while Keo plowed through the tank. At the first lap, 55 yards, he touched the wall with Noel Ryan just slightly behind him, but by the second turn, Keo was a full 3 feet ahead, with Robin Biddulph closely behind Ryan. The same was true at the turn of the third lap, and by the fourth—with a touch at the halfway mark at 2:19 for Keo and 2:27 for Biddulph—Keo was a full 4 yards ahead, while behind him, Ryan and Biddulph were separated by only a foot. In the sixth lap, Keo tore 8 feet ahead of Biddulph, who himself was now a solid 9 feet ahead of Ryan. The crowd roared. In the seventh lap, Biddulph had a burst of energy and caught up, just behind Nakama, and it was a desperate finish to the wall. Even though Australia's best swimmer had clocked a second-half split time of 2:26, he had still finished only a close second.

The clock told it all. Keo came in at 4 minutes 52 seconds. Biddulph finished admirably at 4:53, besting his own time by nearly a full second. The moment Keo could catch his breath, he congratulated Biddulph and then called out to Plummer to please send a cable to his coach back home. The unbelievable had occurred. He had equaled Jack Medica's world record.

Keo's performance in Sydney was unprecedented. He took the 880-yard freestyle at 10:12.6, bettering his own time by an unheard-of 21 seconds, and beating the record of Andrew "Boy" Charlton of Australia. The crowds were on their feet, the coaches and trainers on deck as wide-eyed and speechless as those who had watched Keo Nakama swim the iconic Ralph Gilman race. What in the world did the kid have in him that made him go so darn fast?

With the exception of a single race—the 220-yard in the saltwater Manley Baths—Keo took first wherever he was. And in that one race, when he was second to Biddulph, he refused either to blame the conditions or to sound sour. The press noted that on the night of the Manley race, the wind was unbearably strong from the south and had sent a "diagonal swell" that caused the swimmers to roll and "lose the full advantage" of the race's single turn, but when Australian Olympic coach Harry Hay asked Keo how he felt upon losing to Robin Biddulph and whether he felt the conditions were unacceptable or had slowed him down, Keo responded as he typically did, a good sport and gent. He was quoted as saying, "I like to race a nice clean sporting boy like Robin...He was too good. But it was a fine race and a pleasure."

The feeling was mutual. Where Biddulph could have been frustrated, he wasn't at all. Swimming against a great like Nakama only made Biddulph better. In his first outing against Nakama, he felt, he said, in spite of his lingering bronchitis, absolutely energized to swim alongside Keo. "I feel like a lion," he said. Nakama was in Australia to help Biddulph, to help spur him and other Australian swimmers on.

Indeed, as word of Nakama's virtuosity spread, the crowds swelled in stadiums across Australia. In the course of three months, he traveled from Sydney to Melbourne, across to Perth and Adelaide, over to Tasmania, swimming in twenty-three competitive events and many more exhibitions, breaking three Australian records, beating Biddulph nine times in all and taking six championships.

Australians never wanted him to leave. They renamed him "Kurt" and joked about adopting him. He was just so perfectly adorable, sweet-natured, quirky, and as fast in the water as anything they'd ever seen. They loved that he was developing a bit of an Australian accent. They were miserable when he boarded the *Mariposa*. He did so on March 31, just one day after he was supposed to have left, but the departure was in no way to affect his arrival date. That was written in stone—he would steam into Honolulu Harbor, just as E. L. Damkroger had planned, on April 12.

Throughout the Anzac tour, the Australians were obsessed with Keo Nakama's technique in the water. They studied him, filmed him, and tried to break down his motions so that they could understand them. They were impressed but confounded, saying that they'd never seen the likes of him before, which they didn't attribute solely to his stroke. They noted both Keo's bunched fingers and deep, slow kick, and when they had asked him about it, he had answered with complete honesty: I don't know why I do what I do; I just do exactly what Coach Sakamoto taught me to do, he explained. He said he understood nothing about the propulsive forces that were at work in his form, just that Sakamoto was a genius.

Olympic coach Harry Hay was the most intent on understanding. What he saw was that the kid relaxed throughout the catch—when the hand entered the water—and that he stayed relaxed during both the pull and the recovery—the movement through the water and then the exit of the elbow and the return. Others watching were easily deceived, Hay said; they thought Nakama was tense because his arm in the recovery was straight as a stick and almost parallel to the water's surface before the catch. If one wasn't looking closely, it appeared that the arm and the hand were entering the water simultaneously, as if there were no real catch at all.

What Hay saw was unusual: that flat recovery, then on the pull a brief flutter at the hip but no interruption in continuous motion. Perfect circularity. The pull, he said, was just slightly outside the centerline of Nakama's body, and it was much, much deeper in the water than that of most swimmers Hay had seen in his career. The smooth continuous motion would have cramped anyone else who tried to copy him, Hay said. Nakama was built a particular way—was built special, and the stroke had been tailor-made just for him.

Hay understood. He threw his hands up in the air and shook his head and praised Coach Sakamoto for what he had done. Soichi Sakamoto was a genius: Hay was certain that each kid in the Three-Year Swim Club had his very own stroke, a stroke that worked only for him, which Sakamoto had designed himself.

Harry Hay was precisely right. From that moment in the dark belly of the *Matsonia* in June of 1938, when Duke Kahanamoku had told him that the sharp tool in the water was the stroke, Sakamoto began focusing on finding the perfect, most efficient propulsive stroke for each child in the club.

In the spring of 1939, as news about Keo Nakama was spreading—how he had equaled Jack Medica's middle-distance record, how he was winning every race he swam, how beloved he was Down Under—Soichi Sakamoto was back at the Camp 5 pool, implementing something he called "stroke checking." After calisthenics, he had each swimmer take a single 25-yard lap in front of him and then climb out of the water.

Then, at the edge of the pool, he critiqued the motion, sometimes standing behind the swimmer and moving the swimmer's arms from the elbows, or sometimes from the shoulders or the hands, repositioning each arm in the catch, pull, and recovery until what he saw in the next lap was a movement without drag, without resistance, without wasted energy. And it was, indeed, different for every kid. No body was built the same. Every body needed its own particular stroke, a signature movement. That's what Soichi Sakamoto was working on.

His teaching method was evolving as well. He was learning from each swimmer. Coaching them was a kind of collaboration. He watched them in the water. They would carry out his ideas, and then he would hone them and shape them, and together they learned what worked best. Trial and error. Common sense.

And on the larger scale he looked at each swimmer as a complete individual. He examined each one, and he found in each a particular strength and built on it. He would begin with the bud of something he could see—say, that this one's arms were more flexible in a horizontal movement; this one had more extension circling back. Their particular flexibilities helped him determine the events they should swim, the events for which he believed their bodies were built. He would nurture the potential he saw in them until it blossomed into something.

That spring was all about blossoming in the swimmers. Sakamoto saw a whole new crop rising. Jose Balmores, a young Filipino from Camp 5, was excelling at the backstroke—he was fast and glided so beautifully and for so long on each stroke that his friends began to call him "the Filipino Flash"— and becoming a prime candidate for the individual medley. Another swimmer who began to impress was a half-Filipino and half-Hawaiian boy named Benny Castor, a barrel-chested original ditch kid also from Camp 5, whose strength was in the breaststroke. Sugio "Shangy" Tsukano, the middle of the Tsukano brothers, was turning into a freestyle middle-distance swimmer, and so was Shangy's brother John. Keo Nakama's brother, Bunny, still little, was showing promise in the same events that Keo swam. Little Charlie Oda, who hadn't been able to make it a single lap across the pool, was now more than competent at freestyle; Sakamoto was still deciding which events should be Oda's focus.

Sakamoto had new tricks up his sleeve; while traveling he'd had endless time to think of what he might need to bring the team along. He found an old piano stool and managed to attach it to a frame on wheels, and on top of the swiveling seat he created a platform on which the children could lie facedown and practice kicking against the clubhouse wall.

He began to correct tiny faults he found in the children's breathing. A gasp or a choke did the body no good; breathing had to be steady-steady-steady with no tension in the breath. He bought a metronome and made each swimmer listen to a pace he set for them, with each click representing a stroke; they had to listen to the metronome until they heard the pace in their heads, and sometimes Sakamoto would even squeeze it into their hands. He'd broken it down, in math: if they wanted to meet a certain time in a race, they would have to cross a particular distance in that time, and in order to do so, their stroke rate would have to be: click, click, click. Then, in the water, they were to swim to the beat he'd given them, accomplishing a lap in a certain number of strokes in a specific time. It was a level of precision he had never before thought to have. And it was, in fact, a level of precision that no one else in the United States was practicing. Soichi Sakamoto, without knowing it, stood at the horizon of groundbreaking innovations in the sport of swimming.

In March, E. L. Damkroger conveyed to Sakamoto a strange message: Keo Nakama would be returning on March 15, one month early. It would be best, then, Damkroger said, to get on with the planning of the welcome home celebration, wouldn't it?

It was a rush. Sakamoto originally had things lined up for a month later, so he now asked favors of all those he knew to accommodate Keo's early homecoming. He enjoined all of the Japanese-American civic leaders on

Oahu and on Maui to host lavish, banzai-filled shindigs. The one on Oahu would feature masters of ceremony, including Japanese bankers and Japan's vice-consul. On Maui, HC&S, Alexander House, and the Japanese Civic Association together planned a chop-suey dinner at the Canton Café, an event so popular that the restaurant took reservations, filled up, and had to start a waiting list. Sakamoto lined up speaker after speaker, luminaries to praise Nakama's achievements as one of the "greatest touring records ever established." He arranged for a display case and tables where Keo could lay out his cache of cups, trophies, and banners. And nothing could be more perfect: Keo would steam into town and have almost two weeks before the indoor AAUs at Punahou to rest and to train.

On March 15, all of Hawaii was poised to welcome Keo Nakama home. Sakamoto stood at the Aloha pier among a crowd of hundreds that included members of the Honolulu Junior Chamber of Commerce, AAU officials, reporters, and photographers. Among the throngs stood Duke Kahanamoku, official greeter of all passengers of importance, and E. L. Damkroger, director of athletics on the island of Maui.

When the *Monterey* came into view, the crowd exploded into applause, and as the great ship inched toward the pier, the Royal Hawaiian Band struck up "Aloha Oe," but after nearly every passenger had disembarked, Keo was nowhere to be seen. Sakamoto was gripped by the fear that something horrible had happened to him. He inquired of the crew, then of the ticket office, then of any straggler passing by. One man, an Aussie tourist, had news: Of course the man knew the great ditch swimmer of Hawaii. Why, all Australia knew he wasn't set to leave Sydney until the end of March. And for good measure, the cheerful fellow noted that at least in *his* country, the swimmer's comings and goings had become so important and the boy so famous that whatever he did was, frankly, a matter of public record.

On that horrid day in March, after the Royal Hawaiian Band had packed up its instruments, the *Nippu Jiji* newspaper announced that Keo Nakama had "skipped the ship." Sports reporters complained about the "severe blow dealt local committees and organizations who had been planning receptions for the conquering hero." When the boy had failed to appear on Thursday, said one, he had disappointed hundreds.

The front-page headlines of papers in those days were about a disappointment of a more global nature. In September of 1938, just moments after Halo Hirose had left Germany for home, Hitler's army had goose-stepped into Prague, and on the Ides of March—when Sakamoto was fooled into believing that Keo Nakama would show up at the Aloha pier—in Europe, the Czechs at last surrendered. It was only a matter of time before Poland would fall, and so much more seemed imminent. In Helsinki the Finns were still building stadia and a velodrome and pouring the foundation of a larger swimming pool. But what would happen to Finland, then?

All through the early spring, Soichi Sakamoto walked about as though he were a ship lost in the thickest fog. It was incomprehensible. All of it.

The only explanation was that E. L. Damkroger had intentionally lied to him and then waited at the dock to witness Sakamoto's humiliation. There was nothing Sakamoto could either say or do but shrug and tell others how foolish he had been to have misremembered the date of return, and as for confronting Damkroger, there was no point: the man would certainly deny everything.

In mid-April, Sakamoto returned to the pier. He had confirmed that Keo was indeed aboard the *Monterey* and he was prepared this time, he thought. He'd even wired the ship with a cable for Keo, reminding the boy of the evening's events: it was Wednesday, April 12, and the time trials for the Hawaiian AAU Indoor Championship meet began at the Waterhouse Pool in Punahou that evening. The competition would run through Saturday evening, and Sakamoto wanted to be certain that Keo was shipshape for practice immediately upon arrival home.

This time, Sakamoto had come to Honolulu with thirty-four members of the Three-Year Swim Club. Each wore the new team uniform that Sakamoto had designed and for which the children had raised money in order to buy: white trousers or skirts, and a white shirt underneath a dark, navy blue sweater with the crest of the 3YSC sewn on the front. Another swarm of reporters and photographers had come as well, and standing beside Sakamoto was Duke Kahanamoku.

This time when the band played "Aloha Oe," Keo appeared. A flurry of teammates rushed to him and covered him with leis, and reporters pressed him with question after question. Sakamoto stood by and watched, relieved at last.

The reports asked him about his months of adventure in the Antipodes, whether he had liked it, what he thought of Fiji and Tasmania and of the crowds and all the attention. As demure as always, he answered, "Gee, everything was so fine, I don't know how to express myself," in the most endearing way.

But when the reporters turned to the subject of the Duke Kahanamoku Indoor Meet, at which point Kahanamoku himself began to listen more closely, the boy was dumbstruck. He was, he said, completely unaware of a meet. This evening? he asked. Soichi Sakamoto watched in horror as Nakama blanched, like he had choked on a chicken bone. When Keo's eyes met his, he looked blankly at his coach, tried to signal something, but Sakamoto had to stand and merely watch as the situation devolved into humiliation once again.

Sakamoto had sent a cable to the ship. There was no question. Why hadn't the boy received it? For their part, the reporters just assumed the boy was dazed; the trip must have, they offered, taken a great deal out of him.

Indeed it had. He'd swum nearly every day, competitions galore, and no, he hadn't slept well Down Under; it was summer there, and the heat had been awful. And as for training on the way home, he had to admit he had done none; this time it wasn't just because the pool was so small, it was because the seas had been so rough that the captain had decided it better not to fill the tank at all.

Most passengers had been seasick, Nakama said, including himself. In the past few weeks, he had lost ten pounds. His suit jacket and trousers hung off of him as though he were nothing but bones. So do you think you'll swim tonight after all, a sportswriter pressed. Flashbulbs popped, and Keo was blinded for a moment. "Sure," Keo answered, and looked tentatively at Sakamoto. "If my coach wants me to." Sakamoto stepped in between Keo and the press. Unlikely, he said, with no practice, the seasickness, and the ten pounds lost. Why, the boy didn't have ten pounds to spare! Sakamoto tried

160

to joke. Duke Kahanamoku stepped in and agreed. There was no reason, Kahanamoku said, to push the boy. Everyone knew how capably he swam; his career would be long, and it would be a pity to ruin it by pressuring him to do more now than he was able.

To an outsider, the ensuing photo session would have seemed cheerful, and even the faces of most of those in the photographs are happy, but for Sakamoto, the hour of posing and re-posing at the dock and along the great green lawn that stretched from the pier to the street was excruciating. From time to time he looked over at Keo and saw a gaunt stick of a thing with flowers strung about him. The headlines, which didn't appear until the next day's morning edition, were bloody: "Nakama's Back; Tired, but Willing to Swim." One reporter described the boy as "dazed," but on the evening of April 12, the real story was that Keo had insisted on participating in the time trials. He also insisted, upon leaving the pier that very morning, that Coach take him up to the tank to practice. What Sakamoto saw in the water was encouraging, but he thought better of giving in to the boy's desire to please. Keo pressed him through lunch, a banquet that the chamber of commerce hosted for the entire 3YSC. Sakamoto continued to refuse, but at 7 p.m., Keo Nakama was dressed in his swimming suit and poised upon a block at the Waterhouse Pool, prepared to dive in for the 440-yard freestyle trials. He told Sakamoto he was certain he could do it.

In January, at the Sydney Olympic pool, Keo had swum the 440 and equaled Jack Medica's record. The telegram he'd had the swimming association send home for him had been addressed to Sakamoto. It read: *Happy New Year. Stop. Tied Jack Medica's Record. Stop. Kurt.* Now, Sakamoto watched his skinny swimmer take off into the water. Beside Keo was Halo, and the third competitor was James Tanaka, a promising young man who swam for the Nu'uanu YMCA. At the gun, the boys sprang into the 25-yard Waterhouse tank. Sakamoto stood, arms crossed, watching, completely uncertain that he had made the right decision. Some of the reporters from the Honolulu papers came to stand next to him on the deck, and as the race began, here and there, they offered an observation: how beautifully Nakama was swimming. They marveled at the improvement in his form and said how assured he looked in the water. Sakamoto said nothing. He just watched as Keo, Halo Hirose, and James Tanaka swam a tight heat, tense in every lap; Sakamoto expected Keo to tire, but instead the boy went on, keeping up a rhythmic pace through lap after lap, Tanaka, Keo, and Halo head-to-head until the final splasher when James Tanaka pulled ever so slightly ahead and touched the wall at 5:02.9. Keo was second in at 5:03.4, and Halo was clocked at 5:04—no longer a terribly respectable time for a 440.

Friday evening opened with the finals in the 440-yard freestyle, and Sakamoto was jittery as he watched Keo swim it. The only competitor in the pool was James Tanaka, and the two swimmers fought it out all the way, lap by lap in the Waterhouse tank. Keo was smooth on every lap, his pace and rhythm as steady as in the heats, so much so that he didn't need to push or sprint ahead to gain advantage. When he came to the wall at 4:54.6, six strokes in front of Tanaka, Sakamoto felt as though he could finally breathe again.

The time of 4.54.6 was only 2.6 seconds off the Jack Medica record Keo Nakama had equaled down in the pool in Sydney. *And* it was an island record. So maybe Keo Nakama was out of shape; maybe he was tired and underweight; maybe he had traveled too many miles in the past three months; and maybe there had been confusion about his return, but in Sakamoto's mind the 440-yard time said that nothing he had done had ever hurt Keo Nakama. He only wished that others would see that.

The results of the April meet—and not just Keo Nakama's spectacular performance—should have been enough to vindicate Sakamoto. In all, the club nabbed 19 first places out of 27 events and established 7 territorial records, and that should have marked the end of idle talk.

But it didn't.

The Three-Year Swim Club was no longer just a club, Sakamoto felt. Now it was the pride of Maui and the pride of the Territory. But everyone smelled blood. Sakamoto was indeed wounded. The refrain in the press was the same message that Bud Crabbe, Robert Hughes, and E. L. Damkroger had lobbed at Sakamoto a year before. Why was he working the children so hard?

"Right now, as far as the territory is concerned there is no one who has any right to advise 'Saka' just what he should and shouldn't do with his boys," wrote one sports columnist in Sakamoto's defense, but the popular opinion was that he was going to do the children damage in the long term. "Someone with influence ought to be able to knock some sense" into that hardheaded grammar school teacher, read one editorial. The criticism built and built. After all, Soichi Sakamoto wasn't a swimmer or even a real coach. He'd gotten the children this far, but could he really get the swimmers to the Olympics? It was unlikely he had the know-how, people said. The results of the meets were more than pleasing, but the danger was that he'd kill the children before they'd even have a chance to make it to the Games.

Sakamoto's philosophy with regard to hard work, what he taught the children, was that they had the ability to do more than what was asked of them. One of his favorite sayings during Coach Church was "Let your energy match your fatigue"—in other words, there wasn't a way to burn out. Continuing on was a matter of finding a way to refuel. Energy wasn't finite in a child or any human being. Energy wasn't finite at all; it was something on which an athlete could build. Strength led to strength. Success led to success. But no one was listening. The way that Keo Nakama had looked at the dock on April 12 had made a far better story than his showing at the Punahou meet. Everybody loved a victim. And everybody hated tyrants. It was, after all, 1939, a banner year for dictators.

One critic wrote that although "Great pains have been taken" to develop Sakamoto's swimmers, "greater pain should be taken by those in-the-know to prevent the club from 'hitting the downward trail.'"

Sakamoto was certain now: E. L. Damkroger had set him up in front of the public in March; he'd lied to Sakamoto about Keo's change of plans, and he must have watched with pleasure as Sakamoto made a fool of himself with the very communities on whom he had come to depend for financial support to keep the 3YSC running and independent.

There was something even more suspicious about Damkroger's behavior;

he seemed to be making calculations for something. Damkroger had not long before overseen a major renovation of the sports facilities at Alexander House: he'd gutted the inside of the entire recreation center, and he'd spent what must have been a fortune on six billiard tables, a Ping-Pong table, a shuffleboard court, stations at which children could sit and play cribbage and checkers, a quiet reading space, brand-new bleachers in the gymnasium, new bowling alleys—it was only 15 cents to play a game—and a soft drink concession stand where kids could buy soda pop and candy. But strangest of all was this: Damkroger had had workers dig out the old Alexander House pool in Wailuku and extend it to a regulation length of 25 yards. Just what he planned to do in that pool, and with whom, concerned Sakamoto.

Sakamoto did his best to repair his ties with the Japanese-American community on Maui, and he sought out donors on Oahu. Sakamoto found a friend and benefactor in a man named George Higa, the owner of the successful Honolulu Café. Higa, who was Okinawan, had made his way in the business world in spite of the prejudice against him, and he was famously kind and generous to all comers. He'd let Sakamoto know that whenever he might need help, all he had to do was ask. He freely offered money for the children's travel, and he became the de facto "cafeteria" for the team; when they were in Honolulu, the Honolulu Café was where they ate their meals. And with George Higa, there were no strings attached.

Sakamoto should have seen it coming from a distance. Way back when he'd first returned to Maui with Keo and then Halo in tow from Louisville, he'd sensed ever more certainly that Damkroger wasn't what he seemed to be on the outside. The club's successes—their records in the Pacific meets and four second places in their first-ever national championship bids—set the minds of almost everyone on Maui on the possibility, if not probability, that the two young men—and perhaps others from the 3YSC—had a bright future in national and international swimming. When they'd returned, it had seemed that all of Wailuku had welcomed them with sukiyaki dinners—along with hot dogs, sandwiches, and ice cream. And, he remembered now, it was E. L. Damkroger who always stood to speak. Damkroger called Hirose and Nakama "the envy of all the second-generation Japanese." But when he spoke about Soichi Sakamoto, even in words that ought to have sounded like praise, there was equivocation and even resentment in his voice. *Here was a man—even so untrained, so unprepared—*Damkroger had once said, *an elementary school teacher* hadn't let his own *shortcomings hold him back from developing excellent swimmers. Soichi Sakamoto worked hard. As hard as he possibly could.*

For the rest of the month of April, Sakamoto hardly slept.

He set out to make a splash. He filled an entire page of the *Maui News* with an announcement of a Saturday Victory Hop. Eight local businesses had paid for advertising space in which they congratulated the 3YSC on annexing the indoor territorial championship. The 3YSC had won the day!

But Soichi Sakamoto was losing self-control. Once, at practice, when he'd found a group of boys loafing, he'd hit them hard and knocked their heads together. Another time, at a meet at Punahou, some of the younger girls had innocently jumped into the pretty pool to play, and he'd screamed and cursed, calling them country bumpkins. If he saw anything like that again, he'd put them on the boat back home. They'd also incensed him when, after returning from a Honolulu meet, he discovered that they'd stolen towels from the Nu'uanu Y where they'd been staying. The horrid embarrassment had come to light the following day, when, as they approached the pier in Lahaina in the early hours of the morning, they found Damkroger standing at the dock waiting for them; the people at the YMCA had called ahead. At another meet, Sakamoto's excessive sideline coaching—a euphemism for interfering—ended up disqualifying Halo Hirose and the infraction made the papers.

The worst, the children whispered among themselves, was when Coach had forced one of the girls to sit and eat a steak so she'd grow stronger. It was cooked, but the juices had run red onto the plate, and the girl had cried and asked if she could be spared from eating it. Coach had made her eat and he'd watched her until her plate was clean.

He was absentminded, distracted. To some he appeared like someone else entirely.

Some time before, Sakamoto had purchased a movie projector and a screen, and he began to watch the reels and reels of film he had taken in the past year every night after dinner. The pictures ticked by, showing Halo

Taken at the Flood

Hirose and Keo Nakama in vivid action both in California and in the green lagoon at Louisville. Ralph Flanagan. Adolph Kiefer. Bright light and the clicking and ticking and the fan of the movie projector kept Mary awake and miserable. Her husband had returned from the Mainland in body only; his mind was somewhere else, somewhere in those moving pictures he stared at for hours and hours at a time. His thoughts were in the frames of the film, in between the frames. His thoughts were wheels that turned in the same directions—both forward and in reverse—as the wheel on the projector did. Over and over and over again.

He was becoming a stranger to Mary and she to him; he was diving deeper and deeper inside of himself, closer to the children in the club and further from his own children. He could hardly remember their names. He rarely saw his parents or his brothers and sisters. He meant to. He had even promised his children and his younger brother Benzo that he would teach them how to swim, but there never seemed to be the time for it. He told himself that when the Olympics were finally over, when Sakamoto and the club had met its promised goal, he'd return to those who loved him.

In the meantime, he watched the reels spin in the dark and the images flash before him, while Mary tossed and turned in bed, knowing that for reasons she didn't understand, her husband was going somewhere beyond her reach.

Chapter Nine

YOUTHS OF THE SEA

In 1939, Kamehameha Day fell on a Monday, June 12, which made for a long and festive weekend. Thousands had turned out in the early morning and lined the streets of Wailuku to watch the annual parade with its contingents of uniformed Sea Scouts and the Maui Junior Police battalion, with its *pa'u* riders in their silk culottes, executing elegant maneuvers on horseback.

This year, the Kahekili—the men in orange caps and sashes and the women in black dresses—had outdone themselves. The group marched ahead of their float: a double war canoe, a replica of the one that had once belonged to Hawaii's greatest monarch, the man for whom the day's holiday was named. On the bow of the outrigger on the float was the face of Kukailimoku, the Hawaiian god of war, and in the center of the canoe stood a statue of the legendary King Kamehameha I himself. At the foot of the statue sat a group of living children whose role was to play his court, and on either side of the canoe real bare-breasted men j-stroked the morning air with single-sided wooden blades, creating the fleeting impression that they were not atop a wagon on the streets of Wailuku, but instead propelling themselves on a voyage of purpose across the swells of the Pacific.

Wailuku town was no Honolulu, but in the late 1930s, it was Maui's metropolis. Writer Georgia O'Keeffe visited the island in '39, and she found

Wailuku both charming and maddening. The downtown, she noted, was filled with modern stores of all kinds, a "Kress 10-cent Store, which carried delicacies like Hershey Almond Bars," and the Maui Book Store, where, to her delight, she could buy "a couple of Nancy Drews." "The people amuse me," she wrote, and when she walked the town, she found herself captivated by the spired stone church, the trees that lined the village streets, the wide sidewalks, which, she noted, were not crowded as Honolulu's were with tourists. O'Keeffe didn't consider herself a tourist; she'd been invited by an island pineapple company to paint labels for its cans, and while she traveled to all manner of outposts where she indeed painted extraordinarily beautiful images of flowers, she seemed happier in a place like Wailuku, the only real city on the Valley Isle, enjoying the luxury of what anywhere else in the world would have been modest accommodations: the Maui Grand Hotel, with its crisp linens, fine service, embossed stationery, air-conditioned cocktail lounge, and pretty little gift shop—the nicest shop, O'Keeffe noted, anywhere on the island. And she had found some enticing trinkets: "Ni'ihua shells and ivory, Chinoiserie and Japanese remembrances." Ever the Mainlander, O'Keeffe found herself appalled to discover that Wailuku's single rental car business was in possession of only two automobiles, and that, obviously, if one were in use and the other broken down, there was no transport available at all.

If Wailuku wasn't Honolulu, it also wasn't Lahaina. That town, located on the island's northeast coast, had been the first real commercial town on Maui, a port that served the sandalwood and then the whaling trade. In the years of the latter, it was a garden spot for whalers who had come ashore after long turns at sea. Most of these men, who stood on life's ladder perhaps just a rung or two above the average pirate—and who had a pirate's appetite for liquor—enjoyed the cheap pleasures to be found in brothels and games of chance.

Sakamoto had been born in Lahaina; his childhood house stood no more than a few hundred feet from the old Lahaina Prison—the *Hale Pa'ahao*, or, "the stuck-in-irons place." As late as the turn of the twentieth century, the prison was a temporary residence to all manner of petty criminals, such as sailors and ships' officers charged with petty theft, brawling, and fornicating. Soichi Sakamoto's earliest nighttime lullabies might easily have been the sounds emanating from inside the high coral walls of that jailhouse, the drunken complaints of men who shook the bars of the cells in which they were locked—unfairly, they believed. Perhaps that odd, drunken lowing had formed a part of Sakamoto's character as well: the earnest desire for freedom.

When the whaling industry moved on, Lahaina became a less unsavory port town, and a great deal of trade and shipping moved to Kahului Harbor, which had been dredged and made usable. By the time Soichi Sakamoto had been a youth, the majority of commercial life had migrated to Wailuku, home to the Valley Isle's middle class: bankers, telephone operators, doctors, dentists, dressmakers, and attorneys. The town had a courthouse, restaurants, gas stations, automobile shops, a pool hall, a pharmacy, a meat market, two separate movie theaters, and the two-story-high Maui Dry Goods Store, with a red, white, and blue electrical sign the owners had imported from San Francisco that lit up in the window.

Over the years, Kamehameha Day in Wailuku had grown only more festive. In the early years, missionaries had celebrated the day with hours in church followed by liquor-less luaus. In recent years, though, after the 1920s loosened things up, Kamehameha Day in Wailuku had become one of the most raucous celebrations of the year. The parade wound its way down Vineyard Street, down Central Avenue, past the Maui branch of the Bank of Hawaii and the town's fish and pickle counters, which were shuttered for the holiday. It wove past the grandstands at the Kahului playing fields and stopped there where, after brief speeches in honor of the former king, which were given in English and the native Hawaiian tongue, there were sack races, mule races, and greased pole competitions.

On this day in 1939, the sun broke through the clouds, and all along the fields near the harbor revelers sat with picnic lunches of pork and poi. A choral group from Makawao Akau burst out in the "Hawaii Ponoi," one of the unofficial anthems of the island kingdom, a muddled, mixed marriage of music reflecting the cultures that had colonized Hawaii. Among its strains one could hear "God Save the Queen" and "Heil dir im Siegerkranz." "Hawaii's own true sons," the choir sang. "People of the loyal heart. Your duty . . . to your chiefs . . . is to list and to abide."

The holiday on Oahu was grander by far than it was on Maui. In Honolulu, the parades were longer, the paʻu riders more brilliantly outfitted. In 1939, Governor Joseph Poindexter opened his mansion and allowed the public in. But Soichi Sakamoto had no intention of taking a holiday. Even at the docks, he ignored the long lines of lei sellers plying their wares for a holiday also called Lei Day.

Soichi Sakamoto had no time to celebrate, neither in Honolulu nor on Maui, from which he had just sailed. In the early morning at the Aloha pier he helped his enormous contingent of 3YSC swimmers step onto dry land after a rough overnight crossing in unsettled seas. A rare June squall was on its way; the waves were up, and the swimmers had hardly slept. They hadn't been able to take an interisland steamer, so Sakamoto had put them on a 200-foot-long cattle boat, and all night the cows had stomped and lowed at the cresting of the waves, and the queasy members of the swim team had spent the passage heaving over the railings and into the ocean.

A few of the less-traveled members of the team, the youngest ones in particular, like Charlie Oda, had been awake all night. He and some others had feared that they might capsize if they weren't vigilant. And as Sakamoto helped the children off the boat that morning, he saw that their eyes were rimmed red and their faces gray. It certainly wasn't at all the shape he'd wanted them to be in. They'd come to Honolulu once again for a major competition, one for which they had been preparing all spring. It was an invitational at the Natatorium in which the Canadian swimmer Bob Pirie was to compete, and Sakamoto was finally pleased with his ranks.

In fact, that spring Sakamoto had rigorously developed a strong boys' team with backstrokers, breaststrokers, and enough critical mass to have a 4x200 relay team with an alternate. He'd gone beyond grooming his two lead swimmers, Nakama and Hirose, most intensively. Damkroger had criticized Sakamoto publicly for what he called Sakamoto's undemocratic "star system," complaining that he was developing just a few swimmers at the expense of the rest. The two boys, Keo and Halo, were more like movie stars. Soon, one of them would turn into a Joe DiMaggio and refuse to swim until somebody paid him $40,000 every year.

But Sakamoto had been intentional in his strategy: a rising tide raised all ships. The younger boys hadn't been ready for the Nationals yet. But now, those like Jose Balmores and Charlie Oda and Benny Castor were swimming well enough that they might qualify for the Nationals in Detroit that August.

And although Damkroger also criticized Sakamoto for how hard the coach was working the girls on the team, Sakamoto was happy both with their progress and with the fact that he'd been able to recruit and even retain girls at all. In the late fall of 1937 and early 1938, he'd actively looked in the camps and then beyond, in Wailuku town, where he combed the Red Cross lifesaving classes and the water pageants for girls who could really swim. He even sought those who swam alone and entirely untrained in the Iao Valley pool above town, and by the spring of 1939, he had the makings of a girls' team that would likely peak around the time of the Olympic trials in a year.

Chieko "Chic" Miyamoto was a quick-witted, fast learner with a warm personality, who was tall for her age and versatile. He had her pegged for the individual medley. Toyoko "Toyo" Takeyama, a tiny girl with an elfish face, was painfully shy, but her strength was in the backstroke. Both Chic and Toyo and another girl, Charlotte Shigehara, were camp girls, and generally their proximity to the pool made it easier for Sakamoto to keep them coming to practice, although sometimes he lost camp girls to chores. Camp girls had to light the tirau long before breakfast or wet-mop their houses each afternoon, fighting against the red Pu'unene dust that covered everything.

Many girls who lived in Wailuku or Kahului were challenged by the distance, although some had an easier time than others getting to practice. Mitzuko "Mitzi" Higuchi was the daughter of divorced parents; her father lived in camp and her mother was a laundress for the Maui Grand Hotel. Mitzi, a squat, square girl who always appeared to be squinting, managed to move easily between town and camp; sometimes one parent thought she was staying with the other. Mitzi had a strong upper body and arms from having helped her mother hang hotel linens on the line, and she excelled in the 200-meter freestyle, the breaststroke, and the backstroke.

Those three likely wouldn't be ready for the Nationals this year; their times weren't yet good enough, but he saw them coming around the bend for the trials for the 1940 Olympics.

One of the town girls was the most promising of all on the team. Fujiko Katsutani was 5 foot 4 inches tall and weighed no more than 108 pounds. She hadn't started out good at any stroke in particular, but he'd given her a redwood board and told her how to move her legs like a frog. Then he gradually weaned her from the board as he became more satisfied with her kick. Now she was on pace in the breaststroke to qualify for the Women's National Championship in Des Moines, Iowa, in '39.

As essential as Keo Nakama was to the boys' team, so was Fujiko, or "Fudge," to the girls' team. But Kahului was far enough away from the Camp 5 pool that it was difficult for her to get to practice on time in the mornings; she took the Kahului Railroad, which dropped her off at the Kahului Depot; then, still before the sun was up, she transferred to a bus in order to get a bit nearer to Pu'unene, after which she made a two-mile trek. At first, Sakamoto didn't understand why she was tardy by half an hour or why she had circles underneath her eyes even before morning practice began. "If you're not here by six a.m.," he said, "don't come." The same was true for afternoon practices. In the winter months, she sometimes arrived after 4 p.m., at dusk. Quietly, she'd change her clothes and shower, but it would already be dark when she got into the pool, and the other children had gone through most of their training already.

Fujiko's family was middle-class, struggling to keep a small hotel going. Fujiko didn't suffer from malnutrition or neglect, but, at least in terms of fatherly understanding, she suffered greatly. Mr. Katsutani disapproved of nearly everything his youngest daughter did, and he was particularly unhappy that she had joined the swim club. He had no truck with Sakamoto, but he was afraid for his daughter's reputation, concerned that the amount of time she spent half-clothed in a pool with boys would give others the wrong impression. Fujiko continued to infuriate and defy him, and each night when she arrived home late, her father and older brothers locked the door against her.

Fujiko's mother, Kimiyo, was far more supportive; she had allowed Fujiko's older sister to travel to Japan to study; and while the curriculum there included the traditional feminine arts of etiquette and the minute particulars of the tea ceremony, it also included the study of literature, language, and history. After practice, Fujiko sat in the dark until the boys and her father settled down to sleep, at which point her mother always, with a warm dinner waiting, unlocked the door and let her youngest girl back in.

The girls' performances at the Punahou meet in April had been stunning and promising. The crowd had stood and roared for the girls when the 300-yard medley relay team of Toyoko, Fujiko, and Charlotte Shigehara broke the existing record in the event with a time of 3:49.8, and they had stood again when Mitzi Higuchi triumphed in the 200-yard freestyle over champion Olga Clark. Her time in the 200 freestyle was 2:47.5, proving that Mitzi Higuchi was a rising star. Her picture made all the papers.

But Fujiko Katsutani was already a star, and she was ready for Des Moines: that night, she swam as if the water were air and broke the territorial record in the 220-yard breaststroke by an unbelievable 16 seconds. Now, on the morning of another Honolulu competition, Sakamoto shepherded both the girls and the boys through Waikiki. They were a large group now, and however ill they were from the night's bad crossing, they seemed to be recovering. Morning practice was little more than an exercise in getting wet, but after a hearty lunch they looked alive again. On the deck of the Nat in the afternoon, Sakamoto ran alongside them, clapping out cadences and correcting their strokes when they came up for air.

In the old days, when Lahaina town was Maui's port, Kahului Bay had been a nightmare. Its currents were at cross-purposes, its bottom shallow, and trade winds—sweeping in from thousands of miles away—folded the flat ocean into unnavigable origami shapes; but ever since sugar planters had dredged the area near the shore and built a pair of protective breakwaters, the dangers of the bay sat behind quiet Kahului Harbor, which was divided into two parts: one for commerce, the other well-suited for pleasure boats and wading.

On Monday afternoon a swath of five thousand spectators crammed the docks and piers of the harbor for the annual Kamehameha Day regatta. The competition featured just about every iteration of canoe and surfboard race one could think up: multiples of distances; ages of rowers and paddlers; races between surf paddlers on hollow boards; races between surf paddlers on solid boards; a separate competition between groups of men in fishing boats; squads in traditional outriggers; and even an "open" race in which almost anything resembling a canoe and able to float was allowed to compete. The Kahului home team walked away with fistfuls of trophies, but some of the young people still felt somehow empty-handed. It was only 3 p.m., several hours yet until dark, and the water beckoned.

Among those who waited was a girl named Blossom Young. She had been a member of the Three-Year Swim Club not long before. But it had been an awful year for her, and among one of the awful things that had happened was that Coach had told her she didn't have what it took to carry on, that she wasn't committed enough to the team. It had been devastating enough, but there was more. It had been a year of misfortunes; she had been in two accidents, and her parents were angry with her, worried about her. They were traditional Chinese parents, and they said she had become irresponsible and flighty. Her father had arrived in Maui with a red leather-bound Chinese trunk containing an ivory signature chop, and ancient instruments: an *erhu* (two-stringed violin) and two flutes, the *dizi* and the *xiao*. He preferred Cantonese opera to ballroom music. And he didn't like to have a daughter swimming and spending all her time outdoors. Coach Sakamoto's nickname for her, Blackie, was because her skin had become too tan in the sun. Good Chinese danced ballet and played piano, and they stayed pale.

Blossom and three schoolmates stood at the waterfront. Among them were Amy and Mary Yamashiro, the daughters of Wailuku's most prominent doctor; another was a girl she knew less well. With them was Benzo Sakamoto, Coach's younger brother. Blossom's parents would have approved of the Yamashiro girls, who were rich and of good character, but they would have looked askance at Benzo Sakamoto. Blossom Young had heard that he had begun to earn a legal wage by renting out jukeboxes to pool halls and saloons, but that could have been a rumor. He was a famous pool shark in Wailuku; he even made a living from it.

The four friends were waiting at the dock for another. Rikio Ebisu, an old friend of Benzo's from his Scouting days, was going to bring his boat by and take them for a joy ride in the harbor. Blossom didn't know Rikio Ebisu well, but she knew his boat. Rikio Ebisu was, like Benzo, a boy who had never grown up. He hadn't married yet and still lived at home; his job as a petty clerk was dismal, part-time, and unrewarding. He had named his boat the *Mae West*, a sign of his own outsized grandiosity. The buxom blonde had starred most recently in a motion picture called *Every Day's a Holiday*. She'd been sassy and teasing and Hollywood all over. But Ebisu's *Mae West* was a slapped-together piece of work, from bow to stern just 16 feet and its beam 6 feet wide, open and adorned with only two homemade backless benches and a hastily soldered-on set of rusty rods that served as a rail to protect passengers from falling overboard. The little boat looked like it was meant to hold no more than six, including Rikio, but it was the kind of day when people liked to show off, and Rikio packed the boat with more than twice that number: Blossom Young, the Yamashiro girls, some housewives and teachers, and some men and boys Blossom Young didn't recognize. About thirteen in all.

Benzo Sakamoto, Coach's brother, hadn't climbed aboard. He wasn't coming after all, he said. He'd be waiting for the group at the pier. But Blossom Young, Rikio Ebisu, and their friends insisted that Benzo must get on, and they tugged at him until he stood shakily on the deck of the crowded *Mae West* as Rikio Ebisu unhooked the hawser rope from the pier and put-tered out into Kahului Harbor.

Every motor launch captain seemed to have had the same idea as Rikio Ebisu. He could hardly move a foot ahead at a time. Ebisu tried to circle the harbor, put-putting left and right but coming far too close to other crafts; he couldn't rev the motor, couldn't get ahead. He couldn't show off just what the

Mae West could do. Blossom Young was taken by the broad expanse of sky, the salty air, the way her mop of curls tossed in the wind, the chatter of her friends. So she only half noticed when Ebisu pointed the prow of the *Mae West* at the opening between the breakwaters and gunned the boat ahead.

It had already been difficult enough to keep her balance, but as the launch neared the wash and run-up from the breakwaters, it began to sway side to side. Blossom Young lost her footing and grabbed on to friends, who grabbed on to her as well. The other passengers gripped the rails. Some laughed. One girl tried to raise her camera up and take a picture but couldn't keep herself or the camera steady enough to accomplish it.

The wash grew ever wilder. Ebisu steered the boat toward the mouth of the bay, nearly swamping on the jagged boulders on each side. Somehow, improbably, he made it through, and Blossom at first felt some relief, but the fetch beneath her was choppier than on the harbor's side. Violent white-caps angled everywhere, fickle. Although the sea looked calmer farther out beyond the breakers, when Rikio plunged the boat forward, 10 yards, then 25, the *Mae West* still swerved and lurched amid the swells. Fifty yards more, then 100 yards.

A flat-faced wave slapped against the starboard side. Blossom Young reached out to grab the rail but found herself, with all the others, sliding toward the port side. A group of girls rushed back, and as they did another wave hit, sending all the rest in their direction. Ebisu tried to turn the launch around, but the current made the boat a puzzle piece that simply wouldn't fit back in. Ebisu tried again and again, acrid puffs of smoke pouring from the motor, and when another wave hit, it sent the *Mae West* nearly flying into the air, then tipped it, and with it tipped every passenger into the cold and heaving sea.

Blossom Young's first accident had been in Lahaina in a single-prop plane. Blossom's parents had given her permission to travel interisland to Hilo to attend a meeting of the Future Homemakers of Hawaii. It wasn't the usual thing to send a daughter up into a plane, but the whole affair seemed perfectly safe and modern and Blossom's intentions pure.

Still, one moment Blossom was on the runway at Maalaea Field, and in another, the plane failed to gain altitude and crash-landed into a thicket. Blossom remembered little else but the silence and the plane's single propeller slowing down, spinning until it finally stopped.

The second accident had been in a roadster. It belonged to a friend of Blossom's, and after school one day the driver, Blossom, and two other schoolmates set out for a ride in the countryside. Scarcely did a week go by on Maui without auto fatalities; too often, the few drivers who observed the rules of the road—such as stopping at a crossroads—fell victim to the majority of those who didn't. Dutifully, Blossom Young and her friends had even asked their school principal for his permission to make their country jaunt and had promised that they'd take good care.

The roadster was a dream. It was an open-air marvel, with room enough for two. It was a departure from the boxy family sedans that Blossom knew. It was curvaceous, sleek, and gleaming, with roundly sculpted wheel covers, a curved-glass windshield, and a chassis that rode so low it nearly touched the ground. From the side, its rounded back end couldn't help but remind one of a perfectly proportioned woman lying on her side. It was a post-Depression car, a new kind of conveyance for a young and sophisticated generation—those who fancied themselves adventurous.

As clearly as she remembered the roadster, Blossom remembered little of the accident itself. The driver and another passenger were sitting up front; and, because the car was unequipped with a rumble seat, she and another friend sat on the trunk. They had driven toward the coast. Roads there, both south toward Kihei and north toward Lahaina, were largely unpaved and so narrow in places that when another vehicle came toward you in the opposite direction, you had to pull over to the shoulder, which was sometimes sloped precariously down into an irrigation ditch or a field of tall cane.

What Blossom could recall of the accident was this: that at some places the road not only became narrow but also curved; that the roadster's driver had not taken the precaution to slow down; that in the split second another motorcar came into view, her driver veered suddenly off onto the narrow shoulder in order to avoid a collision. The next thing she remembered was waking and seeing the color red. *Red, red, I must be dead*, she thought, but in short shrift discovered that the red she had seen wasn't blood but the skirt of one of her companions. And, just as in the plane crash, everyone had—unbelievably—survived the wreck.

On the day of the car accident, she was terrified of the scolding her parents would give her. She'd been born with lightning in her veins. But they embraced her when they found her, forgave all, and then made it clear that something must be done. Because, they said, misfortune comes to us in threes.

Blossom Young surfaced to mayhem and struggled to tread water. The boat, completely capsized, thrashed about the waves like a horse off its reins. Some of the passengers, heads above water, still held on to the rails; Blossom made a break to reach them.

Amy Yamashiro was holding on tightly. Beside her were a pair of teenage boys, then the two women who spoke only Japanese, although they weren't speaking, they were hanging on and weeping. Rikio Ebisu was hanging on, too: he scanned the same jagged horizon as Blossom did. The world was empty but for the boat, the knifelike waves, and a young woman hanging desperately on to an ice chest, floating. Above, the sun was blocked by clouds. Had anyone onshore seen them capsize? Should they try to right the boat, turn it over? No, it was too heavy. Splinters and barnacles tore their skin as they crawled up onto the bucking hull until it was awash with blood.

The sorry upturned boat kept drifting farther out to sea. The girl on the ice chest drifted, too, growing more distant. She moaned. At the rail, Blossom tried to distract the others. She told some silly jokes. She sang—loudly—to keep their spirits up. Every once in a while, one of the teenagers managed the semblance of a smile, but most of them, even Rikio, looked at Blossom Young with hollow eyes.

She told them all to stay awake. Stay awake! Her tongue was now coated in salt. Her throat was hoarse. She tried to sing, but she was growing sleepy, too.

Soichi Sakamoto was so hungry. He couldn't understand why, but who can explain the roots of a starving man's hunger? He had traveled: Japan, the Mainland; he had eaten like a rich man on steamers and on Pullmans, and in many more restaurants in his lifetime than anyone he knew, but the food at George Higa's Honolulu Café was, as he always told everyone, out of this world. At Higa's he gorged on the food he'd grown up on: hot rice, Portuguese sausage, *nishimai* stew, *saimin* noodles; and no matter the abundance of food put before him, Sakamoto was always ravenous at Higa's. Even after he had eaten his portion, he always wanted more.

It had rained in Honolulu the previous night, but now the sky was clear, and the sun shone through the café's high windows. The hustle and bustle of a downtown morning was everywhere, tables filled with bigwig architects and bankers, early-bird women in high heels waiting for the Sears department store across the street to open, and businessmen in double-breasted suits.

Sakamoto dug down farther into his bowl. To want more from George Higa made no sense. He helped with everything from uniforms to swimsuits to this food, and, recently, he'd offered Sakamoto money to help get Fujiko Katsutani to Des Moines, Iowa. It would be an expensive trip, requiring aeroplanes to fly across the country in order to get her there on time. Higa gave to the club selflessly, without any expectation of return, and perhaps it was that reason—because the gift was both so pleasing to the tongue and generous of spirit—that Sakamoto couldn't help but enjoy it. That Tuesday morning, he sat in one of the brown booths, his face in his plate, his fork shoving food into his mouth with unbounded pleasure. He ate and he ate and he ate, hoping the children wouldn't see him. But one clearly had. He looked up. It was Mitzi Higuchi, his squat, square squinter; the laundress's daughter, and his rising star.

Taken at the Flood

Mitzi's face was ashen; in her hand she held the morning newspaper, which she gave to him, and then stood there, silent, waiting.

"One Dead, Two Missing, as Launch Swamps at Kahului," read the front-page headline of the *Honolulu Advertiser*. Hundreds had seen the *Mae West* disappear. One man had jumped into his car and drove on the beach road until he spotted the wreck, then drove back to the pier, summoning help. A tug had headed out, going beyond the breakers to pluck survivors from the waves. A handful of women still in their holiday best stood waiting onshore, and when the bodies were laid out in rows, rescuers kneeled down and felt for pulses. Out in the bay, one sampan crew tied up the wreck of the boat and tried to haul it in, and another full of Sea Scouts hazarded the waves. By sundown, the survivors had been sent on to Puʻunene Hospital, but there was one dead, and no sign of another two. The paper said that local fishermen predicted that the bodies would wash up by Camp 1, but most of the rescue teams stayed south at the harborside. They stayed when darkness fell; they stayed when, with the darkness, the storm that had been promising to come all day arrived. The rain washed out all view of the sea.

Sakamoto had the paper with him all the way back to Maui. He'd picked up the *Hawaii Hochi*, too.

The *Mae West* had been overloaded with thirteen aboard. Mary Yamashiro, the younger of Dr. Yamashiro's girls, was the one who had died. Missing were a mechanic from Kahului, the father of six children. And missing, too, was Sakamoto's brother Benzo.

Blossom Young had been on board, and so had others, teenagers now, whom Sakamoto had known as children, some from the ditch days and others who had swum for the 3YSC. And the boat's captain was Rikio Ebisu, who'd quit the 3YSC before it had become something that could have helped the boy in more ways than one.

One newspaper listed Benzo Sakamoto's age as twenty-four, another as twenty-eight; the latter was closer to true. One misprinted that Benzo was the Sakamoto family's firstborn son, but these mistakes mattered little. What mattered were the slight differences between the newspapers printed soon after the accident and the ones published later. The earliest one said merely that Benzo Sakamoto and Matsuo Takeuchi, the mechanic, were "missing." The next, the *Nippu Jiji*, said they were "unaccounted for." And the *Shinbun*—the third and last to have gone to print—reported that someone had actually seen Benzo trying to swim toward the breakers, but all that could be done now was to wait for the ocean to give him up again.

It had rained so much on the Monday night Benzo disappeared that officials called off the rodeo and the doubleheader baseball games as up-country roads and ranches flooded out, but when Soichi Sakamoto arrived back in Maui on Tuesday, he discovered that all night long, Kahului Harbor volunteers—hundreds—had gathered along the seawall, keeping a vigil, lining the piers with gas lanterns, and stoking the embers of enormous bonfires until dawn. And even in the heavy rain, the SS *Waialeale*, an interisland steamer full of passengers, dropped anchor for a while in the bay and cast its searchlights out; then, finding nothing, it moved slowly on.

Now fishing boats and strong swimmers headed out past the breakers to comb the water, while overhead, monoplanes circled, and at the beachline a few pieces of debris washed in: a hat, blue soda bottles, a plank identifiable from the prow of the *Mae West*, and—tragic to behold—attached to that plank was Rikio Ebisu's *omamori*—a Shinto talisman that was supposed to have kept everyone aboard safe. At the pier, the wreck of the *Mae West* seemed as small to Sakamoto as a child's toy. It was barely upright, its iron railing twisted along the gunwales, its wheel gone, its benches, too; the deck stripped of anything and anyone who might have been there.

Sakamoto wouldn't leave the pier. He sat by the ruined boat, with a lantern nearby, furiously thinking. There was everything to do and nothing to do at the same time. At dawn, the bonfires died out and the evening's shift of watchmen headed home, and when a fresh group of volunteers arrived on Wednesday morning, Sakamoto was still there, thinking.

Someone called out. A body was floating in and it was drawing closer to the shore with the tide, but it was bloated, facedown, and still not close enough to reach. Sakamoto and half a dozen men scrambled to the water's edge. What had Benzo or Mr. Takeuchi been wearing the day they disappeared? No one seemed to know. One man ran all the way to the Takeuchis' house and when he returned, he said that for certain the clothes on the body were Mr. Takeuchi's.

Soichi Sakamoto didn't know Matsuo Takeuchi, but pictures of him at his funeral showed him to have been a puckish fellow with thick cowlicked hair and a pair of alert, pit-bull ears. He was thick of waist; his palms were callused, and beneath his stubby fingernails was the gray-brown signature of motor oil—the scent of which may have arrived in a room before he did. Perhaps that's what his children would remember and miss: the smell of sweet gasoline. In death Takeuchi left behind a mystery. In the process of bringing him home, someone checked the man's pockets and found a fat wet roll of bills—$600—a fortune, half a year's salary. Perhaps he had won it by gambling; that was the most likely reason for having so much money on him. People did like to gamble on the regatta. Some were unlucky; others were unlucky beyond belief. And sometimes, but rarely, people were lucky and unlucky at the same time: Matsuo Takeuchi's last day on earth had been both the most fortunate *and* the most unfortunate of his entire life.

By Friday normal life in Wailuku and Kahului seemed to have resumed. Downtown bookstores and photo studios were open for business; so, too, were the meat and pickle counters, and at the movie theaters, you could take in a Japanese talkie, see Tex Ritter in *Where the Buffalo Roam* or Olivia de Havilland in *Wings of the Navy*. Still, Soichi Sakamoto waited at the harbor for his brother. He was feverish with thought. He hadn't been as taken with so many ideas since two years before when he had first come up with his plan for the Three-Year Swim Club.

He had plans now, too. More than he could count.

He sat at the waterside thinking and scheming and planning, and his thoughts were interrupted only when Benzo's body finally appeared, surfacing on the Wailuku side of the rocky breakwater. Fishermen said that he had likely been stuck beneath the stones for days.

The papers hailed Benzo as a hero. He had died, it was said, saving several others' lives, but the papers said a lot of things that simply weren't true: that in high school, Benzo had been a long-standing member of the Chemical Club, a faithful singer in the Boys' Choir, a "famous" athlete on the football and the track teams, and an expert bowler. The truth was, he'd lasted in the Chemistry Club for only about year. He was a good bowler, not expert. His favorite avocation was billiards. In truth, he was more like Soichi Sakamoto had been as a young man: someone who had yet to live up to his potential. Someone, his yearbook photo said, who was more likely to be found "gazing at the ceiling" than working hard. The papers didn't tell the truth, thought Soichi Sakamoto. Because more than all of that, Benzo Sakamoto couldn't have tried to save his own or anybody's life; his older brother Soichi had never found the time to teach him how to swim.

When Blossom Young was first pulled from the sea, she'd been told nothing about the dead; she had even felt a quiet thrill as she was carried through the streets in an ambulance and when the driver had asked her to push the button on the siren for him all the way to the hospital. She knew from previous rides in the ambulance exactly where that button was. At the hospital, the doctors and nurses tended to her wounds, and her parents never left her side; her brothers and sisters crowded around her and joked about all the trouble she had caused. From outside the room, the hospital corridors echoed with the sounds of others—families, their voices sounding relieved, parents reuniting with their children. Only when the ward grew quiet did Blossom's parents tell her.

In the plane crash and in the car crash, no one had died. She had not even contemplated that the boat wreck could have been any different, and her mind became wild with grief. Benzo Sakamoto. Mr. Takeuchi. Mary Yamashiro. Her parents did what they could to comfort her. She had had her three accidents, they told her: the airplane, the roadster, and now the boat. For the rest of her life, she would never have to worry about anything again.

Sakamoto hadn't worried about the team on the Tuesday morning he'd learned that Benzo was missing. He trusted his manager, Mike Ginoza, and he'd deputized him to stay in Honolulu and to coach the team in the meet. The man was more than competent, but everyone, including Ginoza, was glum the rest of that day, and the Honolulu club coaches and officials offered to scratch most of that night's events. Halfheartedly, Charlie Oda and Jose Balmores qualified in the trials for the 100-meter freestyle and Yoshio Shibuya secured his spot in the 100-meter breaststroke.

The team sleepwalked all through that Wednesday, and when news arrived the next day that Coach's brother was still missing at sea, the evening meet brought out a larger-than-expected crowd, and before the start of the events, everyone in the Natatorium observed a moment of silence for Soichi Sakamoto's brother.

Perhaps it was that silent moment that awakened the 3YSC from their sleep. In the races that night they rewrote the record books. Fujiko Katsutani clocked in at 1:18.6 in the 100-meter freestyle. Charlie Oda broke the Hawaiian mark in the men's 100-free. Toyo Takeyama lowered the island time, breaking the previous record in the 200-meter backstroke. And where they didn't make history, swimmers like Charlotte Shigehara and Chic Miyamoto exceeded their personal bests. All in all, the team scored two wins: a 72–30 victory in the men's championship and a 47–10 win in the women's. It was the most decisive victory in the history of the club.

Yes, Keo Nakama and Halo Hirose prevailed over the visiting Canadian, Bob Pirie. Yes, Halo outswam Pirie in the century, and Nakama came into the wall thirteen strokes ahead of Pirie in the grueling 500-meter freestyle. Yes, the papers said that there was no doubt now that the swimmers were headed for the 1940 Olympics. But more than anything, the meet marked the first time that they were a solid team in most events—not just one swimmer prevailing here or there, but an entire club that stood very strong as a whole.

Youths of the Sea

Sakamoto welcomed them home, hugged them all. He led a series of celebrations. To most of the swimmers, he seemed unbelievably like himself, unmarked by the tragedy, but when Blossom Young finally came to visit, she saw Coach Sakamoto wholly differently; she knew that both he and she were changed entirely and forever.

His transformation was, in fact, astonishing. He was a man with more plans than ever. He was a nervous, gushing wreck, a desperate well of ideas. First, he said, shaking, he would invite Bob Pirie to come to Maui from Honolulu; in just a few days' time, everyone on the island would be able to see with their own eyes what the swimmers of the club could do. He had already mocked up a block-letter ad for the *Maui News*: "SWIMMING MEET: SEE BOB PIRIE AND K. NAKAMA RE-SWIM THEIR DEAD-HEAT RACE." And as for dances, he had in mind as many as he could fit into the schedule in advance of the Nationals. Sometime soon—he rushed his words—it would be nice to invite some of the best Japanese swimmers to visit Maui and swim an exhibition race in the Camp 5 pool. And to raise additional funds for new bathing suits and equipment and travel, he would ask his father to donate a brand-new car to the club, which the team could raffle off. Think of that! There was so much to do.

Mary watched him from a distance. She was certain now that he had lost his mind. Where was his grief? It had taken the strangest of turns. In the same situation another man might have taken to drink or cheated on his wife or begun to gamble, but what is known about Soichi Sakamoto is that his grief turned oddly wild.

Each day was one day closer to the Olympics, wasn't it? he asked. In Europe, the cancellation of the Olympics seemed to draw ever nearer. Sakamoto asked Pachi Tsukano to write a club song. He wrote it to the tune of the fight song sang at Notre Dame. "Three Cheers for the 3YSC..." They'd design a club flag and would write a club newspaper, and they would solicit ads from every business in town. The first edition of the newspaper would be a glorious one. It would feature the history of the club, mark its near three years of existence, tell of how it was born, which swimmers were there at the beginning, and reinforce the dream of reaching the Olympics. It should come out by Christmas. He already knew who should write each article.

Taken at the Flood

They could have an aquacade, with races with umbrellas, eggs, and spoons. They'd have Ralph Gilman swim again and hijinks of all sorts: intentional belly flops off the diving board, a water ballet, a skit by a group he'd call Professor Brandt and His Stooges. He'd show all of Maui what real showmanship could be.

And for the winter dance, Soichi Sakamoto said as Mary watched him spin from one idea to another, he would go and buy one of those mirrored balls, the kind that hangs from the ceiling in the dark and that turns on a string and fills a darkened space with broken but beautiful shards of light—so that it seems, even if it isn't true, that the room is full of snowflakes. Like a snowstorm, he said. It'll be just like it is snowing.

Chapter Ten

THE COUP

THURSDAY, THE sixth of July, just days after Benzo Sakamoto's funeral, Robert E. Hughes called to order the inaugural meeting of a new committee under the supervision of the Alexander House Swimming Executive Committee. It was a subcommittee, and its motto was "On to the Nationals." E. L. Damkroger had reasoned the group into being through a fit of anxiety, and he was in the room that day as well.

Around the table were the island's most respected civic leaders: the executive director of the Maui Boy Scouts; the head of the Maui County Fair; a well-known physician from the Baldwin family; Ezra Crane, publisher of the *Maui News*; and, last but not least, Bud Crabbe.

E. L. Damkroger had been watching Soichi Sakamoto. And it was time to do something, he said. There was simply too much at stake now, too much to lose. All evidence pointed to the likelihood that members of the Three-Year Swim Club would be good enough to qualify for Finland in just one year's time, and in that case, men with more experience would now have to take control of the situation. Sakamoto was a grammar school teacher. It had been a miracle he'd been able to take the children this far. It was time to relieve the poor man of the heavy burden he had carried alone for too long.

It was time for others—older and wiser and more business-minded—to take over. If the men in the room—if the island of Maui—wished for these *Maui* swimmers to stay on course, then they needed to protect their *investment.* An ounce of caution now would be worth its weight in Olympic gold in 1940.

Those in the room understood the language of investments. That spring both the HC&S and the Maui Agricultural Company had posted huge losses, the result of three factors—inhospitable weather, having been forced to pay workers higher wages, and the low price of sugar on the international market. No one wanted additional losses.

The committee identified the youngsters they felt it best to send to Detroit. These included four from the Valley Isle. The committee had conferred with the father of Fujiko Katsutani, who firmly agreed with them that his daughter, so young, so tender, and so impressionable, should not be traveling to Des Moines, Iowa—which was so far away and where she would be improperly chaperoned. Her reputation couldn't possibly be served well by being the only girl in a group of boys whose sole companion was a grown, married man. It was unseemly and unacceptable.

The committee appointed E. L. Damkroger as the official manager for the Detroit trip. He would travel with the group, supervising not only the boys but Soichi Sakamoto as well. The group inked into the minutes of the meeting that they conferred upon Damkroger "full authority on all matters of training, swimming and personal conduct."

As for finance, they wouldn't allow Sakamoto to use his own funds. They would immediately begin a fund drive of their own. It would be called "On to the Nationals," and Ezra Crane of the *Maui News* would both announce the subscription drive and help to manage the incoming money.

Efficiently, they worked out travel plans that were foolproof and spit-spot, with nary a moment of improvisation in them, except for anticipated spontaneity. The team would leave for Honolulu July 25 on the *Empress of Japan*, with a stop in Seattle on July 31. The group would then travel by train to Detroit August 1–4, where they would train and enter competition between August 5 and August 22. They would ultimately return to Honolulu on September 7, with an overnight interisland steamer trip to Maui scheduled immediately thereafter so that all the children would be prepared for the first day of school.

As for planned spontaneity, Damkroger carefully calculated the cost of possible educational or entertaining side trips to San Francisco and New York, in order to take in the Golden Gate International Exposition and the 1939 World's Fair and perhaps see a ball game or two. The total for such diversions would come to a mere $8.50 per person.

The committee expected the children to be well-dressed at all times, to comport themselves in a manner equal to real ambassadors for the Valley Isle. They would carry with them paper leis for presentation to local government leaders, hosts, and meet officials. And they were to take their ukuleles.

All that remained now was for E. L. Damkroger to make the final arrangements, pack his bag, and meet Soichi Sakamoto in Honolulu with the news.

The conversation between Damkroger and Sakamoto on the morning of July 20, 1939, was never recorded for posterity; perhaps it is better that way. What is known is that when E. L. Damkroger arrived to deliver his news, he met a man who was already prepared to receive it. Soichi Sakamoto had been up nearly all night making urgent radiophone calls.

He was as prepared as he could be to swallow at least part of his poisonous fate—having now to defer all decisions to Damkroger—but he would not defer to him or anyone else in this: Fujiko Katsutani *would* go to Des Moines. Sakamoto had the money for the trip from George Higa, and he'd come up with a plan to have a proper chaperone for the championships.

When Damkroger arrived, Sakamoto handed him a pile of papers. He had arranged it so female chaperones along the way—maids on the steamer, stewardesses on the airplanes, and women passengers on the trains—would carefully supervise Fujiko, ensuring that everything was on the up-and-up as Sakamoto took her to Des Moines. Every woman along the way would sign the form to prove it, and Sakamoto would give those permission slips to Damkroger, the committee, and the Katsutani family.

As for the family's opposition to the trip, he had thought of that, too. He had radiophoned Mr. Katsutani and secured his agreement. He had also discovered that Mrs. Katsutani was currently in Honolulu in order to meet the ship on which Fujiko's sister, the one who had been away in Japan studying, had returned. After handing Damkroger his travel arrangements for Fujiko, Sakamoto stepped aside to reveal both Mrs. Katsutani and Fujiko's sister behind him, the girl dressed in a fine kimono, and Fujiko beside them carrying her own travel bag.

Mrs. Katsutani politely told Mr. E. L. Damkroger that, yes, it was true: the whole Katsutani family endorsed Fujiko's trip to the Women's Nationals. They were so grateful to Mr. E. L. Damkroger for all his generosity, and Fujiko was ready to leave. They were hopeful she would do well in Des Moines, they were excited for the opportunity, and they would be glued to the radio at home. They attributed the "swimming success of Fujiko-san to the untiring efforts" of Coach Sakamoto. If "queried as to the swimming of Fujiko-san," Mrs. Katsutani told Mr. Damkroger, "Please ask Sakamoto-san."

Last but not least, Sakamoto produced another piece of paper that he handed to E. L. Damkroger. It was a message from the Hawaiian AAU addressed to Soichi Sakamoto, giving its permission for Fujiko to participate in the Nationals at Des Moines. "Backing you 100%," the note read.

Photographs from the crossing reveal what appears to be a jolly bunch. The children posing along the railings of the promenade; the wind blowing in what little hair E. L. Damkroger had upon his balding head. There are few pictures, however, of Soichi Sakamoto and E. L. Damkroger together on that summer's adventure. One such photograph captures the moment just before the group's departure from the Aloha pier on the steamer *Empress of Japan*. In it are the Hawaiian swimmers, ten in all: Peter Powlison and Carlos Rivas of Punahou, James Tanaka of the Nu'uanu YMCA, Barney Pung of Hui Makani, and the rest from Maui, newcomer Bill Neunzig, Jose Balmores, Kiyoshi Nakama, Takashi Hirose, Benny Castor, and—of course—Fujiko Katsutani.

Coach Soichi Sakamoto and the newly appointed 3YSC manager, E. L. Damkroger, could not be standing farther apart from each other in the picture. Perhaps they intended to flank the group—two grown men sufficiently prepared to bring such a large contingent of young people on such a big trip—but the looks on their faces seem to speak of a more pressing cause for the distance between them.

On the far left-hand side is Soichi Sakamoto, his face surprisingly forlorn. It could be by chance, but he isn't looking at all toward the camera; instead, his eyes are downcast and looking off to the side, as if he were distracted by something he spotted out of the corner of his eye, a piece of litter or perhaps nothing at all.

E. L. Damkroger stands on the far right. He is dressed in a dark double-breasted suit fastened together by only one button, and beneath the jacket he is wearing an open-collared aloha shirt. His hands are behind his back in a stance that looks something like a soldier who has been told to be at ease but who cannot seem to fully inhabit a posture of relaxation; and his face has the tight-lipped expression of a man who is at once dangerously on the verge of losing control of his universe while at the same time resolved never to let go of the reins again.

Neither man wrote home on the trip about any tension that may have existed between them; one can only imagine how awful it might have been. On the fourth day of the voyage, Damkroger sat down to compose a letter to the Permanent Executive Swimming Committee back home. He cleared his throat for a few paragraphs, as if unsure of what or how much he ought to say.

"It is by our conduct," he wrote, "and by whatever success we gain at the two National meets," that "we may in some way repay what has been done for us," and he rambled on about how exciting the fourteen-thousand-mile trip he was taking with Soichi Sakamoto would surely be.

Fujiko, who had never traveled by steamer anywhere, was ill without respite from Hawaii all the way to Seattle. She was pale, unable to keep any food down, and so weak that she could barely drag herself out of her closed-in cabin to get a breath of sea air. From her cabin, she used ship stationery to write letters. Some were to her friends back home. She described the *Empress*

of Japan as "a noble ship," and in one letter she wrote, "My heart break when I leave you people...but its [*sic*] better that way cause you wanted me to go." She even wrote a letter to Coach, who was on the same boat. She thanked him for fighting so hard for her to go on the trip, and she told him that her repayment to him was her determination to win at the Nationals.

In Canada, she and Coach Sakamoto split from the larger group, who went south to San Francisco, and there the two began their cross-country odyssey by aeroplane. There were six legs of it on six different flights: Vancouver to Seattle; Seattle to Portland; Portland to Salt Lake City; Salt Lake City to Denver; Denver to Omaha; and then all the way to Des Moines. Each one-way ticket had cost $120, the equivalent of $2,000 today. The planes were stunning, all of them DC-3s that fit one tidily dressed stewardess and fourteen passengers, including Sakamoto and Fujiko, in cushioned seats that swiveled with the touch of a button, so that passengers could take in the spectacular views of the nation as it sped by below. The rides were horribly rough, though. Sakamoto tried his best to eat the meals that the stewardess brought to him on a tray, but most of his time was spent tending to Fujiko, whose stomach wouldn't hold a thing. The engines, with their paddle-blade propellers, roared as loud as a passenger train. On takeoff, the wings bent disturbingly; when it rained, water sometimes came in at the window seams. The temperature hovered around 70 stifling degrees. There was some relief in landing and waiting for the next flight, but there was also once again the excitement and terror of the next takeoff. Sakamoto was thrilled, Fujiko terrified. When at last they arrived in Des Moines after a nighttime trip, she was positively green. The four thousand miles had done her in.

It was Wednesday, July 26, and the trials at Des Moines's modest Birdland Pool were scheduled for that very morning, with finals for all events scheduled in the afternoon. But Des Moines was so hot that organizers had to delay the start of the championships. Anything that had been set for the afternoon was shifted to the evening, as the concrete decks were so searing that they were unbearable to stand barefoot on.

Fujiko's competitors looked fresh, and all of them were haoles from the Mainland: the glamorous Esther Williams; the disgraced 1936 Olympian turned Billy Rose Aquacade star Eleanor Holm; the tiny Nancy Merki, smaller even than Fujiko and all of thirteen years old. One would never have known by looking at her in the water that Nancy had suffered from polio and almost died as a young child.

In her first trials that morning, even sick as a dog, Fujiko finished first in the 200-meter breaststroke with a time of 3:16.3; and in the evening finals, she won the title at 3:16.1—her time slow, but, the press said, an incredible feat considering her epic journey. Just like that, Fujiko Katsutani was a national champion. The press declared her a prospect for 1940, and she easily became the crowd favorite in the few days of the meet.

But Fujiko was unhappy with her time; had she not been so exhausted, she could have broken the standing 1932 record time of 3:12.6. She was even less pleased with the questions that people asked her and the way the press portrayed her. Everyone, including all of the girls, assumed she was Japanese, not American. Sportswriters and fans wondered aloud why the girl wasn't swimming for her own country. It was remarkable, people said, that both Fujiko and her coach spoke such excellent English. And as much as Fujiko insisted that she was a US citizen and a resident of Hawaii, they still couldn't understand. "Hawaiian Tank Star Insists She's—Not Japanese," read one headline. After that, Fujiko stopped answering reporters' questions and grew sullen, even when the reporter from the UPI declared her "the favorite of the huge crowds."

She became about as articulate and forthcoming as Keo Nakama had been upon returning from Australia, but more churlishly so. A scrum of reporters surrounded her. "Do you like swimming?" they asked. "Do you like the Mainland?" She hardly said a word, no matter how much Sakamoto encouraged her not to show her anger. She was disappointed, too, at how few people had attended the meet; the bleachers were empty a good deal of the time—the excuse was the 97-degree heat—but back on Maui, when Keo and Halo had come home from their meets on the Mainland, they had described crowds of thousands and thousands. It was puzzling, and upsetting, too. Why were the women's championships so sparsely attended? Sakamoto felt protective of Fujiko. Some at Des Moines commented that they seemed as close as father and child.

Sakamoto shrugged when she asked, but silently he vowed that next year, in Portland, Oregon, he'd bring a chorus. A whole team. Maybe all of Maui. Just to fill the empty bleachers.

Damkroger had taken the boys on a side trip to San Francisco, and when Sakamoto and Fujiko Katsutani met up again with the group at Ames, Iowa, Sakamoto proudly handed to E. L. Damkroger the evidence of her success: the first-place trophy that Fujiko had won, and then sheet after sheet of affidavits attesting to the fact that she had been carefully supervised—by women—at every possible moment on the cross-country tour. There were signatures of stewardesses on Trans-Canada Air Lines and United Airlines: an Anne Tierney; an R. Daugherty; a Hazel Parry; a Lillian Young. Sakamoto had been certain to document everything and had even requested the signature of the chairwoman of the AAU swimming committee herself along with a business card here and there from attorneys-at-law they had met along the way. He tried not to behave too smugly about it, although he felt smug. But he knew to watch himself on the rest of the trip. Damkroger was in charge—if not of the swimming then of absolutely everything else—and Sakamoto's strategy was to stay as quiet as possible, to show no power and give no opinion, and to let the man have his day. Sakamoto would show his strength at the pool. He knew it would serve him poorly to try to show it elsewhere; he had, after all, already won the war.

Upon reuniting, Damkroger was positively cheerful. He announced that he had been impressed by how well-behaved the boys had been in San Francisco and en route; he seemed drunk with the pleasure of travel and suggested, although it wasn't really a suggestion, that the group ought to take a side trip to New York next, even before the Nationals began in Detroit.

Sakamoto really had no say, and so the group traveled onward to New York, taking up residence at the Taft Hotel, just a block away from the lights of Broadway. Damkroger purchased tickets for the lot to entertainments such as Billy Rose's Aquacade, where they watched a newly returned Eleanor Holm perform, and they saw their own Hawaiian Stubby Kruger steal the show. Sakamoto said nothing as Damkroger splurged some more, buying tickets for all to a play called *Hellzapoppin*, which sent him into fits of laughter for hours. And he said nothing when the group attended a game at Yankee Stadium and toured around the New York World's Fair.

Sakamoto looked on as Damkroger led the children gleefully through tours of every pavilion they could pack into their schedule, but he never wrote home about one of the most interesting events of the trip. Damkroger wrote about it, however, a most unfortunate occurrence at the New York Athletic Club that shocked and angered Damkroger but surprised Soichi Sakamoto not a whit.

Back in 1937, Olympic swimmer Jack Medica had passed through the islands and told Halo and the rest of the 3YSC that should they ever be in New York, they should look him up at the New York Athletic Club. He was a member; they could drop his name, and the club would certainly let them in. E. L. Damkroger knew about the offer, and he insisted that the group go over to the club. Sakamoto wouldn't have, since he knew precisely what would happen.

When Damkroger arrived at the door and announced himself, the children, and their connection to Medica, the concierge took one look at the Hawaiian and Japanese-American kids with Damkroger and summarily turned the entire group away. It was club policy, he explained. Mr. Medica certainly must have been mistaken about sharing the benefits of his membership at the club.

Damkroger, incensed, stormed along the New York sidewalks, seething, steaming. For all the New York Athletic Club members the officials of Maui had entertained, he fumed, he couldn't believe the bitter lack of hospitality he and the swimmers had just experienced. He couldn't understand it; he couldn't believe it; he was stunned to the point where he was filled with fantasies of revenge. And all the while that E. L. Damkroger went on, Soichi Sakamoto said nothing. E. L. Damkroger had never before been turned away from any place he'd wished to go.

Detroit was baking-hot, but it was far more interesting and certainly more welcoming than New York. It lay low along the river, a sprawl of factories and houses and churches and a downtown rising not much more than two stories above the horizon, although those buildings felt like skyscrapers to the children. Detroit was Henry Ford's city, visible only through a haze of coal soot, but it thrilled Damkroger, too, and seemed to pull him out of his foul mood. He led the group on sightseeing trips to the Ford Factory and made sure they took in a Detroit Tigers game. To the children, life was "like a fairy tale." It was suddenly hard to believe their own story: from the irrigation ditch to the Baldwin Pool to Honolulu, Louisville, and now Detroit.

Sakamoto continued to be quiet as he watched Damkroger spend money on frills, but there came a time when he had to gently deliver the news in the most humble, deferring, and Japanese style, as he had been doing throughout the trip, that it was time for the group to begin to train for the meet. Damkroger seemed disappointed, but Sakamoto had work to do. It was the swimmers' first opportunity to compete in a team championship; in Louisville he'd had just Halo and Keo. Now there was a chance, however slim, to earn the team title. That's what Sakamoto told the swimmers they were aiming for at Detroit, nothing less.

The Nationals were held in an odd place; the Detroit Athletic Boat Club Pool was a mere 55 yards long by 40 feet wide with a depth ranging from 4 to 12 feet, and its six lanes were so narrow that backwash from adjacent lanes would hit the swimmers and cause drag, all factors that made the pool as slow as molasses. No one in the press could predict who the winners might be, and every top-notch swimmer and diver had shown. A total of 117 individuals were slated to compete, and the hype machine predicted that it was going to be the best National Men's Championship to date.

Sakamoto could look around and place names and faces from Louisville a year before, and it was, with few exceptions, a welcoming and friendly lot: Steve Forsyth had brought his boy Flanagan again. The two of them mostly kept to themselves, but they weren't unfriendly, just sort of balled up with planning and worry, the way Forsyth had been in Louisville. Steve Wozniak, who had come in third in the mile at Louisville, looked a bit weary. Jaretz looked ready, as did Ed Kirar, and Bob Pirie was also competing; he was a sight for sore eyes. Bob Kiphuth was on deck, sour as ever, and he'd brought with him a new swimmer by the name of Howard Johnson, scion of the famed Howard Johnson chain. But for every Bob Kiphuth in the world there was a Stan Brauninger and an Adolph Kiefer, just about the sweetest people in the world. Brauninger greeted Sakamoto warmly, and Kiefer, who was sick with the flu, sat down on the grass and caught up with the Maui kids.

From time to time, Sakamoto caught Damkroger watching the events, looking helplessly on; he was out of his depth, but Sakamoto did nothing to rub that in. The results of the meet did it for him.

While Flanagan once again aced the mile swim—it was a horrid, hot 32 laps in all—his time wasn't where he'd wanted it to be. At the half-mile mark, backwash from the pool overcame him and he swallowed water from the wake of other swimmers, which slowed him down; Forsyth had wanted his boy to break Jack Medica's mile record time, but Flanagan came in just 3 seconds over it at 21:07. Still, it was Flanagan's fifth national mile title in as many years.

The 220-yard freestyle on that same night was Keo Nakama's chance to shine. Sakamoto hadn't wanted to waste him in the mile, so this was his first event. The 220 was an all-star race between Bob Pirie, Otto Jaretz, Paul Herron, and Halo Hirose, with Keo as the favored to win. It was a tight race; Pirie got ahead by 5 feet at the halfway mark, and he seemed the certain winner until both Keo and Halo rushed him from behind and came into the wall one and two, Keo at 2:16.3.

It was a start toward racking up some team points, Sakamoto thought. Next was the 330-yard medley relay, and Neunzig, Castor, and Hirose did the 3YSC no favors by finishing third, a full 10 feet behind the team from the Detroit Athletic Club. By the end of Friday, the Maui team was in the lead with 17 points to Detroit's 11, but Sakamoto wasn't comfortable with the narrow lead.

On Saturday, the 880-yard relay quartet of Neunzig, Hirose, Jose Balmores, and Keo Nakama clocked in at 9:21, only 1 second below the national record. In the 440-yard, Flanagan took first, although the race had been tight with Nakama until the halfway mark, when Flanagan pulled ahead a good 30 feet, Keo swallowing water in his wake; but the rest of the Hawaiian team racked up more points with Tanaka taking third, Rivas at fourth, and Halo Hirose at fifth.

Even sick with the flu, Adolph Kiefer was triumphant in the 110-yard backstroke; it was *his* fifth consecutive national title and a fifth of a second better—at 1:06.6—than his national record in 1936. The boy might have had a fever, but he was on fire in the water. Neunzig, swimming backstroke for Hawaii, had one of the finest races of his career, finishing close to Kiefer's near-record time. Sakamoto kept track on his clipboard. By the end of Saturday, after Benny Castor had placed fifth in the 220-yard breaststroke finals, Maui had 28 points, and the Detroit Athletic Club was not far behind at 22.

Sakamoto didn't talk much about the results with Damkroger. He was still keeping as quiet as he could about everything. He wanted to draw no attention to himself whatsoever; any glory belonged in the pool with the swimmers, and on the last day of the meet, Sakamoto watched things turn glorious, indeed. That Sunday evening, when the finals began at 8:30 p.m. with only a meager 6 points separating Maui from Detroit Athletic, Maui furthered its lead, first playing small ball in the 110-yard freestyle final, where Halo came in fourth; then, in the 880 freestyle, where Keo fought bravely against Ralph Flanagan in a tight race that had the crowds standing. Flanagan took his usual first place, but the Hawaiian team had second, third, and fourth. Jose Balmores was only fifth in the 300 individual medley, but Sakamoto saw that next year would be Jose's year, for sure. When all was said and done in Detroit, Medica Club of Chicago was third at 28 points, and the Detroit Athletic Club was second at 29 points, but the 3YSC had amassed an amazing 32 points in all—the greatest number ever accumulated by a single team in the history of the US Men's National swimming championships; and Sakamoto thought it was worth noting that Keo Nakama, the inexhaustible hummingbird, the kid who wasn't burning out, had alone garnered 13.5 of those 32 points. As a bonus, Mike Peppe, who was leading a trip to Ecuador for the Pan-American Games, decided to take Halo and Keo along with a great gang of others, including Adolph Kiefer.

When the rest of the crew finally returned to Maui, the 3YSC had its very first national team championship in hand, Fujiko held the national title of 200-meter breaststroke champ, and two of his boys were traveling in South America as members of the All-American team.

It was more than Soichi Sakamoto could have hoped for. Even E. L. Damkroger was ecstatic; he'd had a terrific time on the trip, lots of sightseeing, lots of excitement, and he was pleased to see how well-behaved the swimmers had been. Sakamoto was pleased, too, but he was quiet about it. At home, he let Damkroger do all the talking—and Damkroger could talk and talk. And Sakamoto also listened to the likes of Bob Hughes, of the Permanent Executive Swimming Committee of Maui, say that the Maui boys had done in Detroit what Bob Hughes had expected them to do. It was what Soichi Sakamoto had both expected and hoped for, though silently. To prove his skills and proclaim by his actions alone that he was the coach of the 3YSC, and that the 3YSC was still on its way to the Olympics.

For Halo and Keo, the Pan-American trip was downright libertine; Mike Peppe was more permissive than Kiphuth, Sakamoto, or E. L. Damkroger. He was a hail-fellow-well-met, a dapper Dan with little ego but great flair and a love of any excuse for festivity, generous to and well-loved by all his swimmers and divers at OSU, the sort of coach who doesn't mind when the team hoists him on their shoulders and tosses him unceremoniously into the pool for a soaking. The group traveling to Ecuador played as much as they swam. They played cards together and drank whiskey and beer and gambled and smoked snipes. When they came ashore they visited all manner of cultural sites, including shops in which they found real shrunken human heads for sale. And the girls: Halo went as hog wild as the South American mores would allow. Both he and Adolph Kiefer found a girlfriend in every port, the only downside of which was that South American girls always needed to be chaperoned; even a simple walk down the street meant being accompanied by some burly brother just steps behind.

In early September, Halo and Keo were aboard ship in the Panama Canal. Even there, the world was tight as a piano wire: fifteen soldiers had boarded at the western terminus and remained there for the whole transit. The soldiers had portable telephones to receive orders, a precautionary move to prevent "even the slightest mishap." And then the word came over the radio: Great Britain and France had declared war on Germany.

Back on Maui, Sakamoto was devastated. That last glimmer of hope for the Olympics was fading. The IOC raised a possibility: perhaps a separate Pan-American Games in 1940 could replace the official games. Perhaps those games could be held in New York, Philadelphia, Los Angeles, or Buenos Aires. There was even talk of some sort of event to be held in Helsinki. But on the twenty-fifth of November, the day after Thanksgiving, Count Henri de Baillet-Latour announced with finality the cancellation of both the Summer and the Winter Olympiads. He told the world simply: "We have abandoned them."

In the news reports, a hopeful suggestion remained that maybe there was still a chance for something to happen in Helsinki. Something did happen, but it wasn't helpful for an Olympiad. Instead, Russia bombed Helsinki in December. And, while it would take some time for the IOC to declare it really over, the dream of the 1940 Olympics was dead.

We have abandoned them. Count Baillet-Latour's words haunted Soichi Sakamoto. He didn't know how to comprehend them, because in his own mind, one never gave up, one never gave in. "Olympics First, Olympics Always!" When Halo and Keo returned to Maui by plane across the United States, Sakamoto tried not to show any emotion. He was, in fact, miserable, but what he said aloud whenever he was with them was: "Yes, it's a bit of a letdown." He bit his tongue. He said, yes, it was a "bum-show."

In truth, it was the collapse of everything.

It was nearly Christmastime. The winter had already been full of insults added to injury. At Kahului Bay, he and his family had stood silently during the memorial service for the summer dead, including his brother. That same week, Sakamoto was summoned by the police and the mayor and warned that his Studebaker scam, the raffle he was running that he'd come up with in the days after Benzo's death, was illegal. The mayor was there, as was the town's postmaster, and they informed him that it was a felony to conduct a raffle through the US mail; the penalty was a $10,000 fine or time in jail.

Sakamoto would have to figure out some other way to sell tickets, or it was off to prison with him.

They were bleeding him.

He told himself that he had accomplished much of what he'd wanted to do, that he'd proved his point. He told himself that there would be other Olympics to follow these missing Olympics. He told himself the war would be short, and he'd better keep his swimmers in tip-top shape.

On most days he didn't feel like doing very much, though. He gave the kids a rest. People said that peace could break out at any time. At the library, the December issue of the *Amateur Athlete* arrived, almost as if nothing had happened to the world of sport. On the cover was a slick picture of Elmer Hackney, dressed in his football uniform, a ball in his hand, his elbow cocked back to throw it. Hackney was a back for Kansas State, but he also had the distinction of having broken an American shot put record. Inside was what ordinarily would have been a fascinating article on stopwatches. It was called "Checking Watches," and it covered all manner of topics: how to know the difference between types of chronometers; the importance, when officiating, that a timer string his watch on a leather cord around his neck. Otherwise, there could be time lost, leading to an error of measurement. Watches, the article explained, were more likely to slow down if not kept in like-new condition. But without the Olympics approaching, the article lost some of its interest and importance.

There were few remarks about the larger world, the greater issue. It seemed Avery Brundage still held on to some notion of a Pan-American Games. But he had likely written those paragraphs back in November. From Britain, Lord Sheffield of the IOC wrote that he saw no hope for international athletic events of any sort for some time to come. The writer of an unsigned editorial compared war and sport. "War is hell," he wrote.

Nevertheless, Soichi Sakamoto made sure that the club put on the most spectacular dance. They called it the "Snow Man's Hop." The souvenir program also listed all the dances that the 3YSC would hold in 1940. January was to be the "Resolution Hop," of course; Molina's orchestra would play. On the following page was a list of the championships that the 3YSC had won during the year of 1939, everything from the meet against McKinley High in

March to Fujiko's 200-meter breaststroke in Des Moines, to Keo's 200-meter freestyle in Detroit, and the 800-meter relay team win at the Nationals.

That night, the orchestra played: "Beer Barrel Polka," "Avalon," "Apple for the Teacher." Above the heads of the crowd spun the mirrored ball Soichi Sakamoto had bought especially for the event, while "I Love You Truly" and "Dream of Love" played.

The club had indeed made some money that night on raffle tickets for the 1940 Studebaker. The cops said 50 cents a ticket was okay, as long as it was in person. Second prize was a Frigidaire. The plan was still the same: in March at Baldwin Pool, they'd have a big strong boy turn the barrel and a pretty girl wearing a blindfold would reach in and pick the winning ticket. The third, fourth, and fifth prizes weren't too bad either: each winner would take home a radio.

There were lots of things to do, things to which Soichi Sakamoto could pay attention. It was the time of year for sports roundups in the newspapers, but every article about Sakamoto made it sound like he had died. One headline: "He Did the Most for Sports."

Although it was Christmas, Sakamoto was adrift once more, as he had been some eleven years ago, before he met Mary. Time had slipped by. In 1928, Mary had helped him find his way, but now he was lost again.

His life had once resembled the map of the world pinned to the wall of his classroom: flat, without dimension, until one day he began to work with the children, and the map unfurled, rounding into a vibrant globe as they traveled to the far-off places that had hitherto been mere dots on a map. For a moment, Sakamoto and his swimmers held something like the world in their hands.

No longer.

Now life had reverted back to the flat thing it had always been, and the Three-Year Swim Club seemed like a passing dream, a way of trying to wish a different world into being.

PART FOUR

A TIDE IN THE AFFAIRS OF MEN

1940–1941

Out of the water, I am nothing.

—Duke Kahanamoku

Chapter Eleven

A SEASON OF FLAME

In April of 1940, some five thousand miles to the east of Maui, America's most powerful collegiate and club coaches gathered for an impromptu Irish wake. It was the final night of the 1940 AAU Indoor Championships, and for nearly every sorry soul gathered in the ninth-floor cocktail lounge of the New York Athletic Club, April was the cruelest month of all.

Among those slumped deep into the bar's leather chairs, puffing on less-than-celebratory cigars and drowning their sorrows with liquor, were the likes of Matt Mann of Michigan, Mike Peppe of Ohio, Stan Brauninger of Chicago, and Yale's Bob Kiphuth. They were a ragged group of men with little love lost among them and little in common except for their passion for the same sport and their pessimism about its future.

Three floors below them in the New York Athletic Club locker rooms, their swimmers were toweling off after what had amounted to a wretched meet. Normally a glittering carnival, this year's annual AAU indoor men's swim competition at the 75-foot-long "Winged Foot" had been lackluster. The NYAC pool was historically a fast one; Johnny Weissmuller broke records in it, and the tank hadn't earned its nickname for nothing. But in the spring of 1940, the world outside that tank had slowed nearly everything reliable and expected to a stop. The entire meet had been a congested crush of humanity gathered in an overheated and airless natatorium to witness a set of sorry proceedings—American swimmers just going through their paces and hardly making waves. In fact, the most exciting event had been when, in the still silence before the starting gun, a coach's assistant surprised fans by collapsing from indoor heat stroke.

On April 3 the nail-in-the-coffin news had come from Helsinki. Antti Kukkonen, minister of education and propaganda, had finally shrugged his shoulders and announced with fatigue that because of what he called, with tremendous understatement, "the abnormal situation prevailing between the great powers," no Olympiad would float in 1940—no Summer, no Winter, not in Finland or in Timbuktu.

The great powers had indeed prevailed in making an enormous mess of the European continent. The "Junkers transports—with bomb racks exposed like wolf fangs," which sportswriter Grantland Rice had described vividly as circling over the Olympics in 1936 like "menacing flying wedges at less than 2500," had descended at last upon the world. When Avery Brundage had insisted that sport and politics had nothing to do with each other, he had only to look up in the sky four years later to see he was mistaken. How was it possible that a man of the world could have failed to see that the games on the playing fields of Europe weren't games at all? How could he have looked upon the "imagined community of millions" playing games at the Olympiad and not know that the games were a chimera? How could he have failed to know what one sports historian said so aptly of international sport: that the "friendly rivalry" in which nations come together with a ball or bat "to reinforce the sense that they all belonged together" is merely temporary?

In 1940, the war in Europe had brought the future of sport into question and revealed international sport in particular to be, if not a sham, then at best an empty promise. Outside the windows of the New York Athletic Club that night, the Manhattan sky was so dark that it was impossible to see even a sliver of Central Park or to know for certain it was there. The only thing that was certain was that the men who drank together in the club's cocktail lounge had lost not just their sight but also their vision. It was about this that they were speaking and over which they were drinking.

It was a miserable conversation on which to eavesdrop, which Arthur Daley, veteran sportswriter of the *New York Times*, knew for a fact. He had been listening in on the sidelines of the group for a while before he was moved to shake the group up and out of their blues. Daley leaned in and offered the men a kind of dare: If you were, and I'm not saying you are, Daley proposed, but if you *were* to *have to pick* the fellows for the US Olympic swim team, who'd be on it, huh?

An imaginary roster. The room fell silent at first. None of the coaches wanted to be quoted in any article Daley would write on the matter. Their words could come back to haunt them, but if they spoke as a group, on the condition of individual anonymity, why, sure, they'd play along.

Ordinarily this group of egos rhubarbed about matters as trivial as whose turn it was to order the next round, but tonight they were united in their project, and while men were killing one another all over the world, a strange peace had broken out among America's swim coaches.

The men even agreed on *how* to agree about picking the squad. It would be based on a photograph of the present moment, taking into account: swimmers' performances in the '39 Nationals at Detroit during the previous August; the results of key collegiate races during that academic year of 1939–1940; and they would allow for the admittance of those swimmers of "known skill" who just hadn't had a chance that year to show they had it.

At first there were few surprises: freestylers were Otto Jaretz, Paul Wolf, and Ralph Flanagan—who, despite having just gone pro, deserved the honor. Gus Sharamet out of Matt Mann's crew was an easy pick; Tom Haynie made the cut, and so did Adolph Kiefer in the backstroke. Three Princeton boys and one Eli made it.

But by the time the draft was over, the faces of the team looked profoundly different than they had in '32 or '36 because now three Hawaiians were on the roster: Jimmy Tanaka, Keo Nakama, and Halo Hirose.

The group, the coaches agreed, was far stronger than the one the United States had fielded in Berlin, and if the Games were somehow, magically, to take place, all the young men they'd chosen would be wearing necklaces of gold.

Avery Brundage wasn't in the room that night, but he was occupied with similar, if more typically ponderous thoughts. As an American delegate to the International Olympic Committee, the fate of athletes in every sport concerned him. Present events brought to mind, in a most troubling fashion, those of the past. There was nothing that concerned Brundage more than matters of time, particularly matters of history touching on the ideas of legacy and eternity. He kept the great issues of the world in mind at all times, and it wouldn't be a stretch to say that he always—and often to his detriment—thought his concerns more high-minded than others'.

In spite of all of his—questionable and biased—efforts to keep international politics out of the Olympics and vice versa, which had succeeded in Berlin in 1936, he failed to keep the flame of the 1940 Games alight, first in Tokyo and now in Helsinki. It was as if every knot he had ever tied tight had come undone. The world was becoming undone. And there was little even he could do about it. If he were to force the issue, trying to bring off an Olympiad somehow, it would be only a sham, a trip for biscuits, a swinging of a sword at windmills.

Because of his passion for an apolitical Olympics, Brundage had been called an elitist, a Nazi, an anti-Semite, and much more. Some saw him as a megalomaniac with a feverish and volatile temperament that equaled Hitler's; the two were, in fact, close friends. Others suggested—generously—that there might have been a more personal reason for his intransigence. What, one wonders, would it have been like to be Avery Brundage in the year 1916, for example, in the year of the cancellation of those Games? Brundage had been a superb athlete, a three-time all-around national champ in a suite of some of the most difficult track-and-field events, including an 880-yard speed walk that took place, along with the other nine events, in the course of a single day. He had participated in the 1912 Olympic Games, but just four years later, he became, along with all of the other athletes prepared for that Olympiad, another victim of history. Since that year he had endeavored—to no avail—to keep sport what he believed it should be: the observance of physical exercise as a sacred, pure, and wholly religious moment. The body as a corpus sancti.

Shortly after the impromptu meeting, Brundage wanted to try to make the whole enterprise a little more formal, and he called for an official and larger group of coaches and officials to pick—for every sport—every athlete who would likely have been at the '40 Games. The idea of a mail-in vote from American Olympic Committee members hadn't been exciting enough, although the rosters came out looking similar to the one the drunken men had put together on the night before Art Daley's post.

Brundage cheerfully suggested the handing out of medals and the occasion of some kind of ceremony as well, but May would prove to be as cruel as April, and some four thousand miles to the east of New York, the German army invaded the European Lowlands in a new blitzkrieg.

When news about the April coaches' meeting and the American Olympic Committee's May picks reached Soichi Sakamoto on Maui, he was pleased enough with the inclusion of Halo Hirose and Keo Nakama as hypothetical Olympians, but he was also certain that had the group waited until summer of that year to make their choices, more of his swimmers, including Charlie Oda and Jose Balmores, would have been on the list. And if the coaches had bothered to put together a list of women, Sakamoto was sure that Fujiko Katsutani and Chic Miyamoto would have made that one, too.

That spring, he'd tried to rally himself and break through his own fog; he told the swimmers and anyone else who would listen that his passion for swimming was stronger than ever before. He crammed the Maui swim schedule so chockablock full that even with a magnifying glass it was hard to find a minute when the swimmers weren't immersed in water. He tried to fill the empty space where the Olympics would have been. He raised funds as if the Games were still on and he were desperate for cash: he showed more samurai films in places like far-flung Lahaina, and he opened up and ran a well-stocked concession bar at the Camp 5 pool. He wrote florid letters to Bob Kiphuth, Mike Peppe, and other coaches across the States and invited them to become members of the 3YSC, and when they responded yes—in Bob Kiphuth's letter back he wrote that he was supremely honored to be included in such an august group—Sakamoto drew up new business cards that bore their latest members' names.

At his most grandiose, he floated an idea that knew no bounds. Why, he wondered, couldn't Maui itself host a national championship? He'd begun to speak to AAU officials and to talk to donors about money to expand the Baldwin Pool.

Watching, E. L. Damkroger was astonished and annoyed by Sakamoto's hubris. Once again the man was filling children's heads with useless dreams, and once again, E. L. Damkroger put a plan in action to stop Sakamoto. He formed a new subcommittee of the Permanent Executive Swimming Committee whom he convened in secret and who emerged from out of nowhere with a new system controlling any form of swimming on the island, including Soichi Sakamoto's club.

The subcommittee was now the sole manager of all funds, even those that Sakamoto might have raised himself, and it was also in charge of deciding who could take swimmers off-island for a meet or any other reason; it required a written line-by-line budget for each trip, every penny of which Sakamoto must explain. Furthermore, the subcommittee made it clear that now no swimmer leaving the island could compete under the Three-Year Swim Club name. Instead, a swimmer swam for Maui "under auspices of the Alexander Community House Association." E. L. Damkroger was appointed manager of everything, rendering Soichi Sakamoto, as Damkroger had always hoped to, a man without a kingdom or a throne.

Damkroger made sure that the girls in the club suffered the most. That spring of '40, they were more than stellar. Mitzi Higuchi and a girl named Kay Sugino tore up the lanes in the 400-yard freestyle, and Chic Miyamoto was out in front of them all, breaking two territorial records. In practice, the diminutive Toyo Takeyama broke Mitzi Higuchi's century mark, and Fujiko Katsutani rocketed in the water in the 100-yard breaststroke, breaking the American record in the event. They were headed to the Nationals. Or so they thought.

Damkroger had tried and failed to keep Fujiko Katsutani from traveling to Des Moines, but this year he meant to score a victory: no matter how many girls qualified for the AAU Women's National Championships in Portland, Oregon, Damkroger would keep a stranglehold on who could go.

A Season of Flame

That summer Soichi Sakamoto had called upon his wife to oversee the Portland trip; his duties in Santa Barbara for the Men's Nationals made it impossible to supervise both at once. Mary had proved to be more than competent at taking over in her husband's absence: in 1938, when he was in Louisville, she'd coached the team entirely on her own. And if her husband hadn't complimented her on her work, at least others saw what she had done: the *Maui Shinbun* had honored her for her service to the 3YSC by inducting her into its imaginary "Hall of Fame," and the Japanese Civic Association had presented her with a pretty set of silverware. As the time for the Portland meet drew closer, Mary Sakamoto worked ceaselessly to make arrangements for the girls to travel there.

Once Sakamoto had left for Santa Barbara with the boys, Damkroger did his best to become Mary Sakamoto's puppeteer, and instead of allowing her to take those girls who'd qualified: Fujiko, Chic, Toyo, and Mitzi—who were already inked into the program for events ranging from sprinting to the mile—he restricted the number traveling to two: last year's champion, Fujiko Katsutani, and Mary Sakamoto as her chaperone.

Mary Sakamoto was determined to fulfill her husband's wishes, though, and when Damkroger failed to secure a cabin on a Matson liner, she set to work. The Portland games were drawing closer; it was already the twenty-sixth of July and they had little more than a week to get there in time to participate in the trials. So on a day when she wasn't overseeing the girls in practice at the Nat, Mary went down to the Matson offices to beg for a cabin, but at first no amount of pleading or cajoling worked; she moved from ticket office to ticket office, from liner to liner, until she finally secured cabins in steerage, and the only other cabin left—an expensive one in first class—for herself. Then Mary packed her bags, and without Damkroger's knowledge or permission, she took all four girls to Honolulu in the dark of night. With the financial help of George Higa, they were on their way to San Francisco by August 1.

The only ship available, the SS *President Taft*, was no *Matsonia* or *Monterey*. Neither premium liner nor even comfortable, it was likely the dreariest of passenger boats to ply the Pacific in 1940: a nightmare of a vessel, as equally unsuited to smooth sailing or buoyancy as the twenty-seventh president after whom it was named, and its conditions were as tight as the bathtub in which it was rumored that the hefty Taft himself had once managed to get stuck in.

The third-class cabins of the ship had once had portals, but they'd been painted shut in the same thick metallic white as the cabins' walls; the rooms were lightless and narrow with bunk beds hanging from the ceiling that had mattresses as hard as planks. A basin screwed into the wall served as a sink; an old-fashioned tin pitcher was a faucet; and when the girls closed the door of their prison, as they came to call it, the ventless room became so airless and hot that they took to lying out upon the dirty deck instead.

Mary was stoic, but each of the girls was seasick and no one was able to stomach even the thought of the dining room, which itself was like a dungeon: no linen, silver, or tablecloths; just a collection of rickety chairs around an uneven-footed wooden table, above which, as a gesture of decoration, a dried-up fern sat on a little ledge.

The crew paid no mind to Mary and the girls except to snub them openly, the captain crossing his arms and refusing to give them access to the pool for practice. As much as Mary Sakamoto pressed him, the captain maintained that no one but his bosses in San Francisco could grant permission to use the pool. And upon their arrival in California they had no choice—the time was short—but to get on a train for Portland that was without Pullman cars.

The journey there was a sleepless two days, first through a tinderbox and then through a forest fire. The previous winter had been unseasonably dry, and the summer of 1940 was the worst fire season in recent US memory. From Northern California on up, it had mattered not one whit how many thousands of miles of trunk trails the Civil Conservation Corps had dug nor how many scouts stood at the ready in lookout towers, scanning the horizon; no one had seen such devastation since at least 1934. Lightning strikes from rainless passing storms had ignited acres of forest, and nearer to towns, fires that had begun a month before, with Independence Day fireworks displays, were still burning.

Tall, licking flames and clouds of smoke rose on the horizon, and sometimes the train had to stop until the fire passed, then plunge ahead into the acrid smoke. Mary and the girls and other passengers pressed wet handkerchiefs across their noses and mouths and peered through the ash-caked windows, from time to time seeing forest deer and rabbits scattering for their little lives.

The Women's Nationals were held that year in Jantzen Beach, a playground and amusement park of grand proportion where the girls could see the turning carousel, its pretty painted horses spinning to an organ grinder's tune; a sky-high Ferris wheel; revolving swings they called a Merry-Mix-Up; and the grandest amusement of them all: the fanciest wooden roller coaster in the West, the Big Dipper. When they weren't swimming, the girls could drive in midget cars and walk a swinging bridge and navigate a hall of mirrors with air jets in the floor that animated waving ghosts and goblins.

And that was only Jantzen during the day; at night, its ballroom filled with couples dancing; its Venetian canals crowded with boats that wound their languid way around the park's wide acres toward a spit of land called Hayden Point. At the Elbow Room Restaurant, a sleek diner with an endlessly long counter lined with turning stools, they could stop and get a burger and a malted. Compared to what they'd been through, it was, in no uncertain terms, a paradise.

After their horrid crossing and their smoke-filled train ride, nothing bothered them, not even how, as they made their way throughout the Jantzen complex, they were as much a sideshow attraction as bearded women or sets of conjoined twins. Children, seeing their straw hats and paper leis, had no compunction about running up to them and asking a million questions about the foreign land from which they'd come. Did they wear grass skirts and live in thatched huts? Did they do funny dances and play the ukulele? And at the pool, while the girls did stick out among the crowd of white-skinned bathing beauties, they were never asked—as the other young women were—to pose alluringly in that year's fancy Jantzen swimsuits. Still, none of this mattered anymore.

Their greatest triumph was in the Jantzen pool, and although the press there insisted on calling them "brown fishes" or "brown torpedoes," they were spectacular in the tank.

A Tide in the Affairs of Men

They came into the meet as the favorite for the team championship, with no less than *Amateur Athlete* declaring them the greatest threat to women's swimming in two decades, and with the skies above them sunny and clear, an enormous crowd came to see them swim.

Chic was first on the block in the 330-yard individual medley that had become her strength at home. Against competitors like defending champion Doris Brennan and ace Ann Hardin, a Lakeside Louisville competitor, Chic sped ahead and churned the water as she never had before. In the qualifying heat, she'd swum a solid 4:39.1, but in the finals she led Doris Brennan by a full 10 yards throughout, with Ann Hardin far behind, and came in first at 4:35.7, nearly 3.5 seconds off her heat time.

Chic's was not only the first title of the meet, but also her first title at her very first Nationals. It took a while for others to warm up as much: on the first day, Mitzi Higuchi struggled, placing sixth in the mile, two laps behind the winner; and Fujiko failed to qualify in the heats of the 110-yard freestyle. On the following day, Toyoko Takeyama got a case of stage fright in the 110-yard backstroke and froze; champ Gloria Callen came in first, followed by other veterans.

But later that same day, at 5 p.m., Fujiko Katsutani made a comeback. The sun was still up when she swam the finals in her best event, the one in which she was defending national champion. She'd performed well in the heat of the 220-yard breaststroke, with a time of 3:17.2, and she hoped not to be knocked from her first-place stance in the afternoon. And in that evening's race against Patty Aspinall, Fujiko held on to the championship, a two-time winner now.

The team of Mitzi, Toyo, and Fujiko came in third in the 330-yard medley relay, their points adding up into a heap they'd never before been able to assemble; in the end the four finished in fourth place with 14 points. They'd won enough to return the next year to the championships in High Point, North Carolina, finally a team, a squad, something at last that was their own.

Chapter Twelve

SANTA BARBARA

ON BOARD the *Matsonia* that same summer, traveling to Santa Barbara for the Men's Nationals, Soichi Sakamoto felt as though whatever had once been his and the 3YSC's was quickly disappearing. He suffered panic attacks when looking at his squad, the old familiar faces who'd be headed off to college in a year, a motley collection that he wasn't sure could constitute a team in California.

In part, he was moved to melancholy by the fact that California ought to have been the site of the Olympic trials that summer and by the awareness that, in Japan, the East Asian Games—which were meant in some fashion to replace the Tokyo Games—would draw some seven hundred athletes from as far away as Manchuria, the Philippines, and Thailand—but not Hawaii.

Travel was a pleasure but also a reminder of what they weren't traveling to, and all the boys tried making up for Sakamoto's sullenness with silliness and brand-new nicknames: Bunny Nakama was suddenly "Bunsky"; Mike Ginoza, the team's manager, took on the mantle of "Clark Gable," in part because of his mustache. A kid from Honolulu who had made the squad, Bill Smith, was a voracious eater and a source of great entertainment, literally ordering everything he could off the ship's menu—à la carte—from Yacht Club Sardines to Roast Petaluma Chicken, earning himself the nickname the "Avoirdupois of Table Two." And the group tried to make a joke of it when the air and sea grew colder and colder as they drew nearer to the coast of California, the pool water so frigid that they started taking warm showers just minutes before jumping in.

Sakamoto's greatest pleasure on the crossing was when the group, while playing deck volleyball with a ball E. L. Damkroger had lent them, lost the ball overboard. Halo Hirose had given it a harder tap than usual, and it had disappeared into a mist of cloud, a moment Soichi Sakamoto so enjoyed that he wrote home about it in a letter addressed to the director of athletics on the Valley Isle.

After landing in San Francisco one early morning, still dripping wet from onboard practice and almost missing their connection, the group boarded the modern *Daylight Limited*, a streamliner taking them twelve hours down the coast to a town that, at least to Soichi Sakamoto, didn't look at all as though it was a part of the United States but rather more like Mexico, with its hillsides and skyline of brilliant terra-cotta-colored roofs.

Under the new seven-point system, E. L. Damkroger did most of the planning, such as arranging the team's stay at the YMCA downtown between Carillo and Chapala Streets and securing the loan of a station wagon so they could travel the four miles to and from the venue. But that left them with what Sakamoto called his "none-too-heavy purse," meaning they had little money for food in an expensive town with few inexpensive restaurants. With what little pocket change they had, they ate in crummy cafeterias where the meals still didn't fill their bellies, until Sakamoto told the group that they'd be singing for their suppers, and with visions of a fuller belly, he took out his own ukulele and told the boys to grab their straw hats.

Straw wasn't about to keep them warm at the pool, though. Ski hats would have better served. Sakamoto had forgotten just how deceptively chilly California coast weather was; he thought Santa Barbara, farther south than San Francisco, would be nicer, but the city was situated at the edge of a bay. The sun didn't break through the fog until at least high noon, and when he and the team ventured out for their 8 a.m. workout, the boys had to wrap themselves in sweaters and coats, and Sakamoto had to cajole them just to

dip their toes into the water. When they finally *did* get in, it pained Sakamoto to look at his swimmers wearing suits that now read "Maui." This meet
was the first time they'd be swimming nationally without the 3YSC name.

The name change and the lack of money for food was something for
which he could blame E. L. Damkroger; he only wished he could find some
way to blame the man for the horrid weather, as well.

The Coral Casino Club at the Biltmore hotel was no casino at all but an
exclusive and private beach club, contemporary and sleek and opened in
the summer of 1937. The resort tried hard to be a substitute for the ones in
Monte Carlo and Cannes that no one could visit anymore. It hosted stars
and filmmakers; Gloria Vanderbilt, all of seventeen, would hold her wedding reception there. Legend had it that the place was never intended to be
the site of any swimming competition; the story went that the builders, in
the midst of a poker game, made a deal never to let that happen and instead
built the "Olympic-sized" pool at an irregular 50 meters plus one foot,
although in spite of irregularity, the tank was, on July 4, 1940, decked out
with bunting in celebration both of the Fourth of July and the start of the
AAU Men's National Swimming Championships.

Amidst the socialites and club members on the deck, Soichi Sakamoto
saw some of the swimmers with whom his team had competed in the past,
but he also saw others who had fallen away from swimming and into the high
life: some had relinquished their amateur status and had taken Broadway's
Billy Rose up on his offer to become paid clowns in his gaudy Aquacade; and
even if a swimmer traded swimming for the humiliation of frolicking about
the water in a costume and makeup, at least the money was good. Other
swimmers who graduated college had nowhere else to go but back on deck.
They couldn't make money off of anything to do with swimming without
running afoul of AAU rules and being stripped of their amateur status.

On the upside, the fact that some old rivals weren't in the pool was of
great advantage to Sakamoto's swimmers. Ralph Flanagan was there but not
as a swimmer any longer. Having gone pro, he'd also gotten married in the

spring, and he now traveled along with his wife, the famed American diver Ruth Jump, in tow and wearing fur. With Flanagan in the bleachers, that left room for new winners in the 440-yard, the 880-yard, and the mile. The papers had caught on, calling it a possible "wild scramble...for laurels."

The tension before the meet was high. The Coral Casino put the heater on in the pool and the water temperature rose to a comfortable 74 degrees. Sakamoto said nothing of the sort, but some of the other coaches were willing to go on the record saying that the pool was a fast one, and that there'd be some record-breaking to come. The advantage of having half saltwater and half freshwater also meant, they pointed out, more buoyancy for the swimmers.

The heats began on the Fourth itself, but there were few fireworks for Sakamoto's swimmers. The 220-yard freestyle, which should have been a cinch for Halo or Keo, became a struggle. Otto Jaretz led the whole race, with a steady, methodical pace ahead of Adolph Kiefer, Paul Herron, and the others, ultimately coming in to the wall a full 3 yards ahead of Kiefer for a 1927 American record. Johnny Weissmuller's record had finally fallen; Weissmuller's 2:13.6 was snipped by Jaretz by a mere 2:13.1, Jaretz finally having cut through the stubborn umbilical cord to the distant past. Keo came in with Herron, tying at third with a 2:16.2, and Halo was just behind at 2:16.5.

The 1-mile freestyle took place on the fifth of July in the afternoon. Sakamoto's swimmers were Jose Balmores, Bunny Nakama, and Bill Smith; it was the first time at the Nationals for both Bunny and Bill, and in the race, each had much to do; Rene Chouteau of Yale, the national champ, was in the pool, and his coach, Bob Kiphuth, was about nearby, his steely eyes on his pocket watch.

Chouteau, a raven-haired St. Louis–born Creole of impeccable manners and good pedigree—his family had founded St. Louis—was the greatest threat to all the boys; he had a smooth freestyle stroke, and he'd learned to swim in open water, too, though his training ground had been the mighty Mississippi. But Bill and Jose set the pace in the first quarter of the race, with Bunny and Chouteau behind, and at the halfway mark, Bunny pulled suddenly ahead, while behind him, Bill Smith and Chouteau began to battle, sprinting, fighting so tightly that the fancy crowd rose to its feet. Sakamoto wouldn't have dared to look over at Kiphuth, when who, of all swimmers, Bunny Nakama came in to the wall at 21:31.4. Keo's slender younger brother, with Smith behind him in second with a time of 21:47.2 and with Chouteau in third just .2 seconds behind Smith. Bunny's contribution was significant, and so was Smith's. By the end of the day, Sakamoto's team was in second place with 11 points. Chicago had a solid 18 points.

The sixth of July dawned hot and it stayed hot. Keo had struggled in the morning 440-yard freestyle heats; he didn't look or feel like himself and barely qualified at 5:01.5, though by the afternoon, he was back in order, and his was the hugest victory of the meet so far, a first-place with an astounding 11-second shave off his own time at 4:50.4.

Then, in the high heat of the afternoon, Bunny, Keo, and Jose, with Halo as their anchor, swam a record-breaking 880-yard freestyle relay in the Coral Casino Pool, beating the American mark of 9:20 by a nice, clean 9:17.3. It was a necessary win, Sakamoto knew, and what it did was double duty: Sakamoto's swimmers pulled into first place with 29 points, and, moreover, they held on to their national team title in the relay. Two consecutive years of team firsts. Keo topped that win off with a huge victory in the 880-yard individual freestyle, coming in 4 seconds short of Ralph Flanagan's record while Ralph Flanagan sat fanning himself in the stands. The time, 10:08.6, pushed the Hawaiian team further ahead in the running, and just an hour later, it was Jose Balmores's turn to shine.

The 330-yard individual medley was a thriller and a career high for Jose. He was in the drink with veteran Adolph Kiefer, who led by 10 yards during the backstroke second lap, after which Jose got a surge of power and sprinted the freestyle final lap, losing by inches to the champ but coming in only a yard behind him. Kiefer, at 3:58.6, bettered his two-year-old record of 4:02, and Jose Balmores was second.

By the end of the championships, Sakamoto's spirits were revived. His Hawaiians, his Maui kids, three of whom had started out with him in the ditch, took the team title. The total of 41 points was a huge increase over the previous year's win of 32, and bested once again their own number for the highest number of points accumulated by a single team at a national meet. The headlines ran tall and bold: all of Flanagan's defending titles went in Santa Barbara to the two Nakama brothers, and the word was: if the 1940 Olympics had taken place that summer as planned, the American team would have cleaned up, and most of them would have been from Hawaii.

During the trip, Sakamoto had kept his eye on his extra man, Bill Smith, "the Avoirdupois of Table Two." It was the kid's first foray into major competition, but Sakamoto thought he saw something there: the boy swam with seeming effortlessness, his kick barely breaking the surface right behind him, and he was also friendly, seemed to fit in easily. Another nickname that the other boys had given him was "Honolulu."

For Smith's part, he wasn't paying much attention, though. He liked the Maui group. They were a clean-cut, friendly, and well-mannered lot, Keo Nakama and his younger brother Bunny, a Hawaiian-Filipino boy named Benny Castor, and, oddly, Paul Herron, the former Stanford ace. The group was well staffed; a big blond fellow by the name of Neunzig was manager-type, and a little skinny guy by the name of Mike Ginoza was the team's trainer.

Nakama was already Bill Smith's hero and his favorite. A few years before, Bill, sitting in the bleachers, had seen Nakama swim the famous Ralph Gilman race. Smith was less enthusiastic about Halo Hirose, thought Hirose tooted his horn all the time, and when he wasn't talking about himself he was rattling on about girls.

The Maui coach was a piece of work, though, stern, a stickler about meetings, meetings, meetings. His swimmers were the first ones in the ship's pool in the morning and the last out at night. He ran a shipshape operation, all right. There was no loafing around. He had an individual training program for every swimmer, and he made sure that each swimmer carried that routine out completely to the specifications.

All that was new to Smith, but what was even stranger was Sakamoto's emphasis on form. Smith hardly knew what the coach was talking about: cutting down on resistance in the water and putting more power in each stroke. Sakamoto checked and corrected and shifted Smith's stroke around so much—elbow this way, then pull with fingers that way—that Bill, who had never thought anything was wrong with how he put his arms in and out of the water, started to wonder if there was something all wet not with his stroke but with Sakamoto himself.

On July 24, when he returned to Honolulu—alone—on the *Malolo* in cabin class, Bill Smith decided he hadn't at all been impressed with the Mainland. He'd hardly stepped foot on land in California when he decided it was just a "terrible place," with its looming buildings and clanging cable cars, and he didn't like the disconcerting way that thousands of people on the sidewalks of the city didn't stroll the way people in Honolulu did. They didn't walk so much as half run, and nobody else cared where anyone else was going. Frankly, the whole trip to California with the odd coach made Smith appreciate Hawaii in a way he never had before. He couldn't wait to get home to his ordinary life, a life into which he put some planning. He was, he was certain, to become a football player. More than anything else, he looked forward to the start of the football season. It was what he had dreamed about for years, and when the ship landed and Bill Smith put his feet on steady ground, he put away his swim trunks and searched for a pigskin he could toss around.

Chapter Thirteen

MR. SMITH COMES TO MAUI

Bɪʟʟ Sᴍɪᴛʜ was the haole-est name for a Hawaiian boy, and from time to time his father asked if he wanted to change it to something more *kanaka*—local. But William Melvin Smith Jr. adored his father, William Melvin Smith Sr., and so he was only Bill, Billy, or Bill Jr., at least until he earned a couple of other names.

When he was born in Honolulu in May of 1924, Bill Smith Jr. didn't look haole or even hapa haole; he was a chubby, full-lipped puddle of a thing, with dimpled cheeks, dark eyebrows already filled in, and a hint already of the wide smile he'd have for the rest of his life. His skin was the color of a koa calabash, and his head a mop of jet-black curls.

His father was green-eyed and had, people said, a tinge of orange that showed up in his hair when the light hit it just right—it was a touch of Irish blood—but his complexion was caramel, and his body—round shoulders, short legs, and a full belly—was somehow more Pacific Islander. Smith's mother, Rena, was lighter-skinned but full-on Hawaiian, a Kealoha, the eldest of a clan of sixteen children.

Smith's parents had met through the Mormon Church—Rena was the eldest in a family of sixteen. They shared a love of Hawaiian music; both played the ukulele and sang. And for the brief untroubled years of their marriage, there hung on the wall of their home a sepia photograph of them depicting an idyllic, if dramatized, Hawaiian life: each was robed in island garb, performing in a church pageant.

Mr. Smith Comes to Maui

Smith's father was a big bear of a man, warm in spirit, a cop whose beat was down by the harbor keeping watch over the Matson line. And his mother was a schoolteacher, so committed to church and to music—her father was a bishop—that sometimes she seemed more passionate about those concerns than a middle-class family life.

The Smiths' home was in the hills above Waikiki, in a neighborhood of streets lined with pretty three-bedroom houses filled with families in which most mothers stayed home. When Smith's mother was busy, his father was in charge; he cooked scrambled eggs for breakfast—he said it was just too much work to keep the yolks from breaking—charred hot dogs and hamburgers for dinner, helped the children with their homework, and on weekends treated them to John Wayne and Bob Hope movies. Young Bill loved the cartoons that came beforehand.

Bill Smith's father scrimped to send the children to private Catholic school, though on Sundays the family worshipped at the local ward house. Bill found the huge Kealoha family enveloping and strange; he marveled at the idea that he could have two uncles younger than he was, and he tried to puzzle that out. What he couldn't figure out was the fact that every day, his mother seemed, for reasons he didn't comprehend, to be fading from his life as rapidly as she was from the photograph on the wall.

In other ways, Bill Smith's life was ordinary. At school, the Christian brothers taught him how to write with his right hand instead of his dominant left, and in time he mastered the meticulous cursive required at St. Louis. But at the age of ten, he fell ill. It began with a dull ache in his head and it only grew and grew until it was a violent pain no ice cap could relieve and no darkened room palliate. Within a day, an angry, weeping rash broke out on his chest and stomach, and his temperature inched higher and higher until he became delirious, unreachable. At the Hawaiian children's hospital, the Kauikeōlan, the doctors determined he was suffering from a virulent strain of typhoid.

In those days, there was little to do but pack the patient in ice and hope that the fever didn't strike the brain. For three dark months, Bill Smith Jr. lay feverish in a cot at Kauikeōlan, surrounded by other children with illnesses of all kinds—spinal meningitis, sleeping sickness, and polio—and

223

he himself was plagued in the dark with night terrors and in the days with half-dreams. Sometimes he felt the presence of a nurse beside him. Sometimes the visits of physicians who prodded him punctuated his hazy twilight sleep. His father seemed always to be there. But his mother seemed never to appear. None of the people who came into the room could make him better. He longed to stop feeling so lost to the world; he couldn't eat, couldn't speak except to mumble what he knew was nonsense. Everything in the world had tilted and wouldn't right itself.

When he at last woke from his long stupor, his dark hair had fallen out and he could neither stand nor move his legs or arms. At last, his father hoisted him from the bed, and Smith went home, limp, in his arms. But even home was a crooked confusion. It wasn't the pretty three-bedroom house in the hills above Waikiki but a house by the ocean, down in Waikiki itself, Smith's father explained. No, they didn't own it; they were renting it. And no, his mother wasn't there with them. She had decided to stay at the old house. Eventually, his father fessed up that the two had divorced.

The best his father could do to help Smith was carry him across the road to the beach and lay him in the sun, take him in the water, and hold him like a baby. Eventually the boy could move his arms and legs, but he still couldn't stand. Back at school at St. Louis, his friends were glad to see him alive, and they carried him—and his schoolbooks—from room to room. The Christian brothers began to teach him how to hold a pencil again, how to write in cursive, but it took a year before he could make real loops with his hand and more time to stand again on wobbly legs. It was an improvement, but he had far to go.

He was nearing his teens. Sometimes he thought about his mother, so near, just up in the hills and alone in the big house without them. He and his father and his sister stayed at the beach, but they moved again and again from tiny house to tiny house. Soon he stopped thinking of her so much, and though he knew where to find her, he lost track of her, and she of them, and the beach across the road from whichever house in which he lived became the center of his newly wakened world.

The sand was his backyard and his living room. Restaurants like the

Mr. Smith Comes to Maui

Unique and the Honolulu Café became his kitchen and his dining room; his father had arranged a tab there, and Smith could eat as much as he wanted. His sister and he became latchkey kids, and as Smith's strength grew, he turned into a Waikiki beachboy.

Duke Kahanamoku and his friends—the Hui Nalu club that used to meet under the shade of a hau tree—had been the first generation of beachboys. Kahanamoku was more of a sportsman than an opportunist and a racketeer, but in his time, the other beachboys sat at Honolulu Harbor, on the long teeth of the wooden wharves and docks, awaiting the arrival of steamships. As ships neared, the beachboys swam to them and dove for the bright coins that the passengers tossed from above; daringly, they climbed ships' foresails and flung themselves off hundreds of feet into the water, in gorgeous arcs that drew gasps and applause.

During his sojourn in Honolulu at the turn of the century, the writer Jack London observed that the beachboys were like "a perfect fusillade of small dark objects," springing from "every height and ringbolt and sill." And the more tourists who arrived in Waikiki, the more ambitious the beachboys became. In the mornings, before hung-over visitors emerged from the hotels in search of sun, the beachboys sat on a stone wall near Sans Souci—earning them the nickname "the stonewall gang"—and when the guests began to straggle and stumble out, they rented them towels and chairs and private canopies; they offered coconut oil rubdowns called *lomi-lomi* while selling fragrant leis.

For a dollar per person, the boys took the adventurous types out on outrigger canoes, or carried the women on their shoulders while they stood on surfboards. There grew among some of the boys and visiting women a secret intimacy. At night back then, anything could happen. A divorcée or a dissatisfied housewife on vacation didn't mind if a dark-skinned, muscled "native" type walked her back in the dark to her hotel. Sometimes the two peeled off in a direction away from the hotels for romance and clothes-less midnight swims. It was something a woman certainly couldn't have done back home in Peoria.

Trouble finally arrived in the form of the infamous Massie case, which

A Tide in the Affairs of Men

hinged on a white woman's accusation that a group of native boys had brutally raped and beaten her, charges so inflammatory that none other than Clarence Darrow—he of the Scopes trial—came to town to defend the boys. In the meantime, the beachboys' reputation was tarnished.

Smith's world was one without gravitas or purpose. He had nearly become a man, but he was a young Jack Dempsey–type, and with his weight hovering at 185 pounds, his father worried that his tendency toward plumpness was a sign of laziness. He should become something more. Study math. Study science. Become, say, a civil engineer. The answer was that the boy should take up swimming, not just floating in the waves, and he steered him away from the beach and to a club swim team at the Natatorium.

Smith was drawn to the Nat in the same way that other kids in Waikiki were. He loved the 33-foot diving tower, and he loved swimming—against the rule—under the decks of the pool. He loathed work, and he tired easily doing the required 100-yard laps, and after less than two weeks, deciding he could find something better to do, he snuck off, heading back toward the surf until his father took him by the scruff of the neck and walked him back over to the Nat and into the ranks of the Hui Makani swim team. Smith Sr. told the Hui Makani coach to give the boy more than an ounce of discipline and to take some pounds off of him, too.

It's doubtful that Harvey Chilton, the head of the Hui Makani swim club, was the best candidate to straighten out young Smith. Chilton, himself a former beachboy, was a colorful character with a checkered past. He'd struggled most of his own youth to stay on the right side of the law.

At the age of twelve he'd served as a choirboy at his church, but when he hit his teens he turned to crime; a detective spied him through the keyhole of a guest's room in one of the big hotels and charged him with larceny.

That episode over, Chilton began to spend the rest of the nine or ten or twelve lives he seemed to have in him. He turned himself around, became an athlete, anchored the 1-mile relay in track, and played baseball until he landed in jail on a charge of assault and battery: he'd attacked another player in the middle of a game. Motorcycles were new, and he liked that they were shiny. He ran with a crowd of motorcycle enthusiasts who gathered down in Kapiolani Park and showed off their vehicles. Somehow, though, in the summer of 1913 he lucked out.

He'd run into the president of the Hui Nalu, a man by the name of W. T. Rawlins, an attorney and a friend of bigwig swimmers. Rawlins thought he saw something in Chilton and took him on as an errand boy at the Nat, fetching towels and rubbing down big-time swimmers, including Duke Kahanamoku himself.

People called Chilton a trainer. Rawlins once said that Harvey Chilton could get Duke Kahanamoku, postrace, into fit-as-a-fiddle shape just fifteen minutes later. Rawlins so prized Chilton that he let him tag along on one of the champ's junkets to San Francisco. Just as it seemed he'd set himself right, though, the devils on one of Chilton's shoulders overcame the angels on the other, and for years it was common to see the young man's name not in the sports columns of the *Honolulu Star Bulletin* but in the public crime log whose headline read, "Sidelights of Police Court Scenes," as if those named there were actors in a light theater farce.

But Harvey Chilton's luck changed when one day he saw a fellow by the name of Warren Kealoha thrashing about in the surf and brought him to Rawlins's attention. Kealoha became a top-rate swimmer and went on to the Olympics, swimming for Chilton's newly formed club, the Hui Makani. And by the fall of 1939, when Bill Smith joined the ranks of the Hui against his will, Chilton was described as a man with the ability to see "great possibilities in others." Perhaps *that* was his talent, as he couldn't seem to develop such possibilities in himself.

Chilton grew into a flamboyant and ridiculous figure around town. By his mid-fifties he was bloated and wobbly, seemingly given to drink. He was pear-shaped, his head square as a wood block, his jowls sliding down the sides of his face as if the man were gradually but inexorably melting into himself. He dressed in fancy suits at least two sizes too small for his girth, and he walked around bulging or unbuttoned and in a pair of shoes that were flat and large, like the kind you'd find on a carny clown. The total effect was that of a figure misplaced in the world, someone who was better suited to camping it up under the lights of a burlesque show stage than strutting about with authority on a pool deck.

How he succeeded in developing Kealoha, and then young boys like Barney Pung, was a mystery. Chilton was short on discipline, inattentive to detail. He'd get the kids in the water, then order up a few exercises in the pool Monday through Friday for about an hour or two. It might have been that the laps in the Nat would strengthen just about anyone, and in the case of those with natural talent, it would strengthen them well above the capacity of the rest. Young Bill Smith was one of the naturally talented ones. In spite of his early illness and his resistance to his father's push, the kid began to swim pretty fast.

In his very first race for the Hui he'd cramped up toward the end of the mile swim, but by the end of the season, having just turned sixteen, he swam a junior division mile in an impressive 23 minutes and 2.3 seconds. It was a new Hawaiian record, and his closest tail had been a good 45 yards behind.

Smith hadn't paid attention to his pace or his improvement because Chilton hadn't. But in late May, after Smith broke the record, Chilton started to mouth off that Smith was going to do even better. Chilton could prove it. He called up the local AAU office and discovered to his amazement that Smith's time had already qualified him for the Men's Nationals. The kid was going to Santa Barbara, California, and the competition was less than a month away.

The AAU hadn't given Bill Smith money. He'd have to prove himself in Santa Barbara to warrant a wad of cash at the next Nationals; that was the way the AAU finances worked. It cost $185 for a round-trip from Honolulu to San Francisco, and even though the figure included train fare, food, and incidentals upon arrival in California, it was a heap for his father to gather together. Bill Sr. had recently been promoted to sergeant, but at a salary of only $2,400 a year; and he had a large, new family to care for—he had remarried a woman with children. He had to work hard to make the trip happen, and just as Smith Jr. boarded the boat and the band began to play "Aloha Oe," his father reminded him that the trip, while the boy had earned it, was a privilege, and that swimming with a great coach was a privilege, too.

Mr. Smith Comes to Maui

Everybody had a different version of how Bill Smith ended up living with Coach Sakamoto on Maui. The way that Bill told it, it was his father's idea. When Smith returned to Honolulu in the summer of 1940, all he'd wanted to do was get on the gridiron, but his father was dead set against the idea; Big Bill had played football in his youth but had a lifelong back injury that made him gun-shy about putting his son out on the field.

Therefore, Smith's father gave him no choice: swimming was the sport from now on. But his son was reticent at first. Sakamoto was, he'd seen, a strange sort of man. Quiet, solitary. At the pool, Smith found himself wondering why Sakamoto never talked to other coaches, why he was wound so tightly. And if he had to swim, he might as well stay on with Harvey Chilton, who didn't demand too much of him. True, he had learned ten times more about swimming in one week with Sakamoto than he had in a year with Chilton, but that wasn't any reason to go hog wild and do something crazy like his father had in mind.

At home Smith's father had moved his new family back up to the hills above Diamond Head, not a three-mile walk away from Smith's mother, whom Smith never saw. His father's new wife had three girls and a young son, so the house was filled with a crowd of six, including Bill and his sister. The two boys slept in bunk beds in one room and the girls in bunk beds in another.

Bill told the story two ways. In one he made it sound like he begged his father and Sakamoto to allow him to go to Maui. In another he enjoined Mitzi Higuchi to help. Whenever he, Mitzi, his father, and Sakamoto were at the Nat at the same time, he sent Mitzi running back and forth between his father and Coach. "Go talk to my father," he'd tell her. Then, "Go talk to Coach Sakamoto."

But Sakamoto remembered the whole affair in his own way. He believed Bill's father was, for reasons he never fully voiced, the driving force behind the move, not Bill. Sure, Bill had "suffered" under Chilton's coaching, and Sakamoto knew that he could do a better job to bring out more in the boy; he'd already done it at Santa Barbara. But there seemed to be something else, something more—as if Bill Sr. wanted to get the kid off of Oahu and away from a latchkey life. Sakamoto couldn't put his finger on it. Maybe it was just that Bill's father wanted a better day-to-day life for his son.

But for Sakamoto's part, the opportunity to have Bill Smith train with him every day was tempting. He saw potential in him in Santa Barbara. And Sakamoto faced impending loss. Bill Neunzig had decided to retire. Mike Peppe had begun wooing Keo. Benny Castor had already left Maui to take a job on some kind of secret "government project" in the Midway Islands.

It was more or less a mass exodus.

Sakamoto hoped it was the right thing to do: he said yes. It was decided. Bill Smith would come to Maui, live with Sakamoto's family, and train with him. He would attend Catholic school until the tenth grade—that was as far as it went on Maui—and then study at the new Baldwin High School. The arrangement pleased Bill Smith Sr., and the two men shook hands.

As soon as Bill Smith arrived on Maui, Sakamoto sat Smith down to give him the straight-up. He placed their chairs directly across from each other, and he stared into Smith's eyes with a piercing, inescapable attention.

"You want to be a world's champion?" he asked the boy.

"Yes," he said, a little surprised Coach would ask him.

He wasn't sure what Coach was getting at.

"Would you like to be like Keo Nakama?" Then Coach asked after a bit, "Would you like to be a very wonderful and modest person and a gentleman?"

"Yes," Smith answered. Of course this was what he wanted. This was why he'd come.

Then Sakamoto laid it out.

There was more to being a champion swimmer than just learning to swim well, he told Smith. To be a world champion like Keo, you had to be both modest and "gun ho," saying the term as he always thought it was pronounced, without the second "g." And you had to be a good listener. You had to always listen.

Smith nodded and nodded. He tried not to say anything, to just listen for now.

"You want to go to college?" Sakamoto asked.

Smith nodded again.

Because that was the focus of the club now. That was how the swimmers were going to get ahead. Win championships, be champions and real gentlemen. That way they would get scholarships on the Mainland.

Keo is going to go to the Mainland, he told Smith now. Mike Peppe wanted him to transfer immediately to Ohio State University, to leave Hawaii, to swim for one of the best college teams in the world.

"You do what I tell you to do," Sakamoto told him, "and you can be like Keo Nakama; you can have what he is having now."

Once the pool opened up again, Sakamoto designed Smith's daily practice schedule. It was torture bookended by a shower. It started with 5 minutes of calisthenics; 4 laps to loosen up, with Coach checking strokes; 72 laps freestyle; 50 laps backstroke; 36 laps kicking on back; 20 laps with inner tube, using only arm power; 10 laps on back, with inner tube; a 25-yard sprint; two 50-yard sprints; one 100-yard sprint; 600 yards paced; a 20-yard sprint.

Sakamoto started having him do two-lap swims, four-lap swims, and ten-lap swims two or three times a day, depending on whether school was in session. And before every practice, Sakamoto always gave him a full half hour of weight training.

Smith wasn't at all used to the weights. Chilton certainly hadn't required the use of them. And Sakamoto had developed even more sophisticated equipment in the past year. He had real barbells now instead of buckets with cement, real hand weights for curls. Sakamoto had also devised a pair of new machines; in addition to the wall pulley weights, there was a pulley bench and a leg machine. Coach had Smith lie on the bench, and the bench slid on wheels mounted on top of an angled frame.

The leg machine was on an angle and 10 to 15 feet long. With a body bench on wheels on top of a metal pipe frame, Smith had to push off the wall and slide down the frame and pull himself back again—not unlike the mechanism of a rowing machine but on a steeper incline. There was more.

A Tide in the Affairs of Men

Calisthenics included sit-ups to strengthen the abdominal muscles and push-ups as well. Then Sakamoto sent Smith and the other swimmers out onto the nearby quarter-mile track to run laps.

Sakamoto had also refined his swimmers' strokes. He made swimmers take two laps in the pool and then stop, during which time he let them rest but also critiqued their form. And everything was done by the pace clock. It was enormous, one-handed, and encased in a plywood box. Sakamoto said it was the swimmer's job to keep an eye on that clock at all times.

He'd also come up with a way not only to make his swimmers faster but also to ensure that they could jump into any competition pool knowing they would win. He worked them and worked them until their time was well under anyone else's. He and Bill, in particular, set goals. And then they set out to meet those goals.

They broke a 400 freestyle into four 100s, and they set the planned time with the intention of lowering and lowering it each time. Smith had to hit the marks, to make the correct number of strokes, achieve the planned pace and then go further. The advantage was that the faster your pace, Sakamoto said, the more time you have to rest in between each 100. Swim fast, rest. Swim hard, rest. Swim hardest and fastest, rest a little longer. Make your time lower and lower in each 100, and get a nice long relaxation period. Then you do the next 100.

Smith had to bring the time down until he earned the big rests, and then he had to pull it all together without stopping—four lightning-fast 100s. Smith got to rest after the race, after he had made his goal pace. Today, they call the practice "negative splits." But Sakamoto's name for it was "goals" and "sacrifices." You had a goal? You had to decide what "sacrifices" you were going to make to get there.

He kept a stopwatch. He used the metronome to set Smith's pace. He squeezed the pace from the metronome into Smith's hand, stroke, stroke, stroke, stroke, stroke. And he made Smith pay attention to another clock: the one inside his body. Smith had to count his heartbeats, keeping track of how the numbers rose and fell during a workout.

Sakamoto didn't think in variables, and he didn't let Bill Smith think in variables either. They had "absolutes." No wiggle room. They didn't talk about being sick or having a bad day. They talked about pace. And they talked about time all the time.

The days and nights became routine. School, practice, and then, on the way home from practice, Sakamoto dropped Charlie Oda off in Kahului; he was the kid with the longest walk and the least pocket money. Dinner, and then after that Sakamoto gave Smith "inspiration discussions," after which Sakamoto went into his room to watch the movies he had taken of swimmers. Alone.

Maui was an island, but it was more like a country town. At six o'clock everything closed up. At home, Smith continued to find Sakamoto and his family odd. Coach was the sort of man who could be lonesome even when in the company of others. He could laugh and play the ukulele for a crowd, be polite enough in company, but he was not one for small talk or joking.

He seemed to have organized his life around other people, and yet he was not fully comfortable or conversant with them. He rarely spoke, except to speak of swimming, and he never talked to the swimmers unless the subject was swimming or something to do with it. And he never spoke of himself, what he thought, what he felt, who he was, or anything about his past. Once in a while he might say, apropos of nothing, that he'd heard the trout were running in Maui's freshwater streams or that pheasants were on the slopes of Haleakala, but he never went on from there, and Smith just sort of figured that Sakamoto was a genius and that all geniuses were a little offbeat.

For his part, Sakamoto tried to restrain himself from being a coach to Bill all the time. He tried to don the role of nurturing father, advising him about rest, homework. And he genuinely meant well. He wanted Smith to succeed in school; having a swimmer actually live with him made him ever more aware of the engulfing quality of the life he had created for the team. He meant to leave time for Bill to study. He knew Bill was tired, and he watched him fall asleep before he even had time to open his books. He felt bad about that. Once, he even told Smith that after they left the swimming pool, they weren't to think of swimming, but of other things. But that never happened. All they did was talk of swimming.

Swimming, after all—Sakamoto believed—was a means to an end: to travel, a free college education, a job later, and a better life. Bill was listening. He started to step it up, not just in the pool, either. Soon, he started wearing a tie to school. Other boys did so, too, but when Bill Smith dressed up, it was a big deal. Usually he wore just a pair of wide-wale corduroys, a thin white belt he sometimes forgot to buckle up, and a T-shirt and bare feet.

In turn, Sakamoto began to take Smith more seriously. Sometimes he took out his home movies and made Smith watch them, too. And it wasn't passive watching but close looks at everything. Sakamoto had taken miles of film of world champions wherever he had traveled, and he broke down every moment of every performance to Smith. He said that you have to pay attention to the subtleties, not so much in what others do, but in what you can learn from them and apply to your own swimming.

Sakamoto continually pressed Smith for what he wished to achieve. Did he want to break the Hawaiian record in the 100-meter free? If he did, then Sakamoto pointed out the path. Do you want to break the world record in the 400-meter free? If he did, then Sakamoto pointed out how to get there. For every aspiration, there was a path to follow.

Smith and Coach were now family. Smith felt Sakamoto was a father to him and found he didn't miss his father or even think about home. And he didn't think about his mother at all. Sakamoto took Bill Smith on as "son" and "brother." He started calling him "Brother" or "Brother Bill." He didn't say why, but it felt like the right thing to call the boy. Then he started calling him the more pidgin "Brada." Coach might have called him a brother, but all the kids took to calling him something even sweeter. First, he was known as "Brala." But when that didn't seem quite enough, his moniker became "La-La." That would be his nickname from now on.

The Sakamotos lived in a three-bedroom house with what was now a family of four children: Raymond, Donald, Janice, and little Rene, an adopted baby. With Smith joining them, it would be something of a squeeze, but they could manage. Janice had been sleeping in a little storage room, just behind the garage and right off the furo. They moved her into the house proper, and made room for Smith back there instead. The space was ample. Sakamoto ordered a big enough bed for the six-foot Smith. He ordered a dresser and mirror as well. And the closet, though small, was sufficient to hold Smith's few belongings.

In a relatively short life, Bill Smith had already had three families, each so very different from the others. His first had been with his mother and father and sister Leilani, but it hadn't been a family like those that lived on the same street in the same neighborhood as they. His mother had been aloof. She was a woman quite before her time, with two careers: the first during the day as a schoolteacher and the second at night as a performer in a women's musical group, her most passionate commitment, which didn't make her the sort of woman who would do what was expected of her.

The second family had not been without discipline or order—his father was a strong presence and a good influence—but it had been something of a loose and unbounded existence, living in rented houses, eating in restaurants all the time, hanging out at the beach. The third family had not really been Smith's. When his father had remarried, Bill was old enough to know that, regardless of how warmly his stepmother welcomed him, he didn't really belong.

The Sakamoto family was something else entirely. For a man who liked Hawaiian music and Hawaiian life, Coach's family was old-school Japanese. Coach did nothing around the house; he barely spoke to his children or to Mary. And Mary bore the weight of everything. She cooked—very well: the family joked about Smith's appetite, saying that any meal with Bill Smith was a 400-meter eating event.

Mary cleared the dishes. She washed them. She drew the furo for her husband, steamy, ready every night, even when he came home late. All Sakamoto did was wipe his automobile down every day with a wet and soap-less sponge until it looked brand-new, in "A-1 condition." When Bill offered to help clear the table or to help Missus weed the yard, Coach told him that he shouldn't. One day, though, Smith came home to find Missus literally digging a hole with a pick and shovel, working through dirt and rocks; he began to help her, and after they were done, they put a roof on it and covered the roof with rocks and dirt, and he helped Missus stock it with food and gallons of water.

Yet another family to which Bill Smith now belonged, even if that family had been effectively stripped of its name, was the 3YSC. Smith hadn't expected that when he signed on to train with Coach he was signing on to much more. Most everyone was under the impression that for all intents and purposes, the club had vanished along with the hopes of the 1940 Games, never mind being erased by Damkroger. The patch sewn on the front of his fellow teammates' one-piece swimsuits read "Maui."

Soichi Sakamoto wanted to ensure that the group would bond. On the first day of practice with Smith, he announced the formation of the "We Stick Club," a club within the club. He gathered the team together, and he explained what the new club was. *We stick together no matter what.* And everybody had to have a personal goal. Everybody had to write that goal down on a piece of paper, and then Sakamoto sealed it in an envelope and hid it away. The initiation ceremony involved blindfolding them, which Bill found odd, and then Sakamoto held out a long bamboo stick for each to hold on to. He told them to grab the stick and had them say "We Stick," vowing their allegiance to the team and to the vision of great swimming they had always had and would always have in the future.

That wasn't Bill Smith's only initiation, though. He got to swim in the ditch. When he arrived, there was some kind of contagion in the pool, and for safety's sake, Sakamoto had to shut the tank down and drain it. It would take about a week to drain it, clean it properly, and fill it back up before anybody could get in again, so Sakamoto had his swimmers practice in the ditch one more time. It made Bill feel like a real member of the club. And soon, he saw, the other members easily accepted him. He clearly could swim, after all; he'd joined the Hawaii contingent at Santa Barbara with records already under the belt of his Jantzen swimsuit. He had "whipped" the club's Honolulu competition, and at the Nationals he'd further proven himself to have potential. He wasn't the brightest, but neither was he a hardhead or hollow head like Halo. He was simple, straightforward, and modest in spirit, and he didn't swagger around and bowl down every pin in his path.

Keo, heading off to the University of Hawaii for his freshman year, gave a quiet nod to Smith. He could leave the island knowing that he wasn't leaving the club completely: he'd still swim under the team banner in Honolulu and on the road with the gang, his points adding to the club's kitty. And he mollified his regret in leaving Maui by knowing that his replacement in the middle- and long-distance events was solid.

Halo didn't bother to nod, but Smith likely didn't notice. Halo was headed to UH with Keo, and he was busy getting out of town. Ever since the trip to Germany, he'd been itching to get off the island, to have the bigger life he felt he had earned by swimming well. The world was much larger than Pu'unene, and not only were the pools of grander scale, but he had also come to believe that he belonged in the racing lanes with university and club swimmers like those with whom he'd traveled—the big boys in the big leagues. But when applying to the University of Hawaii, he was stunned to discover that he was considered "academically retarded," in the words of the university. He knew he wasn't stupid; the fault lay with Coach. Sakamoto, who always made sure others did their homework at the pool, had never insisted that Halo do his. Instead, he'd always have Halo in the water working harder than anyone else and telling him not to slack off in swim training. Why hadn't Sakamoto paid as much attention to his education?

Why hadn't Coach released him long ago, perhaps to Punahou, where he would have gotten a better education? If Halo had gone to Punahou, then maybe Bob Kiphuth, who had encouraged Halo so much, would have taken Halo on as a student at Yale. After all, hadn't Kiphuth shown his interest in him in Germany in 1938? "Keep 1940 in mind all the time," Kiphuth had written on the back of Halo's etching of the Brandenburg Gate. It was code that Kiphuth had wanted Halo to come to Yale and train there for the

Olympic Games, instead of on Maui. If only Halo had known. He was sure that during all these years Coach Sakamoto had kept him on Maui for a selfish reason: in order to build his—Coach's—own reputation. Whenever opportunities arose for Halo it was Coach who stood in his way. Keo was Coach's favored son; he always had been. Coach had pushed Keo to get a scholarship at OSU, but he hadn't done the same for him. Favoritism. From then on, Halo always had a bitter taste in his mouth about Soichi Sakamoto and nearly everything that had happened in the 3YSC.

Chapter Fourteen

BLITZKRIEG

THE ADVENT of the Duke Kahanamoku meets in 1937 had changed the Hawaiian swim season so dramatically that by 1941, it was hardly recognizable. For years, June had been the single month in the calendar for meets. In those days, even in the driest spell in Hawaii swimming, a local could look forward to attending at least two Hawaiian AAUs in the late spring. The AAUs were the climax of the season, when swimmers vied to qualify for the national championship meets on the Mainland.

But when Keo Nakama beat Ralph Gilman in the first Duke Kahanamoku Outdoor Meet in 1937, things started to change, and fast. The Duke meets, both the indoor and the outdoor, added almost another two weeks of cheerful spectatorship, the first at Waterhouse Pool at Punahou and the second at the Nat. Then things went wild from there.

The success of the Three-Year Swim Club led to meet after meet after meet—and not just small ones, but meets of prodigious size and importance. With each successive national headline the club made and each national championship title it won, the number of planned or spontaneous invitationals, spectacular dual meets, or special-occasion competitions grew exponentially. From May to August of 1941, the Territory's swim fans might as well have glued their behinds to the bleachers at the Waterhouse, the Nat, and any other swim venue to be found—including open-water ones—and swimmers might have been better off sleeping in their bathing suits. It was high noon after the dawn of the Second Golden Age of Hawaiian swimming.

A Tide in the Affairs of Men

By 1940, the 3YSC had already copped two men's national team championships (Detroit and Santa Barbara), broken American and world records at home and abroad, and in the women's events had two national titles, from Fujiko Katsutani's two-year 200-meter breaststroke wins and Chic Miyamoto's spectacular individual medley crown at the Portland Nationals. Day and night, Aussie, American, Canadian, and British aqua stars started steaming into port on the Matson line's white fleet, looking to test their skills against the increasing prowess of a whole new generation of Hawaiians.

In the spring of 1941, Maui's swimmers were readying themselves for a packed season. Ever dissatisfied with the few opportunities for competition that his kids had had on the Valley Isle, Soichi Sakamoto continued with a whole system of preseason "practice" meets that he crammed into the schedule between January and March, and then when the season itself began in March, he created even more in-the-water opportunities for the club. All that time in the water—in addition to daily practice—was paying off.

Bill Smith's life was a total-immersion swimming experience, whether he was in the Camp 5 pool or at the Sakamoto dinner table. His nightly in-house "tutorials" had him living the sport in his waking hours and in his sleep.

Sakamoto had developed for Smith a new training regimen, the intricacy and intensity of which was likely unprecedented in the history of swimming.

It was a twice-a-day routine, with each session consisting of 5 minutes of calisthenics, 4 laps, a stroke check, 6 slow laps, 72 fast laps, 30 slow laps of inner-tube arm stroking, slowly, then 4 fast inner-tube laps, 4 fast-kicking laps with a board, and 1 fast-kicking lap for a time trial with the board—just to *start*. Then there were 10 more laps, then 20 laps just for practicing turns and push-offs or open turns, then 6 laps for starting (diving in) and for fast finishing. Sakamoto liked to emphasize making fast dive-in starts off the blocks and also keeping the stroke intact toward the end of the race instead of panicking and going to pieces in the last 10 yards when fatigue would weigh heavily. In order to practice pace and hitting the wall, the next part of the routine was hitting the wall, doing a 100-yard sprint, then two repeats of 50, then two repeats of 25 yards, timed. At the end, for good measure, it was 600 yards for endurance.

Blitzkrieg

To make matters more complicated, Sakamoto broke down Smith's 600 endurance yards to maximize the benefits. He had benchmarks for his new swimmer: at 25 yards into the 600, he wanted Smith to be at 11.8. At 50 yards, he wanted him to be paced at 26.8. Next was 100 yards—56.8—and 220 yards—2:17.8.

And there was more. At 440 yards, Smith was to hit 4:46.4. At 500 yards, it was 5:26. And at 600, Sakamoto wanted him to hit 6:37 on the nose, a set of requirements after meeting which most swimmers of that era would have dropped dead. The workout ended with a taper of 6 laps Sakamoto put in for Smith to cool down, but all in all, Smith was doing 3.3 miles, or 5,825 yards, of swimming twice a day.

Smith's preseason paces, unsurprisingly, far exceeded the expectations of any members of the Hawaiian press, not to mention Soichi Sakamoto's. Smith's month of April was simply off the charts. He cut his time in every freestyle event in which he was training, and he did it methodically, second-by-second and day-by-day, as if he were whittling a plank of wood down to a toothpick, at times not twenty-four hours passing without a direct Smith assault on the time clock. One Saturday afternoon, for example, he swam a 100-yard freestyle time trial at a more than respectable 54.1 seconds, and then, after a good night's sleep and a meal or two, he was back in the water on Sunday cutting at least half a second off the previous day's pace.

In the course of a single meet during the preseason, he'd approach a territorial record in the heats, coming at it with his teeth bared, and by the final of the event on the same day, he'd have bitten the head right off it. As May approached Smith came so close in practice to Jack Medica's Olympic and world records in the 400-meter freestyle that he had to remind himself that there was nothing mechanically amiss with his stopwatch. Keo had equaled the 400 record; Bill was likely to better it.

It was the 400-meter that Sakamoto knew would be Smith's métier, and his regime for Smith was as specific as it got to make it so: Sakamoto's target time for Smith was 4:39 in practice, and Sakamoto set the pace as thus: At 50 yards, Smith should be at 25.8. At 100 yards, he should hit 55 seconds. At 200 yards, he should be just 1 second shy of 2 minutes at 1:59; at 220 yards, 2 minutes and 12 seconds; and then at the 400 mark—before the 40-yard sprint to the finish—he was supposed to arrive, still breathing, at a nice 4:12, and then hit the 4:39 like no one's business.

With one eye closed, Sakamoto could see it coming. The boy had become a real swimmer in the past six months, toned, exchanging fat for muscle, exchanging laxity for precision and a lack of care for commitment. Now Billy "La-La" Smith was perfectly poised to announce himself as the new Hawaiian swim king that spring, and all anyone had to do was set him at the edge of a Honolulu pool and pull the trigger on the starting gun.

Smith's official debut of the '41 season was in a dual meet against the University of Hawaii big boys in the Puʻunene Athletic Club pool. Keo Nakama, studying then at UH, had intended to sail over for the competition—and it would have been a fun one, too, to see the old teammates race—but he had been struck with a sudden case of appendicitis and was recovering in the hospital. Even without Keo there, though, the crowd got a show. Smith swam a thrilling 220-yard freestyle against Halo Hirose, who was swimming for the Rainbows now. In that matchup, Halo Hirose kept decent pace for the first 25 yards, but then La-La pulled away to win by a margin of about ten strokes. Before Halo even had the wall in sight, Smith hit it. Smith's mark of 2:10.4 not only broke Keo Nakama's standing territorial record of 2.11 by a second and a half, but it also took Smith's own pace in the event down by a full 2 seconds from a time trial he'd done just one week before.

Up next for Smith and the club was a little trip to Honolulu for an impromptu battle with some of the best swimmers in the States. Paul Herron, Adolph Kiefer, and Tom Haynie stopped by with frequent visitor, Coach Stan Brauninger, and freestyler Otto Jaretz happened to be on the same boat. The setup was a battle at the Nat during the first week of May, followed by a repeat battle at Punahou just one week later.

J. Lyman Bingham, vice president of the Amateur Athletic Union, also just happened to be breezing through the Territory on a trip to assess the islands' track and swim team programs. Local AAU officials planned to wine and dine Bingham, fly him to Molokai, and tour him around Hana, but the highlight of his trip was an unplanned coincidence: watching Sakamoto's boys meet up with Brauninger's crew.

Jaretz, Kiefer, and Stan Brauninger, with a load of other swimmers, arrived on the *Matsonia* a week before the first meet, and they practiced over at Punahou for a few days while Smith and the club prepared at home. Smith and company took a Sunday night interisland steamer over the day before the trials, and as they did, the presses at all the Honolulu newspapers were rolling out sentences that all sounded alike: young Billy Smith was coming home from Maui to face "the stiffest competition of his life." That kind of public relations material was like honey for the crowd, and Wednesday the seventh of May turned out to be the date of one of the sweetest and most satisfying swim meets for fans in Hawaiian history.

No fewer than twenty-five athletes represented the Three-Year Swim Club; Sakamoto's ranks were thick with kids in both the novice and the men's and women's divisions, and he had boys and girls in nearly equal measure. Not only would the up-and-comers in the club get a chance to compete, but they'd also see the impact of Sakamoto's coaching on their teammates.

Jose Balmores had, just the weekend before, smoked the backstroke and breaststroke events in the preseason. His 150-yard backstroke was at 1:44.2. In the women's division from Maui, Chic Miyamoto was becoming a freestyle whiz, and Mitzi Higuchi could outswim anyone she wanted to in the individual medley; while 100-pound Fujiko Katsutani was still the heavyweight champ in the women's breaststroke.

It was kismet; the alignment of planets; a conspiracy of the gods to wow mere mortals; or maybe the Natatorium's caretaker, Wally Napoleon, had poured magic into the water that night instead of blue rock, but whatever did it, record after record fell, and, with equal opportunity, visitors and locals knocked on history's door all night.

Otto Jaretz did away with Johnny Weissmuller's 1922 80-yard freestyle record in a time of 40.3. Adolph Kiefer broke his own world record in the 150-yard backstroke, bringing his 1937 time from 1:37.2 all the way down to 1:35.6. Then Kiefer topped that stunt by breaking yet another mark—also a world record—the 1938 100-yard backstroke mark once held by the swimmer Albert Vande Weghe. Kiefer pulled back Vande Weghe's number of 1:02 to an astonishing 1:00.4.

Chic Miyamoto broke two Hawaiian records: In the 100-meter backstroke event, she conquered Toyo Takeyama's 1939 mark of 1:27 with a blazing 1:23.2. In the 300-meter individual medley, she eclipsed the 1929 record of none other than the infamous Eleanor Holm. Holm's record had stood at 4:49.8 for twelve years, and in one night Chic Miyamoto came in at 4:40, nearly 10 seconds shaved off the record. It was Chic's best outing to date, and her performance said loud and clear that she'd be headed to the Women's Nationals that summer in High Point, North Carolina. Then Honolulu ace Carlos Rivas smashed yet another Hawaiian mark, this one in the men's individual medley, stealing the 1931 astronaut's helmet from the head of Olympian Buster "Buck Rogers/Flash Gordon" Crabbe. Rivas took the film star's mark of 4:05.8 and replaced it with a searing 4:01.5.

It would have been hard to find a fan in the stands at the Nat who wasn't ecstatic, but it wouldn't have been at all difficult to point out the night's nervous Nellies: Bill Smith Sr. was in the crowd, and Soichi Sakamoto was on deck.

Bill Smith Jr. was calm as a cuke. He was loose and happy; his seventeenth birthday was a week away, and the night had already been splendid. What he was about to do was less a test for him than for the two older men. Bill Sr. often wondered if he'd done the right thing in sending his only son off to Maui to become a star, and Soichi Sakamoto wanted to see if his own foster-fathering had done the trick.

A still-sweet-sixteen Bill Smith Jr. vindicated both his dads that night. In a single race he changed both the course of swimming history and the history of the 3YSC. In a race to the chase, in the 400-meter freestyle, side by side with Tom Haynie, Paul Herron, and Otto Jaretz, Smith stole in one dazzling gesture Olympian Jack Medica's standing world and American records. Medica's 4:44.5 was now in Smith's hands at 4:44.1.

Sakamoto watched as Stan Brauninger looked on in astonishment. He knew that Brauninger respected him; he knew that over time the Chicago coach had seen Sakamoto's boys improve. But now, Sakamoto saw that Brauninger couldn't quite contain himself: Billy Smith was Sakamoto's latest prodigy, a curly-haired kid from paradise who, at only sixteen, made two standing records disappear right before Stan Brauninger's eyes. When Brauninger could pick his lower jaw up off the deck and reattach it to his face, he hurried over to Sakamoto and told him that Bill Smith was going to be the best swimmer in the world. He hadn't seen anything like him since he'd discovered Kiefer. No high schooler was supposed to be able to move through the water the way Smith did.

And Brauninger had a brilliant idea. If Smith was on a roll, why not see just how many records he could break? How about a shot at every freestyle mark in history and then some? He wanted to put Smith in the pool the following week and do time trials at every single distance they could think up, from those in the books to those that had never yet been inked there, and Sakamoto was game. In a week's time, his newly adopted son would have a chance to swim at Punahou's Waterhouse Pool in every freestyle event, including those with non-citizen American records, American citizen records, and world records, not to mention Olympic records as well.

After that, everybody needed a rest except Bill Smith. Even just a few nights after Brauninger's wacky suggestion, the kid went on to break two more records; first, the American mark in the 200-meter freestyle alongside Haynie, Herron, and Jaretz with a time of 2:10.9, and then against the Brauninger clan in the 800-meter freestyle, Smith stole Ralph Flanagan's 1936 American record—Des Moines, 10:07—and owned it now in Waikiki at 10:03.

All that week, Sakamoto had Smith stay in Honolulu, working out in preparation for Punahou, and on that Friday night, the young Smith's seventeenth birthday, Brauninger, Sakamoto, and a crowd of thousands watched a competition that might as well have been the first ever Mr. Smith vs. Mr. Smith Swimming Extravaganza.

An extravaganza it was indeed; Brauninger clocked the boy at every

A Tide in the Affairs of Men

interval he could think of: distances from 50, 100, and 200 for yards and meter lengths at 400, 500, 600, and on up through 1,500. There was a 25-foot mark and a 25-yard mark, too; a 500-meter; a 600- and 700-meter, a 780-yard event; and an even-numbered 1,000-yard swim. That night, Smith proved he was swimming's greatest rising star since Duke Kahanamoku: he broke world records Olympian Jack Medica had set back in 1934, and he clipped 3 seconds off the world mark for the 880-yard freestyle; he cut 3 seconds off the 900-yard freestyle and almost 4 seconds off the 1,000. In the sprints, he clipped 3 seconds off the 55-yard world's mark, and the night went on and on until the crowd was spinning in their seats. When all the times had been properly recorded, Stanley Brauninger was dizzy. He pulled out his hankie, wiped his brow, and exclaimed, "If there are any other records around, they had better be locked up good and tight in a safe." Soichi Sakamoto knew that Brauninger was right.

There was no doubt now that Bill Smith Jr. was the reincarnation of Duke Kahanamoku. He shared his heritage, his height, and his weight. He was loose-limbed, plenty rugged, healthy, and Hawaiian. At Duke Kahanamoku's height—a twin-like 6 feet 2 inches—it was almost all too perfect. Even Smith's father was a cop like Kahanamoku's, and Smith was Mormon like Kahanamoku, too.

American swimming was ripe for a new hero, and the nation's newspapers and magazines knew what to do with one when they found him. The first half of the twentieth century had seen the rise of a new kind of sportswriting in America called "Gee Whiz" journalism, perfect for depicting—and creating—the nation's athletic legends: the then-unblemished sports heroes such as Babe Ruth, Ty Cobb, Knute Rockne, Bill Tilden, and Duke Kahanamoku, whose stories were capable of capturing an entire nation's fascination. Readers in the United States came to expect on their doorsteps every morning a sports page as full of hyperbole as a balloon with helium. The most peerless of all the "Gee Whiz"-ers was a reporter by the name of Grantland Rice, who ran a syndicated column called "The Sportslight" (picked up in some 250 papers nationwide) and who once proclaimed that "when a sportswriter stops making heroes out of athletes, it's time to get out of business." The apogee of the form was in the '20s and '30s, and in the spring of 1941 plenty of Rice imitators were still on the job, just in time to make legends of the members and the coach of the Three-Year Swim Club. Sakamoto's scrappy ditch swimmers arrived on the scene straight out of central casting, and no one was more perfect for the leading role than William Melvin Smith Jr.

Smith was a sportswriter's—and a nation's—dream. From the beginning of his life, he had all the personal makings of a legend, but at that historically preconscious moment in the spring in 1941—war in the Pacific, in Smith's own backyard, would begin in the islands at the end of that year—he was perfectly poised to be embraced by America, and reporters nationwide swatted at their typewriter keys and composed a story called "The Bill Smith Myth."

The usual calculus for the American sports hero included talent, a great backstory, and a big and quirky personality, and Bill Smith was positively formulaic. He was also both comfortably familiar and more than a little exotic. He was a mixed-race kid whose bloodlines called for reams of newsprint, an American moniker and a Pacific Island nickname: "Malolo," meaning the "Flying Fish." In the hands of sports reporters, Bill Smith Sr. became an Irish cop who hailed from urban Detroit, and Smith's mother became a dark-haired *waihine*, or island woman, with mysterious ways. Bill Sr. was always responsibly out on the beat in urban Waikiki while the Mrs. was back home at the hut doing native things; and Smith's magical, multicultural alliance had made it possible for the boy to have risen from death like Lazarus—a properly Christian image with a twist of island hooey.

Photographers started dragging the estranged divorced couple out into the light, posing them together beside their son and asking the entire family to sit barefoot in the grass and perform "war chants" or "soft hulas." Newspapers and national magazines carried the remarkable story of Smith's return from the brink of death, his ascent from "the crippled ... wonder boy," whom typhoid had wasted to nothing. According to journalists, disease had reduced the kid to a "hopeless weakling" with "not a strand of hair on his brown head," who would have died—in the words of *Collier's* magazine—if his "tribal mother...wise in the ancient practices of her race" hadn't "slowly, lovingly massaged" her son with coconut oil and held him in the "blue green waves" off Diamond Head until his limbs came back to life again. The story was largely the same wherever it appeared, only sometimes it was Smith's father who took the boy to the beach at Waikiki, laying him down on a reed mat in the sun or teaching him how to float upon a surfboard. Sometimes, for good measure, either Bill Sr. or Mrs. Smith was credited for giving Bill Jr. "life-saving blood transfusions."

As for Smith's coach, newspapers and magazines had a field day. Americans were more than a little prickly about Japanese-Americans at that precise moment, so sportswriters made of Sakamoto a slightly comedic, slightly menacing caricature: a "wily" Japanese with "diabolical" contraptions; a samurai-type who kept Billy Smith on a diet of fruits and vegetables and an exercise regimen of eight hours a day. Smith's teammates were "ditch-wrigglers," rendered harmless as enemies on the battlefield but made quaintly formidable in a swimming pool. That summer, the Three-Year Swim Club story was everywhere—in every newspaper and major magazine, from *Time* to *Newsweek*.

They may have been an entertaining story for others, but as the group headed off to the Men's and the Women's Nationals, they felt they had become a family to one another for the first time. The Maplewood/High Point trip was the first one on which Sakamoto took a horde of boys and girls together; in previous years, the Men's and the Women's Nationals had never been scheduled in a way that allowed for a shared trip. In 1938, Sakamoto didn't have a team of girls; in 1939, the squad had been all boys except for Fujiko, who headed off to Des Moines. The 1940 Santa Barbara Men's Championships were early and the women's were late in Portland. But now, the club was traveling in full-force, the core group now including some from Honolulu, too, including Bill Smith.

Sakamoto and Missus both traveled on this trip, a kind of mother and father with their brood. Missus became a sympathetic ear for the teenage concerns the swimmers had never been able to share with Coach; in the past when they'd approached him about anything emotional, they'd been rebuffed. "Oh, no, no, no," Coach Sakamoto used to say to them. "Don't let it bother you." But with Missus, they could be lovesick, homesick, optimistic, worried. It didn't matter; she was there.

On the boat, they ran down the narrow corridors, laughing and talking in loud voices. Missus looked over the "day's activities" card each morning with them, choosing what they'd do on board. Coach kicked himself for having forgotten to reserve deck chairs for the group, but he opened up his stateroom for daily meetings to strategize about the coming competitions.

On the train they kept themselves entertained by playing cards and rushing back and forth between their seats and the club or dining car. Missus busied herself counting up money and balancing the team's books; Coach absorbed himself in studying the rules and regulations handbook of the AAU and memorizing his swimmers' times.

At Maplewood, they took up residence in a tourist court, a cross between a trailer park and a motor hotel, settling into an on-the-road way of life as if it were the one they lived all the time at home. Missus shopped for food: enough fruit juice for many thirsty mouths, pounds of tomatoes, peaches, eggs, and loaves of bread—she found the prices mostly reasonable and was pleased that a milkman delivered five gallons to their door each morning—and she cooked the meals outdoors and washed the dishes and pots in a makeshift sink beside a rough-hewn wooden countertop, tending to all of the children, and her husband, as if she were their mother.

Maplewood had greeted the Maui family like a group of dignitaries, the reception as full of pomp as the one that Soichi Sakamoto and the Maui Boy Scouts received in 1930 in Japan. The swimmers were celebrities, rainmakers, and oddities, and local officials and an enormous crowd swarmed them at the train station. They were also the featured guests in a two-hour-long parade, in which no fewer than fifteen identical gleaming convertibles lined up in the streets with a squad of Maplewood beauty queens, an entourage of local police, and banners flying everywhere. One of the swimmers was lucky enough to get to ride on the back of a policeman's motorcycle, holding on to the cop with one hand and with the other carrying a loaf of bread someone in the crowd had offered as a gift. The parade took them on a tour of the great sights of St. Louis, from the very place where Lewis and Clark had begun their expedition west to Sportsman's Park, where that summer Stan Musial played in the outfield and pitcher Mort Cooper chewed aspirin during every game.

Their swimming reputations preceded them: Bill Smith's sweet-sixteen exploits in May in particular drew reporters closer and closer, fixating on the team's strangeness with magnifying glasses. No matter how ignorant reporters' questions could be, each swimmer worked hard to be polite. Mary, especially, tried to hold her tongue when faced with an offensive question or assumption about Hawaiian life. "Rice eaters," the swimmers were called in headlines, and their great swimming was thought to be the result of the island voodoo food. "We also eat potatoes just like you do," Mary once shot back when yet another reporter remarked on the heaping bowls of rice on their lunchtime table.

The papers' photographers took pictures of the group when they were eating: all crowded together in a nook just big enough for a skinny four-foot-tall Frigidaire and a rickety table piled high with toast and vegetables and meat. And rice, of course. They took pictures of Mother Mary cleaning up, all while wearing a bathing suit in the print of ferns and orchids, or with her hair pulled back with a flower behind her ear, or while she was hanging the swimmers' suits from a rope laundry line that she'd strung cleverly between two shady maple trees.

They took a picture of Halo chomping on a slice of summer watermelon, eating it in what the caption said was "Hawaiian style," right off the rind; of Sakamoto striding about in long pants and a white sleeveless T-shirt; of Bill Smith shirtless and in unbelted, unbuttoned corduroys. And the reporters never failed to point out to their newfound friends that not too far down Manchester Avenue from the tourist court stood a bar called Johnny Ryan's Pub, which offered a drink called the "Hawaiian Cooler, a concoction mixed by expert barmen," that was delivered to one's table accompanied by a lei.

Blitzkrieg

Both the Maplewood pool and the High Point pool were segregated, and the cities around them, too. Maplewood's tank was supposed to contain water so pure that you could drink it, and it was divided up in perfect little lines with bright white cork balls floating on the surface. The kids had grown to dislike the segregated buses so much that sometimes, just like a big gang of brothers and sisters, they put Charlie Oda out on the road to hitchhike and hid behind some brush until a car stopped. When the driver—white— saw a whole horde of strangers rushing toward his vehicle, he peeled off as fast as he could go. It gave them no end of pleasure and fed the stories they would take home and tell for years.

The suspenseful buildup to the meet was extraordinary. Maplewood would include not only championship but also open events; both men and women would compete over four days; and every defending champion was on deck to hold on to his or her crown; and the proceedings, like the welcome at the train station and the parade throughout the city, were grander than at any other Nationals event Sakamoto had ever seen.

To start the program on opening day, a bugle blew, the American flag flew, and organizers let go a dozen doves—it turns out they were actually squabs bought at a local poultry market and unable to swim past the boundaries of the pool—that were meant to announce to all the world that St. Louis was host to one of the greatest swim meets in America.

Mary and Sakamoto dressed up for the event, Mary in a pretty pleated skirt, a pair of white heels with little bows on them, and a white pukka shell necklace; Coach wore a pair of cuffed pants and a straw hat and, as always, had his movie camera slung over his shoulder.

Independence Day had been a month before, but the Maplewood pool was still decked out in red, white, and blue bunting hung in intervals along the stone walls of the bathhouse, and in the box seats and bleachers, the gallery was gaily dressed as if for a holiday.

Maplewood marked the team's fourth national championship meet in as many years: there'd been Louisville in '38, Des Moines and Detroit in '39,

A Tide in the Affairs of Men

Santa Barbara and Portland in '40. The previous summer in Santa Barbara there had seemed to be a pall over events and an absence of friendly faces, but now the group felt more welcoming again with Mike Peppe of OSU and Stanley Brauninger. The same officials were there as always: Larry Johnson of the AAU was a referee, as well as Max Ritter, with whom Halo had traveled during the 1938 Germany trip. What had happened in the course of just a few years was remarkable not only in terms of the swimmers' achievements but also in the feeling of community they now had beyond Pu'unene, beyond Maui and Hawaii. They were part of something larger now, part of a society of swimmers.

On August 8, Maplewood was 100 degrees in the shade in the bleachers, but by the time the trials began in the evening, a crowd of some four thousand had shown up for the festivities. The pool was a boiling pot of water: even though officials claimed that they had drained it so that it would be cooler, it was reported that the 480,000 gallons in it were a "sun-cooked" 85 degrees.

In Louisville, Sakamoto hadn't had enough critical mass—just Halo and Keo—to have won team points, but after Detroit and Santa Barbara, Maui had won team championships with figures previously unheard of. At Maplewood, they exceeded their team points, holding on to the championship but with an unprecedented, excessive, and record-breaking 71 team points, 50 full points ahead of the second-place team, Chicago, with 21.

In the 400-meter freestyle, Bill won at 4:47.6, coming in along the cork with Keo 10 yards behind, then Bunny and Charlie following, in that order. The boys took the 800-meter freestyle relay final, and Keo Nakama, recently recovered from his appendectomy, shaved .8 of a second off Ralph Flanagan's 1935 1,500-meter freestyle time. Jose stroked to first place in the 300-meter medley race, besting Adolph Kiefer's 1940 time.

When the affair concluded with a beauty pageant in which a queen was crowned—the winner awarded first place for personality, charm, and figure, among other attributes, and the runners-up compensated with $10 and $15 each—the men got on the train back west, bringing with them their third national championship in as many years. In Maplewood they had been so beloved that one family by the name of Keshner—owners of a Black Angus cattle ranch called "The Good Earth"—promised to name their son after one of the club's swimmers. The couple hadn't had a child yet, and no, they weren't expecting. But when they did, they said, they'd name him "Keo" Keshner.

They had never been more successful, more integrated, more celebrated, or happier than they were at Maplewood. They were the 3YSC again, forever now, together, inseparable, unstoppable—"all for one and one for all," as Coach had always said.

As the men of the 3YSC headed west, the women went south on their way to High Point. The North Carolina town was a thriving hive of nearly fifty thousand people whose lives were organized around hosiery, furniture, and other manufacture; and as much action as there was at the swim tank, there was more entertainment all around when the girls were out of uniform: informal teas, watermelon cutting parties, Southern barbecues, and a visit to the R. J. Reynolds Tobacco Company. It was the women's version of a close encounter of the Southern kind.

Mary Sakamoto played ukulele for the crowds. Chic, who was dubbed a "pretty Maui Miss," retained her medley title on the first day of competition, and the rest hadn't done too shabbily either, Fujiko holding on to her 220-yard breaststroke event and Toyo placing admirably in backstroke. When the meet was done, they first took a train down to New Orleans before heading west to catch up with the boys in Los Angeles. The last competition on the trip was called "the Hawaiian Islands vs. the Pacific Coast Championships," a showdown between Mainlanders and their brothers from the Territory.

That summer was both wonderful and strange. It was wonderful to be loved, and it was strange to be attended to with such curiosity, which seemed to have its foundation in something more than wonder. To the press, diver

A Tide in the Affairs of Men

Sammy Lee of Occidental College was a "gum-chewing Korean." Bill Smith was a "kinky, red-haired Hawaiian (English) fellow," who might have been a curious island water sprite but who was also somehow solidly American. *Time* magazine called the "Nakamo [*sic*] brothers" heroes on "the flashiest team seen in the U.S." in many years. And in the *LA Times*, Dick Hyland wrote about the group: "It's probably odd for a native Californian...to think too highly of the Japanese," but "then there are Japanese and there are Japanese."

But there was something magical about Maplewood, what would turn out to be the team's third and last national title of their youth. There, Soichi Sakamoto experienced something that he had never experienced before: the feeling that he himself was part of a family. A real family, it seemed to him—with a mother, Mary, and with a father, he himself, and with children, all the members of the 3YSC. Even thousands of miles away from home, it had felt like home for the first time ever.

Never had he felt so proud of his children. Never had he loved Mary so much. Never had he felt that as a father he had succeeded in ways he had always wished to succeed. At home somewhere were his own children. They had long ago become specters at the edges of his awareness, at the periphery of his life, and to them, he, too, had become a kind of ghost. In this reality, he had not succeeded as a father at all. Only in his air castle dream of a family had he become a loving—and beloved—patriarch. His real children would, in fact, never really have a chance to know him. But what he took home from Maplewood that summer was a sense that he was known, and that he knew others, and that he loved them, and he was loved by them, as well.

There was a grand welcome, first in Honolulu. There, Mayor Petrie met the delegation at the dock and "led them in a parade up the main drag and on to the capitol where acting governor Hite commended them...and the Junior Chamber of Commerce hosted a luncheon in their honor." Sportswriters were delirious about the national championship wins. Red McQueen of the *Honolulu Advertiser* declared Soichi Sakamoto the "world's greatest coach."

Blitzkrieg

Of the parade it was written that "they should have had a squad of the city's finest, bearing a palanquin or a sedan-chair" reserved for the man who had returned Hawaii to aquatic greatness.

Sakamoto and the swimmers arrived back at Kahului by sampan on a Thursday morning, where the august figures of the Permanent Executive Swimming Committee were waiting, neither to berate them nor to check their bags for stolen towels but instead to take them to a chop-suey dinner and laud them for hours. After all, no other team or any club in the United States had amassed as many points as the Three-Year Swim Club had that year.

The year had been a total blitzkrieg for the Maui swimmers, but there had been blitzkriegs of other sorts in the wider world. When the team returned home it was to a Maui where preparations for war had intensified. There were ominous military exercises outside of Pu'unene, announcements of maneuvers, and rehearsals of blackouts. Bob Hughes of the Permanent Executive Swimming Committee now led the blackout committee, ordering when all lights had to be extinguished on the island so a hypothetical enemy wouldn't be able to see houses from the sky. Some residents of the Valley Isle mistook the sounds of target practice by the 299th infantrymen at Camp Paukalo for an early Chinese New Year, but as the paper announced, it wasn't. And that summer the Department of Justice began systematically to fingerprint and register all "aliens" above the age of fourteen.

Maui had grown strange. On the sugar plantations, much was changing. The companies had been forced to introduce cane-hauling trucks, and in a few years, it would change the entire labor system on the island. That summer the Iao Theatre ran a special showing of *Gone with the Wind*, and fieldworkers who had the money to pay for a ticket could sit and watch as Vivien Leigh cried out that she'd never go hungry again, while behind her the plantation world went up in flames.

Marian Anderson, the world's greatest contralto, arrived in Maui that summer to give a stunning concert in the new Baldwin High auditorium. The Maui Rotary Club put the event together, and the place was "filled to capacity." Anderson, a divinely talented African-American singer, sang "Ave Maria," "O Don Fatale," "Amuri Amuri," and "Crucifixion," and wowed the crowd with Handel, Scarlatti, Bizet, and Schubert. But she didn't fail to sing songs of the American South, such as "Deep River" and "My Soul's Been Anchored in the Lord," and when she did, the crowd gave her a thunderous ovation and presented her with strands of crown-flower leis.

It was still a struggle to be black in America, and in those days it had become as much a struggle to be Japanese-American, as well. On the Mainland and in Hawaii—including Maui—the US government was preparing with much forethought for the imminent incarceration of those of Japanese ancestry, whom they suspected of forming a so-called "fifth column," or underground network of pro-Japanese spies.

On Maui, authorities at the Japanese Civic Association held a patriotic rally in the Baldwin High School auditorium and invited Robert Shivers, FBI territorial head, and T. G. S. Walker, coordinator of Emergency Disaster, to address the more than one thousand people, most of Japanese ancestry, who came out to demonstrate their loyalty and to hear it questioned. The evening began with a rousing rendition of "America," after which Director Shivers reassured the audience of their safety. No vigilante groups were forming, he said, nor did aliens need fear being sent off to concentration camps should a war begin. Smiling, he reminded the group that because the various races on Hawaii lived so harmoniously and were so integrated into American society, the Japanese-Americans on the islands wouldn't come under the same scrutiny as those on the Mainland. He said nothing of the kinds of preparations that were indeed already occurring there, and he squelched rumors circulating about the construction of prison camps on the nearby island of Molokai. Still, Shivers stressed, citizens ought to do their duty and report suspicious activity of any kind to the proper local authorities. That, he said, was merely a matter of precaution and a requirement of good citizenship.

Mauiites left the meeting feeling uneasier than ever, having become even more aware of the cloud of mistrust hanging above their heads. In the wake of the rally, a local boy by the name of Ichiro "Iron" Maehara, the son of the Pu'unene Japanese School principal and one of Soichi Sakamoto's former students, wrote an ardent editorial about the transformative power of baseball. Maehara had swum in the ditch with Coach Sakamoto, but he was best known for his talent on the diamond. There, he argued, he—and so many other Japanese-Americans—demonstrated their love of and loyalty to America by playing the most inarguably American game of all with such passion.

Still, some of Japanese-American life went on as usual, with traditional activities such as the "Doll and Kimono Pageant," sponsored by the Japanese Women's Club. The *Maui Shinbun* began to run ads for stamps and war bonds, with a complete list of what contributions could buy for the Marine Corps, the US Navy, or the Army: A quarter bought a dozen bandages; 50 cents got 12 yards of barbed wire; it cost 5 bucks to buy a single steel helmet; $184 got the Army a submachine gun. And for $15,000 you could buy a brand-new pontoon bridge. War bonds were an equal opportunity event: even prisoners in jails could contribute. E. L. Damkroger erected a billboard on the lawn at Alexander House and took pride in changing the rising numbers listed there. By just the middle of September, he had raised $5,696.33, with more to come.

As Christmas of '41 approached, Sakamoto painted the names of those who practiced the most and who improved the most on wooden plaques that he hung on the wall in the clubhouse. Mitzi, Remy Balmores—Jose's sister—Charles Oda, and Chic Miyamoto found their names there. The club's end-of-the-year festivities were to include a second annual Snowman's Hop and a free public aquacade on the evenings of December 28 and 29. The pool would be lit up, and the event was to include the entire club and a performance from the Baldwin High marching band. There would be formation swimming and Hawaiian singing and dancing and comedy stunts and dives. Sakamoto planned once again to take his mirrored ball out of storage for the hop and let the light play on it as if there were stars on the walls and ceilings of the Wailuku Armory.

On a Sunday morning in early December of 1941, Bill Smith was out to sea—literally—swimming in the surf and preparing for an upcoming open-water swim, when a boy swam out to tell him the news. "You're crazy," Bill said, and he kept on swimming. Only when he returned to Sakamoto's house a few hours later did he begin to understand what was going on. He had difficulty reaching his father on Oahu and later learned that Bill Sr. had been on duty the morning of the seventh, right in the middle of his beat at the water's edge. He'd escaped being blown to smithereens by a bomb that landed just thirty feet away from him, and he'd lived to tell about it.

In Waikiki that morning, at around the same time that Bill had been out in the waves off Maui, Duke Kahanamoku, now a member of the Outrigger Club, had already completed his early swim in the surf and was breakfasting at the Snack Bar with his new wife, Nadine Alexander, a perky dance instructor employed at the Royal Hawaiian Hotel. The two had recently married and settled down into a solid life together, and a Sunday morning like this spoke of the calm predictability of their domestic lives.

Suddenly, though, the door to the Outrigger flew open and through it came an Army Air Corps member who told Duke, the club's manager, and several families sitting nearby what was happening not far down the road. Some had assumed that the noise came from nearby antiaircraft exercises, but now they knew, as Kahanamoku put it, that this was the real thing. As sheriff, Kahanamoku had to report for duty—somewhere. "This is it," Kahanamoku cried out to Nadine. "Baby, we have to go." And they were gone.

Outside, war reigned. Halo, who was studying at the University of Hawaii, covered his head and scrambled toward the ROTC building, wearing a T-shirt, khakis, and *zoris*—traditional wooden slippers. He and roughly 370 other recruits were being called in for active duty. On arrival, officers gave them each Springfield rifles and five rounds of ammunition and split them up into units, each unit guarding key installations: the Board of Water Supply, the headquarters of Mutual Telephone, the city's electric generators and its fuel storage tanks. Halo and his troop went to the height of Diamond Head to watch for any incursions on land. When he tested out his rifle, though, he found that he was helpless, as were his friends. The Springfields had no pins. They were just ROTC practice weapons, and no one had ever thought they'd need to be ready for war. Halo watched the land and sea that lay below him, and he waited, unarmed, for the worst.

Keo was thousands of miles away in his dormitory room at Ohio State University in Columbus. The news had hardly sunk in when Mike Peppe sent a message to the fraternity house. Peppe wanted to see him. Posthaste.

Blitzkrieg

Outside it was growing dark and terribly cold, and the walk to the pool seemed eternal. Keo thought: *I'm done for. They'll send me home*, although he tried not to imagine what they would do to him there. At the natatorium at last, he knocked on the door of Peppe's office and found Peppe on the other side, shaking. Peppe told him to sit down.

It's not good, he explained. But it's not just bad for you. It's not good for us, either. He pointed out that Carl Wirthheim, the team's assistant coach, who was in the office with them, too, was German. "And I'm Italian, see?" he reminded Keo. Between the three of them they were possibly in deep. Peppe talked about "playing it cool," but Keo wasn't clear about what he meant until later. After they had listened and listened to the radio, they looked outdoors, and, seeing no one about, they decided to chance it and run. "Lay low and don't show your Japanese face too much," Peppe told Keo—although it was difficult to know how to do that and for how long he should—and then the three men split up and ran like hell to get back home without somebody deciding to hang them.

Back on Maui, the publisher of the *Maui News* personally saw to it that the press rolled off war editions and that newsboys distributed them across the island. It was Ezra Crane's duty to get out the news. "BLACKOUT TONIGHT," read the back page in the biggest letters that could fit on it. And the front of the fourth edition said, "Japanese Planes Attack: Game Off," referring to the dual football meet that had been planned between Punahou and Maui High.

By the time the fourth edition made it to the football field, the Punahou team, who had sailed over the night before, and the Maui players were already suiting up. Pundy Yokouchi, one of Sakamoto's early swimmers, stopped cold when he got the news, and everybody, without talking much, took off their shoulder pads, put their helmets under their arms, and walked across the field toward home, looking now and then at the sky.

In Pu'unene, another of Sakamoto's swimmers, Johnny Tsukano, was in his house with his family in McGerrow Camp. It was awfully quiet, he thought, strangely quiet, except for the news coming over the wireless and the occasional sound of people in the neighborhood crying out "bakatari," meaning "foolish," to describe the Japanese bombers. That is, until after dark, when he heard the sound of cars driving in, headlights blaring. One. Two. Three.

Of course, General Shivers had lied at the rally. Even on Maui there were two concentration camps already: one at the Wailuku County Jail and the other in Haiku, near the post office and in the shadow of the pineapple cannery where Soichi Sakamoto spent a miserable summer sticking labels on cans. Now there were tents and barbed wire.

The first man that the G-men took prisoner was Mr. Maehara, the Japanese school principal and husband of Mrs. Maehara, the woman who used to protect Johnny, his brothers, and the other camp kids from the luna back in the old days when they used to be chased at the ditch. Everyone in camp knew Mrs. Maehara was a good woman and Mr. Maehara was a patriot. He had an American flag in each of his Japanese School classrooms, and he made his students say the Pledge of Allegiance six times a week in both Japanese and English.

Mr. Maehara lived just a few houses away from the Hirose family, the Balmores family, the Ginozas, the Nakamas, and the rest of his own family, too. In the dirt path in front of their home, Mrs. Maehara and the couple's children wept as they watched the men put Mr. Maehara in a car and drive away.

Reverend Miura was next. He was the Buddhist priest at the Camp 5 church. He spoke the most beautiful and completely fluent English, and he regularly gave sermons about America, the advantages of the American system, and the duties of American citizenship. He was taken on a Sunday. Church was canceled. He wouldn't have a chance to say things about America anymore.

In the dark that night, forty-nine people in the camps of Puʻunene would vanish.

When Mr. Tsukano, Johnny's father, looked out the window and saw the authorities begin to take Reverend Miura, he seemed to lose his mind, because he dashed out of the Tsukano house, bounded down the stairs, and ran to the Miuras'. There, he stepped smack in the middle between the FBI and the holy man.

Blitzkrieg

Mr. Tsukano cleaned the Mighty #8 train every day; he was a simple man, one not generally given to demonstrations of feeling, but now he clasped his hands together in front of him, raised them to his forehead, and bowed to the reverend, blessing him in Japanese before the FBI agents could take him away. Later, when he thought about what he had done and the danger his behavior could have caused him and his family who had so far escaped suspicion, he knew he had been stupid.

But Johnny Tsukano, original ditch swimmer and card-carrying member of the 3YSC, wept tears of joy at what his father had done. It had been courageous; it had been unexpected, bold, and it had been the right thing to do. Sometimes instincts had to be trusted, children like Johnny Tsukano had learned, to withstand a deluge racing toward you.

PART FIVE

FALL SEVEN TIMES, GET UP EIGHT

Nana korobi, ya oki

1944–1948

Chapter Fifteen

GO FOR BROKE

GLOBAL WAR ended the golden age of global tourist travel. Bombs had hardly stopped raining down on the ships at Pearl Harbor when the Navy turned wherever it could for vessels to replace or stand in for the burned or battered USS *Arizona*, the *Maryland*, the *California*, the *West Virginia*, the *Oklahoma*, the *Nevada*, the *Tennessee*, and the *Pennsylvania*. Welders took torches to anything big enough to make a cargo or trusty troop ship, sealing the famous double-hulled cruise liners of the 1920s and '30s to make them even more watertight, commandeering the *Queen Elizabeth* for the Atlantic fleet and plucking the grand cruise ships of the Matson line from the Pacific. No longer could the ships sail the seas gleaming a brilliant and conspicuous white; instead painters slathered them from funnel to hull and stem to stern in coat after coat of warship gray. The Navy shuttered tight the portals and unscrewed every bulb from every chandelier, preparing for blackout while sailing. All along the gunwales, where tourists just shortly before could stand to feel a brisk sea breeze on their faces, now stood turrets from which gunners could pivot and pepper approaching U-boats or aim upward and try to push an enemy bomber higher into the sky.

Belowdecks, the ships were husks of what they used to be—emptied of armchairs, pool tables, books, and bandstands—now room-less, stripped to the rivets. Gone were the grand pianos and the feather beds; gone were the murals in the dining rooms, the champagne flutes, and the silver trays. Ships that had once sped vacationers to San Francisco, Los Angeles, Auckland,

and Pago Pago in style were troop ships now, their ballroom ceilings steel, and from those beams hung hundreds of Army-issue hammocks swinging low in row after row after row.

In galley kitchens, which had once served the grade-A meat on which boys like swimmer Diamond Martin had in 1938 gorged themselves to the point of "steak-itis," in 1944, Army chefs boiled up big tasteless pots of chow. Beside them men performed KP duties—men like Charlie Oda, who was now a soldier on his way to the Mainland and beyond.

Oda wasn't alone. He was just one of more than four thousand Japanese-American volunteers who were needed as warm bodies to replace the cold dead on the advancing Allied front in southern Europe. With Oda were some fifty other Maui soldiers, and 2,686 other Hawaiian-born Americans of Japanese Ancestry (AJA) volunteers, among whom were more than a handful of Pu'unene's original sugar ditch kids, including brothers Pachi, Shangy, and Johnny Tsukano, and one of the greatest swimming stars in the world, Halo Hirose. They were core members of those who had gathered in Soichi Sakamoto's elementary school classroom on another June day just six years before. Back then, they had shown up to sign on to the 3YSC, but now their names were on a different roster: they were enlisted men of the United States Fifth Army, most of them in the Third Battalion, headed to the shores of Africa to join other Japanese-American soldiers already struggling abroad to take back Europe. And with them, too, were plenty of other boys from Maui Nei. On board were more of Soichi Sakamoto's loyal swimmers: the can-do Hiroshi Shigetani, the pointy-chinned Yoshio Shibuya, and many others. There were also those from Pu'unene who hadn't swum a stroke but were as brave and loyal as any. None, including Barney Hijiro, one of Sakamoto's former students, and Halo, had had the chance to serve their country in the ways they'd wished in 1941; none had had an easy way to prove their true worth and loyalty to their nation. When Halo and hundreds of others of Japanese ancestry had shown up at ROTC headquarters across America for duty on December 7, 1941, they were turned away as enemies. In the meantime, they had worked for the famous Varsity Victory Volunteers, digging trenches, mining quarries with picks and shovels, and constructing barracks. Halo had also been a fireman and built roads, hoping—along with the other young men of the VVV and AJA volunteers across the United States—that by doing so, these Japanese-American patriots would also rebuild the bridge of trust between themselves and the rest of America's citizens. For the first time, Halo Hirose performed the hard labor to which he had never been subject on the plantation in Pu'unene: forty-eight hours per week at an Army-level wage. At a time when the government would soon empty the West Coast of those of Japanese ancestry, Halo Hirose and the rest of the VVV members had sent a letter to Washington pledging their fidelity to Uncle Sam and offering their heartfelt wishes to be useful in whatever way their country saw fit. Only in early 1943, with the war at a critical stage, had the government deemed the Halo Hiroses, the Charlie Odas, the Johnny Tsukanos, and some fifteen hundred Mainland AJA behind the barbed wire of concentration camps fit to put on US Army boots.

Charlie Oda had traveled by ship to Detroit for swimming, but Halo Hirose had the most tested sea legs of all of the boys from Pu'unene: eight great voyages, round-trip: to Louisville and Germany in 1938; to Michigan and then on to South America in '39; Santa Barbara, California, and Missouri in the two years that had followed. Although they'd worn the 3YSC colors to Honolulu many times, neither the Tsukano brothers, Takeshi Kitagawa, Yoshio Shibuya, nor most of the others had ever been to the Mainland; they'd only heard stories from the old days, and they never tired of hearing them again.

The tales that Halo could tell of his voyages aboard the *Matsonia*, *Lurline*, *Monterey*, and *Mariposa* made it difficult to imagine how the stripped-down ship on which they now sailed had once been so grand, the same class of ship that young men from Pu'unene in white linen suits had promenaded about with ukuleles.

Sakamoto's star swimmer and other AJA from Hawaii and the Mainland now crammed into the ship's crowded holds, bathed in basins of cold salt water, waited in line twice a day for slop, and buttoned up their heavy coats as a foreign coast drew near. They breathed air so foul in the bowels of the ship that one soldier said it was "thick enough to chew."

After the ocean journey, it was another two thousand miles by rail to their destination. America's train system had been retrofitted for new uses: the most recent passengers had been Japanese-Americans "evacuated" from the US West Coast and sent to the hastily built internment camps of Topaz, Manzanar, Tule Lake, and Heart Mountain, each situated in the hard heart of the nation's desert wastelands. After the signing of Executive Order 9066 in February of 1942, America's trains had carried mothers and fathers and children, grandmothers and grandfathers, too, some with tearful faces, others stoic as stone, but each bearing with them only as much as they could carry. Now the trains' passengers were Japanese-American once again, but they were serving as troop carriers, the fancy Pullman sleepers holding as many as eight soldiers to a berth.

The troops traveled onward through Nevada, Colorado, Utah, and Wyoming. For security and secrecy the troop train windows were curtained in black, and the cars hardly paused long enough at any whistle-stop to be noticed or for the men to get out and stretch their legs. Although once, alone among a sea of wheat fields in the town of North Platte, Nebraska, the men had been cheered when locals gathered at the station to hand them magazines and fruit, not as much a fanfare as the hordes that had met the swimmers at Maplewood in '41, but still something to boost morale as they traveled through the country, headed south.

Back in the thirties, folks in that part of the country thought of the town of Hattiesburg, Mississippi, population twenty-five thousand, as the center of the universe because it sat at the axis of an imaginary compass, equidistant from the smaller Dixie destinations of Gulfport; Jackson; Mobile, Alabama; Natchez; and Meridian. Atop the tallest building in Hattiesburg's downtown, an enormous sign was perched in the shape of a wagon wheel and lit up with letters in the night that declared the place to be "The Hub." The town was quaint in the way only Southern towns of its like were: warehouses and stores clumped up around the train depot, streets wide and dusty, here a bookstore and a bar, and there a pretty pink-green limestone post office.

As Halo Hirose and the swimmers of the 3YSC had seen in Kentucky and Missouri just a few years before, Hattiesburg was divided into black and white. Down the town's main thoroughfare a man named Billy Boucher— he could have been from anywhere nearby—piloted a single, sorry streetcar and made sure the coloreds, as he called them, sat in back. At the town's courthouse, which looked as though it had been lifted right out of Richmond or Atlanta, local judges meted out a different kind of justice depending on the color of a person's skin.

To the south of town by some twelve miles on a country road lay Camp Shelby, where Halo Hirose and his fellow Japanese-American soldiers were to train. It had sat in that spot since the First World War, among the old timberland that had once made Hattiesburg a lumber town. Abandoned shacks from that time stood next to the country road to Shelby, still roofed in cedar shank shingles and propped up on heart-pine joists once split and hewn skillfully by hand. Beyond those shacks lay the largest military deployment station in the entire United States, 134,000 acres containing 800 buildings—barracks, ammo depots, mess halls, and the like—and about 250 miles of Army streets, some named, seemingly without irony, Main or Second Avenue.

Shelby was one of the two places in America where the Army trained in isolation from the rest of the nation's troops; the Japanese-Americans of the 100th and the 442nd might have seemed to Caucasians to be a monolithic lot of Asian ancestry, but they were of course as different from one another as any group of men could be. One half of the group was called the "buddhaheads": these were men from Hawaii who spoke pidgin and had so-called island ways; the others were "kotonks," Mainland boys whose English was impeccable and whose manners were considered lily-white but who, the island boys said, made a *kotonk* sound when their heads hit the ground during fistfights. The two groups often failed to get along. In the beginning they were divided by culture and also by rank because, while all commissioned officers were white, it was from the ranks of the kotonks that the Army chose the 442nd's noncommissioned officers, and the tensions could therefore run high.

They would find themselves united, though, by a matter that concerned both the groups but of which the buddhahead Hawaiians were far less knowledgeable. Visiting the nearby internment camps where both Mainland and even some Hawaiian Japanese were imprisoned opened the buddhaheads' eyes to what their Mainland cousins had been facing. They were united, too, in the strange and unpredictable ways in which Southern locals treated them. Halo had seen this ambivalence before, the way that one white man might welcome a Japanese-American soldier to sit in his restaurant while another might send him packing.

Some Hattiesburg townspeople told the Japanese-American soldiers horrible stories about "coloreds," how they were vile and unclean and needed to eat in separate restaurants and weren't fit to use the same restrooms or swim in the same public pools. Unlike Halo and Charlie Oda, who had seen the divide before, most Hawaiian AJA were shocked at the treatment they saw given to African-Americans.

The 442nd included three infantry battalions as well as the 522nd Field Artillery Battalion, the 232nd Combat Engineers Company, an antitank company, a cannon company, a medical detachment, and the 206th Army Ground Forces Band. Shelby was a peculiar place in other ways as well. Out of the sight but not out of the minds of the soldiers in the 100th and 442nd was the fact that by late 1943, one of the largest POW camps in the nation would be housed there, where Germans who had served in General Rommel's Afrika Korps would live out the remainder of the European hostilities usefully occupied by picking cotton.

The German POWs lived in more rugged quarters, but the one hundred thousand US soldiers at Shelby lived in hutments, wood-framed structures that sat about three or four feet up off the Mississippi red clay, and were covered in part with canvas but also with real wooden shutters. Inside each hutment was a row of Army cots and a potbellied stove, should cold weather ever happen to visit.

It never did.

At Shelby the mercury rose as high as 122 degrees in the full sun, but most summer days it just hit about 110. It was humid, too, the air full of mosquitoes, and there was no breeze that could whisk those swarms away. Chiggers bit hard and often; ticks lodged under the skin. Locusts chanted from dusk straight up until reveille, and soldiers learned quick enough that however pretty those coral snakes were, you should never pick them up— although the slithery things were often served for dinner at the prison camp.

At Shelby the rank and file were Japanese-American, but the commanding officers were tall white men. Some spoke with Harvard accents, and none understood a word of pidgin. "Move to the clearing," an officer would say, and it would take the buddhaheads an especially long time before they figured out that the officer meant for them to go to the "no more trees place."

The towering officers taught the soldiers to toss live hand grenades at imaginary enemies; they taught them how to stab straw men with bayonets and to shoot nine-pound M1s on the rifle range until their shoulders ached; they taught them how to dig a foxhole, how to dull their shiny helmets so they wouldn't gleam in the sun and draw a sniper's attention. They taught them how to crouch down in a slit trench when a tank approached and how, while crouching, to cup the muzzles of their rifles to keep the dirt from falling in. The officers taught them not to clank their dishes together, because in war, they warned, dishes were giveaways as good as cowbells. The soldiers built temporary bridges; they humped four miles in fifty minutes. Halo and the Mauiites grew skinny, wiry, and tired, and at night they fell off to sleep in the middle of reading a page or two of *Tactics and Techniques of Infantry*.

There was training, but there was also rest. There was plenty of fun to be had. Some liked to sit around with the other buddhaheads and clean rifles and "talk story." Sometimes Halo and the others got passes to go into town, where they bought Superman and Allied comic books and soda pop, but Halo Hirose preferred to carouse and drink with the kotonks; he fancied himself to be among the likes of them. He and his buddies ventured far off base, to towns at the end of the spokes on the Hattiesburg hub, where there were girls for wooing and hotels for staying overnight. Mostly, Halo and his friends found themselves welcomed in such towns, but once in a while, they'd be met with glares or refused rooms or seats in restaurants. It was hard to predict when it would happen, but sometimes all of a sudden a local would decide that the Army uniform the Japanese kid was wearing didn't make him the good kind of Japanese.

Back on base, sports were big: there were baseball, football, and basketball teams, with a gym that stayed open late at night. The Army encouraged it all, funded it, and an unsung local hero by the name of Earl Finch was Shelby's biggest booster.

Finch was twenty-seven years old and shy. He had been rejected from the service because of a heart defect, but he was so enamored of the Hawaiians at Shelby that he became their greatest supporter, a "one man USO." Poor as sin, he lived with his elderly parents, but he and his mother cooked up real Southern-style barbecue for the islanders and found a way to import shoyu, bamboo shoots, tofu, and mangoes, so Charlie Oda and the others called him Mr. Aloha.

In August of 1943, Finch took them to the Southern AAU swim meet in New Orleans, some 112 miles away, not to watch but to compete. He paid for the train fare, covered their stay at the Roosevelt Hotel, and even hired a truck to drive them back and forth to the University of Southern Mississippi pool for practice. Charlie Oda, Johnny Tsukano, Halo Hirose, and five others from the Japanese-American combat team competed in that meet against the best Southern watermen and walked off with a first-place trophy—a statue of a swimmer poised at the edge of a swimming pool.

With the kind of freedom that condemned men sometimes feel—that the world is their oyster for a moment—they walked with pleasure along the streets and sidewalks of New Orleans, thoroughfares almost as wide as the ones back home in Honolulu. In the French Quarter, they played tourist and rode in horse-drawn buggies across the cobblestones and thought up other trips they'd like to take.

Some trips, however surreal, were to the Jerome Relocation Center, the closest Japanese-American prison camp—ten hours by bus. Jerome sat on swampland about 120 miles southeast of Little Rock. It was rife with typhoid, flu, and malaria, and it was home to thousands of Japanese-Americans who were imprisoned there. Many of them were Japanese from Hawaii, and the pretty girls at Jerome got bused in to Shelby for bimonthly dances. Not everyone felt comfortable about the visits, but Halo Hirose did.

Whenever the Jerome girls stepped off the buses, Hirose found he could woo more than one at a time—an apple-cheeked girl named Elie, a studious-looking high schooler named Ruth, a curly-haired beauty named Sono. And more. Some handed him photographs of themselves and wrote on the backs in looping curls of script: "To a very swell person whom I'll never forget," "Halo, my dear," and they promised to pine for and write to him when he was overseas.

Halo Hirose would indeed leave soon, along with the other Maui water-boys and the rest of the Shelby recruits. As the Fifth Army and the first wave of Japanese-American Allied troops from the 100th Battalion had made its way north in Italy toward the Gothic Line, hundreds of soldiers had already fallen in battle. News arrived at Shelby of the kinds of injuries that AJA had already suffered overseas: close-range wounds like lacerated livers and bullets straight through the throat. The Army needed replacements to get to Arno, in the north of Italy. For as long as anyone could remember, as early as their days in the ditch, Coach Sakamoto had told the swimmers of the 3YSC that as long as they had two legs and two arms, they ought to use them. So far, the swimmers all had both limbs, but as the great ships on which they sailed got ever closer to the coast of Africa, they would soon leave behind the certainty of keeping them.

Bill "Malolo" Smith would endure a war that wasn't bloody in any way. Mostly, it was wet, and pleasantly so. He spent a quiet senior year at Baldwin

High in 1942, still doing laps and reps in the Camp 5 pool, competing in the few meets on the island, from time to time climbing up on the Sakamotos' roof to look out for submarines off Maui, and thinking about his college choices. Matt Mann of Michigan called; so had Mike Peppe of Ohio State. Bill Smith didn't necessarily have a preference between the two schools, but Keo Nakama was in Columbus, and being a Buckeye with his island buddy sounded good. He signed on and traveled east.

OSU had always been a football school, but Mike Peppe, the college's swim and diving coach, was changing all that. Peppe had Keo, and now Smith, and those two swimmers would make OSU into a premier aqua-mecca. At OSU, Bill Smith led a proper collegiate life, rooming with Nakama at Delta Epsilon, an athletic fraternity filled with football and baseball players and runners. And because his training with Peppe was nothing compared to what it had been like with Coach Sakamoto, Smith had plenty of time to fool around on the gridiron with friends like Jimmy Campbell and Russ Thomas, both of whom would grow up to join the ranks of the Detroit Lions.

Smith chowed down on plate after plate of American food in the dining hall. He carried textbooks beneath his meaty arms, and he dated white girls. In the winter, it was bitter cold in Columbus, so he took to wearing shoes with fancy argyle socks and putting on a woolen sweater. When he studied, he huddled up by the radiator in his dorm room in coat and hat and gloves.

He was chilled, but the greater cold of the war was far away. He was such a star—*the* Bill Smith—that he didn't have to worry about being drafted too quickly. In his first season with the Buckeyes he continued to make swimming history. At the outdoor AAUs, held in New London, Connecticut, he swam his best national times ever, shattering three world-record marks, taking home three national titles and outswimming again and again the boys still left at Kiphuth's Yale and Matt Mann's Michigan.

In September of 1943, Smith's sophomore year, the Marines saw fit to call him up. Smith didn't mind the military, but the Marines did not appeal to him. Sure he had a say in it, he lumbered down to the recruitment office to choose his own destiny. It turns out he did have a say, and instead of becoming a Marine, the military made Smith into a sailor, a Navy man.

Go for Broke

In that branch of the military, Smith did in fact have a great deal to contribute. It was well-known and much discussed back then that at least 50 percent of the sailors killed at Pearl Harbor had died from drowning. Fifty percent of the Navy couldn't swim. The statistics had made the news. And it had been Chicago Towers backstroker Adolph Kiefer who'd come forward to head the Navy's effort to teach its sailors how to swim. When Kiefer had trained at Norfolk, the Virginia naval base, he used to go down to the dock and watch US boats come in with sorry sailors. The sight had kept Kiefer up at night. Finally, he'd persuaded his superiors to let him go up to Washington, where he reported in person that the US Navy was still, even after Pearl Harbor, losing more men to water than gunfire.

"What good [is] a 5-man gun crew," Kiefer asked the Navy brass, "if one of those 5 couldn't swim and fell in? With one man down drowned, what good [is] a 5-man weapon?" Kiefer returned to base with funding, and he became the architect of an ambitious program to make sure every sailor went off to war knowing how to keep his head above water. Kiefer knew the best swimmers in America from his competition days, and because he was so well liked he was able to call up an army of twelve hundred swimmers in all. Kiefer was training men how to teach survival swimming—nothing fancy—and sending them off to bases everywhere, where they met all manner of recruits who felt assured they could conquer anything but the water.

That was the "army" Bill Smith wanted to join, and Smith got his wish.

He did his basic training at the Great Lakes naval center in northern Chicago, and after getting certified at Bainbridge Island, Maryland, he headed back up to Chicago to serve his country for the rest of the war with other Great Lakes instructors who trained more than one million sailors during the course of the war—including the first African-Americans to serve. It was noble work, and there was also a personal upside: during his wartime service, Bill Smith was nearer to a pool than any of his 3YSC teammates—in the water itself.

Kiefer and Smith formed the Great Lakes swim team and traveled the nation, swimming in meets nearly as often as they had before the war, and Smith's fame only grew in magnitude. Art Daley of the *New York Times* called him the "Greatest Swimmer in the World," and other newspaper writers loved Smith and his backstory even more now than before Hawaii had been bombed. Fans loved the thought of a hero American islander, and they came out to meet him in hordes. The cartoon book series *True Sport Picture Stories* featured Smith in a full-color eight-page spread that devoted more colorful ink to him than it did to baseball's batting great Stan Musial.

Like all of the coverage of Smith before it, the comic book carried on with the Smith Myth, and the narrative kept taking new twists and turns. Bill Sr., Smith's father, had become English and Hawaiian now, not an Irish cop from the Mainland city of Detroit; and Rena Kealoha, Smith's mother, was suddenly half Irish. Bill Jr. was said to have been a competitive swimmer since the age of nine, never mind a great football player as well.

But in perhaps the ultimate act of mythmaking, the comic book that featured Smith told an interesting version of the relationship between two men—the first by the name of E. L. Damkroger and the second, Soichi Sakamoto. E. L. Damkroger was a patriotic lug of a fellow who ran a charity on Maui, and Soichi Sakamoto was a "Jap-Hawaiian" genius of a swimming coach. The two men were the best of buddies, partners in crime, and in one of the colorful panels, they're pictured hunched close together, serious-looking but friendly as they plot the future. The facsimile of Sakamoto declares excitedly, "Yes, Ernie, I think he's ready," meaning Bill Smith, to which E. L. Damkroger responds with equal enthusiasm that they should take him to the big time now.

Whether his mentors were friends or not, Smith did enjoy the big time throughout the war. During an AAU Indoor Championship meet at Michigan, he won four gold medals. And when Smith was ready, he wrangled a transfer home. He got stopped for a while in Camp Shoemaker in California, where he taught and still swam for Great Lakes, but when he finally sailed back to Hawaii, he spent the remainder of the war in a hardship post as a lifeguard.

The Towers Pool sat in a quiet residential area not far from Pearl Harbor, and it was reserved for top brass and their families. Admiral Towers, for whom the pool was named, lived right across the street. Along with two other Navy guards, Bill Smith's duty was to sleep in the pool house but be up by 6 a.m. and have the pool open and ready for when Admiral Towers

Three-Year Swim Club girls team at the Camp 5 pool, March 1939. Pictured: (back row, l–r) Hiroko Abe, Bertha Ching, Tamiyo Shiramatsu (or Shiramizu), Chic Miyamoto, Lulu Nakagawa, Fujiko Katsutani, Mitzi Higuchi; (middle row, l–r) Yoshie Higashida, Toyo Takeyama, unidentified, unidentified; (front row, l–r) Doris Yoshino, Kay Sugino, unidentified, Charlotte Shigehara. *Courtesy of the Alexander and Baldwin Sugar Museum*

Three-Year Swim Club girls team at the Camp 5 pool, summer 1939. Pictured: (standing, l–r) Bertha Ching, Toyo Takeyama, Mitzi Higuchi, unidentified, Yoshie Higashida; (front, l–r) unidentified, Fujiko Katsutani, Hiroko Abe. *Courtesy of the Alexander and Baldwin Sugar Museum*

At the Women's National Championships, Jantzen Beach, Oregon, August 1940. Pictured: (l–r) Toyo Takeyama, Fujiko Katsutani, Esther Williams, Chic Miyamoto. *Courtesy Moana Smith*

Soichi Sakamoto at the Three-Year Swim Club booth at the Maui County Fair, fall 1940. *Courtesy of the Alexander and Baldwin Sugar Museum*

Duke Kahanamoku congratulates Bill Smith on breaking his third world record and fifth American record at Punahou's Waterhouse Pool, May 16, 1941. *Courtesy of the Alexander and Baldwin Sugar Museum*

The 1941 Hawaiian AAU team arrives in Maplewood, Missouri, for the Men's Nationals, August 1941. Pictured: (standing, l–r) Armin A. Wahlbrink (Maplewood meet director), Paul Herron, Grace Crockett, Bill Smith, Fujiko Katsutani, Toyo Takeyama, Charlie Oda, Chic Miyamoto, Carlos Rivas, Mary Sakamoto, Bob Tribble, Soichi Sakamoto, Mayor Frank L. Martini; (kneeling, l–r) Halo Hirose, Keo Nakama, Bunny Nakama, Jose Balmores. *Courtesy of the Alexander and Baldwin Sugar Museum*

Midday meal at Maplewood, Missouri, tourist camp, August 1941. Pictured: (clockwise from bottom left) Bob Tribble, Keo Nakama, Jose Balmores, Bill Smith, Bunny Nakama, Fujiko Katsutani, Mary Sakamoto, Chic Miyamoto, Paul Herron, Carlos Rivas. *Courtesy of the Alexander and Baldwin Sugar Museum*

Buster Crabbe and Mary Sakamoto, Los Angeles, August 1941. *Courtesy of the Alexander and Baldwin Sugar Museum*

Finish of first heat, 200m freestyle, won by Bill Smith at Maplewood Municipal Pool, August 1941. *Courtesy of the Alexander and Baldwin Sugar Museum*

Front page, Third War Extra, *Maui News*, Monday, December 8, 1941. *Courtesy of the Maui News*

Bill Smith, circa 1945, Honolulu. *Courtesy Moana Smith*

Fifth Army Olympics, at Mussolini's Il Foro Natatorium, Rome, July 1944. Pictured: (l–r) John Tsukano, Halo Hirose, Shangy Tsukano, Charlie Oda. *Courtesy Sono Hirose Hulbert*

Private Halo Hirose with other members of M Company, 3rd Battalion, 442nd Infantry Regiment, Camp Shelby, Mississippi, spring 1943. *Courtesy Sono Hirose Hulbert*

Halo Hirose and Ohio State University swim and diving coach
Mike Peppe, circa 1946. *Courtesy Sono Hirose Hulbert*

Bill Smith at Olympic
Trials, River Rouge
Park Pool, Detroit,
July 1948. *Courtesy of
the International
Swimming Hall of Fame*

Bill Smith discussing time trials with Olympic coach Bob Kiphuth at Empire Pool, July 25, 1948. *Courtesy Yale University Athletics*

800m relay gold medalists, U.S. Men's Olympic team, August 3, 1948. Pictured: (l–r) Bill Smith, Jimmy McLane, Wally Ris, Wally Wolf. *Courtesy Moana Smith*

Testimonial dinner honoring Coach Soichi Sakamoto, Hawaiian Village Hotel, May 23, 1971. Pictured: (sitting, l–r) Mary Sakamoto, Soichi Sakamoto; (standing, first row, l–r) Evelyn Kawamoto, Fujiko Katsutani, Chic Miyamoto, Mitzi Higuchi, Toyoko Takeyama, Thelma Kalama; (standing, second row, l–r) Keo Nakama, John Tsukano, Halo Hirose, Benny Castor, Bill Smith; (far back, l–r) Sonny Tanabe, Charlie Oda, unidentified. *Courtesy Lee Matsui*

Puʻunene Elementary School, Puʻunene, Maui, 2012. *Courtesy Julie Checkoway*

arrived to take a swim. The rest of the day, he watched over the wives and children of top military folk, and in his spare time, he swam competitively. There was probably no one in the Navy who spent more time in the water during World War II than Billy "the Fish" Smith Jr. And it would prove to serve him well when the war was over.

While Smith was in Honolulu, thousands of Japanese-Americans in the 442nd Regiment and 100th Battalion were lying dead on battlefields from Italy to France. Charlie Oda and the 3YSC boys arrived in Europe just in time to take the places of those men. Their Atlantic crossing in the late spring of 1944 was ten to twelve days in rough seas, during which time they read and reread comic books they'd picked up in Hattiesburg, shot craps, and came up on deck from time to time to watch the ocean or to stand aft and stare at the long line of vessels of which they were a part.

When they landed at Naples, they split up for good into the companies with which they had trained at Shelby, knowing that southern Italy might well be the last place they'd ever see one another.

Charlie Oda had started out in H Company, and he'd liked it, but just before deployment he and his buddy, a cheerful grunt from the Big Island named Ranz Matsumoto, had been reassigned to D. Both Oda and Matsumoto had bonded with the H gang and felt "shanghaied." Neither had much respect for the men in D, for reasons they chose not to say out loud. The way they covered up the curve was to begin a running inside gag: they joked they were the only guys in Company D with IQs high enough to do more than tie their shoes.

Oda and Ranz Matsumoto became part of Cannon Company, and at Naples, the heavy equipment they hauled required they hump it overland to Civitavecchia while the rest of the Third Battalion took a safer route north by water.

Their first day of combat was June 26, 1944.

It felt more like maneuvers in basic than like combat at first, and since Cannon Company was at the back of the pack, on the first night Oda and

Matsumoto heard shots but no artillery, no counterfire, just sporadic harassment, and one or two shells lobbed into the air to light up where the Allied troops were camped every once in a while.

On the second day of combat, Ranz Matsumoto, he of the high IQ, didn't do anything stupid. He was just unlucky. He was assigned to drive a jeep through a little valley of no-man's-land when a German sniper picked him off. That left Charlie Oda with the highest IQ in D Company. The whole thing didn't sit right with him. He'd seen violence of all kinds on Maui, but not like this. And now he was surprised to find himself all of a sudden in the middle of real war.

Oda's company and others in the 442nd fought through the towns of Pastina and Lorenzana in Italy; they drove on to take a little hilltop town of Luciano, and they arrived south of Pisa to occupy the last bit of high ground near the Arno River. From there they could see the famous Leaning Tower. They were close now. Along the march, Oda found the Italian people so war-weary that they didn't even stop thieves who stole their property, ruffians who shot their cows or drop-kicked melons in their measly gardens like footballs.

The 442nd carried on. In their first campaign alone, they drove the enemy back an entire fifty miles and won a commendation. They went on to France, through Nazi holdouts in Bruyeres and Belmont. They were introduced to the viciousness of tree bursts, when enemy munitions like "screaming meemies" hit the trunks of giant pines, sending shreds and shards so large and sharp they killed men. In the forest they hid out in foxholes, and if they didn't see every tree burst with their own eyes, they felt them shake the forest and shatter the world around them.

After the pines of Mississippi, they couldn't have imagined a forest as thick, or dark, or cold with snow, but these woods proved even more menacing. As winter fell, at night the towering pines seemed almost human. The soldiers had to limit their movements among the trees in the frigid black of night, and sometimes, without a moon above, they couldn't even see their own hands and a soldier had to grab the shoulder of the man in front of him and march on blind.

Go for Broke

At Biffontaine, in the Vosges, they fought their most challenging battle of all, the one for which they would be remembered and decorated, a singularly bloody engagement about which entire books have been written. It was called the "Rescue of the Lost Battalion."

The campaign came about because the Thirty-Sixth Division of the 141st Regiment of Texas were trapped behind enemy lines for seven days with neither food nor water nor anyone to save them. They were certain to perish. But the Fifth Army sent the 442nd Infantry in, and the Japanese-American men of that segregated unit strove inch by inch up the rugged hill, at the top of which the German soldiers were dug in and waiting.

It was a ruthless battle in blinding rain and with hardly any cover at all. They bled for every patch of earth. Instead of doing what they had been trained to do in basic—conceal themselves, camouflage themselves, and surprise the enemy—they did what was completely against all rules of engagement. In order to save the Lost Battalion, they had to head out into the open, seen perfectly clearly as they crossed rugged terrain without cover, facing machine-gun fire all the way. They might as well have just shouted out "Kill me." Instead, they thwarted all common sense, and they advanced courageously. The myth is that what they shouted as they forged ahead was the now familiar phrase "Go for broke!" but in truth, some of the men said, they were too frightened to shout anything.

Man by man, the regiment threw itself at and up the hill, live bodies replacing the dead again and again. The 442nd succeeded in rescuing 200 men, and in the effort sacrificed 600 of their own and suffered 4,000 wounded.

Sometimes in the middle of the nightmare, there were the strangest moments of peace. Once, during a lull in the fighting, nearly the entire 442nd was stopped in Rome to rest. Halo Hirose had spent the past month holed up in "old farm houses" on the way to Anzio and the Gothic Line as part of a machine-gun platoon that fired tracers for the "big guns" in the rear. By the time he'd reached Rome, he'd come down with an awful case of dysentery—from eating "too many green apricots" along the road, he thought—and he was laid up in the hospital.

"You must be an important person," a uniformed major said when he approached Hirose in his bed one day. Hirose was wanted at Division Headquarters. There, he was met by a Nisei captain by the name of Kometani and by a group of other soldiers who were apparently important, too: none other than Charlie Oda, Johnny Tsukano, and Shangy, who had also been pulled from combat for an unknown purpose.

They were a ragged band of Hawaiians: Hirose still half doubled over with stomach pain; Charlie Oda sore but in decent shape; at least one of the Tsukano brothers largely intact; but Shangy Tsukano had been wounded: the look of his left arm, curved oddly at the wrist, made his brother tear up. The group was being drafted, Kometani told them. He was smiling, and so it seemed like he wanted them to think it was a joke, but then he explained that he was commandeering the Hawaiians to take part in the Allied Olympic Games, right there in Rome. Kometani expected them to swim and win big for the Fifth Army in Europe.

The Fifth had settled into vast headquarters in the northeastern sector of Rome, in a complex once home to a military school for Italian brownshirts. The place, which sat at the foot of a hill called Monte Mario, was known as Il Foro Mussolini, or "Mussolini's Forum." Il Foro was Mussolini's architectural masterpiece. It was centered on a sports arena on the same capacious scale as those of the Greco-Roman Empire with an indoor swimming pool, and it was the site that just a few years before had been the foundation for Italy's foiled 1940 Olympic bid. In 1938 Halo Hirose had seen Hitler's version of over-the-top Fascist constructions, but Il Foro rivaled anything Germany had to offer. A sleek marble obelisk rose high and white and gold-tipped into the sky and led to shade-less piazzas stretching on and on, and below one's booted feet, fancy Latin-inscribed marble read "Many Enemies, Much Honor," along with some other of Il Duce's idiosyncratic and Machiavellian proverbs.

Go for Broke

Charlie Oda wasn't much for proverbs, but he admired the statues that ringed the outdoor arena: gargantuan naked wrestlers, runners, archers, and even baseball players posed as if about to engage in sport. He marveled at the pure, white likenesses of gods that greeted him at the stairways of the main building. And he was struck by the main building itself, which housed not just a theater but also a chapel and a fifty-foot-high ceilinged natatorium.

The natatorium was yet unfinished and was eerie and echoing, half-decorated with what were to have someday been elaborate mosaics. On one wall a sea monster swam among what looked like a group of horses. On another wall were the outlines of cartoonish runners running in tandem. On another, a diver—as if in separate frames of a film—appeared again and again but in different parts of a plunge, springing off the board, flying out in the air, revolving, and then with downward-pointing fingers extended, falling into a kind of nothingness. Mussolini had fancied himself a swimmer, which is perhaps why he had paid so much attention to the pool. He'd never used the larger natatorium, however, but swam in a smaller one nearby; it was decorated with images of bears and walruses.

Charlie Oda had passed through Mussolini's war-torn world. He'd seen the good that the dictator had accomplished: the modern apartments and houses that had taken the poor out of the slums, and pristinely constructed schools. He'd also seen the body of the dictator hanging, famously, among collaborators and his mistress, from the bare steel rafters of an Esso gas station near Milan. Now he was a kind of interloper in the dictator's playground. The swimmers began practice at the far end of the bigger pool and bunked in Mussolini's military academy. None of them was in terribly great shape, but that hardly seemed to matter.

The meet itself took several days. The *Stars and Stripes* covered it with glowing praise for the Nisei swimmers. Mussolini's Il Foro echoed with the hoots and hollers of an occupying army. The others elected Halo Hirose both captain and coach, and Hirose himself swam respectably: mid-war 100-meter backstroke in 1:20.4 and a strong 50-meter freestyle. He placed second in the 100-meter, and he anchored two winning relay teams that included Charlie Oda.

Oda won the 1,500-meter and the 400. Johnny Tsukano won a gleaming gold cup for his first place in the 100-meter breaststroke. The event was as sweet as it was exciting. It was a moment out of time and space. A moment together once again in a 50-meter regulation-size pool and a surreal victory celebration in a place where they and the whole Fifth Army had stolen a crown from a tyrant. They took hundreds of photographs of one another. And when they parted, they each stopped at the post office to mail a load of them to Coach.

It wouldn't be until 1945 that swimmers like Charlie Oda, camped in a bivouac, or Halo Hirose, somewhere on the road, would receive word that the war was over. And it wouldn't be until one day not long after that Halo would begin to grasp the ways in which the war had changed not just the wider world but his own as well. He was among those soldiers in charge of POWs in the European prison camps, and one day he heard a German voice call out his name. When Halo turned to see who summoned him, he found it was one of the prisoners, and that the sorry man he saw behind the fence was one he'd swum against so many years before in Germany. It was none other than Olympian Helmut Fischer. That was another life, an age ago, but the man who called his name was the same one who had befriended him and whom Halo had beaten in a pool and who now, along with the man's country and leader, had been vanquished by Halo and another group of "all-Americans" on the bloodstained land.

The story of the German prisoner was one that Halo would return home to tell not once or twice but many times, and over the years, the prisoner/swimmer's identity was lost in time. Records show, though, that of all the German swimmers the prisoner could have been, he was likely an Olympian. The rest of his teammates were otherwise accounted for, meaning they had died in the war, but somehow this single German swimmer had survived.

The result of who fell in battle and who survived seemed, and likely was, a matter of cruel chance or dumb old luck. Halo Hirose in particular uncharacteristically played down his role in the war, saying that mostly he

Go for Broke

saw little combat and that he spent a great deal of his time in Paris, never saying much about what he had done there except that he'd met some pretty girls. Charlie Oda was modest about his contribution, too; his explanation for why he'd survived was that he'd been at the back of Cannon Company. But when Halo and the rest of the group could gather and account for themselves, they found, astoundingly, that all of Coach Sakamoto's swimmers had survived the war, even Jose Balmores and Benny Castor, members of the Filipino infantry. There wasn't time enough in the world for them to talk story about why this was; all they could do was count themselves among the lucky and the living:

PFC Charlie Oda
PVT Takashi "Halo" Hirose
PFC Takeshi Kitagawa
PVT Bunmei "Bunny" Nakama
PVT Hiroshi Shigetani
PVT Mitsuo "Pachi" Tsukano
PVT Yoshio Shibuya
PFC John Toshio Tsukano
CPL Tsugio "Shangy" Tsukano

Plenty of Maui boys had died—some from Sprecklesville, Paia, Haiku, Hana, Lahaina, and more—but not Coach Sakamoto's ditch wrigglers, as they were sometimes called. Had it been something magical in the water of the ditch or some bit of wisdom they'd absorbed from Coach's endless Sunday sermons? Or was it the good luck of the *senninbari*, or a thousand-stitch belt, that each man received from his mother upon leaving and then wore under his uniform for the duration of the hostilities? It was, after all, an amulet for good luck; each stitch, it was said, was sewn by a different woman. They didn't know. They never would be able to. There was nothing to do with their good fortune but to be forever grateful.

Chapter Sixteen

HOME FRONT

Bᴀᴄᴋ ᴏɴ Maui all those years, Soichi Sakamoto had kept up with his swimmers by post; he wrote them doting letters and sometimes enclosed silly pictures of himself. In one letter he sent Halo a photo in which he posed bare-chested, as if he were some kind of girlie pinup, and he wrote a cheeky comment on the back suggesting he had a fine physique, "didn't Halo think so?" Given the circumstances, there were few other ways in which he could think of giving Halo, or any of them, a good laugh, and laughs were what he was certain they needed.

Sakamoto could report on little from the world of Pu'unene, couldn't safely comment on anything that really mattered to him: how barren his life on Maui was now, how trapped he felt, how changed the world of Pu'unene was. He saw change come that first Sunday in December 1941 with the arrests, and then so much more. Island-wide, he saw the smoke that hung above the towns and sugar camps; the clouds were not the plumes that came from harvest cane-burns but from bonfires onto which every Issei and Nisei tossed all Japanese signs and symbols. Sakamoto's mother didn't throw her son's American instruments on her pyres, but instead, along with everyone else in Waikapu, the instruments came from her own homeland. These were the ones she had once wished her son would play but that she now no longer urged him to take up: the *kugos*, angled harps, and the *shamisens*, the three-stringed lutes meant for a Japanese son.

It was dangerous to forget to dispose of such things. Once, a man on the island ventured outdoors to tend to his barking dog, forgetting that he was dressed in a *yukata*—a traditional Japanese cotton robe. He was shot at and then hauled off to jail for his misjudgment. Sakamoto himself had little evidence of a Japanese past to keep, but just enough to worry over. He had a few mementos of the old world that he couldn't seem to part with, like the scores of photographs he'd brought home from his Boy Scout trip in 1930. For the duration of the war and even beyond, he would stash them in a secret place: the pictures of himself on the delicate, arched bridges of city parks or among a crowd of cheerful fellow Scouts who were now to be despised as sons of the wretched Empire. He tucked away the photos of his brothers Bill and Benzo clowning in the countryside, the pictures of the leader of the Scout trip shaking hands with the most famous Kabuki actor in Japan, and the ones from when Sakamoto and his mates paraded in Hibaya Park past the then-exalted mayor of Tokyo. So much mischief and intrigue could be made from those photos—from the pictures of Mount Fuji to the pictures of him solemnly marching past militarily outfitted boys and men of the nation that was supposed to be his enemy.

He and Mary had given their own children English names right from the start: Raymond, Donald, and Janice, but those who'd named their children Japanese names now changed them to Ralph and Ann and Warren, Ruth and Charlotte. Sakamoto never changed either his first or his last name; he instead went mostly by his nickname, "Saka," but there were others on the island who everybody knew used to be called "Oda" and now called themselves, a bit ridiculously, by the Irish name "O'Day."

For Sakamoto's parents and their friends there was no more speaking Japanese. Sakamoto watched quietly as the territorial government shut down not just Mr. Maehara's Japanese school in Puʻunene, but all the others, too. There was no more calligraphy: no hiragana or kanji. No more teaching of the tea ceremony, no more Samurai Saturdays at the picture shows. For Sakamoto, it ought to have mattered little; he hardly saw himself as Japanese, but it was difficult to watch what happened to his parents and their Issei friends. It was good-bye to the apples and oranges at the New Year festival. It was good-bye to Bon dancing and Sumo wrestling, farewell to the bonsai that men like Halo's father, Denkechi, used to tend with care. If anyone hid bonsai in their gardens or their homes, they must have trimmed them only with less-than-precise, trembling fingers.

Issei mothers whose sons had joined the 442nd no longer prayed for them at the Hongwanji, the Buddhist church, but instead made sure to be seen in pious worship in the pews at Christian churches like the Pu'unene Congregational.

Sakamoto's Scouts no longer camped out or held their jamborees; instead, they were encouraged to stalk the plantation villages and the streets of towns, handing out $50 fines to anyone who dared to light a cigarette after curfew and collecting newspapers and aluminum pots and pans for the war effort. Everyone, including Sakamoto, volunteered—just like his swimmers in the VVV—most strenuously to prove their fidelity to the American cause. Those of Japanese ancestry turned the tracks and football fields and once-prized baseball diamonds on the island into victory gardens, working glove-less to plow over what remained of the now-frivolous past.

Maui became home to some one hundred thousand troops from the Mainland as well—the entire Fourth Marine Division, in fact—who took up living in miles-long rows of barracks near the HC&S plantation in Pu'unene. Both day and night, from the airport just to the north of the plantation, the noise of the everyday became not just the whistle of the factory or the cries of the lunas but the sound of the great, lumbering Flying Fortresses that always "thundered overhead." The entire island was in a state of constant vigilance and in regular receipt of bad news from overseas. At Pu'unene School and the Camp 5 pool, Sakamoto had only a shell of a team. They were young boys; the older ones had enlisted, and most of the girls had dropped out of sight. Fujiko Katsutani took sewing lessons and helped out in the family business. Other girls wound bandages and volunteered at blood drives.

Those who were still part of Sakamoto's re-formed 3YSC weren't able to reach the heights of his old swimmers who were gone now. The new generation of swimmers paddled around in the Camp 5 tank, waiting for their chances, but the war meant that they hadn't a chance. Night meets were ver-boten because of the blackouts, and travel off the island was nearly impossible because of the fear of submarines. In 1943, Sakamoto was crestfallen when he couldn't take his team—a mix of old hands and some rising stars including Bunny Nakama, Chic Miyamoto, and even Bunny's kid sister Lillian, who had been showing promise for a while—to the AAU Outdoor Championships.

Sakamoto, along with Damkroger, oversaw the public school meets, and Sakamoto kept up with his 3YSC and all-Maui meets, most of which the team still won. But often the most daunting outside competitors who joined in the men's races weren't exactly visitors from afar: Sakamoto invited Marines from the local base to put a swim team together and try their luck in the Camp 5 pool. Mostly, the Marines lost, which was always a morale boost for the older swimmers, but it didn't help assuage the fact that Sakamoto and the rest were effectively trapped on Maui. Anyone wishing to visit Honolulu had to seek permission from the island's new Home Security and chief information officer, Mr. Ezra Crane, former publisher of the *Maui News*. Additionally, E. L. Damkroger still had to rubber-stamp all sports events, and he, at least for a while, continued to be reluctant to stamp too many.

As for what was going to happen to sports in the rest of the world, the famed Gee-Whiz writer Grantland Rice remarked that it was "beyond anyone's guess." Not only had Soichi Sakamoto's Olympic dream gone up in smoke, but also anything else he'd wanted. He awaited the few letters that his swimmers sent back home; he wrote more than he received. He heard from others the names and whereabouts of those from Maui who were injured or who had died before they were published in the news. It must have been excruciating to be Sakamoto at this time in history: he was a man of action, impatient, full of ideas and energy, not one to wait things out easily, and now what was inside him simply had nowhere to go.

Thankfully, in 1945, as the war in Europe was winding down, Soichi Sakamoto received from Oahu the surprising offer of a job: the president of the University of Hawaii recruited him to coach the University of Hawaii swim team. The position was full-time and required him to leave Maui, but he'd be paid the first dollar he'd ever made in all his years of coaching. There was hope again in starting anew.

To Sakamoto and to many others, Maui was a wasteland. To that wasteland, only some had returned. Mr. Maehara, head of the Japanese school, returned for a time after being imprisoned in a Mainland internment camp for years, but he found his school shuttered and his eldest son dead. The boy had died on his thirty-second birthday, serving in the 442nd in Italy. Reverend Miura returned from the prison camps, too, to find what was left of his church.

On Hawaii, as on the Mainland, the war had decimated the college athletic squads, including the U of H swimming Rainbows, but Sakamoto now had the chance to rebuild the squad and also to start his life over again. There was nothing left for him on Maui, really. He'd trained a young man, a former diver by the name of Mac Nakano, first as a manager and then as a coach, and Nakano stood poised, but patient, for Sakamoto to hand him the torch.

As was customary, Soichi hardly—if at all—consulted Mary or the children, presenting the move as a fait accompli. He put their Paukukalo house, just north of Wailuku, up for sale, put his family and beloved automobile on an interisland ferry, and by the summer of '45 had settled into a modest bungalow on McCulley Street in downtown Honolulu, not far from the university pool up *mauka*—toward the mountains—or the Natatorium down *makai*—toward the sea.

For both tanks, he had elaborate plans. At the university he would groom a fresh group of rising undergraduates and the returned soldiers who had come back to study on the GI Bill, and down at his old haunt, the Natatorium in Waikiki, he started up a new swim club with children separated into proper age-groups.

Sakamoto reached out beyond the university to the kinds of kids in Waikiki whose lives he'd helped to transform on Maui—they were the suntanned kids of the slums, the scrawny boys and girls who'd been the lookers-on, sitting in the bleachers of the Nat when Sakamoto and his team had practiced below them in the water. Sakamoto called his new group of kids the Hawaii Swimming Club, and he gave it a motto with a most familiar ring. "Olympics First, Olympics Always!" would be the cry that his new children, his adoptees, would shout until their throats were sore and until at last the warring world would settle down enough for the Olympics' return.

Sakamoto had continued to pay attention to the news; he hadn't left Maui on a whim. Just the previous year, in 1944, the papers reported the tentative discussion of the re-formed and reborn International Olympic Committee. By 1948, they hoped—and Soichi Sakamoto silently prayed—there would be a chance for the Games again. Sports reporters started throwing around the names of cities: Stockholm. Los Angeles. Maybe even Rome if the country could be stabilized and all forms of enmity, resentment, and bad blood could become a thing of the past. Sakamoto didn't care where the Games would occur; long ago he'd loosened his grip on the broken promise of Tokyo and then the wasted wish of Helsinki.

What he wanted now was one more chance. Escaping Maui was the first step. The swimmers of the 3YSC would return from war—if they returned at all—and he hoped they would, *all of them*; but he knew all too well that by 1948, they would be old men. Time and fate and circumstance would have washed away whatever spirit of the water had been in them from youth.

At nearly the same time Sakamoto took his leave of Maui, Keo Nakama took his of Columbus, Ohio. He'd spent his war years at OSU: the wide and archless feet that had served him as well as flippers in the swimming pool, taking him to the apex of his sport, had ironically made him IV-F, disqualified for service. Nakama watched the men go off to war, just as he had watched so many others leave. When Bill Smith left for the service, Nakama had managed his grief at the loss of his dear friend by throwing himself into his studies. He would likely never see Europe, in war or peacetime; that was his cross to bear.

At OSU he had achieved so many dreams, and in his senior year, he captained Mike Peppe's squad but also helmed and played second base on the

OSU baseball team, captaining the squad in his senior year. He was thrilled that at last others called him by the nickname he had always longed for: not Keo, but "Casey" Nakama. Casey Nakama at the bat.

His war years hadn't been uncomplicated, though. After the Sunday in 1941 when Mike Peppe told Keo to try to hide his Japanese face as much as possible, any harassment he encountered, at least on OSU's campus, was mostly good-natured. Friends and strangers alike took to calling him "Tick-Tock": he was, they joked, an enemy who had a bomb hidden somewhere on him. Keo took the ribbing in stride, but off campus, it was harder to do so. When he traveled with the squad for collegiate meets, he never knew what kind of reaction he would get when he stepped out on the deck.

Mike Peppe was a constant supporter and defender, Keo said. Once at a meet, an admiral who had been in the bleachers openly criticized Peppe for having a "Jap" on his team, and the argument that ensued between the admiral and the tiny Peppe escalated, Keo said, until Peppe hauled back and slugged the fellow in the face. A far more dramatic situation occurred at the 1942 AAU Indoor Championships at Yale, the details and import of which Keo Nakama would never forget. The meet took place in the famed Payne Whitney natatorium, Bob Kiphuth's home turf.

The Payne Whitney was a masterpiece. It had no fewer than two pools: an upstairs 50-meter practice pool and a downstairs competition pool, the latter engineered to be the fastest pool in the world. It was deep—no shallower anywhere than 8 feet—and lined on either side with gutters that cut down on chop. For the comfort of the audience, there was excellent viewing from any seat in the house. It would have been hard to miss a moment of any drama that occurred there.

The date was April 5, four months after the bombing of Pearl Harbor and the commencement of the bitter war with Japan, and it was at the height of America's hysteria and paranoia toward those of Japanese ancestry still among them. On February 19 of that year, a little over a month before the AAUs, Franklin Delano Roosevelt signed Executive Order 9066, giving full discretion to the secretary of war to remove both Japanese-American citizens and resident aliens from their homes in "restricted areas" and to transfer them posthaste from those coastal regions to inland prison camps.

During this atmosphere of extreme racial tension, Keo Nakama, the only Japanese-American swimmer in the AAU at the time, came to Yale representing the OSU swim team in his freshman year. Going into the meet, Keo's toughest competitor in the middle- and long-distance races was Yale's national collegiate titleholder Rene Chouteau. In the only final scheduled on the meet's opening night of April 2, Keo soundly eclipsed Chouteau in the 1,500-meter freestyle by nearly a pool's length before a large crowd of Yale fans. Nakama began the long-distance race sprinting and never looked back. Two years before, his brother Bunny had once outraced Chouteau in the mile event at Santa Barbara.

Throughout the 30 grueling laps, Keo paced himself perfectly, never reaching exhaustion, lapping all of the competition and leaving behind not only Chouteau, who struggled at second place, but also a swimmer named Dan Green from Dallas in third, and another Yale Blue, Richard Peters, in fourth. In doing so, Keo also established a new American record of 19:35.2, as well as, of course, a new Payne Whitney tank record.

In the *New York Times* the next day, Nakama was hailed as a spectacular racer. His win over Chouteau made Keo a likely entry, it was said, in the 1,500-meter race that was slated for the Pan-American Games planned—if not counted on—for Buenos Aires in November of '42.

The *Times* and other newspapers carried plenty of news about the war as well in those first days of April. The horrifying word out of Kunming was that the Japanese were beheading nine out of ten British soldiers they captured. The Army announced that in May a third draft of American soldiers would commence. The Japanese were continuing to advance in Burma, and American and Filipino troops were reported to be engaged in hand-to-hand combat with the Japanese in the Bataan Peninsula.

It was in that context that two nights later, on April 4, Keo Nakama stepped onto the pool deck for the finals in the 440-yard freestyle, the AAU championship event. At the sight of him, the crowd erupted into jeers and boos and snide remarks; they hollered for "the Jap" to go back home. The response was ugly and riotous, until Mike Peppe came forward and made his own voice heard over the din.

"The Ohio State team," Peppe shouted, "has on it only loyal citizens."

The crowd still grumbled.

Keo Nakama, Mike Peppe continued, "is Japanese-American." He emphasized the latter word. And today, he told the crowd, our boy will swim. The fans in the Payne Whitney fell into a deep silence and remained quiet as Keo stood up on the block, but when Rene Chouteau climbed up on his, the crowd broke out in wild applause and hoots and whistles. The starter raised his gun, and in that moment there was a taste for blood in the natatorium. When the swimmers leaped into the water, the noise and ruckus and rancor only became louder.

The race began head-to-head, but Keo soon sped 2 feet in front of Chouteau and carried the lead through lap after lap, but only by a tenuous 2 feet. The crowd screamed and stood, leaning in, the majority in the gallery rooting for Chouteau. Nakama fought hard, and Chouteau fought behind him in equal measure, but still behind in 15 of the laps. In the last lap, Chouteau attempted a takeover and swam with all his might, but Nakama held his scant lead of 2 feet to come in to the wall at a grand 4:42.4, with Chouteau coming in .4 of a second behind, both men clocking a new Yale record—and Nakama proving his worth before a crowd of disbelievers who looked on in horror as Keo Nakama, having leaped out of the pool, promptly fainted. Exhausted, he was unconscious, unwakeable. The Yale swimmers carried the Ohio State champ to the locker room, and it was hours before he again came to.

As a civilian at OSU, Nakama had proven himself an American to the greatest degree, not only in the swimming pool but also on deck and in service to the military. Through a program not unlike the one in which Bill Smith and Adolph Kiefer participated, Keo trained many a sailor to swim at the nearby Navy Recognition School. It was a responsibility he attended to with gravity; many of his swimmers had been officers from the Ivy Leagues, some with such an antipathy toward the water that he'd had to gently coax them in. He taught these men, in part, the way that Coach had taught the children in the ditch: to dunk their heads, to look around, to become unafraid of being under, to imagine that the water was a pillow or a kind of bed. That was floating, he said, and he taught them to tread water because that was the skill they would need the most in a disaster.

In the fall of 1943, a letter appeared on the desk of the Cleveland, Ohio, news bureau; it was from a Princeton lieutenant whom Keo had taught not long before, with tremendous patience and attention, to conquer his fear of the water. The lieutenant had been aboard the famed and ill-fated ship *Helena*. The *Helena* had barely survived the attack on Pearl Harbor in 1941, only to be sunk in August of 1943 by a surface-fired torpedo in the Kula Gulf, the same location in which future president John F. Kennedy would narrowly escape death in the wreck of the PT-109. Of the men on the *Helena* 165 were lost; only one man, Keo Nakama's student, lived to praise his former swim instructor. "Tell that little Hawaiian boy I was in the water for more than an hour," the letter read, "and without his patient teaching, I wouldn't be writing this... He saved my life."

When both his time on the diamond and his amateur swimming days were over, Keo Nakama packed his trunk to return to Hawaii. His pursuit of a graduate degree in physical education and his student teaching, the latter for which he had been only modestly paid, was seen as coaching, and it officially stripped him of amateur status. According to the rules of the AAU, any athlete who took pay in his sport would be disqualified. Since Keo had a child now, he would once again have to take up the mantle of responsibility and help support his still-struggling family. In truth, he had little choice in the matter.

When Keo left Columbus, he was treated to a hero's farewell on the occasion of his official retirement from amateur swimming. At banquets, university officials and state notables showered him with praise. On the sixth of August, the United States had dropped the atom bomb known as "Little Boy" on Hiroshima, followed by the plutonium bomb "Fat Man" on Nagasaki on August 9; and on August 10, Keo Nakama stopped for one last swim meet in the town of Akron, Ohio, his last AAU National Championships.

He was ill with a stomach bug and had to withdraw from the 1,500-meter race; then he suffered defeat to Jimmy McLane, the boy wonder of the time, in the 800-meter freestyle, but in the last races of his amateur swim career, Keo Nakama copped his final 200- and 400-meter freestyle titles, the last official crowns of his young life.

When he reached Hawaii at last, the war with Japan was over. In Honolulu the press and public greeted him at the pier and toasted him at restaurants, just as they had so many times before. They draped him to the eyebrows with leis, and then Nakama began to carry on with his life. He wasn't the sort of person to look back in anger. Regarding the regulation that had pushed him out of the swimming pool, he simply referred to it as a "funny kind of rule," and he laughed it off. Then in the spirit of his mentor, Coach Sakamoto, he took a job in Honolulu as a high school teacher and coach. Both professions seemed a fitting way to spend the rest of his life, and Nakama looked ahead to his future.

At home, he spoke little about the past, taking after Duke Kahanamoku in his unwillingness to linger on difficult memories, particularly the slings and arrows of prejudice. Perhaps each man saw no point in sharing the stories if they couldn't yet leverage any change in the present.

Nakama's life settled down into the ordinary: teaching, visits with Sakamoto, and time with friends, but he had come to live in Hawaii in the midst of a great cultural transition. Kamaainas had great respect for the sacrifices of the 442nd, great pride in the contributions of the Hawaiian-born Japanese, some of whom were still deployed in Europe, but it would take time before Americans of Japanese ancestry on Hawaii would be welcomed and embraced as full US citizens and members of the Hawaiian community. It would be yet another year—1946—before President Harry Truman would address the 442nd and congratulate them for having fought the enemy abroad and prejudice at home, triumphing over both foes. However, it would take many more years before AJA across the United States began to feel they'd been given their full human and civil rights.

Home Front

Bill Smith was back in 1945, and he and Keo were terribly glad to see each other. In the days before Thanksgiving of '45, Smith invited Keo to meet him for lunch and a catch-up. When Smith came home from Shoemaker to Honolulu, local officials had welcomed him back much more warmly than Keo Nakama had been. They praised Smith for both his service and his swimming, and they held a huge bash in his honor at the Outrigger Club, where, in the course of a speech-filled evening, the "Flying Fish," was presented with both a platinum watch and a lifelong membership to the exclusive club.

Smith and Nakama planned to catch up at the Outrigger. The club had suffered through hard financial times during the war. It had been sitting smack-dab in the center of a war zone, its beach cordoned off, many of its dues-paying members either off-island, at war, or dead. It had flirted dangerously with bankruptcy; and though it had come down from its early days, it was said to be gearing up for a return to its state of former glory and snobbishness.

When Smith and Nakama arrived for lunch that November day, they were sideswiped by what happened. No sooner had they sat down at a table than the manager accosted them and brusquely told them to leave. Smith was puzzled. The manager had to explain that it had been the Outrigger's "unwritten policy" from time immemorial never to accept "Orientals" either as members or as guests. Smith was welcome, but the manager looked meaningfully at Nakama.

Smith was furious. He grabbed Keo and stormed out of the club, pounding his big feet on the pavement of the club's parking lot. In some sort of attempt to mollify him—after all, he was a club member—the manager came out and tried ridiculously to make small talk as if nothing had happened. Were Mr. Smith and Mr. Nakama planning on participating in the upcoming Thanksgiving swim meet between the Outrigger and local *huis*, or groups, the manager wondered. He certainly hoped they would. But Bill Smith shot back venomously to the clueless man, "What do you think?" And he and Keo took off. Smith resigned from the club, effective immediately.

Whether or not Bill Smith told the story to others, it nonetheless made it to the local papers, even hitting the *LA Times* and newspapers as far away as Pittsburgh. For that entire winter, it was the shame of Honolulu, a source of great unhappiness and a deep sense of injustice throughout the swimming community. Local papers reported that Walter Napoleon, head of the Natatorium's Athletic Club, "withdrew his own team from the Turkey Day meet; of the fourteen on [his] squad, two, he pointed out, were 'Oriental.'" "I don't want my boys," he said, "to go into any place where they're not wanted." The president of the Outrigger Club wouldn't budge. "It [was]," he told the press, "a ticklish situation." He regretted the "fumbling manner in which Nakama had been treated," and he apologized for the "slight." He even acknowledged Keo Nakama's great contributions to "aquatic sports," but the Outrigger was a private club, after all. And private it would stay.

All over town, people in the Japanese-American community asked the obvious question that the episode raised. Never mind membership. If Keo Nakama was good enough to study at Ohio State University; if he was good enough to represent the Territory abroad in Australia and South America; if he was heroic enough to save the life of a Princeton lieutenant; and good enough to teach and coach schoolchildren, then why wasn't he good enough to be served a meal at the Outrigger Club? And if Keo Nakama wasn't good enough, then who in the heck was?

The incident died down by the turn of the year, and Nakama rarely mentioned it, but Bill Smith was still racked with guilt. He had amends to make. Most of his debts to Nakama and the rest of the 3YSC swimmers weren't because of the Outrigger incident, but now the scales had tipped quite over. Throughout the war, his teammates had paid a debt far deeper than he had to their country; after the war, Smith was seeing that they still were. He felt he owed them now, particularly Keo. He would have to find a way, any way, to pay them back; though it might be some time before he discovered how.

Sakamoto wasn't the sort of man to let such an incident stand for long. He immediately set to planning a grand swimming meet in Keo Nakama's name. The first annual Keo Nakama Swimming Invitational would rival the

Duke meets of the late 1930s. There had been nothing like them since the war, and Sakamoto wanted a spectacle. Bill Smith might have become Sakamoto's brother, but Keo had always been his son; and the way Sakamoto saw it, Keo had been the one person who had done more to revive the sport of swimming in the islands than anyone else.

Keo was humbled and gobsmacked by the honor, and he demurred, but Sakamoto still insisted, and the meet, held in the Waikiki Natatorium in July of '46, was indeed a combination of a P. T. Barnum production and a Billy Rose production. Sakamoto's inner orchestra leader had risen from the dead. The show featured every kind of swimming event imaginable, sanctioned and unsanctioned. There were parades in which the Royal Hawaiian Band marched and played, a beauty contest and the crowning of a "Nakama Queen," and entertainments ranging from a clown show to a water ballet to stunts performed by Johnny Weissmuller.

Sakamoto, master of all ceremonies once again, oversaw everything: the hanging of colorful banners and stringing of lane lines, the lettering of signs and invitations to city officials. He invited Mike Peppe and OSU swimming stars who had been Keo's teammates and dear friends. The meet was two weeks long, and Duke Kahanamoku was charged with handing out the trophies and certificates. The bleachers were filled to the brim—even the hau trees were peopled by locals sitting on the branches—just like it had been back in '37 when Nakama was the fresh-faced, bony boy who'd thrashed in the same tank and outswum an Olympian.

To underwrite the fete, Sakamoto enjoined George Higa, owner of the faithful Honolulu Café, who had also paid some of Keo's college bills, to help, and Higa in turn brought in another generous patron: his bosom friend Ralph Yempuku, another Okinawan and a great Nakama fan. Together Higa, Yempuku, and Soichi Sakamoto set out to throw a swimming party like no other.

Although Halo Hirose, Jose Balmores, and Bunny Nakama swam in the competition and attended every fete, and though all the swimmers gathered at the Nat had also had their dreams deferred, Sakamoto intended the meet to be an unabashed celebration of just Keo, who had always been his prized favorite.

If Halo Hirose harbored ill will about the event—for example, that it was named for Keo, whom Sakamoto had always preferred—he didn't come out and say so. Such things would irk him for years, but he put on a good face for the events and turned to celebration as consolation for loss. He smiled, mugged for the camera, danced at all the dances, and made sure his arm was around this or that pretty girl. His grin was as wide as anyone had seen it since before the war, and for all anyone knew, Halo Hirose was lighthearted, there to celebrate his good old friend, swim buddy, and neighbor from Pu'unene's Camp 5.

In the previous year, Bill Smith, just out of the service, had swum under the banner of UH and the Hawaii Swim Club, but in the fall of '46 he was planning to head back to Mike Peppe's tank to swim competitively for OSU. He had to finish up his university degree, and he still had a few years left on the college circuit. Smith, like his teammates Councilman and Fetterman, was ready to get back in the thick of things again. The swim world was coming alive once more. College teams were rebuilding. International meets were beginning to approach pre-wartime numbers. A sports reporter for the *Washington Post* joked that the exchange of athletes from shore to shore had become a regular "reciprocal lend-lease" deal, and intercontinental events were becoming as "commonplace as cross-town rival[ries]." The trend boded well for the Olympics. Soon Americans would be popping over to London regularly for a visit and a spot of tea.

Sakamoto was certainly paying attention to the trend. He was anxious to travel again, although the prospect hadn't yet presented itself to him or his university team. In the meantime, though, he watched as invitations flew from far and near to Bill Smith: the Europeans were smart enough to want the Flying Fish back on the invitational circuit to scout him out before he ambushed them come '48.

The French Grand Prix of swimming was set for late August 1946, shortly after the inaugural Nakama meet, and the French invited Smith to swim against French freestyle titleholder Alexander Jany, otherwise known as the "Dolphin of Marseilles." Sakamoto may have been behind the response Smith wrote—Sakamoto was, after all, constantly looking for ways to set the world aright again, and maybe this was one of those opportunities. Smith RSVP'd to the French that he'd come only if Keo Nakama could join him on the junket as both coach and manager, but the French responded right away, and curtly: they likely couldn't bear the additional expense; they hoped that Smith would reconsider.

Then Smith made a most generous offer, given his dislike for Halo Hirose. He offered Halo the spot in Paris. In no extant materials is there any evidence that Halo Hirose was grateful for the trip; rather, he seemed to have considered it a kind of birthright. He was still Esau-like in his bitter disappointment in Nakama's good fortune, and as with everything, he appeared to regard the trip as though he were indeed Isaac's accursed and discarded son.

Sakamoto unhappily continued to see in Halo the kind of entitlement the man exhibited as a young child. And observing protocol seemed to be another weak point in Halo's makeup: there's no record of any letter in which Halo might have had the decency to ask—or even to tell—Mike Peppe about a trip to Europe, although he knew he'd be gone through at least September, missing the first month of both schoolwork and preseason training, which could hurt Peppe's '47 roster.

Halo Hirose packed his bags for Paris. His wartime scrapbooks were already chock-full of photographs of pretty girls he'd met on leave, beauties named Giselle and Marie; in fact, his French collection was even more impressive than his gallery of Camp Shelby dishes. The chance to return to the City of Lights was too perfect, and Soichi Sakamoto witnessed how his former charge wasted hardly any time with the usual formalities that ought to accompany such a bon voyage.

The story of Halo Hirose's trip to Paris that Sakamoto came to know was murky, a mix of truth and fiction that Halo fed just about anyone. No one doubted the veracity that Hirose had gone to France, but when he returned, they had difficulty believing what he said had happened there. The tale had too many holes to be taken entirely at face value. For eight solid months he was mostly unaccounted for, during which time only some of his whereabouts and activities could be ascertained by tracing one or two newspaper clippings. A single headline in the *New York Times* shows him to have participated at the Paris Grand Prix, as planned. The Associated Press reported that Hirose competed against the Frenchman Alexander Jany but that he had come in a very slow fourth to the Dolphin in the 200-meter freestyle.

The tale of Halo's AWOL year was as mysterious as it was geographically sprawling. In Paris, he said, he had met an Egyptian prince. He believed the name was Lazuli Ratib, but he wasn't entirely sure. He did know that the prince was fourth in line to the Egyptian throne, which was why the man was driven about at all times in a sleek black limousine with the number 4 on it.

According to Halo, the prince had accompanied the two Egyptian competition entrants to Paris, one a diver and the other a swimmer by the name of Taha El-Gamal. Most of the other details were sparse and irregular. The prince had apparently been staying in the same hotel as Halo, and the two took a liking to each other, after which the prince invited Halo to travel with him onward, first to Morocco and then to visit the prince's home country. The way Halo told it, he was the special guest of the royal family and he saw everything that one read about in ancient history books, from the Sphinx to the Pyramids. An AP story, reprinted in the *New York Times* on November 4, 1946, reports that Halo won the 100-meter freestyle in Cairo in the Egyptian National Championships.

It's all possible, but teasing out just who this prince was takes a tremendous amount of work; even scholars of the royal family are unsure just who he was. What is known is that throughout Halo's travels to Germany and South America and across the United States as a young man, Halo Hirose had developed a larger sense of possibility, of his own agency, and of his ability to escape from what he felt was Soichi Sakamoto's self-interest and tyranny. It's easy to see how Halo might have, at least for a time, become both the guest and part of the retinue of a royal. On the other hand, it is also known that 1946 was a tremendously tumultuous time in the history of modern Egypt, as factions fought violently against one another in a push for independence from the British. It's hard to say if travel would have been easy that year; perhaps for a prince in a limousine it was.

The way that Halo told the story to anyone who'd listen was that, since he wasn't eager to return Stateside by the end of his time in Egypt, the prince paid for his ticket to Paris, where, because of an airline strike, Halo was delayed getting home. His extra time in Paris left him penniless, destitute, and from there, he'd had to call upon old friends.

One photograph in Halo's collection from his time in Paris raised another set of questions that no one has yet been able to answer. The photograph depicts Halo standing in front of Notre Dame, togged to the bricks, dressed in an argyle tie, double-breasted suit, spats, and an ornate medal around his neck. In the background of the picture are two men, one middle-aged, the other older. The middle-aged man is wearing a pair of wool jodhpurs or perhaps driving trousers, the sort typically worn on a jaunt. On the back of the photo there are a few clues to who at least one of the men might have been. The signature reads "A mon ami Halo"—To my friend Halo— and is signed, "Amore, Bilal." Beside the signature is something curious stamped in red ink; confusingly, it is the precise name and address of a well-known leftist newspaper called *Combat*. During the war, *Combat*, founded and edited by Albert Camus, Jean-Paul Sartre, and André Malraux, was a significant voice of the French resistance, and in 1946, it was still in publication. Bilal doesn't appear on the masthead, but it seems he was associated with *Combat*. Exactly how is unclear, and Halo never explained to anyone what he might have been doing spending time in postwar France— or perhaps in wartime France, too—with men who had the sort of political influence Camus and Sartre had. It's just more of the mystery of Halo Hirose.

When Halo finally returned to school at OSU, Mike Peppe had little patience for his stories; he reprimanded Halo and made sure that he paid the full price for any NCAA rules the swimmer had broken in the course of his trip abroad. However, Halo seemed not to mind at all. He appeared both unrepentant and satisfied that he had accomplished something important while he'd been away. What that was he never said. But he did maintain that the trip had been the most important one of his entire life.

The year 1946, the year that Halo Hirose slipped through the cracks, was that sort of time: a time between things when much could be lost and more could be found. On Maui an enormous strike of unionized plantation workers marked the end of the reign of sugar on the Valley Isle. Workers either sought better employment elsewhere or gained better wages at HC&S, but the upshot was that the camps at Puʻunene began to disappear. It was a time of rising and of falling. The rising of the voice of Japanese-Americans and the falling of an empire of cane.

As if to underscore the moment most dramatically, to make Maui remember that the change had come, an earthquake the magnitude of the temblor in Japan in 1923 cracked the ocean floor around the Hawaiian islands and caused destruction that would be remembered for half a century. Hilo, it was said, was the hardest island hit, with hundreds dead beneath the rubble, but on Maui, the scourge came in the form of a triple tsunami, a tidal wave that swept the homes of wealthy islanders out to sea, and while it didn't kill the rich, it changed their lives forever.

In that same year of 1946, the larger world was changing, too, if not at the speed of tidal waves, then at the pace of a globe tentatively becoming more accustomed to the reign of peace. In the fragile peacetime, the leadership of the International Olympic Committee resolved to hold the Fourteenth Olympiad in London in the summer of 1948; and no sooner had the group made the announcement than an entirely different war broke out once more—this time not on the battlefield but in the newspapers, in the mail, and around conference tables when and wherever the International Olympic Committee met to discuss how best to proceed.

With the London Olympiad in the blueprints stage, long-running and bitter debates surfaced once again. And the familiar figure who stood at the stove and stirred the brew was the same one who had been there, it seemed, forever: none other than Mr. Avery Brundage.

After seventeen years of vilification in serving the cause of athletics worldwide, Brundage hadn't disappeared. He was no longer the president of the AAU in the States, but he had moved his way up in the International Olympic Committee to the position of vice president. Since the cancellation of the 1940 Games, Brundage had succeeded in consolidating his global power behind the scenes. His penchant for cultivating both leadership and unpopularity had continued unabated. Throughout his career he had left controversy and collateral damage in his wake. In 1936 he had stripped popular gold medalist Jesse Owens of amateur standing on the grounds that post-Berlin, Owens had capitalized on his Olympic fame. In the same year, Brundage had tossed US Olympic Women's Swim Team member Eleanor Holm from the squad after what he considered an unseemly display of drunkenness aboard the *Bremen* as it sailed from New York to Europe. His insistence on participating in the '36 Games at all and his alliance with Hitler continued to haunt him and to define his legacy, and his critics said straight out that Brundage was nothing more than an elitist and a racist.

There were plenty of arguments in which Brundage had the opportunity to embroil himself as the London Games approached. Putting a global event like the Games back together after a global conflict meant having to deal directly with the ravages of war, the continued economic and political instability of nations everywhere, and the delicate, walk-on-eggshells politics required of even those in sport when addressing the complexity of a new world order. For those—like Brundage—still naive enough to believe that an international sporting event of the magnitude of an Olympiad was separate from international politics, London provided oodles of evidence to the contrary.

The conundrum of amateurism was in the air in advance of the London Games but with a new twist: talk in sports circles centered on a notion called "broken time," which wasn't, in essence, an attack on amateurism but merely a practical solution to an immediate problem. In a postwar world, many athletes had had to take jobs merely to survive, not in the field of athletics but in work central to the rebuilding of their countries, in factories and on construction crews throughout Europe. Britain, along with other European nations, introduced the notion of broken time as a way of encouraging working athletes to take a leave of absence from their jobs in order to participate in the London Games. Athletes were unlikely to take leave unless they were compensated for pay lost during the weeks of the Olympiad. "Broken time" gave countries the opportunity to reimburse their athletes—if they so chose—not for participating in the Games but for being unable to support their families while doing so. Many Europeans supported the idea, but as was his wont, Avery Brundage found any situation in which athletes pocketed money for *anything* sports-related to be profane. In response, Brundage easily dusted off a tale he had invoked many times before, about the downfall of the ancient Olympics: a tale in which, though once the Games had been pure, they fell into tawdry and meaningless exhibitions of moneymaking at the expense of athletics. It had been Brundage's lifework to make certain that nothing like that could ever happen again.

Regular meetings of the IOC went on and the issue went round and round, both in private conversation and in the sports pages. In 1947 Brundage traveled to London for a look-see at the city's progress and then went on to one of the IOC's regular meetings, this time in Stockholm. And there, by hook and by crook, he quashed discussion about "broken time." The arguments about broken time had broken down; the committee was exhausted and still at loggerheads. Brundage seized the stalemate to persuade the IOC to postpone the discussion about "broken time"—and so, in his mind, the redefinition of amateurism—until after the 1948 Olympics.

Most fundamental to defining the 1948 Olympics was the question of which nations would be allowed to participate. Worldwide sentiment was against the inclusion of wartime aggressors. In the Germany/Japan fight, Brundage would walk away the loser. He firmly believed that Germany and Japan should be allowed to participate in the London Games. His belief was echoed by an unlikely ally. The gruff boxer Jack Dempsey told the press quite simply that "as much as we hate them...we've still got to live with them."

The issue dogged the IOC, but in the end, neither Germany nor Japan would be included.

When Brundage returned from his overseas trip, he and the US Olympic Committee convened in the familiar and well-worn leather armchairs of the New York Athletic Club. There, he encountered much easier problems to solve. Seizing on an idea of Bob Kiphuth's that the US swim team ought to travel separately from the rest of the US Olympic squad, the AAU's Larry Johnson suggested that the swimmers travel by air. While it would be expensive to do so, the airplane trip would help the swim team bond together, and it would keep them out of the ruckuses that too often occurred on board ship during the Atlantic crossing—episodes of drinking, carousing, and gluttony. From his armchair at the athletic club, Brundage couldn't suppress a rare smile. It was a small but sweet victory for Brundage, who never wanted to revisit the infamous Holm incident ever again.

Brundage, though, was not alone in his unhappiness about the exclusion of Japan and Germany from the Games. Bob Kiphuth shared Avery Brundage's belief that without Japan and Germany in the mix, the London Games would bear the stain of illegitimacy. In swimming in particular, Kiphuth, who had spent the majority of his career as a swim coach assessing Japanese and German competition, felt that the Games would be false and lopsided without the participation of the strongest swimmers in the world.

In lieu of spying on the Germans or the Japanese, Kiphuth at least did reconnaissance on Allied nations. He and his usual traveling companions, Max Ritter and Larry Johnson, headed over to Europe in August of '47 to make an inspection of the competition, and after a brief stop in London, where, like Brundage, they looked over the construction, they headed to Monte Carlo for the European National Championship. The Monte Carlo meet proved a washout for the United States. With the sole exceptions of two backstrokers, Philly's Joe Verdeur and Kiphuth's own Allen Stack, both of whom Kiphuth felt assured were prepared to go to London, Kiphuth saw little that impressed him in the Americans. In fact, the most formidable middle-distance swimmer was Alexander Jany, who in the course of the meet broke the world record in the 400-meter race with a time of 4:35.2. When Kiphuth came back to the States, he engaged in his usual doomsday predictions: Alex Jany was going to vanquish any American swimmer in the 400, hands down.

When asked about the Russians, Kiphuth simply admitted, "We know very little about them," a statement resonant of the concerns of governments around the world. The Russians were an unknown quantity in many different ways. Kiphuth was concerned about their swimming capabilities in the middle distances and the breaststroke, but Western governments were more concerned about Russia's military—and in particular nuclear—capacity. If the Russians showed, Kiphuth said, they'd be full of surprises.

Chapter Seventeen

DETROIT, REDUX (1948)

BY 1948, Mike Peppe had rebuilt his swim squad from a tried-and-true, if aging, roster. He'd lost some of his stalwarts to graduation, some to war, but he was sentimental and profoundly loyal. He welcomed Bill Smith and Halo Hirose back, and he had a soft spot for those military veterans who had cheated death.

Diver Miller Anderson participated in 111 combat missions as a pilot during the war, on one of which he'd been shot down, his left leg so torn away from his torso that he would have lost it if it had not been secured by a metal plate. He'd been captured by the Germans but swiftly recaptured by the Allies, and the latter had been able to save his leg. By the time Anderson returned to Columbus, his leg was sewn back up, but it wasn't completely healed. On the springboard, Miller was a changed man, and he compensated for it. He had to cut back on the amount of practice he put in, and he invented both a new method for leaving the board and a new dive, which was more complicated than any attempted in the sport to date: a double twist followed by a half somersault.

Halo Hirose was back on the roster as a sprinter, Bill Smith had also returned to Columbus, and Bunny Nakama, Keo's brother, had come out to swim as well. Even aged and hobbled, the swimming Buckeyes eclipsed the university's famed football team. Mike Peppe's swimming and diving squads had become the greatest in college athletics in the nation. Peppe himself continued to be a respected international figure as well; recently, the USOC had honored him by appointing him head diving coach for the upcoming Games in London.

As OSU headed into the 1948 swim season, Peppe assessed the threat from swimmers in their prime and also those rising fast at other colleges. Joe Verdeur, a big blond-haired, blue-eyed backstroker from Philadelphia, swam for LaSalle College, and he was as close to a reincarnation of Adolph Kiefer as was humanly possible. Verdeur was as big as Bill Smith had been at the age of seventeen, and even though he was large for a backstroker, his clocking was out of this world. He'd earned the nickname "Rubber Man" because people said that his arms weren't made of flesh at all—maybe foam, Bob Kiphuth suggested. The kid was so crazy-flexible that every time he swam in a race he dislocated his shoulders but was never worse for the wear.

Allen Stack was another backstroker, but one with a different strength than Verdeur. Kiphuth's protégé, Stack was a big lug whose size was unusual for the backstroke but whose 6-foot-5-inch frame enabled him to reinvent the event. Sportswriters noted that Stack would "put his arm in the water and pull through like a normal backstroker, but as he brought the arm to his side he would bend it a little at the elbow and push with his hands toward his feet." One noted that "it was long, looping, and seemingly effortless." And it was a game changer.

Wally Ris, another competitor, was a dashing, dark-haired Chicagoan and a born 100- and 200-meter freestyler who now swam for the Iowa Hawkeyes. He had been a teammate of Bill Smith's on the Great Lakes squad during the war, and 1947 had been Ris's best year yet. All three—Verdeur, Stack, and Ris—were shoo-ins for the Olympic squad.

Against the likes of those swimmers, that spring season Peppe's boys didn't hold up as well as he'd have liked. His divers did well, but his swimmers fell short. Peppe particularly kept his eye on Smith and Hirose—his two most likely candidates for the Olympic squad—and his fingers crossed. In a home meet in February versus Matt Mann's Wolverines, the Buckeyes barely sank Michigan by 2 points. Bill Smith had a sinus infection that had kept him out of the pool in the days before the competition, and in the 220-yard freestyle he was a full 2.8 seconds slower than his own world record pace, a now antiquated mark. This poor performance gave men like Michigan's Matt Mann the notion that Smith was on his way out, and the idea of a washed-up "Malolo" gained momentum.

In what was considered another crucial test, 175 swimmers from 34 colleges and universities gathered in Ann Arbor in March to compete in the NCAA Swimming Championships, seen as a prelude to the Olympic trials to be held in Detroit that summer. Sadly, at the Ann Arbor meet, more rumors flew about Smith. He swam well against Wally Ris in the 220-yard freestyle, but he looked physically unfit. He was overweight and bloated with a double chin. His new nickname became "the Whale." And as for Halo Hirose, he embarrassed himself at Ann Arbor, flailing in at fourth place in the 100-yard freestyle. There was no way that Peppe could let his guard down and uncross his fingers. Although both Smith and Hirose would be competitors at Detroit, they would be underdogs as well.

Mike Peppe's training program had never held a candle to Sakamoto's; it reflected Peppe's personality and his overall belief that swimming ought to be as much fun as it was hard work. Bill Smith admired Peppe, but he knew that in order to train properly for the Games, he'd have to leave him. Reluctant to say so directly to Peppe, he offered instead the disadvantage of staying at OSU and practicing in a pool that was only 25 yards long. It gave a swimmer the benefit of the frequent wall, meaning the frequent turn and push-off. Smith wanted to measure himself in a 50-meter pool, the same length as the one at the Detroit Rouge Park and the one in London.

Smith knew that it wasn't just about tanks, though. Only one man knew how to prepare him properly for the greatest challenge of his life. That man had trained him as a teenager to break world records and had turned him into an Olympian so many years before. With the swim season over and with Peppe's support, Smith dropped out of school; local papers said it was "to rest," but Bill knew what his purpose was. It was the beginning of April, and Smith put out his thumb and hitchhiked across the country before sailing for home, willing the ship to move as fast in the water as it possibly could.

No one ever explained why Halo Hirose didn't choose to join Smith in returning to Sakamoto, not even Halo himself. Smith wondered if maybe he was short of money, but he knew the most likely reason as well as anyone who had been closely watching Halo through the years. Halo had come not only to resent but also even to hate Coach, and that bitterness, combined with his longtime refusal to train hard under anyone, made him rely heavily now on what charisma and natural ability he had in him after the long war and at a dangerously advanced age.

And, in truth, Sakamoto likely didn't expect to see Halo come home. Years ago, he had given up on saving him, and Halo was certain he'd needed no one to save him from the very beginning of his swimming life in the ditch.

Since his arrival at UH in 1945, Soichi Sakamoto had built a decent UH swim program. His women swimmers in particular had stayed loyal, interested, and enthusiastic. Mitzi Higuchi and Chic Miyamoto were still on the roster in '48 and swimming like gangbusters locally, and Sakamoto was cultivating a new and very promising swimmer named Thelma Kalama and another named Evelyn Kawamoto. Sakamoto had full faith that Kalama would make the Olympic squad, likely on the 400-meter medley relay team.

But as for the male swimmers Sakamoto had in his UH tank, he had his doubts. He loved the old ditch kids who had returned to him from war: Jose Balmores and Charlie Oda, both of whom were studying at the time at UH; and Yoshio Shibuya, who signed on as team manager. But if Oda and Balmores wanted to go to the Games in London in '48, they had some work to do.

In qualifying for the Games, Balmores was as much at the mercy of the Olympic events as his own swimming abilities in '48. There had always been a disconnect between American and European events—yards vs. meters, of course—but more significantly, Balmores had always specialized in an event

Detroit, Redux (1948)

the Olympics had never sanctioned: the 300-meter individual medley. Even though US sportswriters continued to argue that the 300-meter medley was the highest form of swimming—as high as the decathlon in track and field, because it required the mastery of three key strokes and skill—the Europeans had always considered the event a purely American invention.

Since the beginning of the modern Olympic movement, the swimming events had been in flux. It was perhaps only a matter of time before the likes of Balmores would see a 300-meter individual medley race, because even in short-term Olympic history there had been events far stranger than the dreaded medley. In Olympic days, strokes still varied so much from country to country that the earliest Olympiads could feel more like water carnivals at the Tower of Babel: swimmers sometimes did whatever it took to reach the finish line first.

At the first modern Olympic Games held in Greece in 1896, the planners settled on some basic rules and acceptable strokes, but the most popular of the swim events—there were four—was the 100-meter freestyle specifically for *sailors*. The 1900 Olympic Games in Paris were still a hodgepodge, with an obstacle course event in the river Seine. Four years later swimmers vied for medals in St. Louis in the "plunge for distance": athletes leaped enthusiastically into the water, attempting to maximize the amount of time and distance they could glide forward without having to move their arms or legs at all.

In Stockholm in 1912, Duke Kahanamoku's first Olympics, the Swedish Olympic Committee considered adding a "400 metres team" relay in which swimmers did whatever stroke they felt like doing. Antwerp, 1920: Americans arrived "heartsick" to find that, because of the war, there had been no time for Belgians to build a pool, so events took place in an ancient "city moat" so cold that "many swimmers had to be rescued from [it because of] hypothermia."

In London in 1948 there would be only six swimming events for men. For American swimmers, used to a larger number of events—in both distance and type—on the American collegiate and club circuit, trying to get on the Olympic squad was a little bit like trying to put on a pair of clothes that were just too tight. It was a shame, but Sakamoto decided to have

Balmores concentrate on his strongest skills now: the backstroke and the freestyle short-course events; if all else failed, putting Balmores up against the powerful Joe Verdeur might get Jose a spot on the 4x200-meter men's relay squad, where there was often room to squeeze someone in at the last minute.

Charlie Oda had little skill in the backstroke, and he was at risk in distance and endurance in the 1500, but Sakamoto had no choice but to prepare him in those. Oda had done well abroad, even in the Army, and when he'd come back he'd been a faithful swimmer and enthusiastic member of the UH squad. Others adored him; in the previous year he'd been elected captain. Even if he were to go to Detroit for the purpose of morale, it would be worth the effort.

Bill Smith's strength, no question, was in the 400-meter. That's where he'd first made his mark in 1941, and it was what his body was most used to training for. Smith had, however, lost the 400 to a very young Jimmy McLane, and no matter how much Smith trained for Detroit, McLane was going to be his most dangerous competitor. McLane didn't have just youth on Smith; in addition to being ten years younger, as only a junior at Philips Andover academy he had cut a spectacular 19.5 seconds off Keo Nakama's former record in the 1,500-meter freestyle. What McLane had in even greater abundance than youth was physical fitness.

Bill Smith would jump into the Rouge Pool in Detroit with seventeen championships under his belt in events ranging from "sprints to middle distance," but if he couldn't get fit, nothing mattered. Each time Smith had arrived back home in Honolulu—way back in 1945, and then more recently—Sakamoto had taken one good look at him and known on the nose what he had to do with the swimmer. His greatest work would be in teaching the "Avoirdupois of Table Two" to push himself away from every table.

The swimmers were disadvantaged by their age—they'd passed their prime—but age was Sakamoto's great strength. Coaches only grow in wisdom over time, and Sakamoto was a more skilled and seasoned coach than he had ever been. He had access to better equipment than ever, and his position at UH buoyed his spirits. His standard training regimen now involved 25 laps of swimming, 25 laps of stroking while attached to an inner tube, 25 more kickboard laps, starting and turning practice, breathing exercises, and then intense sprints: time trials at 20-, 50-, 100-, 220-, and 300-yard distances and then, for most, even sprinters, a long 600-yard finish. And that was in addition to land training, for which he now had the use of resistance machines on steel frames and the financial resources to purchase everything from real barbells to state-of-the-art kickboards.

He had deepened his understanding of technique. He knew now how to get swimmers over the bow wave that formed in front of them; how to help them control their body rotation so that it strengthened rather than weakened their propulsion; and he knew how to work closely and intimately with swimmers with different types of bodies to cut down on drag. Finally, he'd figured out how important a fourth step the arm stroke was: he'd always thought of the underwater movement as a pull; but he now saw that it also included a push that gave extra propulsion.

He was primed, and he started the group off immediately. The Detroit trials were in July. They had three months to get there in good shape. If he'd thought about it, he might have called them the Three-Month Swim Club. And they had a new goal to meet.

However, UH hadn't yet brought its pool up to date. It was slow, and it was only 25 yards long. It was fine for some kinds of practice but not for endurance, proper turning, timing, and more. Each morning Sakamoto started the group out at the UH pool for calisthenics and technique, and then they headed over to the Natatorium to work on pace and endurance. For others, afternoons at the Nat were prime recreational time. Although the war had shuttered it, it was now open again to the public and to swim clubs, and it was filled with youngsters at play who rose in the mornings and called out to one another, "You goin' tank today?" Kids from the nearby slums sunned themselves in the bleachers. They dove from the 10-meter tower, shrieking and laughing and shooting up splash, but when Sakamoto's team arrived at the Nat, they stopped and stared at the procession of swimmers and managers with their fancy equipment and their seriousness of purpose, and they kept watching the practice until nightfall.

Sakamoto's game plan for Detroit was to have Smith and Oda in two freestyle events. They would each swim in the 200- and 400-meters. Smith's third race would be the 100-meter sprint, while Oda's would be the 1,500-meter. That way each had a chance to win a spot in either an individual event or a medley. Balmores would enter the 200-meter breaststroke and later swim the 200-meter freestyle to gain a spot on the 800-meter freestyle relay, so if all else failed, his three boys at the very least had a chance at a berth on the relay team.

In the midst of the pre-Detroit training, an unexpected letter arrived for Sakamoto. He hadn't seen a New Haven, Connecticut, postmark in years; perhaps the last time had been when Bob Kiphuth had accepted Sakamoto's invitation to become an honorary member of the 3YSC. Bob Kiphuth's current letter extended to Sakamoto an invitation to be "an associate coach" at the Games. The title was honorific.

It seemed, at first glance, a generous offer. Over the years the relationship between Kiphuth and Sakamoto had grown only more distant. They had to have respected each other, but they must have also feared each other and harbored jealousy, because the enmity between them was "palpable." They avoided each other at meets. The more successful Sakamoto's swimmers had become, the less friendly Kiphuth was and the more withdrawn and self-protective Sakamoto was. The louder Kiphuth's voice was—the more dominant and established a figure he was on the national scene—the more Sakamoto silenced himself. He intentionally skipped coaches' meetings and social gatherings, and he spoke softly when in the company of those he thought his betters. It had been a strategy Sakamoto had developed in his years on Maui: to connect with no one more powerful, to rely entirely on himself. It had served him well enough with Damkroger, Crane, Bud Crabbe, and the rest.

Detroit, Redux (1948)

But at the national level, Soichi's fierce independence had cost him what might have been an opportunity for collegiality and even a rise to prominence. In his heart of hearts, though, he'd had to protect himself all these years from the reality that, even if he had tried harder to insert himself into the mainstream, as a man of Japanese ancestry, as a country hick and rube and grammar school teacher, it would have been a miracle had anyone chosen truly to embrace him.

Upon receiving Kiphuth's letter, Sakamoto was honored. He shared the letter widely, and the papers printed it and celebrated that Soichi Sakamoto had at last been acknowledged for his contributions and would stand among the nation's other great coaches, precisely where he belonged.

It didn't take long, though, before Sakamoto read between the letter's lines. The invitation was, in truth, "left-handed." Kiphuth said nothing about underwriting Sakamoto's trip, something Steve Forsyth had complained about back in Kentucky in '38. And the closer he looked, Sakamoto could see the true emptiness behind Kiphuth's gesture. Bob Kiphuth's invitation was for Sakamoto to serve as an "associate coach," but both men were well aware that the only other coaches of the US team were called "assistants." Assistant coaches stood on deck and were involved in the athletes' training. Not unlike the invitation Sakamoto had offered Kiphuth to join the Three-Year Swim Club, the invitation that Kiphuth now extended to Sakamoto was a gesture, nothing more. Kiphuth was a "member" of the 3YSC club only in name. Bob Kiphuth was essentially letting Sakamoto know that, if the Hawaii coach could come up with the cash, he was welcome to think he was important while he sat up high in the nosebleed seats in the bleachers of the Empire Pool, far away from the action.

Others read between the lines, as well.

The offer wasn't generous; it was in spirit unkind. Upon realizing so, the communities of which Sakamoto was a part rallied on his behalf. On both Maui and Oahu, groups announced fund drives to raise money for Sakamoto's ticket to London. At the U of H, the Footballers' Club began to scare up cash. And back home on the Valley Isle, something truly remarkable began to occur.

It seemed that time hadn't softened Bob Kiphuth's ways of being in and

315

seeing the world. But it had changed others profoundly. E. L. Damkroger had lost his eldest son, Ernest Leaphart Damkroger Jr., in Europe in 1944. In his grief over the boy whom he and his wife had affectionately called "Poggie," the head of athletics at Alexander House set about at last to write the book he had always intended to. It was the culmination of his life's work, and it was called *Recreation Through Competition*. It was not a rigid manifesto but a thoughtful handbook, complete with charts and graphs galore, designed to guide others in organizing community athletic programs for underprivileged youth. Damkroger dedicated the book to his son.

The ice between Damkroger and Sakamoto had melted. After Poggie's death and before he'd left the island for the U of H, he and Damkroger had shaken hands and entered a friendly partnership, one in which Damkroger provided support for Sakamoto's swimmers, without strings attached, and Sakamoto agreed to have his group swim as the 3YSC of Alexander House. Now, in the face of Sakamoto's humiliation, Damkroger announced the "Send Sakamoto to London" fund, and he was the first to contribute to it.

Old Ezra Crane would never become less imperious in business, but during the war one of his duties had been to pay visits to the Japanese-American mothers whose sons had died while in the 442nd. He abhorred doing it, never had a taste for it, but he did it nonetheless, and he had since become quietly contemplative whenever the subject arose in conversation. In the *Maui News*, of which Crane was again the publisher, he implored the citizens of the island to give generously in support of the London fund. In an editorial titled "Maui Cannot Fail," Crane wrote of Sakamoto that "all through the years he stood at tank-side and taught, coached and trained, without remuneration and oftentimes, we suppose, without much appreciation being shown for his self-sacrifice." It was essential, he said, to show "that Coach has not been forgotten."

The money was intended to fund not only Sakamoto's travel expenses but also a gift: a brand-new Kodak movie camera—color—with which the islands asked Sakamoto to record what he saw at the Games and to return home with reels of memories to share. His title was "Observer," and it was understood that Soichi Sakamoto would serve as Maui's proxy witness. He would stand in for those at home—villagers, swimmers, and anyone else who, however ardently they had wished or passionately they had tried, had never been able to make it to the Olympics.

The funds overflowed. By the time of the Detroit trials, the figure came nearly to $5,000, and the donor list read like a who's who from every era and corner of Soichi Sakamoto's life: Dynamite Nakasone, one of the first ditch swimmers who now proudly owned his own upholstery shop; and Chow Shibuya, the swimmer–truck driver who had begged Sakamoto to start a swim club in the first place. There were envelopes from Sakamoto's first Scouts from old Troop 27 of Waikapu. Parents of swimmers gave generously in gratitude for what Sakamoto had done for their sons and daughters: Boss Yokouchi, the Katsutanis, the Nakamas, Denkechi Hirose. Pu'unene locals pitched in: Reverend Miura, Mrs. Maehara, Sakamoto's former colleagues at the elementary school. And it was impossible to overlook the kindness of a humbled Rikio Ebisu, captain of the ill-fated *Mae West*. Since the accident, the contrite Ebisu had served without pay as an official at swim meets across the island.

Sakamoto's father, Tokuichi, and his brother Bill contributed, as well as hundreds of others; friends like George Higa, who had always been there; and then there was a list of those who didn't wish to be acknowledged for their gift but who instead were known simply as "Admirers."

The fund drive was so successful that it raised double its goal of $5,000, an amount that enabled Sakamoto not only to go to London but that also completely underwrote the Hawaiian team's trip to the Detroit trials. Instead of having to take a long sea journey and train ride across the country, the delegation flew instead in speed and style on Pan American Airways, first to the West Coast and then to Michigan, a trip that took a mere two days.

In the first week of July, more than four hundred swimmers descended upon the city of Detroit. By the end of the week, less than a tenth of them would prove themselves in the "trim Brennan pools" at Detroit's Rouge Park and earn the right to leave for England. Sakamoto and his swimmers prayed they'd be among the lucky tenth. They had twenty days.

317

But it was the 3YSC swimmers about whom Sakamoto was most concerned. The others had time to compete again, but for the boys of the 3YSC, this was it. As in the old days, the group carried with them paper leis to gift to anyone they might meet. A new tradition was to bring along a bowl of rice for luck. They dressed as spiffily as in the past, the boys debonair in blue suit jackets and the girls in dresses. All had sporty white hats.

Detroit greeted them once again. Sakamoto, Oda, and Balmores had been here in '39, during a journey of firsts. The very first team championship. Fujiko's first individual title in Des Moines. The jaunt to New York, Billy Rose's Aquacade, the baseball games, Joe Louis's barbecue shack. The horrid rejection at the New York Athletic Club and Sakamoto's painfully fragile relationship with Damkroger.

They had changed. And Detroit had changed mightily, too. The war had been the cauldron of their transformation and of the city's as well. Detroit's automobile factories had retooled and had ceased building cars. Instead, they built M5 tanks and jeeps and Flying Fortress B-17s at a rate of one of those massive crafts per hour. Now, in 1948, Detroit had returned to the manufacture of automobiles, but it would never be the same Detroit that produced a '39 Ford. Everywhere one looked the streets were crowded with new and shiny cars that little resembled those of the past. The 1948 Cadillac looked like nothing so much as a fighter jet: Detroit's designers had modeled it on a "secret military aircraft" and turned it into a thing of beauty with "one...unbroken, flowing...line that continued from the cowl...of the craft...all the way to the tip of [its] tail," an icon of both war and peace.

The looks of cars weren't the only change. The very face of Detroit was completely different. After strikes and strife, the city had been unionized; it was now more prosperous. It was also more diverse, as the African-American population had more than doubled since the war. The demand for new houses was insatiable. Timber-framed houses rose everywhere one looked, and the United Auto Workers had succeeded in bringing to workers on the line good wages, benefits, and a quality of life they had never seen before. The apex of that life was the summer of '48. The city would be torn apart again in the 1950s, roiled by racial turmoil and economic downturn, but for the moment, that summer of '48, it was shining; and the place that

318

Detroit, Redux (1948)

built the vehicles that helped the United States win the war had come to have a new nickname: "the Arsenal of Democracy."

This time, the swimmers took up residence at the Hotel Wolverine on Elizabeth Street. It was a storied spot where Duke Ellington, Glenn Miller—the famous bandleader who had long ago disappeared over the English Channel—and every visiting ballplayer or Tigers recruit used to stay. Next door was a spiffy cocktail lounge called the Tropics that had seen better days but was the perfect kind of welcome to the visiting Islanders, with its fake rain-on-the-roof bar and tiki decor.

The downtown was booming, exciting, filled with businessmen and businesswomen and construction workers carrying beams over their shoulders. There were new restaurants, and of course, the ballpark was nearby. This trip, though, there'd be no visit out to watch a game at Tiger Stadium, even though it was awfully tempting: bad-boy Dick Wakefield was playing. Bill Smith had crossed paths with notorious Number 77 during the war—at Great Lakes, Shoemaker, and in Honolulu—and that week in Detroit the Tigers were playing the Yankees. And there'd be no tour of the Ford Factory either.

There was just too much to do to get ready.

Sakamoto had picked the optimal number of days—ten—for pretraining and acclimatization to the Brennan Pools. The pools were a ways from downtown, on the city's west side in a pretty green park called Rouge, so he had to factor in travel time. On Sunday, Sakamoto got the troops into gear and started workouts. The first session was from 6 a.m. to 10 a.m., when the pool was largely abandoned. The second session was in the late afternoon, when most other swimmers had gone home for naps.

The newspapers harped on the early arrival of the Hawaiians and how stealthily they came to and went from practice, as if they were keeping a state secret. Sakamoto had no real secret, though. He had plans, and he had hopes.

Still, local reporters were particularly unkind to Bill Smith. George Puscas, longtime sports editor of the *Detroit Free Press*, challenged the readers of his regular column, "Love Letters," to bet on events with the most "improbable" odds, especially Smith's, in exchange for a whole yard of kielbasa. Puscas implied that Smith's chances were, if not long, then "wide," and he referred to his physique in much the same way. It was becoming an old joke.

Keith Carter of Purdue and Bob Sohl of Michigan would challenge Balmores in the breaststroke, and "Rubber Man" Joe Verdeur of La Salle College and "Gentle Giant" Allen Stack of Yale would push Balmores in the backstroke and the individual medley. The top freestylers against whom the Hawaiians would compete were Wally Ris of the University of Iowa; Alan Ford, formerly of Yale; and Michigan State standout George Hoogerhyde. But the most formidable and threatening competitor in the freestyle, however baby-cheeked he was, would be little Jimmy McLane.

McLane was an enfant terrible, a prodigy. In 1944 Bob Kiphuth called McLane, then only thirteen years old, "the World's Best Swimmer," a title that Bill Smith had held, at least informally, after Arthur Daley's similar declaration in the *New York Times* in 1942. In '44 McLane had been about the size of Keo Nakama in '37; he was a little taller than Keo, but he was a withered 116 pounds when wet, and he had a pair of big feet that served him as well in the water as Keo's had once done. In fact, in July of 1944, McLane became the youngest swimmer ever to hold a national title in the 4-mile swim; and the swimmer whom he'd vanquished on that day had been Keo Nakama himself. In 1945, in Keo's last stop in Akron, McLane had robbed him of his national title in the 800-meter freestyle. In '47, in Tyler, Texas, McLane outswam Bunny Nakama in the 1,500-meter freestyle and was described in the *Chicago Daily Tribune* as "the top American hope in the 1948 Olympics." Now, at seventeen, McLane was nearly a decade younger than Bill Smith.

The prelims began Wednesday the seventh and Sakamoto kept a close eye on Halo Hirose and Bunny Nakama. Even though the two Ohio State students weren't technically swimming under Sakamoto's umbrella, they were as much his swimmers as Oda, Smith, and Balmores. They were young men whose careers, even some eleven years after the start of the 3YSC, he still felt responsible for, having placed his earliest hopes on them.

In Wednesday's 100-meter freestyle heats, Bill Smith's least likely chance for an Olympic berth, he came in predictably far behind the pack. Halo Hirose's most likely chance at a berth was in the 100-meter. In the second heat, Halo Hirose swam a 58.8, qualifying for the finals, but in the finals themselves, he failed to qualify for the team. Wally Ris, Keith Carter from Purdue, and Alan Ford secured 1-2-3 spots for London.

On Thursday and Friday, the 400-meter freestyle heats and the finals were to be Bill Smith's litmus tests. Smith had come a long way since his arrival in Honolulu in April and his training with Sakamoto. He'd taken off the weight. He was at exactly 210 pounds. His best time in training in the 440-yard freestyle at home was 4:49, and Sakamoto's thinking was that Smith would be at 4:42 in Detroit: 2.5 seconds below the world record. In the heats, Bunny Nakama and Charlie Oda, who were entered alongside Smith, faded away early, each coming in far over the 5-minute mark. But Smith made it through to Friday, which was when he and McLane would shoot it out.

In the finals on Friday, McLane was on fire. From the beginning of the final 400-meter freestyle, McLane pulled out and just drowned everyone behind him, including Smith, who touched three lengths later. McLane came in at 4:45.6—faster than Smith had been swimming at home—and Smith was a second over his home time at 4:50.4. That still put McLane in the #1 berth, Smith in the #2, and a fellow by the name of Bill Heusner in the #3 spot for the Olympics. Smith had secured his place, even having lost to McLane. Bill Smith was going to London. So far, though, no other 3YSC swimmer was going with him.

There was nothing built into the meet that could give Oda, Balmores, Nakama, or Hirose any advantage. The most logical order of events in swim competitions is to start with sprints, then middle distance, then save the longest distance event—the 1,500-meter freestyle—for last. But for reasons no one could explain, the organizers of the Detroit meets had messed with convention, which would spell trouble for any swimmer not completely up to snuff.

On the very last day of competition, the 1,500-meter would precede the 200-meter sprints, so anyone trying to qualify in the 1,500-meter would be thoroughly exhausted by the time the 200 sprints came around. On Sunday, July 11, the grueling 200-meter finals would be the last event in which a swimmer could bid for a berth on the Olympic squad—one final chance to travel through the looking glass to the London Games.

The prelims for the 200 took place on Saturday, and for Sakamoto's boys, the heats were disastrous. Charlie, Jose, and Bunny were shut out, and when it was his turn, Halo came in a dismal ninth place. None qualified for Sunday. But Bill Smith had an idea. He talked to the other men who had already qualified and proposed something radical. When they'd all agreed, they headed on over to the officials.

Smith and the others sought permission to do the following: Smith and McLane agreed to "scratch themselves" out, which meant make it to the wall and then ask the officials to cross out their times as if they'd never swum at all.

Four others who already had berths—Ris, Ford, Heusner, and Verdeur—asked if they could legally "dog," meaning swim as slowly as possible, so that at least two others, including Halo Hirose, would have a chance to qualify for the Olympic team. The officials agreed it was dodgy in the United States but that it didn't violate FINA, the European rules. As for Kiphuth, if the scheme allowed him to strengthen the team, he wholeheartedly approved. He was flush with an elastic $50,000 budget. And he added a kicker: Why stop at two?

He knew he'd be the subject of tremendous criticism later, accused of stacking the deck against nations that didn't have the kind of reserves that the United States had, and Germany and Japan weren't even a factor. What's more, only four of the swimmers on the squad had qualified in their own events. Why not put a distance swimmer in "fancy diving"? asked the *New York Times*. But at the moment, Kiphuth didn't care one bit. It was likely one of the few times in his life when Soichi Sakamoto felt unabashedly thankful for Robert J. H. Kiphuth.

Detroit, Redux (1948)

Halo Hirose seemed to be grateful to Bill Smith for the chance to redeem himself. He hugged and thanked Bill before the race began. With six other swimmers still to contend with, Halo had his final shot now. His competitors were George Hoogerhyde, Bob Gibe, Wally Wolf, Eugene Rogers, Ed Gilbert, and Ralph Sala of Stanford—the latter a distance swim champ. On that Saturday morning, the scheme played out in stages: all of the swimmers dove in at the same time, but Smith and McLane swam swiftly and scratched—disqualified themselves—with the officials immediately.

Hirose hit the water along with Hoogerhyde and the hungry rest, while behind them, the doggers—Ris, Ford, Heusner, and Verdeur—took their sweet time. They merely aped the swimming strokes and kicks, making the "crawl really look like a crawl," the *New York Times* reported. Sakamoto watched the proceedings through the lens of his brand-new movie camera. Something was going terribly wrong. For all of the careful planning, the second chance at second chances, Halo fell behind now, horribly, distantly, instead of speeding ahead of the pack, whom he ought to have beaten. And through all 4 of his laps he stayed behind.

The ancient Greeks were the architects behind the Olympics; they also invented tragedy. In Greek drama the tragic hero is a man of stature who lives in ignorance of a single fatal flaw in his character that will be his undoing. One poor choice, the flaw is revealed, and the man's life is ruined. He awakes to a nightmare that the audience had seen coming the whole time. Bill Smith and Soichi Sakamoto were the audience to a tragedy that Saturday.

In the chilly waters, Halo Hirose unraveled, stroke by stroke. His hubris had always been his belief that he was exceptional. That the rules didn't—or needn't—apply to him. He wanted to be an Olympic swimmer. But he'd never worked as hard as the others. He'd never practiced enough. All of his life he'd cut corners, choosing pleasure over sacrifice. He'd trusted only himself, and he had harbored resentments against others. His fatal flaw had been his preference for ease. When Bill Smith had left Columbus, Halo had stayed behind. Preparing for an Olympic bid in Peppe's short pool hadn't served him. Neither had staying away from Coach. He was a sprinter by nature, but the wall had always been his crutch. Sakamoto had seen that early on, how Halo would have to work harder if he wanted to be a champion.

The first six who came in were Wolf at an even 2:14; Dudley and Gibe a half second later; Gilbert at 2:14.8; Hoogerhyde at 2:15.3; and Rogers at 2:15.8. Sala followed, and Halo Hirose was dead last. He wasn't going to the Olympics. Not now and not ever. He was now among those swimmers at Detroit in the summer of 1948 who would retreat into the American heartland or into the shadow of their own disappointments. In fact, no one would know where Halo Hirose took his sorrow; he'd be missing during the next few weeks, unheard from during the Games. He'd be untraceable.

That had also been his habit.

Chapter Eighteen

GOALS AND SACRIFICES

THE AUSTERITY Olympics could not have been more aptly named. Every borough in the city of London was pocked with bombing-damaged sites. Through the holes in buildings one could see the remnants of family life: a fallen table, a turned-over wash bin, or a charred bureau of clothes.

Cities in the wake of war have historically had difficulty gearing up for an Olympiad. Antwerp in 1920 was "ill-prepared following almost ceaseless bombardment for four brutal years" of the Great War. Back in 1920, the condition of the army transport vessel used to carry the American team from New York to Europe led to a literal mutiny of the athletes: the ship, which had been used to transport the war dead, smelled horribly of corpses.

The construction of roads and buildings and the renovation of sporting arenas and fields met blockade after blockade: Petrol was nearly impossible to come by. So was lumber. The purchase or import of nearly any commodity required a government license that got tied up forever in red tape. The IOC had decided intentionally to keep the celebration in London austere. It would have been not only impractical but also impolitic—even frightening— had the Games carried a whiff of the excessive pomp and nationalism of the 1936 Games, which had left a bitter taste in the mouths of fans.

At the same time, the postwar conditions in London precluded even the ambition for anything grandiose. The still-standing stadia and the less-gouged playing fields of England—whatever had withstood the blitz—would have to serve. Wembley Stadium, which had been turned into a greyhound track after the war, was both run-down and ill-suited for real track and field. It took both persuasion and sweat to repurpose it. In the former case, stadium officials had balked at the notion of allowing the Games there, since Wembley would lose significant amounts of its revenue on dog racing during that time.

There were many such tempests in English teapots. Original plans had called for the building of a new pool, but money ran out. The old Empire Pool near Wembley would have to do. But it, too, required much attention. Since the war began, no one had seen the water in it. It was there, but it was boxed in below the skating rink built above it, and the place would have to be retrofitted both for swimming and for water polo events, after which it would have to be used for the boxing competition—organizers had sorted out a way to build a boxing ring above the pool once they excavated the skating rink and found the tank.

There had been talk of an Olympic Village, but that was also not to be. It was expensive and impractical, and the resourceful organizers instead brilliantly repurposed old Army barracks and the dormitories at universities to house athletes. Some athletes were to be put at storied Richmond Park. Others would stay at nursing hostels. Still others, including the US Olympic Men's Swim Team, would stay in bunk rooms at Uxbridge, while the US women would stay at a college near Wimbledon. Some problems irked visitors more than others. It was said that in both places the cots were awfully hard. And the accommodations offered visitors literally no towels. Tell that to a swimmer.

Spectators who had attended the games of '32 or '36 pronounced the situation in London positively dreary; one man reported that "the most festive sign" he saw upon arriving at Wembley Stadium "bleakly announced, 'Welcome to the Olympic Games. This road is a danger area.'"

The British were still under a rationing system, from tea to meat to chocolate. The ration for British athletes was twenty-six hundred calories per day. Chocolate was nearly as scarce as it had been during the war: each person was restricted to just eight ounces of the stuff per week. Whale meat wasn't rationed, but only the bold would brave it. However, visiting nations were resourceful. Many brought their own food. In all, British customs saw three hundred tons of comestibles arrive, some of it the likes of which the Brits hadn't seen in years or, in some cases, ever at all. The Kiwis brought butter and mutton drippings. Mexican athletes arrived with stores of tripe and liver. The Czechs carried in twenty thousand bottles of mineral water. The Danes shipped in 160,000 eggs. And among the treasured pleasures of the French were cases upon cases of Mouton Rothschild, purely for drinking. Cooking wine came in separately.

For all of their shortcomings and challenges, it was said in admiration that the Brits made use of the infrastructures of the war with skill and ingenuity. One strange but interesting aftereffect was that the British had within their borders a captive labor force: four hundred thousand German POWs were still in England, and they were put to work pouring concrete and fixing up Wembley Stadium.

What the Games lacked in bodily comfort they made up for, at times, with moments that stirred the heart, and whatever hunger Soichi Sakamoto might have felt was instead sated by the momentous Olympic displays laid out in a kind of banquet before him. The IOC had succeeded in finding the ruins of the Berlin Games' ceremonial flag, missing since 1936, and they raised it over London. But there was the new to celebrate, as well. A new scoreboard at Wembley bore the words of Baron de Coubertin. Coubertin was many years dead now, his heart buried in the soil at Olympia, but he spoke from the grave: "The important thing in the Olympic Games is not winning but taking part. The essential thing in life is not conquering but fighting well."

The IOC had also decided that at the opening ceremonies, it would carry on with a stirring tradition: the torch relay. It was no ancient ritual; Hitler had introduced the epic journey by foot from Olympia in 1936. The organizers had questioned the wisdom of repeating a ritual, however beautiful, that might evoke the potent images of the Nazi past. In the end, they had decided in favor of the relay, because their symbolic act would be to take the torch out of the hands of a dictator.

The contemporary resonance of the torch relay is meaningful, but it cannot compare with that of the torch's 1948 journey. From the moment it was lit in the still-recovering country of Greece on July 17, until its arrival thousands of miles to the west, the relay would speak of the traumatic past and more hopeful present. It would travel lands made wretched by war: it would pass through Katakolon, where the British had begun the liberation of Greeks, to Corfu, where the Luftwaffe had destroyed the island's noble architecture. At every exchange stop—from Modena, the site of massacres, to Milan, where Mussolini's corpse swung in the bitter wind, to Switzerland and France, Luxembourg, Dover, and across the river Thames—it was meant to tell a tale of resurrection.

July 29 was a hellish-hot 93 degrees. Athletes perspired in their heavy regalia; Boy Scouts crouching too long passed out, although fainting was, in truth, a far better fate than the one suffered by three soldiers who earlier that week had died of heat stroke. Trumpeters of the Household Cavalry played glorious flourishes; the members of the IOC entered the arena in top hats and tails, and the Lord Mayor of London led the King and Queen of England to a reserved box, where they sat among other royalty from the Continent and from Persia.

There was fanfare and speechmaking and flag raising, the pronouncement of the Games' opening, the release of thousands of pigeons from wicker baskets, and the punctuation of cannons and a twenty-one-gun salute by the King's Troupe of the Royal Horse Artillery, just outside the Wembley gates.

In through those gates marched the representatives of a strange, new world order that the war had brought about. A procession of nations altered by battle or forged in it entirely. Two athletes wearing turbans represented Mali, a new country. Athletes from India, a nation separate from Pakistan for the first time and roiled by the recent assassination of Mahatma Gandhi, marched in wearing pale blue blazers.

In presence there was also absence.

For the Games, those absences were the result of global turmoil: Palestine had threatened to boycott if the new State of Israel were included; Russia had not been able to organize itself in time; and the ghosts of whole peoples, of Europe and beyond, paraded by with the living. Nearly thirty Olympians, from Jewish Hungarian fencers to Dutch gymnasts, had perished in Nazi concentration camps, and so many Allied and Axis athletes had lost both lives and limbs in battle against one another. Certain countries' athletes appeared far war-wearier and more sloppily shod than others. From Sakamoto's vantage point in the Wembley stands, he couldn't help but notice the absence, too, of the swimmers who had been his, and who but for an accident of history would have been Olympians.

There were still intimations of the war that Smith couldn't have ignored. The IOC told athletes, for example, not to use the Olympic salute when passing by the royal box: it too closely resembled the Nazi one. And most athletes obeyed, walking with arms held tightly at their sides; the only strange exception, one witness noted, was the single "Colombian banner bearer," who, for reasons unclear, broke into a "spontaneous goosestep."

In the heat, Lord Burghley, chairman of the Olympic Organizing Committee, began what seemed an endless speech, which in spirit echoed the one that Count Baillet-Latour had delivered years before—but then uselessly—at the 1939 IOC meeting on the Nile. "Your Majesty," Burghley began, "the hour has struck. A visionary dream has today become a glorious reality. At the end of the worldwide struggle in 1945, many institutions and associations were found to have withered and only the strongest had survived." The moment was meant to be the official and formal opening of the Games, and it was met in the stadium with "the deafening applause" of "the multitudes," but for so many in the stands, like Soichi Sakamoto, the Games had begun one hour before, in the moment when there had risen in the stadium and on the field the most spontaneous and heartfelt of demonstrations, a moment of new beginnings.

It came after the march of delegations—alphabetical with the exception of Greece coming first according to custom and the British hosts coming last—through Wembley gate and along the newly laid cinder track, after Sakamoto had watched all of the athletes assembled in orderly, military fashion on the green infield: a dutiful assemblage of discreet rows of color, each country distinguished clearly from the next.

Just then, the torch, its journey from Olympia thwarted for eight long years, appeared in the hand of the bearer at the stadium's gate. The torchbearer, dressed in trim white shorts and a sleeveless shell, entered the stadium, the magnesium flare in his right hand, his arm bent at the elbow, the flare as high in the air as he could hold it. The runner, as was the plan, circled the track at a pace somewhere between walking and running, so perfectly slow as to pierce the hearts of the assemblage of onlookers and athletes in their prim formations.

Far above, Soichi Sakamoto looked for those he knew on the field. Bill Smith, of course, but there was also Thelma Kalama, whom he had coached in Honolulu and who would swim at these Games in the women's 4x100-meter freestyle relay. And near them, though he couldn't quite make him out, was a young man by the name of Emerick Kotoro Ishikawa, one of the original ditch kids, who had traded in his swimming trunks to become a weight lifter years ago and was also here in London representing the US men's team.

The bearer rounded the track, and as he did so, he passed out of view of some athletes, and so the group moved with him, toward him. They rushed the track, not on it but to its edges, as if they couldn't get enough of the sight of him and of the flame he carried. Suddenly, the world as it was represented in rows on the infield spontaneously dissolved into oneness: no boundaries, no borders, just athletes beside one another in a giant crowd, united in the act of straining to see something that bound them entirely together after such a long time apart.

The torchbearer in his white outfit completed the oval, the last meters of his journey becoming a sprint and the kick in his steps enough to bring tears to the eyes of even the most stoic observers. He stood then before the Olympic cauldron, faced the stadium a moment, looking as perfect as a statue, and then he turned. From the stands Soichi Sakamoto had the best view of all: of the gorgeous chaos of the athletes on the field, of the torch as the bearer dipped it into the bowl, and of the holy flame flaring once again for the first time in twelve years—and flaring for him for the very first time of all.

He was, he knew, the farthest from Hawaii that he had ever traveled in his life, but he knew in his heart that at last he was home.

More than five hundred athletes from thirty-seven countries—itself an Olympic record—registered in the swimming and diving events alone.

Goals and Sacrifices

The Olympic swim committee hadn't anticipated the numbers and had to scramble to find enough practice pools for all of the visiting teams.

A part of Empire Pool would be open for practice to each of the thirty-seven nations for a mere two hours per day. The rest of the time they had to travel to distant pools. It was the height of summer. London's public baths were indeed "public," and officials had to cut deals with small-time government types. In the end, the swim committee had to settle for having the teams practice in off-hours, during closing times, and at other inconvenient and odd times of the day and night in more than twenty-three separate venues across the city. It was an inconvenience, but there were many inconveniences, and the swimmers seemed largely to adjust with good humor.

When the Americans did have their time at Empire, Bill Smith was blessed with an embarrassment of riches: he essentially had with him three coaches, two of whom felt particularly and personally his. There was Kiphuth, of course, remote as always; but Mike Peppe could serve as support and advice; and up in the bleachers sat Soichi Sakamoto, carefully observing Smith as the swimmer made his way through his paces—a regimen far more taxing than that of anyone else in the pool.

Sakamoto arrived in London on his own and had taken quarters not far away from Uxbridge, and each night after dinner, he quietly appeared at Bill Smith's dormitory. There was no prohibition to his being there, at least not technically. While he hadn't taken up Bob Kiphuth's offer to be an honorary coach, he was still Bill Smith's coach, and he had been for going on eight years. He had no intention to interfere with either Kiphuth's or Peppe's coaching, at least not in their sight, but he knew from the experience of the past several months that Bill's best chance was when Sakamoto was there with him to remind him of who he was and what he needed to accomplish. More than any other reason, that was why Sakamoto had ultimately come to London—not for his own pleasure but for his commitment to his swimmers and to the vision and yet-unfulfilled promise of the Three-Year Swim Club. He admitted to himself that he felt a thrill at what he might—if the stars aligned and Bill was on target—be able to contribute, yet he trembled at the very real possibility that his efforts would once again come to nothing.

Bill expected to face challenges from his own Jimmy McLane and also

Alexander Jany, the world record holder in the 400-meter free from 1947. Jany's time was 4:35.2 in Monte Carlo. Sakamoto had brought paper with him, and he sat with Bill and went over the 400-meter again and again: the split times in particular, the pacing for each lap; and at times, other swimmers from the American team gathered around them, listening, watching; no one had ever coached them with the same specificity. They listened in while Sakamoto reminded Bill of the psychological factors that would help him win: how he ought to go over every lap in his mind before sleep and when waking, and how Bill needed to remember that he was swimming not only for the US Olympic Men's Swim Team, but also for another team he still belonged to, the one he had joined on Maui in the fall of 1940. It was imperative to win for America, but it was redemptive to win for the 3YSC.

The rest of the American team had traveled to England by boat, and when they arrived for the first time before the opening ceremonies, Bill Smith was buoyed by their presence. At that first meeting, officials handed out the uniforms the group would wear in the ceremonies. For men there were two pair of trousers, one pair gray flannel, the other white linen, a blue blazer, and white hats; for women, crisp white skirts, high heels, and white berets.

Very little of the outfit fit, even the blue blazer, and Bill thought it funny and a good subject for a letter. He had met a girl back home whom he was sweet on. Her name was Peedee Riley, and he had come to feel about her the way that Soichi Sakamoto had felt about Mary—that their marrying was inevitable.

"The Americans," he wrote to Peedee, "are probably the best dressed team here." And he described how the hat barely covered his head, how the arms of the sports jacket were weirdly too long, and that the teeny white sweater he'd been given would far better suit Peedee than him; he promised to bring it home to her. He loved the uniform belt, though. It was clasped with a bright buckle, on which was imprinted the Olympic emblem. It was a "beaut," he wrote, before signing off in his best St. Louis School cursive, "Cheerio, darling," and marking the envelope with his temporary but completely wonderful address: "The Olympic Swim Team, London, England."

Bill noticed the uniforms, but what Sakamoto noticed was the swimming in practices. Sakamoto was intrigued, for example, by how things had changed. With the exception of the breaststroke, athletes observed more things in common in terms of technique and stroke. In just a few years, during which he had been sidelined and unable to travel, somehow globalization had brought swimmers from many countries together in agreement about form, if not technique. It was heartening to see the world come back together.

For days it had rained in London, starting with a downpour on the twenty-ninth, torrential, drenching, and tragic for those who were supposed to have started track and field at Wembley. But now at Empire Pool, a bit of sun shone through the glass roof, where crews of men had spent ten days scraping the ceiling of its wartime coat of blackout paint, and in the rafters, flags of all nations hung, the Olympic flag the largest. Among the flags, sparrows flitted and twittered.

Officials had done whatever they could to make all of the Empire Pool shipshape. No one, wrote the *News of the World*, had seen the pool since the beginning of the war, and here it was, for the world to see once again. The gallery was large enough for eight thousand, and while on the first day the arena was sparsely filled, the overall mood was high. Bunting draped the tables where the scorekeepers sat. Press lined the deck, and sanctioned cameramen pointed movie cameras at the special portals that had been built in the sides of the pool and through which they could film the swimmers in motion, partly underwater.

The officials stood at the ready—turn judges primly dressed in dark coats and white bottoms, along with timekeepers clutching shiny new Omega stopwatches—on the makeshift bridge. Precision, of course, was important. Heat times determined lane placement, with the best pacers in the center lanes, which had less wash.

Who would take those center lanes wasn't really in question. With the Japanese gone, all expected that some other nation would lead, and in spite of Bob Kiphuth's dire predictions, the odds favored the United States. Ever dramatic, Kiphuth had said he was tired of reading in the European press that the United States was going to come in gangbusters. That was a crock. He was just too levelheaded, he said, to court any optimism. The Games were a farce anyway without the greatest Japanese swimmers, who were the real competition for the US.

Maybe the Olympics *were* already in American hands. For years Britain and those on the Continent had been at the disadvantage of subscribing to traditional and antiquated notions about training, coaching, and the like. European coaches were still trainers, and while theory about track and field had developed in the Nordic countries, swimming still lagged behind. The Brits and many other nations still believed that excessive training would exhaust the athlete physically or psychologically "dull the driving force of enthusiasm," blunting the edge of one's desire to get back into the water again. Europeans still smoked cigarettes like chimneys, and the paucity of healthy food in the postwar didn't afford them the luxury to think much about nutritious eating. And the clearest disadvantage for countries other than the United States was the fact that, however much athletes might have wished to practice, many still lacked regulation pools, and some didn't even own time clocks.

During practice at the Empire Pool, the American swimmers drew applause even from their competitors. Construction workers nearby stopped and extended their lunchtimes to watch diver Sammy Lee spin off the spring-board and do five full rotations before easing into the water. They lingered to see Miller Anderson, with the steel plate in his leg, rehearse again and again his back somersault to get it just right.

Soichi Sakamoto was in the gallery watching, too. He appreciated the grace and finesse of the divers, but his eyes were fixed on Bill Smith. The press had criticized Smith for loafing through his practices, but Sakamoto knew full well that what Smith was doing was focusing on technique over speed, which was exactly how Smith was supposed to prepare. The press ought to have been worrying about other things, like how crowded the Empire was in the afternoons and alerting officials about the level of chlorine in the pool; it was far too high, and all of the swimmers complained about irritated eyes. But the press had already declared the winner in the 400-meter freestyle: Jimmy McLane was a shoo-in, and Bill Smith was a "Hawaiian paddler who was at his peak during the war before the Games were wiped out."

The men's swimming competition began with the 100-meter prelims. There were forty-eight entries, an enormous group. In the first heat, seven sprinters from France, Australia, Hungary, Spain, Sweden, Brazil, and India lined up on the bath-side to dive at the pop of the gun. Alexander Jany qualified in his first heat, his sister Ginette watching nervously as he did. And Wally Ris, Keith Carter, and Alan Ford were first in theirs.

Jany was favored in the finals, and his sister Ginette was so thrilled for him that she ran alongside the pool cheering him on in frantic French, but her dramatic enthusiasm unfortunately did neither of them any good. Jany lost his lead at the 50-meter mark, and the Frenchman came in fifth; Ginette collapsed on the deck and was promptly stretchered away. Almost as an anticlimax, Ford came in second and the Hungarian Geza Kadas surprised the fans at third. It was clear to those watching that had Kadas not had a collision with the lane divider 3 yards from the wall, he might well have taken first. The swimmers were now on notice about the Hungarians. Kadas was the dark horse to watch in all of his events.

Smith's first day of competitive swimming was Saturday, July 31—the 400-meter freestyle—and it was his only chance in an individual event; he'd been preparing for it from the age of seventeen, and his personal best in the event, from Detroit, stood at 4:50.4.

Sakamoto watched from the bleachers, surprised at how few fans were in the stands for the prelims. In heat 1, Jimmy McLane had no competition in any of the other lanes: he came in a full 20 seconds ahead of a Hungarian, a Brit, an Argentinian, and the Spanish, Bermudan, and Egyptian swimmers with a time of 4:42.2, his heat time exceeding the Olympic record of famed middle-distance foe Jack Medica by 2.3 seconds. There wasn't anyone in the stands, including Soichi Sakamoto, who didn't think that 1936 Berlin records would fall in these Games, but McLane started it off with a bang.

Heat 3 had everyone on the edge of their seats. From the block, Alexander Jany, the favorite, was so far out front that it was clear he would win. Behind him was a squat Yorkshire gent, Jack Hale, who had assumed he might qualify only for the semis and had thus been content to stay behind the Frenchman. But when he saw Jany swimming with such arrogant languor, he started sprinting toward Jany, who at first had no idea of the threat that Hale now presented. The two battled it out to the wall, where Hale tied Jany at 4:53.3, all of Empire applauding the Yorkshireman's performance.

Then, in both heats 4 and 5 of the 400-meter, all eyes were on the Hungarians, who surprised everyone by emerging first. The two men were Gyorgy Mitro, slow at 4:56, and his countryman Geza Kadas, with a time of 4:52.8. Going into the sixth and last heat, Bill would contend with an Australian named John Marshall, who had looked good in practice. When the race began his anxiety was his fuel, and he sped out in front of the entire field—Yugoslavian, Colombian, Icelandic, British, and Pakistani swimmers—and blazed even Marshall with a time of 4:45.3, shaving an unbelievable 5.1 seconds off his personal best.

Sakamoto was beside himself, and so was Bill. That night, Bill ran the race in his head again and again, preparing for the semifinal on Monday, August 2. Jimmy McLane had the first chance to qualify for the finals, swimming against John Marshall of Australia, Jack Hale, the Hungarian Gyorgy Mitro, and four other swimmers. Although McLane was the winner, he swam a logy 4:49.5 in a tight race, barely scraping past McLane at 4:50 and Mitro in third at 4:50.8. But here was the kicker: unlike his electric time in the prelims, McLane's time was 7 unbelievable seconds *over* his time in the heats two days before, and also 4 seconds *over* Bill's time in the heats the previous day. Sakamoto and Bill looked on with excitement.

There were only two semifinal races, and it was in the second that Bill

Goals and Sacrifices

dove into the water, with Hungarian Geza Kadas, Frenchman Alexander Jany, and Argentinian Alfredo Yantorno. If he had anyone to worry about, it was Jany, despite the fact that Jany had a bad day two days before. Smith had never been in the water with Jany, and so he was wary of the world record holder, but then he saw Kadas coming. Kadas was right at Bill's heels; he'd rallied hugely over what he had done on Saturday and surprised the field by going head-to-head with Bill, who tore desperately to touch the wall first but failed with only .6 second between himself and the breakout Hungarian. Jany was far behind Kadas at 4:51.3, just 3 seconds off Bill's time.

In the end, the top dog in the 400-meter semis was none other than Geza Kadas, with Bill Smith next, and Jimmy McLane behind. It was likely cold comfort for Bill to be complimented not on his swimming but on how gentlemanly he was to his fellow swimmers. Many noted how Smith wouldn't leave the water until all of the other competitors had left first. It was something Sakamoto had always taught him.

After such an intense competition, Smith had nothing else to do that day. He was not slated to swim the 4x200-meter relay; Bob Kiphuth had instead put in his reserves, Bob Gibe, Bill Dudley, and Ed Gilbert and Eugene Rogers, likely with the intention of sparing his best 4x200 swimmers like Smith and Ris from overexhaustion. Gibe, Dudley, and Gilbert swam effortlessly in the lead against the Hungarians, but when Rogers dove in as anchor, he fell behind Hungarian Szatmari and caused the US team to lose by 2.3 seconds, with 8:55.9 compared to the Hungarians at 8:53.6. The Hungarians weren't just good; they were great competitors. Their time was 2.1 seconds under the Olympic and world records that Kiphuth had watched the Japanese rack up before his very eyes in Berlin in '36. It had been a nightmare for Kiphuth when the Japanese came in a gaping 11.5 seconds under Kiphuth's all-star Americans: Medica, Flanagan, John Macionis, and Paul Wolf. Today's nightmare was to see that even with the Japanese off the slate, the Hungarians—who had placed third in the '36 finals—had the potential to win the relay finals here in London.

Kiphuth, who had assumed he had the 4x200 wrapped up, was mortified. He knew he had to do something other than put his second string in the next day.

Olympic athletes describe various ways that terror strikes them before competition. Some say their stomachs knot up so bad they think they've got a case of appendicitis. Others describe the yips: shaky hands, the sudden inability to toss a discus or a javelin. Some are breathless; some are sleepless; some are cotton mouthed or suffer tunnel vision; and some experience something of all these afflictions, and more.

On August 3, Smith was tied up in knots. Kiphuth had entered him as anchor in the 4x200-meter. Kiphuth had decided to put in only his ace sprinters, Ris, Wolf, McLane, and Smith, who was now in the hot seat. He was shaking. There was far too much at stake.

High up in the bleachers, Sakamoto knew exactly that the American 4x200 team faced more than they could have expected. The Hungarians, who had done so well in the prelims, now made the smartest move of all. They took dark horse Geza Kadas and made him their anchor. The significance was in no way lost on anyone at the Empire, particularly Bob Kiphuth, Soichi Sakamoto, and Bill Smith. How could anyone forget that in the 100-meter Kadas would have won over Wally Ris but for a collision with the ropes? And who could forget Kadas in the 400-meter prelims? Now the dangerous Kadas would be swimming head-to-head against Bill Smith in the first Olympic finals competition of Smith's life. The Hungarians had stacked everything they could up against Smith and his teammates.

At the gun, Ris and Szatmari were immediately head-to-head in the leg; when Ris handed over to Jimmy McLane, McLane was equally challenged by Mitro; the two never left each other's sides; in the third leg, it was Hungarian Imre Nyeki against Wally Wolf, and Wolf, try as he might, could gain no advantage whatsoever.

It truly now was up to Bill, who dove in just as Kadas did, and for 2 endless laps Bill couldn't shake him. But at the turn with 100 meters, 2 laps to go, Bill opened up a slender lead on Kadas and then maintained it, racing to the wall with a burst of energy and touching 2.4 seconds ahead for first.

The time was 8:46: a world and Olympic record erasing the nightmare of

Goals and Sacrifices

the Japanese win in 1936. Gold for Bill Smith and the American 4x200 relay and the fastest 200 meters of Bill Smith's life.

That night when Sakamoto visited him to go over the 400-meter freestyle for the next day, he felt confident. If he swam as well as he had that day in the relay, he was all set; he had no doubts. But later that night, he was a wreck. Half waking, half sleeping, and fitful in his cot at Uxbridge, he swam the next day's race in his head over and over again. He was old. Too old. Diver and war vet Miller Anderson, who had done so well in practice, had choked during his events. Smith and Anderson were of the same vintage. Anderson had been vanquished by a slender Mexican ace of Jimmy McLane's age, and he had been injured in a fall.

On the morning of the 400-meter final, Bill Smith woke to find himself drenched in sweat and then all too aware of just how much he was detached from himself. His mind sped, and one moment he remembered everything he had ever learned; the next moment he'd forget.

The 400-meter final pitted him against no less than the greatest competitors of his career. He was going to have to outswim Kadas again; he had John Marshall to contend with, who had been second to him in the prelims; and he didn't want to rule out Alexander Jany—after all, going into the Olympics everyone had said that the 400-meter was Jany's to lose. This was Jany's métier. He was the world record holder in the 400-meter, and no matter how slow he'd been until today, that was still completely true. But now it was Jimmy McLane, the very teammate with whom he'd just won gold and a likable, sweet young man out of the pool, who was his greatest foe in it.

When the post came, there was not one but two letters to Smith from his sweetheart, Peedee Riley. He tore both of them open and read them over and over again, the thin onion paper in his shaking hands, her encouraging words in his head. When he was done reading, he suddenly felt shot through with adrenaline. In a letter back to Peedee before he headed off for the race he told her that now he felt as though he could take on a herd of elephants.

The feeling didn't last.

At Empire, he took Mike Peppe aside and confided that he was terrified. "That's a good thing," Peppe said, and patted him on the back. He told Bill Smith he ought to use his fear and his desire to push himself in the race, to take advantage of it and let it fuel him. The best thing, Peppe said, was to just "go all out," not hang back in the early laps like he had against McLane in the 400 in Detroit but this time take a different strategy and hold on to the lead from the beginning and keep it until the end.

Sakamoto had coached Smith otherwise: to stick to the program, to keep the paces and the splits in the 400 that they'd planned on forever. But in the frigid Rouge pool back in Detroit, Smith had done just that. He'd taken Sakamoto's advice, but even achieving his personal best—4:50.4—Bill Smith had come in second to McLane. Sakamoto had always coached to go steady-steady-steady.

Smith's head spun. The natatorium echoed with announcements in French and English. Nearby print reporters crowded around a single table where there were a mere five phones with international lines to be split among all of them, and the BBC was broadcasting live from a roomful of wires to a world full of viewers and listeners. Citizens of the UK would watch the event live on television for the first time in history, and in the United States, the closest equivalent was to listen to a radio broadcast. On Maui, in Honolulu, in Ohio, and all over America, Bill Smith's former teammates were tuned in to see if—and how—Billy "La-La" Smith would bring to a conclusion the story that they and their teacher had begun eleven years before at noon on June 7, 1937, in a classroom in a school on a sugar plantation in the little village of Pu'unene.

Up in the bleachers Soichi Sakamoto took measure of Bill Smith's odds. The heats had put McLane in lane 6, the fastest at Empire, and Smith was in 5, beside him. McLane shook out his limbs. Officials called for readiness. Bill Smith tensed, tried to relax like Soichi Sakamoto had always taught him. He leaned forward, and the gun went off.

Goals and Sacrifices

In 1937, when Keo Nakama had been all of fifteen, he had swum against an Olympian of Bill Smith's size. He had struggled in the water and splashed and choked his way past Ralph Gilman.

Now, at the Empire Pool in London, Bill Smith didn't struggle; he went all out, like Nakama had once done. He took the lead from the beginning and tried not to look back.

Above in the gallery, Soichi Sakamoto must have felt that something was terribly wrong. At the first 50, Smith was out in front too early. Below, however, Bill carried on. He held the bulge at the halfway mark of 200 meters, only suddenly to feel Jimmy McLane behind him. McLane had been in last place, but now he nipped at Bill's heels, and then was right beside him.

You want to be a world's champion? You want to be the world's best? You want to be like Keo Nakama?

Sakamoto had never spoken of maybes.

Bill Smith fought to keep his lead. He fought through the fifth lap, the sixth, the seventh, and on the eighth and final lap, he had one last chance to beat Jimmy McLane.

It has always been unspoken, but it had always been understood: from the time that Bill Smith joined the Three-Year Swim Club in 1940, it had become his duty to redeem Coach Sakamoto's dream.

When Smith touched the wall that day, he broke a new Olympic record. He swam the fastest 400 meters of his life, beating out Jimmy McLane by 2.4 seconds. On the rostrum, Bill Smith stood at the topmost tier, McLane just inches below him on the stand at #2, and John Marshall of Australia at #3. Behind him, the Stars and Stripes rose and his national anthem played. Technically, the gold medal was his. But he knew better. As soon as the music died down, he grabbed his clothes, tossed them on over his suit, and flew into the bleachers and the arms of his coach.

They stood there like that for a long time, weeping. Smith knew full well what he had just done, and Soichi Sakamoto knew it too. Until now, Smith couldn't truly have understood what it was like to live so long with a dream deferred, but now he knew at least something of it: he knew what it was like to be caught in the middle of a dream, to be suspended in time with your longing unsatisfied, because that's what the final moments of his 400-meter race had been like. The last ten yards between his reaching for the wall and touching it had been endless to him. They had felt unbearable. He could hardly have believed a measure so seemingly short could be so impossible to breach. But he'd had his coach's dreams and his teammates' unfinished quest in his fingertips that day. And because he did, those last ten yards, the excruciating distance between wishing and wanting, between hoping and achieving, were the greatest responsibility he had ever borne, and the roughest water he had ever had to cross.

Friday, September 29, 1961

Thirteen years later, the water was not only rough, it was brackish, salty, dangerous; the tide was high, and it had the power to pull a man off course in a second. The wide-open ocean made the Waikiki Natatorium look like a bathtub. The dark of night made the Kaiwi Channel look like a big mistake.

For months, Keo Nakama had trained to accomplish what those preceding him had failed to do. For all time and twice that year, the 27-mile-long channel that ran between the islands of Molokai and Maui, and all the way to Oahu, had conquered every swimmer in the world, including Danish-born swimmer Greta Anderson.

Like any channel swimmer, Keo Nakama wasn't foolish enough to be alone. When he dove into the sea near Luau Point on Molokai, the hour was 3 a.m., the sky still dark blue, the water deceptively warm, but his team included experienced sea captains and fishermen friends with whom he'd charted out a course. Divers on surfboards paddled beside him; beyond them a short distance was a sampan and a cabin cruiser; and ahead in the dark, a trawler hauled a shark tank, just in case.

As a young man Keo Nakama had been slender and frail. Now, at the age of forty, he had grown heavier by about twenty-five pounds and thickened in the middle. He loved his Sunday baseball games and racquetball matches at the local Y with friends and beer, and he had given up swimming long ago. When, in midlife, he'd gotten it in his crazy mind to cross the channel, he'd had to set goals for himself. It had taken nearly a year to prepare. His regimen included running 1,600 meters around the track twice each day and swimming two miles, plus resistance training and calisthenics, too. In his years as a competitive swimmer he had many times pushed himself to the point of exhaustion and unconsciousness; this time he wanted no friend as much as endurance.

But at only one hour out, he wasn't sure what he *would* be able to endure. The glassy sea had turned to open water, and he entered a realm of knifelike waves. He had been seasick on boats but never during a race, and he was getting queasy. Some twenty-four hours before, he'd had what he thought was a good idea for dinner: a juicy steak, and he'd wisely eaten nothing since, but now, though, his stomach churned and he threw that dinner up. From beside him on the surfboards, voices called out and asked him if he was okay. Did he want to continue? In answer, he gagged, swallowed what felt like gallons of salt water, wiped his mouth, and swam forward through the murky puddle of his own half-digested food.

He stroked forward, but buffeted by whitecaps, he vomited twice more. Just when he began to think that the nausea was unbearable, a man-o'-war snuck beneath him and stung him mercilessly on the chest and arms. Then for hours he swam through swarms of them. At least, he thought, the pain distracted him from the nausea.

When the sun rose, it was both a welcome and a daunting sight. There was light by which to swim, but soon the rays would beat down on him and burn his skin. When his stomach finally settled, he called out for a packet of high-protein concentrate, and, struggling to swallow it and tread water at the same time, he swam on with the knowledge that he would be under the sun for the rest of the day.

One o'clock: Swells that rose five feet high washed over him. Two o'clock: The waves washed over him. Three: He was becoming delirious. He was a helpless baby his mother had left in the crib. He was a runt of a kid after a game of Hardhead. He was a young man in a pool on the East Coast of the Mainland swimming his heart out to prove he was American. He was a man against whom so many doors had closed. He was a failure. A has-been. He had become an overweight, middle-aged man who played racquetball with his buddies at the Y and who liked to drink beer. He was nothing but a schoolteacher, too, and he was a swimming coach. That's all. His mind was a muddle. He tried to focus.

For the longest time, there had been no sign of the mountains of Oahu on the horizon, but then when they seemed to appear on the horizon, instead of coming closer, they played a trick on him and receded. The sight was like his life itself: The more he aimed toward them the farther away they were.

He was a fool.

Minutes passed muddily, every stroke a struggle. He tried to stay with the strokes, but his mind—like his goggles—fogged up with the idea of the crossing as a whole. He had lost perspective on the venture that surrounded him. By twenty minutes past four, he felt a current come out of nowhere and begin to push him back. He tried to swim against it mightily, but it kept pushing.

And then suddenly something gave way. He wasn't sure what it was. The current was still strong, but the pain fell away, and the world seemed to fall away, and where there had been surfboards and boats and the shark tank, beside him now swam children, a hundred of them, maybe more. His goggles were still fogged, and he couldn't see precisely who they were, but he knew where they were from. He had known them all his life. And skinny, naked, and strong, they swam beside him, stroke after stroke after stroke, all of them pushing together against the same great sea.

On and on they swam together, as if somehow they'd formed a team. Together, they were more than something they could ever have been all alone. The children kicked their feet and wheeled their arms, and each rotation of those wheels was something like a promise toward the future, a promise they had once made long ago, and which was turning forward once again in time.

Not everyone would make it to the shore, Nakama knew, so he gathered courage for himself and for all of them, recommitted himself to the task, and swam on—to make it for them. The mountains were coming closer now, and from somewhere in the distance someone called out that the bay was coming up. Smiling, Nakama turned to give the news to his companions.

Goals and Sacrifices

They were so close, he wanted to tell them, so close. Perhaps they'd join him in the triumph after all.

But the swimming children were no longer there. Where they had gone in body he wasn't certain, and at first he felt a stab of terror until he realized that in spirit they were with him; he could feel it. He knew he was not alone now, and he knew he no longer had to be afraid.

Could anyone on shore have seen him and the swimmers? One man, squinting into the sun, might have made them out. That man had been standing on the shore for years, waiting for all of the children to come in. It was toward that man that Keo Nakama swam. That man had taught him everything. He'd taught him how to float and how to speed-float and how to breathe. He'd taught him how to dress himself, how to wear shoes and comb his hair, how to speak proper English, how to keep his body clean. He'd taught him, too, how to swim through the capricious waves of life and how to overcome them. He'd taught him commitment; he'd taught him that commitment was an exercise of will, and that will was the constant application of one's choice.

The coral reef near shore was shallow, and Nakama's fingers, knees, and toes were bloodied up; but he was painless and soon, he felt himself no longer swimming but walking toward the beach, emerging from the rushing surf on the power of his own big, archless feet. A crowd of thousands awaited him, some near the water's edge, some high above the cliffs of Hanauma Bay, and still others perched, he thought he saw, in the branches of some nearby hau trees, waving banners. The swim had taken fifteen hours and a half, but those who saw him would go on to tell their children and their grandchildren that, even having crossed the channel all the way from Molokai, Keo Nakama came out of the ocean looking like a man who'd just finished up an easy swim on a lazy autumn afternoon.

Still, he knew what it had taken for him to make that crossing. It wasn't strength or physical endurance. It was something that his coach had taught him long ago.

You want to reach your goal? his coach had always asked. And the right answer wasn't yes, you *wanted* to, but instead, yes, you'd *do* so. You want to be a champion? his coach had asked. And the right answer was to swim against the current of your circumstance. Every moment of your life, every day, in everything, and not just in the pool, you had to make that choice. Every moment of your life, come storms, come twists of fate, come waves that threatened to overcome you, if you wanted to become a champion, then every minute of your life you had to be one.

Afterword

KEO NAKAMA was inducted into the International Swimming Hall of Fame in 1975, in recognition of his 13 NCAA and AAU national titles, 27 national championships, 5 Pan-American Games titles, 5 Australian national titles, and 8 Big Ten titles. During his swimming career, he held world records that spanned the mile (1,760 meters) and the first-ever crossing of the Kaiwi or Molokai Channel. He coached swimming on Oahu and taught for years in the Oahu public school system. In 1964, Nakama was elected to the Hawaii legislature, and along with others of his generation, he was one of many Japanese-Americans integral in the dramatic transformation of Hawaii's state government from Republican to Democratic, a movement that gave those of Japanese ancestry a voice in Hawaiian politics. He served as a legislator for five terms, but true to his character, he admitted that he didn't love politics. He and his wife, Evelyn, were the parents of seven daughters. All of his life, he continued to be interested in and active in baseball; he played a regular Sunday softball game well into his seventies and served as a scout for the Detroit Tigers. Since 1946, the world's swimming stars have traveled to attend the Keo Nakama meet on Oahu each summer. Over the years the meet rebuilt bridges once again with Japanese swimmers, including that nation's greats such as Hironoshin Furuhashi, Shiro Hashimuzi, and Masaru Furukawa. Australians and Americans have come to the meet as well; in the early years, the likes of Jon Henricks, the diver Sammy Lee, and Shelly Mann, a butterfly gold medalist, were among those. Over the years, organizers arranged for the appearance of celebrities at the meets. In the early days they included Edward G. Robinson, John Wayne, and Danny Kaye. The

Afterword

year 2016 will mark the sixty-eighth anniversary of the Keo Nakama Swimming Invitational; the meet's longtime organizer, Keith Arakaki, is one of Nakama's former swimmers. Keo Nakama died on September 8, 2011, at the age of ninety-one.

After his disappointment at the 1948 Detroit Olympic trials, **HALO HIROSE** was a standout swimmer at Ohio State. He was named All-American swimmer in both 1938 and 1939, and along with Keo Nakama, he was nominated to the "ideal" 1940 Olympic swim team by influential coaches of the AAU. After college he returned to Hawaii, married, and was a loyal civil servant, eventually becoming the state prison program's chief probation officer. In his spare time, Hirose coached young swimmers, who adored him because, as they said, he treated each swimmer equally, "no matter if you were the slowest swimmer or the fastest." Hirose's coaching philosophy was a tremendous point of pride to him; he never promised his swimmers more than he knew he could deliver to them, and he never played favorites. Hirose was able to send his only child, a daughter, Sono, to Punahou School, and on to college. While he kept in his garage a massive collection of memorabilia from his 3YSC days, to revisit it was sometimes a source of regret. Sono Hirose Hulbert remembers that when she grew up, her father often told her, "Don't dream, honey," because, he said, dreams didn't always come true. For his tremendous contributions to swimming in the late 1930s, including the number of world records he broke and the national championship teams on which he swam, he was inducted into the Hawaii Swimming Hall of Fame and the Ohio State Sports Hall of Fame. He also volunteered with retired ex-swimmers to help run Coach's swim meets. People remember him at those meets as a starter, standing with a pistol poised in the air, dressed in a Japanese *habutai* silk shirt and draped silk slacks, wearing stylish shoes, his right ear stuffed with cotton to muffle the noise of the muzzle blast. Of his tendency in life to take the path less traveled, he said once, "I was a bit on the rascal side, a free spirit," an observation with which many would agree. Halo Hirose died in Honolulu at the age of seventy-nine in September of 2002. In 2011 he was posthumously awarded the Congressional Gold Medal for his service in the 442nd Infantry Regiment.

Afterword

FUJIKO KATSUTANI gave up swimming entirely after the 1941 AAU National Women's Swimming Championships in High Point, North Carolina, never knowing that she had officially qualified for the 1940 Games, and took up a job as a clerk at the Maui Book Store. Only sixty years later did she learn that her second national championship crown in the 200-meter breaststroke at Jantzen Beach, Oregon—a sanctioned event—had made her an official member of the US Olympic Women's Swim Team. The certificate had failed to reach her through the mail, but it was signed by Avery Brundage. Fujiko Katsutani married another 3YSC swimmer, Yoshizaku "Zuke" Matsui, who was also a veteran of the 442nd. The couple had a daughter and a son and lived in Maui all their lives. Fujiko Katsutani is an inductee of the Hawaii Swimming Hall of Fame. Katsutani died at the age of eighty-four in 2009. She, Keo Nakama, and Halo Hirose, along with Bill Smith, Jimmy Tanaka, and others who had qualified for one or more of the three canceled Olympiads, have been awarded the honorific title of "Mythical Olympians" by the International Swimming Hall of Fame.

BILL SMITH won two gold medals at the 1948 Olympic Games, the first in the men's 4x200-meter freestyle relay, and the second in the men's 400-meter freestyle; in both he broke Olympic and world records. He garnered 15 national AAU championships and 8 NCAA championships; he held 18 American records and 7 world records; and he was inducted into the International Swimming Hall of Fame in 1966. After the 1948 Games, he became the water safety director at his beloved Waikiki Natatorium, and he held that position for more than thirty years. Smith began with six lifeguards on the beach in Waikiki and grew the corps to more than three hundred guards, skilled watermen who risked their own lives at the beaches to save the lives of others. He also coached swimmers for twenty-five years, his ideas based on the teachings of Soichi Sakamoto, particularly the philosophy that hard work and sacrifice come with rewards. He married his sweetheart, the former Moana "Peedee" Riley; Moana Smith was named Mrs. Hawaii in 1964. Throughout his life, Smith continued to take care of his body, to eat right, and to exercise, as he had learned from Soichi Sakamoto. Even at the age of eighty-seven, he exercised every day. Bill Smith died February 8, 2013, on Oahu at the age of eighty-eight.

Afterword

SOICHI SAKAMOTO coached and mentored some of America's most out-standing swim champions. He is credited with having produced Olympians Bill Smith Jr. ('48); Thelma Kalama ('48); Evelyn Kawamoto ('52), Richard Cleveland ('52), Ford Konno ('52 and '56); Yoshi Oyakawa ('52 and '56); Bill Woolsey ('52 and '56); Fujiko Katsutani ('40); Sonny Tanabe ('56); and George Onekea ('56). He helped train other American Olympians such as Gail Peters ('52); Burwell Jones ('52); Shelley Mann ('56); Al Wiggins ('56); Richard Hanley ('56); and Frank McKinney ('56 and '60). He also coached national champions Harry Holiday, Ivanelle Hoe, Julie Hurakami, Catherine Kleinschmidt, and Jerry Miki, among others. He coached national championship teams in the years 1939, 1940, 1941, 1946, 1949, 1950, and 1951. Sakamoto coached at the University of Hawaii for twenty-one years, from 1945 to 1966, and founded both the Three-Year Swim Club and the Hawaii Swim Club, the first age-group swimming clubs in the Hawaiian Islands and a model for some hundreds of swim clubs that followed it. The philosophy of the Hawaii Swim Club today is still Sakamoto's vision: to develop in youth competitive athletes, but more important, to use "swim-ming as a means of teaching... children life values."

While he has never been formally credited for his technical innovations in the sport of swimming, sports historians point to his development of a very early form of interval training; active, passive, and sprint-assisted training; the first weight-resistance land-training program; year-round dryland; and more. He was among the first coaches in the United States—possibly alone with Steve Forsyth—to focus on stroke technique in his swimmers. In 1966 he was inducted into the International Swimming Hall of Fame. On Maui a pool at the War Memorial Aquatic Complex was dedicated to him and bears his name. His marriage to Mary Sakamoto spanned sixty-four years, and when she became ill, Sakamoto retired from his job at the University of Hawaii and rededicated himself to taking care of her until her death. The Sakamotos were parents of two sons and two daughters, the grandparents of twelve, and the great-grandparents of ten. Soichi Sakamoto died of pneumo-nia in Honolulu in 1997 at the age of ninety-one. Dayton Morinaga, writing for the *Honolulu Advertiser*, said that in the days after Coach's death, "the tears shed... could fill an Olympic-sized swimming pool." In the summer of 2015, he was inducted into the Outrigger Duke Kahanamoku Foundation Hawaii Waterman Hall of Fame. I find it among the greatest of ironies that words that suit this glorious amateur perhaps the best come from a man Soichi Sakamoto mightn't have very much liked. It was Avery Brundage who was quoted thus in an article in a 1956 *Sports Illustrated* article entitled "The Embattled World of Avery Brundage": "If there's one thing that annoys me," Brundage said, "it is the misuse of the word amateur as a synonym for beginner, for someone who is not well-equipped or fully trained. The word does not mean that! Go to etymology. Go back to the origin of the word. What does it mean? It means, one who loves, one who has devotion to."

If any amateur ever loved, if any ever had such great devotion, I believe it was indeed Coach Soichi Sakamoto.

Among the original members of the 3YSC still living at the time of this writing are **BLOSSOM YOUNG TYAU**, **YOSHIO SHIBUYA**, **MITZI HIGUCHI**, and **CHARLIE ODA**. Tyau and Shibuya live in Honolulu; Mitzi Higuchi on Maui; and Charlie Oda in Denver, Colorado. In the course of my researching and writing this book, Keo Nakama, Spencer Shiraishi, and Pachi Tsukano have passed away. May they rest in peace.

Author's Notes

> The past is not preserved for the historian as his private
> domain. Myth, memory, history—these are three alterna-
> tive ways to capture and account for an allusive past, each
> with its own persuasive claim.
>
> —Warren Susman

> There are only two mistakes one can make along the road
> to truth; not going all the way, and not starting.
>
> —Gautama Siddhartha

Among my purposes in writing this book was to make available to writers,
researchers, and the families of the 3YSC swimmers all of the materials
I have used and an awareness of how much material is extant about Soichi Sakamoto's Three-Year Swim Club. In their time, the club was covered by scores of major—and minor—newspapers in the United States and
abroad, and in magazines as varied as *Time*, *Newsweek*, *Collier's*, *Reader's
Digest*, *Liberty*, and *Amateur Athlete*.

For this reason, the number of citations hovers well above five thousand,
and so, for each chapter in the book, I have acknowledged major sources/
influences and origins of particular phrases and quotations and ideas. However, the complete citations and annotated bibliography are available for
download online.

For those wishing to trace the precise and disparate sources for all data
and ideas—there might be five sources within a single sentence—please see

the online notes. This is unconventional in terms of traditional and academic histories, but it is a judgment call on my part for this particular book of narrative nonfiction.

The received legend of the 3YSC—as I encountered it five years ago—was the result of the rich, cultural process of "talk story," an oral storytelling tradition. I celebrate that tradition here, and I wanted specifically to present a narrative that both honored and acknowledged the story's possible mythical elements, while at the same time unpacking them respectfully and correcting them, where possible, through research and hard data.

I have relied heavily on extant interviews with the original 3YSC members and the many hours of interviews with those members still living. That said, Chris Conybeare, in preparing for his half-hour documentary *Coach* in 1984, conducted the first set of interviews on the occasion of a reunion of camp residents and swimmers at Pu'unene. Many of the swimmers were well into their seventies.

My own interviews took place with the original club members when they were well into their nineties, in Hawaii, both on Oahu and in Maui, during the years 2011–2015. Using those interviews and remembrances, I then examined the historical record in the form of the voluminous newspaper and magazine articles about the club in its time—many of which sources are themselves contradictory and contain elements of myth—but that provided me an opportunity to corroborate or correct the accounts of the original charter members.

Similarly, I have used the swimmers' scrapbooks, personal souvenirs, and the online narratives that some members of the 3YSC have published. These have helped me check the accuracy of others' accounts.

My next set of interviews was on-island or by telephone with the children and relatives of the swimmers, who were not only the heirs of the received stories but who also had inherited a tremendous archive of materials, including scrapbooks, photographs, trophies, souvenirs, and correspondence, most of which their parents or relatives never explained to them, and that came to them—and then to me—in the form of stuffed-to-the-brim paper shopping bags, enormous duffel bags—one big enough to hold several pairs of skis!—cardboard and plastic boxes, all of which were hiding under beds or in garages and sheds, the contents sometimes loose, sometimes framed, sometimes in the form of mimeographs. I am certain I have only scratched the surface of what is out there, and I encourage those who have additional materials to preserve them via archives that can digitize them and properly care for them. I also relied on two or three previously conducted oral interviews with the swimmers.

There are hundreds of primary sources on which I relied—from the contents of photographs to train ticket receipts, to certificates, inscriptions, trophies, and more, and these are detailed in the general notes below and online. With the exception of one scholarly article, there are no significant secondary sources and no scholarly writing about the club.

A note: a few conversations with Sakamoto's swimmers took place over the telephone or by Skype, but the majority of my interviews with experts in the various fields I needed to speak with in order gain a foothold in the research took place largely by phone. Just some of the areas I believed were required of me to know about in order to tell the story included, at least for a layperson coming to materials for the first time, the following: the history of the Territory of Hawaii; the development of tourism in the twentieth century; Japanese immigration; sport in the early twentieth century, and the development of coaching and swimming practice from the nineteenth century through 1948, just prior to the Cold War; and swimming pool technology. In the process of writing, I found that certain materials, central to a deeper and scholarly understanding of some of these areas, were too digressive for a popular audience. These involve areas as specific as the history of the construction and the engineering of the east-Maui irrigation system and a history of the Big Five sugar plantations. Those matters are also addressed in the notes.

The abbreviations for my interviews with subjects follow the pattern: BS (Bill Smith); MH (Mitzi Higuchi); CO (Charlie Oda). For purposes of clarity—since many of the girl swimmers married, changed their names, and also changed their nicknames, I use their childhood nicknames and maiden names in citing their interviews: MH (Mitzi Higuchi); Blossom Young (BY). The complete key appears below.

Citations relying on the use of detail from personal memorabilia—from

Author's Notes

train tickets to steamer receipts to trophies, insignia, and family photographs—are noted in the following way: BSE (Bill Smith Estate); HHE (Halo Hirose Estate), and so on.

Because Chris Conybeare was able to conduct personal interviews for his documentary *Coach* with those swimmers still alive in 1984 and with Coach Sakamoto himself, I have relied heavily on those. Hence, the pattern for use of those interviews is: JTCT (John Tsukano, *Coach* transcript); KNCT (Keo Nakama, *Coach* transcript), and so on.

My coding for oft-cited newspapers and magazines is similar: *Maui News* (*MN*); *Maui Shinbun* (*MS*); *Nippu Jiji* (*NJ*); *Hawaii Hochi* (*HH*); *Honolulu Advertiser* (*HA*); *Honolulu Star Bulletin* (*HSB*); *New York Times* (*NYT*); *New York Herald Tribune* (*NYHT*); *Chicago Daily Tribune* (*CDT*); *LA Times* (*LAT*); *Washington Post* (*WP*); and so on. Newspapers are in English, except if noted.

Provenance and provenience of photographs has sometimes proven challenging to determine with 100 percent accuracy. Part of this also has to do with a generous tradition of sharing materials in Hawaii and in the Japanese-American community. Part of it is generational. We are far more careful and anxious today about intellectual property. I have, however, endeavored to be as precise and as respectful of ownership and origin as is humanly possible, given the nature and state of the archival material and into whose hands it has fallen. It seems to have been a practice of the swimmers to take photographs and distribute them widely to friends. It was also a practice to pass these photographs on to news outlets. Similarly, swimmers requested copies of photographs from news outlets and sometimes remembered those photos as their own.

Compounding the challenges of ensuring 100 percent accuracy in all cases is that individuals cut clippings from newspapers and pasted them into their scrapbooks without dates, headlines, or attributions of publication. And some of the archives—both nationally and internationally—have kept poor records or have suffered, at least in two cases, floods or other natural disasters that have wiped out some or all of the original materials. I have often had to rely on copies in the hands of private individuals and interpolate the origin. I have done my very best to indicate in the extensive notes my thought process and deductions about a photo's provenance.

In the identification of individuals in photographs I have used the following resources: where neither archival photographs nor captions indicate clearly who is in a particular photo, I have cross-checked with living members of the 3YSC, many of whom, frankly, are at an age when eyesight is a difficulty. They've done an excellent job in broad identifications, especially in early photographs. From there I've cross-checked newspaper lists and narratives with photographs and have also used simple facial recognition software to identify individuals.

While *The Three-Year Swim Club* is necessarily a mosaic of sources, I have found several secondary sources central to informing my own understanding and interpretation of the phenomenon of the club in space and time. These are biases on my part and certainly open to discussion. These include Philip Curtin's exhaustive history of the production of sugar in the early times of the Levant to the present: *The Rise and Fall of the Plantation Complex*; the collected, and collective, work of the Center for Labor Education and Research at the University of Hawaii, particularly the series of studies in the *Rice and Roses* film series. I have, of course, used the Official Olympic Reports for both the 1940 and the 1948 Games, but I have also relied in part on Janie Hampton's well-researched book *The Austerity Olympics*. Many of my assumptions about sport and Nisei life are informed by Brian Niiya's book *More Than a Game*, and underlying my understanding of the cutting-edge nature of Sakamoto's training regimen is Anson Rabinbach's *The Human Motor: Energy, Fatigue, and the Origins of Modernity*. Fundamental to my understanding of Sakamoto's regimen is that he developed it in the context of a sugar plantation where men and women performed work by hand under difficult conditions and for many hours per day. Sakamoto's presumptions were that his swimmers were neither fragile nor endowed with limited energy over the course of their lifetimes. While the production of sugar wasn't fully mechanized when Sakamoto developed his regimen, he needed only to look to the cane fields just beyond the Camp 5 pool to see the extraordinary resilience, energy, and the

Author's Notes

"steady-steady-steady" labor of which human beings—in extremis and for survival—are capable.

A request: I ask for a generosity of spirit on the part of the reader with regard to the use of sources. Because even some secondary materials about the club are derivative of primary materials that are derivative of oral materials, I believe that perfection on my part is impossible and error inevitable with regard to precise attribution in every case. I look forward to readers' input, corrections, and suggestions, as we all move forward in reconstructing the narrative of the Three-Year Swim Club.

Section Notes

Interview/source key for individuals/estates: The individuals below are the most often cited in the book. Where there initials appear alone, this is an indication of my own interviews with them; where the initials are followed by "CT," the interviews were conducted by Chris Conybeare and appear in the transcript of his documentary. Initials followed by an "E" indicate that the materials came from the estate of the individual. In the case of Soichi Sakamoto, he is almost always SSCT, but because he bequeathed part of his estate to the Alexander and Baldwin Museum, I refer to materials from that collection as SSSB (Soichi Sakamoto Scrapbook).

AK—Adolph Kiefer
BN—Brian Niiya
BS—Bill Smith
BSCT—Bill Smith, *Coach* transcript
BW1—Bill Woolsey
BW2—Bruce Wigo
BY—Blossom Young Tyau
CC—Chris Conybeare
CMCT—Chic Miyamoto, *Coach* transcript
CO—Charlie Oda
COC—Colin O'Connor
COV—Charlie Oda, video

DD—David Davis
FK—Fujiko Katsutani
FKCT—Fujiko Katsutani, *Coach* transcript
GK—Gaylord Kubota
GKCT—Gaylord Kubota, *Coach* transcript
HHHY—Halo Hirose and Hiroshi Yamauchi, interview questionnaire
HY—Hiroshi Yamauchi
IH—Ivanelle Hoe
JM—Jerry Miki
JO—Janet Ogawa

Section Notes

JP—Jan Prins

JTBL—John Tsukano, *Bridge of Love*

JTCT—John Tsukano, *Coach* transcript

KA—Keith Arakaki

KNCT—Keo Nakama, *Coach* transcript

MH—Mitzi Higuchi

MSCT—Mary Sakamoto (Missus), *Coach* transcript

PK—Peter Kennedy

PT—Pachi Tsukano

SHH—Sono Hirose Hulbert

SS—Spencer Shiraishi

SSCT—Soichi Sakamoto, *Coach* transcript

SSOS—Soichi Sakamoto (other source)

SSSB—Soichi Sakamoto Scrapbook

ST—Sonny Tanabe

TS—Tom Sugrue

TW—Tim Wise

WS—Warren Shibuya

A note on diacritical marks: For the lay reader and because a non-Hawaiian speaker/writer is more likely to get them wrong than right, I have limited the use of diacritical marks.

A note on swim times: It's all too easy to look at the times and records of the past and to assume that those men and women were lesser athletes than those living today. In 2012 the *New York Times* charted out the speeds in the 100-meter freestyle over history in order to explain the seeming disparity in swimmers' performances between the start of the modern Olympics and today. When examined carefully, the disparity is slight. We might be faster today, but *why* we are doesn't necessarily or fundamentally make us better; rather, it makes us better equipped. See http://www.nytimes.com/interactive/2012/08/01/sports/olympics/racing-against-history.html?_r=0.

Epigraph

In her foreword to Rita Goldman's *Every Grain of Rice: Portraits of Maui's Japanese Community* (Virginia Beach: Donning, 2003), Barbara Watanabe of the Nisei Veterans Memorial Center in Wailuku translates the phrase "Okage Sama de" as "Because of you, I am." JM points out that another translation is: "I owe everything to you," and in colloquial speech it can simply mean "Thank you." Here I mean it as it is also said colloquially: "I am what I am because of you."

Preface

Descriptions of Maui from the air are from Philip Kinsley, "Feudal System Works Well in Hawaii Islands," *CT*, 4/3/32. A note regarding the name Puʻunene: long before sugar planters arrived in the nineteenth century, the term roughly translated from Hawaiian as "trash heap," but one explanation is that once there was a cinder cone on the site and also many geese, hence the literal translation "goose hill." For obvious reasons, I have not included an extensive history on sugar plantations, issues of land and power, and sugar production on Maui. Excellent sources, however, include Alice Clare Morrow and Jack Morrow, *Maui: A Few Facts About the Valley Isle* (Waikapu, HI, 1930); the authors claim but cannot support the idea that the ill-fated Captain Cook encountered cane growing on Maui in 1778; local historians claim that a Chinese trader appeared on the island in 1802 with a stone mill and a boiler but that after attempting to raise one crop, he abandoned the project. In essence, though, the production of sugar on Maui began in earnest with the signing of a reciprocity treaty between the United States and the Kingdom of Hawaii in 1875. The treaty allowed planters to sell sugar in the US completely duty-free. The plantation on which I am trespassing in this section is Hawaii Commercial & Sugar Co., known as HC&S. For a detailed history on all the sugar companies on Maui, including their development and mergers, these sources are particularly helpful: George Cooper and Gavan Daws, *Land and Power in Hawaii: The Democratic Years* (Honolulu: University of Hawaii Press, 1990); and William H. Dorrance, *Sugar Islands: The 165-Year Story of Sugar in Hawaii* (Honolulu: Mutual Publishing, 2005); Julia F. Siler, while telling the story of the downfall of the Hawaiian Royal family, covers very well the arrival of the Charleston-born Claus Spreckles and other "high chiefs of sugardom" in the islands in *Lost Kingdom: Hawaii's Last Queen, the Sugar Kings, and America's First Imperial Adventure* (New York: Atlantic Monthly Press, 2012). The video *From Cane to Sugar: A Tour of Hawaii's Last Sugar Producing Mill* (Alexander and Baldwin Sugar Museum, 2010), is an excellent overview of methods. Sarah Vowell's book *Unfamiliar Fishes* (New York: Riverhead Books, 2012), is a swift read about Maui and sugar and the personalities that built the industry on Hawaii.

Section Notes

Part One

The epigraph is from Shakespeare's *The Tempest*, act 4, sc.1, Prospero.

CHAPTER ONE: *To Race with Giants*

Aquacades were an equal and popular part of competitive swimming meets in the early twentieth century. They died out as (1) the number of events in swimming increased; and (2) swimming became less an audience entertainment than a legitimate athletic event. The most famous showman of the aquacade era was Billy Rose, the theatrical producer and one-time husband of Fanny Brice, who began his show at the 1937 Great Lakes Exposition, expanding it to the New York World's Fair in 1939. See "The Rose on the Water," *NYT*, 2/28/37. Details of the August '37 Natatorium aquacade come from major Honolulu and Maui newspapers, including *MN*, *MS*, *NJ*, and *HH*, but principally: Andrew Mitsukado, "In Duke's Swimfest," *HA*, 8/21/37; Louis Leong Hop, "Maui Dominates Duke's Swimfest," *HSB*, 8/19/37. Various members of the 3YSC give accounts as well: SSCT; JTCT; and KNCT. Meet programs were essential in establishing order of events and participants, and most information on the San Francisco O's club comes from: George Schroth, "Club Swimmers Hawaii Bound," and E. O. Bondeson, "Hawaii Invaded by OC," both in the *Olympian* (magazine of the San Francisco Olympic Club), 7/37 and 8/37, and heavily canted toward the O's success.

Details on twentieth-century tourism in Waikiki are found in *Hawaii, a Primer: Being a Series of Answers to Queries* (Honolulu: T. H. Mercantile, 1908); *General Information Regarding the Territory of Hawaii* (Washington, DC: United States Government Printing Office, 1937); *The Hawaiian Almanac and Annual: The Reference Book of Information and Statistics Relating to the Territory of Hawaii, of Value to Merchants, Tourists and Others*, vol. 49 (Honolulu: Thos. G. Thrum, 1922) and other volumes; William F. Kennedy, "The Lure of Honolulu," in *The Hawaiian Almanac and Annual for 1927: The Reference Book of Information and Statistics Relating to the Territory of Hawaii, of Value to Merchants, Tourists and Others*, vol. 53 (Honolulu: Thos. G. Thrum); Robert L. Wiegel, "Waikiki Beach, Oahu, Hawaii: History of Its Transformation from a Natural to an Urban Shore," *Shore and Beach* 76, no. 2 (2008): 3–27; Masakazu Ejiri, *The Development of Waikiki, 1900–1949: The Formative Period of an American Resort Paradise* (PhD diss., University of Hawaii, 1996); Camilla Fojas, *Islands of Empire: Pop Culture and U.S. Power* (Austin: University of Texas Press, 2014); names of individuals visiting Waikiki in 8/37 are from newspaper accounts and ship manifests. Shirley Temple details are in "Temple: Philip French's Screen Legends," http://www.theguardian.com/

film/2009/nov/22/shirley-temple-screen-legend, accessed 5/5/15; "Shirley Temple Greeted," *NYT*, 8/6/37; and Shirley Temple, *Shirley Temple: The Real Little Girl and Her Own Honolulu Diary* (Akron, OH: Saalfield Publishing, 1938), and all local Honolulu papers.

FDR's remarks while traveling are found in Franklin D. Roosevelt, "Campaign Address at Kansas City, Mo., October 13, 1936," in *Works of Franklin D. Roosevelt* (New York: Random House, 1938). Liliuokalani Kawananakoa was not a member of the royal family: "A Lazy Princess," *Toledo Weekly Blade*, 9/21/22. A thorough discussion of the "sit down strike" as new in the US labor force appears in Edward B. Lockhart, "Sit Down Strikes in America Becoming a Frankenstein to Both Government and Labor," *NJ*, 3/9/37.

Materials on Duke Kahanamoku come from newspaper clippings, various biographies, and critical works, including Joseph L. Brennan, *Duke: The Life Story of Hawaii's Duke Kahanamoku* (Honolulu: Ku Pa'a Publishing, 1994); James D. Nendel's fine dissertation, *Duke Kahanamoku: Twentieth-Century Hawaiian Monarch* (PhD diss., Pennsylvania State University, 2006); Sandra K. Hall and Greg Ambrose, *Memories of Duke: The Legend Comes to Life; Duke Paoa Kahanamoku, 1890–1968* (Honolulu: Bess Press, 1995); and David Davis's *Waterman: The Life and Times of Duke Kahanamoku* (Lincoln: University of Nebraska Press, 2015). Davis debunks a number of DK legends, including the number of Olympics in which the swimmer participated. Davis argues that it depends on whether one counts what was possibly or not a place for DK as an alternate on the 1932 American water polo team. Davis also debunks the eel-wrestling tale and notes that Duke's brother, David, "passed" as Caucasian. Stories of DK in Europe come from Robert C. Allen, *Creating Hawaii Tourism: A Memoir* (Honolulu: Bess Press, 2004).

The story of DK's unhappiness with the new generation of Hawaiian swimmers in 1937 is told in Dick Hyland, "Island Tank Brigade Belies Duke's Pessimism," *LAT*, 8/22/41. Sol Bright wrote the eponymous song "Duke Kahanamoku."

Primary source materials regarding the Waikiki War Memorial Natatorium are from Ralph S. Kuykendall, *A War Memorial: A History of Hawaii* (New York: Macmillan, 1933), chap. 20; CJS Group-Architects, *Final Historical Background Report: Waikiki War Memorial Park and Natatorium, Kapiolani Park, Honolulu, Oahu, Hawaii* (Honolulu, 1985), includes more original architectural details. The shoddy construction is described in "Work Rushed on Pool for Waikiki Meet," *WP*, 1/2/27; other sources include materials on the website of the Historic Hawaii Foundation Resource Center, http://historichawaii.org/waikiki-war-memorial-natatorium-background/pool-engineering-facts/; see Todd S. Purdum, "Pockmark on Paradise's Landscape," *NYT*, 11/7/99, for a very negative response to the renovation of the Nat; see Rod Ohira, "Restoring the Natatorium: City to the Rescue," *HSB*, 7/7/97, for a more moderate perspective; and the website of the Friends of the Natatorium (natatorium.org), for a very pro-renovation/preservationist perspective. The Nat is listed on the National Register of Historic Places and the Hawaii Register of History Places. An excellent history of pre-Nat baths and small pools in Waikiki can be found in Robert C. Schmitt, "Pipes, Pools, and Privies: Some Notes on Early Island Plumbing," *Hawaii Journal of History* 16 (1982). Newspaper and other accounts continually incorrectly report, intentionally or not, Keo Nakama's age. Sometimes he is fifteen in 1937; sometimes sixteen. His birth date is May 21, 1920.

Sports historians have long disputed where the six-beat kick originated. This article is the smoking gun: "It Took Time to Develop the Kahanamoku Kick," *NYT*, 2/20/16; Kahanamoku's head position in the water vs. the Aussie's head position low in the water, "Kahanamoku Kick Latest in Swimming," *NYT*, 2/14/15; live descriptions of the 400-meter race at the Nat on 8/37 are from interviews with MSCT; JTCT; SSCT; and descriptions of Ralph Gilman are from KNCT; MSCT; JTCT; and SSCT; Nakama's collapse described in Wallace Hirai, *NJ*, 8/21/37. Halo Hirose discusses Keo Nakama's tendency to swim himself to the point of exhaustion and the frequent times he had to be revived in *HH*, "Three Year Swim Club Questionnaire," which was part of Hiroshi Yamauchi's project for the Hawaiian Swim Legacy Project.

CHAPTER TWO: *Hardhead*

Soichi Sakamoto's backstory is pieced together from disparate materials: The few stories Sakamoto ever tells of himself are in SSCT, where he discusses his ethereal nature, his dreaming of "air castles," his conflicts with his mother, his distaste for teaching, and meeting Mary, among other topics. I've used ships' manifests, immigration papers, birth certificates, photos, online family trees; of the story of meeting and marrying, among other things to explore the Sakamoto family tree going back to Yamaguchiken. Tokuichi Sakamoto's immigration papers are particularly useful. Physical detail of Sakamoto's parents comes from the following sources: ships' manifests and the descriptions of passengers found on them; observation of photographs in SSSB and elsewhere. Excellent details about the push and pull factors in Yamaguchiken are available in Jonathan Frederick Dresner, *Emigration and Local Development in Meiji Era Yamaguchi* (PhD diss., Harvard University, 2001). The *Maui News* Centennial Edition, 2000, recounts the scourge of the plague on Maui and locals' attempts to rid the island of it. The Fire Horse legend is recounted in "Superstition May Cut Japan's Births," *NYT*, 1/9/66.

Section Notes

The description of dusty Waikapu is from Henry M. Whitney, *The Hawaiian Guide Book, Containing a Brief Description of the Hawaiian Islands, Their Harbors, Agricultural Resources, Plantations, Scenery, Volcanoes, Climate, Population, and Commerce* (Honolulu, 1875), 38.

The surname Sakamoto is common in all parts of Japan, but especially in the west and the Ryūkyū Islands. It is listed in the Shinsen shōjiroku, and so some bearers have connections with ancient nobility.

Census material and oral histories establish that Tokuichi Sakamoto worked as a clerk at Hackfeld's. Items sold at Hackfeld's are from advertisements in the *Maui News*, 1900–1906. Hackfeld's was a sugar "factor" in Hawaii; after World War II, the German-named company changed its name to "American Factors." Materials about late nineteenth-century Waikapu and its lack of culture come from Henry M. Whitney, *The Hawaiian Guide Book, Containing a Brief Description of the Hawaiian Islands, Their Harbors, Agricultural Resources, Plantations, Scenery, Volcanoes, Climate, Population, and Commerce* (Honolulu, 1875), 38. The description of the first T. Sakamoto store and Tokuichi Sakamoto himself comes from the photograph published in Franklin Odo and Kazuko Sinoto, *A Pictorial History of the Japanese in Hawaii, 1885–1924: Commemorating the Centennial of the First Arrival of Government Contracted Japanese Laborers in Hawaii* (Honolulu: Bishop Museum Press, 1985).

Descriptions of the goods in the first T. Sakamoto Store appear in the oral histories taken by Michi Kodama-Nishimoto, research coordinator, "Stores and Storekeepers of Paia and Puunene, Maui," College of Social Sciences Center for Oral History, University of Hawaii at Manoa, online database. Description of the goods sold in the second store come from my informal discussion on the street with Les Vida, neighbor of the Sakamotos, and his father, Les Vida Sr., in his home.

The history of ginseng in Korea appears in the booklet *Outline of Ginseng Administration and Laws and Regulations Relating to Ginseng Industry* (Kaison, Korea: Bureau of Ginseng Administration, 1910); the ills that Ninjin Homesuey cures are listed on a sign found at Alexander & Baldwin Sugar Museum, Maui, and another at the restaurant Waikapu on 30, owned by Barbara Kikuchi, on Maui. The restaurant is the site of the old T. Sakamoto Store.

There are two sources for the story of Sakamoto's being hit by a car: the newspaper article "Boy on Bicycle Hits Auto Has Ribs Broken," *MN*, 3/14/19; and Sakamoto's personal account in SSCT. The two couldn't be more different: the *MN* claims that *Sakamoto* hit the truck, which is highly unlikely; I find it interesting that the driver is the deputy sheriff, hence, he assumes no blame. Sakamoto's sense of a life of higher purpose and the band in which he played; Sakamoto's connection with the natural world; castles in the air all appear in SSCT; the description of Sakamoto's singing voice is in HHY. The description of the band in which he played and the story of Sakamoto running off to Waikiki are in SSCT. His illness in his senior year of high school is not identified in any of the existing oral histories.

I have used census and ships' manifests to determine the following: that Sakamoto's mother's face was significantly scarred and that his father had inward-turning fingers, "Ship Manifest for Tokuichi Sakamoto and Wife Traveling to Japan and Back in 1928." Sakamoto's daughter Janice Lamm says that her mother was born in an orphanage in Tokyo in JLCT.

Sakamoto had an older sister named Motoyo or Moto. I do not mention her in the book, as I was unable to find information about her with the exception of census data from the 1940s when I believe she was married and living on Oahu. Takeo Sakamoto's date of birth is from "Hawaii, Births and Christenings, 1852–1933," index, FamilySearch (https://familysearch.org/pal:/MM9.1.1/FWSM-1BL), accessed 9/29/2013; Takeo Sakamoto, 5/23/09. Newspaper accounts tell of his accomplishments, such as "His Model Plane Flies," *MN*, 4/11/28; "Boy Scout Assistant Sakamoto Takes His Fourth Photo Award," *HSB*, 8/5/31. Bill also was very involved with the Boy Scouts, and worked as an assistant to Pop Hutton, head of the Boy Scouts on Maui; he is described as a crack golfer in "Sakamoto Thrives on Wet Course," *MS*, 10/26/37.

For further information on the curriculum at the Territorial Normal School, see Linda Louise Logan, *Territorial Normal and Training School: An Institutional History of Public Teacher Education in Hawaii* (master's thesis, University of Hawaii, 1989). The school was indeed far more progressive than Sakamoto may have thought at the time; at the same time its setting was rural, many of its students did not have complete secondary school educations, and some spoke poor English. The dissertation chronicles the improvement, in the '20s, of standards for applicants. Sakamoto attended the college in a very transitional period of time.

For information on early beachboys and their culture, I've turned to "Oral Histories of Waikiki," College of Social Sciences Center for Oral History, an online resource, and in particular to the story of John C. Ernstberg, seventy-six, former beachboy musician and retired lifeguard. I found Isaiah Helekunihi Walker's article, "Hui Nalu, Beachboys, and the Surfing Boarder-Lands of Hawaii," *Contemporary Pacific* 20, no. 1 (2008), tremendously interesting in exploring the "liminal space" where Hawaiian men and white women were able to spend time together.

A list of camp kids' nicknames comes from a file at the Alexander Baldwin Museum, and from interviews with living members of the 3YSC, who remember their classmates fondly and explained some of the stories behind the names. In the 1984 documentary, Gaylord Kubota describes the Pu'unene camps as "resembling today's subdivisions," and I respect that description, but I feel it connotes suburbia when, in fact, camp life was in little way like it. Pu'unene camp life in its specific detail is described in several excellent sources: GKCT; CSCT; Spencer Shiraishi, *Plantation Life and Beyond: Adventures of a Boy Scout, Swimmer, Coach and Boy Scout Leader* (Kahului, Maui/Lexington Kentucky: CreateSpace, 2010); *Uchinanchu: A History of Okinawans in Hawaii* (Honolulu: University of Hawaii, 1981); Hawaii United Okinawa Association, 2009; various interviewees provided detailed information about day-to-day life, including PT; WS. Childhood games like elephant pods and slingshots come from a variety of sources including CMCT; JM; PT; CMCT; FJCT; Katsugo Miho describes the game Piowee or "peewee" in "The Hawaii Nisei Story: Americans of Japanese Ancestry in World War II," http://nisei.hawaii.edu/page/home. Pachi Tsukano told me in detail the rules of the rather horrifying game of Hardhead. Ruben Alcantara, *Filipino History in Hawaii Before 1946: The Sakada Years of Filipinos in Hawaii* (Lorton, VA, 1988), was extraordinarily helpful not just about Filipino life but about camp life in general.

Sakamoto's parents' business trip was recorded in ship's manifests; it was by triangulating this with the interviews that I was able to determine that Sakamoto married while his parents were away. Sakamoto's account of meeting and marrying Mary differs in places from the account of Keith Arakaki, so I've stuck with Sakamoto's original version from SSCT. These differences include his story of working in the pineapple factory, the number of times he spotted Mary before he saw her at the dance in December of 1928, the number of days before they eloped, and some details in Sakamoto's parents' response to the marriage.

Details about Mary and her family background come from MSCT and SSCT, and also my examination of census materials and family photographs. Her work at the telephone company is confirmed in archival photos. My description of the wedding photograph is the result of my having studied the photo. The price of the wedding ring comes from KA. Mary's full name and her family history come from census materials, archival photographs, and KA. The story of Sakamoto's difficulty in attaining the Eagle Scout badge are numerous, although HHHY is one of the best. The particular story of his near-failure at the swim test appears in both SSCT and in Rick Yasui, "Soichi Sakamoto," *MS*, 5/2/39, where Yasui, his actual instructor, describes in great detail what happened. The Scouting handbook Sakamoto would have used was the 1927 *Revised Handbook for Boys*. Sakamoto's trip to Tokyo is chronicled largely in "Maui Boy Scouts Leave in June for Long Visit Land of Nippon," *MN*, 2/26/30; "Japan Prepares Grand Welcome to Maui Scouts," *MN*, 4/3/30; "Maui Scouts Party Are Due to Arrive Japan Tomorrow," *MN*, 6/25/30; "Letter from

Pop Tells of Voyage Boy Scout Party," *MN*, 7/9/30; "Maui Boy Scout Party Lionized on Japan Visit," *MN*, 7/23/30; "Maui Boy Scouts in Japan," *MN*, 7/26/30; and "Climb Up Fuji Ever Memorable Maui Boys Scouts," *MN*, 8/6/30.

CHAPTER THREE: *A Wide Awakening*

I used two key sources for materials on the 1940 Olympics: Sandra Collins, *The 1940 Tokyo Games: The Missing Olympics; Japan, the Asian Olympics and the Olympic Movement* (New York: Routledge, 2008); and *The Report of the Organizing Committee on Its Work for the Twelfth Olympic Games of 1940 in Tokyo Until the Relinquishment* (Tokyo: Isshiki, 1940). Other sources include Brian Niiya, *More Than a Game: Sport in the Japanese American Community* (Los Angeles: Japanese American National Museum, 2001).

Collins discusses Hidejiro Nagata in detail, but I have also used as much other material as possible. "Foreign News: Reds Mopped," *Time*, 1/30/33; "Jap Civilians Named to Aid in Rule of Occupied Points," *LAT*, 2/4/42; "Japanese Sees U.S. as 'Easily Fooled,'" *NYT*, 3/13/38; "Political Veterans Join Tokyo Cabinet," *NYT*, 11/29/39.

"Host to Lindberghs During Tokyo Sojourn," *Baltimore Sun*, 8/31/31; "Pleads for Understanding Here of Japanese Position," *NYT*, 5/1/32; "Educators to Proceed with Tokio Conference," *Daily Boston Globe*, 8/1/37; "Hidejiro Nagata, Served in Japanese Cabinet, 72," *NYHT*, 9/18/43.

The story of the Kanto earthquake is from Collins. Details of the Reconstruction Festival appear in Collins but also in "Tokyo Heralds Rise of Modern City This Week," *NYHT*, 3/3/30.

Many sources describe the earliest days in the ditch, including DeLima's punishments: KNCT; PT; JTCT; SSCT; HHHY; CO. PT tells the story of Mrs. Maehara and the stable. Sakamoto's description of watching the children in the water is from SSCT. For a detailed discussion of the ditch system throughout Hawaii, I have used Carol Wilcox, *Sugar Water: Hawaii's Plantation Ditches* (Honolulu: University of Hawaii Press, 1998).

CHAPTER FOUR: *The Pursuit of Greater Ventures*

Biographical materials about and the story of Jigoro Kano's involvement with the 1940 Olympic bid come from Joseph R. Svinth, "Fulfilling His Duty as a Member: Jigoro Kano and the Japanese Bid for the 1940 Olympics," *Journal of Combative Sport* (May 2004); and Sandra Collins's book. Newspaper articles have been key to this section as well. "Japanese Olympic Delegate Firm in Belief Tokyo Will Stage 1940 Olympic Meet as Scheduled," *NYT*, 4/17/38.

Section Notes

The order in which Sakamoto taught the children swim skills comes from an article that appeared in "Sakamoto, Sage of Swimming," in *Reader's Digest*, 8/41, reprinted from *Liberty* magazine. In it, Sakamoto describes in great detail the process by which he believes beginners ought to be taught, including speed-floating. The early "kid races" are described in "Keo Nakama," taken from the "62nd Annual Keo Nakama Invitational Swimming Competition Program," courtesy Keith Arakaki and available at http://www.hawaiiswim.org/legacy/index2.html. They are also in KNCT; HHHY; JTCT; and PT. Those interviews plus an examination of entrants in official swim meets in 1932–1934 help establish when some of the children started racing competitively outside the ditch. Details about all of the other sports teams Sakamoto coached and the high opinion of him in Waikapu appear in Urban Allen, "Men You Know in Sports," *MN*, 1/34.

Details about the life of Okinawans on Maui and the prejudice they faced come from my interview with IH and also from the text *Uchinanchu: A History of Okinawans in Hawaii* (Honolulu: University of Hawaii Press, 1981).

There are numerous participant accounts of the children swimming against the current, including SSCT; JT; CO; PT; KA; BS. The story of how the ditch swimming started is recounted well in Seabrook Mow, "Hawaii Swim Club Honors Nakama," *HA*, 7/9/2001; description of traveling to and practicing in Iao Valley Pool are found in SSCT; CO, in particular. The story of how public opinion led to the building of the Camp 5 pool is to be found beginning in "Swimming on Maui," *MS*, 5/23/34; and the description of opening day, the speeches, and the races are included in "New Pu'unene Sports Plant Opens Sunday," *MN*, 5/9/36; and "New Pu'unene Field Opened, 5000 Attend," *MN*, 5/13/36. WS points out that Sakamoto didn't abandon the ditch training when the Camp 5 pool opened; rather, he moved the training farther upstream to a part of the ditch nearer the pool. The thumbnail of Frank Baldwin is from "King of Canebrakes," *Time*, 5/4/48. Baldwin and his wife are described in great detail in Irma Gerner Burns, *Maui's Mittee and the General: A Glimpse into the Lives of Mr. and Mrs. Frank Fowler Baldwin* (Honolulu: Ku Pa'a, 1991).

There are vast materials on the Filipino strike in the spring of 1937. Principally, I have used local newspapers, relying on the following key articles: "Field Boss Attacked in Pu'unene," *MS*, 4/19/37; "Cane Knifer Brought Before Court," *MS*, 4/20/37; "One Faction of Laborers Are on Strike," *MS*, 4/23/37; "Filipino Strikers Demonstrate in 2 Maui Towns," *NJ*, 5/2/37; "Several Hundred Laborers in May Day Demonstration," *MS*, 5/3/37; "Governor Asked to Intervene in Pu'unene Strike," *NJ*, 5/7/37; "Filipinos Plead Not Guilty When Arraigned Today," *NJ*, 5/8/37; "Sugar Strike Threatens Territorial Finances," *NJ*, 5/24/37; and "Quezon Plea Before Maui Cane Strikers," *NJ*, 6/4/37.

Section Notes

Very detailed stories of the first meeting of the 3YSC appear in PT; JTCT; KN. I relied heavily on Pachi Tsukano to remember who was in the room that day and BY to identify who the "original members" of the club were. There are also photographs from this period of time, including one of the 1937 Pu'unene school swim team division champions, and numerous newspaper articles in which Sakamoto's swimmers are listed. Estimates of the number of children range between 75 and 150. Most often SSCT says that it was one hundred. Dialogue from that day derives from the memories of the swimmers, particularly CS; from the list of items Sakamoto had written down on the board (as reproduced at the Maui County Fair exhibit in 1939—see photo insert); and from SS throughout interviews and his very short pieces of writing. Description of how crowded the pool was in the early days appears in Charles Young, "Sports Teams Publicizing Valley Isle: Nakama, Hirose Fine Prospects: Maui Swimmers Have Chance for National Honors," *MN*, 6/5/37. A few Individual 3YSC membership cards are preserved in SSSB.

Part Two

"On such a sea" is from Shakespeare, *Julius Caesar*, act 4, sc. 3, 218–24.

CHAPTER FIVE: *An Exercise of Will*

Details of the visit from Brauninger and his swimmers, including Medica and Kiefer, appear in "Junior Chamber of Commerce Delays Swims Till Saturday," *NJ*, 8/23/37; and "Kiefer Shatters Record, Nakama Presses Jack Medica," *NJ*, 8/30/37. Jack Medica's praise of Halo appears in the latter story as well.

The stories of Halo Hirose's family and family history in Shimaneken and HH's childhood in Camp 5 are from SHH; BS also characterizes HH in his interview with me. The stolen watermelon story is from HHHY himself. BS describes Halo's nature. PT provided the story of how Halo got his nickname in the ball game.

There are numerous accounts of routine practice sessions in the Camp 5 pool, including BS; BSCT; CO; CSCT; JT; CMCT; FKCT; and in MH interviews. IH; BY; and JM called Sunday talks "Coach Church" and "Sakamoto's Sermons." All adages are again from photos of archival materials in a private collection. The account of approaching workers is something SS gives many times, but it is principally and most thoroughly recalled in SSCT. Details of the materials Sakamoto scrounged appear in numerous interviews, throughout CCCT and KA; ST; JM; PT; BY; and more.

The notion of Maui as "sports crazy" is from Rita Goldman, *Every Grain of Rice: Portraits of Maui's Japanese Community* (Virginia Beach: Donning, 2003). Information about sporting activities in Hawaii, from the early missionaries to the start of the twentieth century, comes from Gerald R. Gems, *The Athletic Crusade: Sport and American Cultural Imperialism* (Lincoln: University of Nebraska Press, 2006). The story about George Patton is from http://piiholo.com/history.html. The Baldwin family history of polo playing appears in numerous articles mentioned in the book, but particularly "Polo Ponies Burned," *LAT*, 2/1/25; and "Baldwin Is Rated at 5 Goals in Polo," *NYT*, 1/23/26; and "Team Composed of One Family Wins Polo Title in Hawaii," *NYT*, 8/30/29. The Baldwin family also had a racetrack on Maui in the early days, and that information is in "Great Racing," *MN*, 5/10/02.

For a broader, critical understanding of kamaaina culture and power in Hawaii, I very much like John F. McDermott Jr., Wen-Shing Tseng, and Thomas W. Maretzski, eds., *People and Cultures of Hawaii: A Psychocultural Profile* (Honolulu: University of Hawaii Press, 1980), in which Maretzki and McDermott explain the "refraction" of the word *kamaaina* from the American Southern antebellum term "cousins." In addition they write extensively about intermarriage, travel, leisure, and sport among kamaainas. I particularly like Noel Kent's phrase "interlocking directorates" to describe the business models of kamaaina sugar companies and their related holdings in *Hawaii: Islands Under the Influence* (Honolulu: University of Hawaii Press, 1993). Among my favorites of his descriptions is this: "At the Castle and Cooke building...the Kohala Sugar Company scheduled its annual meeting at 9:30 a.m., Ewa Plantation followed at 10:00; Wailua Agriculture was at 10:30, and the Helemano Corporation at 11:00. It would be surprising if the...meetings did not subsequently adjourn to the Pacific Club for drinks at 11:30."

E. L. Damkroger recounts his difficulties when arriving on Maui in 1924 in his book *Recreation Through Competition: A Handbook for Coordinating Community Sports Programs* (New York: Association Press, 1947). It is in this book that Damkroger outlines his philosophies, systems, and his differences with Soichi Sakamoto, and though he doesn't mention Sakamoto directly, he refers to his disdain for his "star system." Damkroger is profiled numerous times in Maui newpapers from the time of his arrival: "Damkroger Promoted to Asst Dir. of Alexander House Settlemt," *MN*, 8/22/25; "Kendall in Unfair Attack," *MN*, 5/8/29; "Editorial," *MN*, 5/15/29; Urban Allen, "Men You Know in Sports: Ernest Leaphart Damkroger," *MN*, 2/34; his run-ins with other coaches and their negative opinion of him appear in "Cary Is Sorry Coach Kendall Spoke Out of Turn," *MN*, 5/15/29. Maizie Cameron Sanford shared in casual conversation with me that some people in town enjoyed calling him "Damn-kroger." Damkroger's work concerns appear in articles such as "Plan Another Water Frolic in 1938," *MS*, 11/30/37.

Details about Ralph Gilman's return are scant, but Sakamoto speaks of it in SSCT and it is reported in "Ralph Gilman to Make Home on Valley Isle," *NJ*, 11/23/37; the article also mentions that he will give an exhibition swim shortly thereafter. Gilman declares his enthusiasm for Nakama's and Hirose's future prospects in Urban Allen, "Hirose, Nakama Churn Water for Fast Times in Workouts," *MN*, 3/16/38. His involvement in the spring 1938 aquacade and with the team are from "Gilman Gives Exposition," *MN*, 5/3/38. It is of note that later Sakamoto attempts to get the Hawaiian AAU to give Gilman back his amateur status so that he can swim for the 3YSC, but this becomes impossible. One can only wonder how things might have turned out differently had the AAU agreed.

In the spring of 1938, when Sakamoto makes his calculations about how much time he has to shave off his swimmers' times, he makes use of national records set in 1937 from "Notable Progress Made in Swimming," *NYT*, 12/26/37; and, I suspect, from *Amateur Athlete* magazine, 12/37. I have made a chart of the times for each of his swimmers in key events in key races through the years from *MN*; *MS*; *NJ*; *HH*; *HA*; and other newspapers.

Sandra Collins chronicles Jigoro Kano's performance in LA in 1932 and his challenges before his trip to Cairo in 1938. Additional information on the founding of judo is available in many places, including: http://judoinfo.com/kano4.htm; http://www.intjudo.eu/Hall_of_Fame/KANO_Jigoro_18601938; and http://umjudo .com/JudoHistory/HistoryKano.htm. Collins and Brian Niiya offer the most complex reading of the Japanese performance at the 1932 Olympics and the relationship to Bushido, military, and physical culture in Japan. For a highly scholarly reading of the swimmer as samurai, see Andreas Niehaus and Christian Tagsold, eds., *Sports, Memory and Nationhood in Japan: Remembering the Glory Days* (New York: Routledge, 2002).

CHAPTER SIX: *Owing to the Protracted Hostilities*

The money raised by the Japanese-American community appears in "Include Sakamoto in Hawaii Team," *MS*, 6/3/38. All details of interior and exterior of the SS *Matsonia* come from discussions with Michael Grace, who shared with me historical photographs and provided materials from his website, http://www.cruisingthepast .com. The minute details of the Aloha dinner are from the signed menu owned by SSH. Details of the trip as a whole, including the sea voyage itself, are from a variety of articles, including: "Sakamoto, Hirose, Nakama Sail for Mainland Swimming Meets," *MN*, 6/25/38; Soichi Sakamoto, "Boys Train on Steamer," letter reprinted in *MN*, 6/26/38. HHYT provides the names of the songs Sakamoto composed.

The encounter aboard ship when DK tells SS about the importance of stroke appears in SSCT. Nendel, in his thesis, *Duke Kahanamoku: Twentieth-Century Hawaiian Monarch* (Pennsylvania State University, 2006), writes extensively about the relationship between DK and HH and KN.

Section Notes

Duke Kahanamoku's reputation in LA appears in "America's All-Time No. 1 Swimmer," *LAT*.

The arrival of the team is chronicled in "Aquatic Stars Appear Here," *LAT*, 6/26/38; and "Swimming Stars from Hawaii Practice for Aquatic Meet," *LAT*, 7/1/38; "Aquatic Show Opens Today at Coliseum," *LAT*, 7/2/38; and Cal Whorton, "Mainland Medley Team Nips Hawaiian Swim Trio," *LAT*, 7/4/38.

The story of the Aztec hotel comes from HHHY, but he states that the hotel is the Mayan, which is too far away. I am assuming that he has mixed these hotels up, as one is nearer Los Angeles. Discussions of the prejudice DK faced throughout his lifetime appear in numerous locales, including the work of biographers Nendel, Brennan, and Davis. It is Brennan who says that DK had an "infallible memory."

Details of the meet results throughout California appear in the following articles: "Maui Stars Shine," *MS*, 7/9/38; "Maui Stars Win Events," *MS*, 7/13/38; "Capacity Crowd at San Francisco Meet," *HA*, 7/19/38; "Mrs. Roger Williams Writes of Swimming Meet in San Francisco," *MN*, 7/23/38; and "Sakamoto Writes on Meets," letter to the *MS*, 7/29/28.

The positive aspects of the preparation for the 1940 Games in Japan appear in numerous articles, including Yasutara Soga, "Olympics Three Years Hence and Spiritual Spoils," *NJ*, 1/16/37. On Maui, things look bright for the Games, as evidenced in advertisements for Tokyo trip savings plans, in *NJ*, 3/8/37; that the entrance, however, into a treatyless period between England, America, and Japan bodes ill for the relationships appears in "Naval Building Race Between England, United States, and Japan, Is Believed Inevitable," *NJ*, 1/5/37. Hitler's indefatigability appears in "Hitler's Rise to Leadership and Germany's Return to World Power," *NJ*, 2/12/37.

News that reaches Maui about the Japanese invasion and occupation of Nanking appears in "Japanese Completely Occupy Nanking," *NJ*, 12/13/37, but is cited here because there is a flashback in this chapter. The dissolution of the 1940 Games is chronicled in many newspapers in the course of 1937. The behind-the-scenes Japanese/German relationship is presaged in "Japanese Kimono Will Be Presented to Adolf Hitler," *NJ*, 1/5/37.

The challenges Jigoro Kano faces when trying to clean up his colleagues' messes prior to both the 1936 IOC meeting in Berlin and the 1938 meeting in Cairo are varied. Sandra Collins details the machinations of the Italy, Germany, and Japan deal over the Olympics and attributes the deal to the need of Germany and Italy to cease arms shipments to Ethiopia. Lord Aberdare raises the specter of danger to athletes attending the Tokyo Games in "Hits Olympics in Warring Land," *NYT*, 2/2/38. The sarcasm about the amity of the Games appears in C. M. Gibbs, "Gibberish," *Baltimore Sun*, 3/9/38. See also Charles Scribner, "Participation at Tokyo: Some Reasons Given Why We Should Not Enter the Olympic Games," *NYT*, 6/23/38.

The story of the limp opening meeting of the Cairo congress appears in "King Farouk Greets Delegates at Olympian Meeting Inaugural," *NYHT*, 3/11/38. Other details of the congress appear in Olympic Report of 1940; Sandra Collins, *The 1940 Tokyo Games: The Missing Olympics; Japan, the Asian Olympics and the Olympic Movement* (New York: Routledge, 2008); and John Kiernan, "Memories of the Nile," *NYT*, 4/15/38. Jigoro Kano's argument as to why Japan is still suited to hold the Games appears in "Japan Will Hold Olympics, Says Representative," *CDT*, 4/17/38.

Details of Kano's judo performance before New York reporters is found in "Super Jujitsu of Japanese, 79, Floors Callers," *NYHT*, 4/17/38. Jigoro Kano's death is reported in "Dr. Kano Dead, Japan's Agent for Olympics," *NYHT*, 5/4/38; "Jigoro Kano, 78, of Olympic Group," *NYT*, 5/5/38; and Royal Brougham, "The Death of Jigoro Kano," unidentified clipping and date are reprinted on judoinfo.com. Kano's age in May of 1938 is variously given as seventy-seven, seventy-eight, and seventy-nine.

The story of the burial of Baron Pierre de Coubertin's heart in Olympia appears in a variety of places, but principally, "Baron Coubertin's Heart Buried in Olympia Stadium," *NYT*, 3/27/38, and in Hampton.

Internal conflict in Japan about the Games appears in "General Sugiyama: Tokio War Minister Urges Japan Abandon Olympic Games," *LAT*, 3/8/38.

The announcement of the cancellation of the 1940 Olympics in Japan appears in numerous sources, but the one most likely to have been seen by Soichi Sakamoto on the morning of July 14, while he was staying at the Del Monte Hotel, was "Tokio Orders Suspension of Olympics," *LAT*, 7/14/38. Discussion of Finland as the next logical place for the games appears thereafter, but first in "Finland Favored for Olympics," *LAT*, 7/14/38.

CHAPTER SEVEN: *Keeping 1940 in Mind All the Time*

Details of DK's travel home with the rest of the All-Hawaiian group are from ships' manifests. Another, more confirming announcement of the movement of the Games to Finland appears in "Sports Lovers Happy That Finland Will Get 1940 Olympics," *NYT*, 7/19/38.

Details of train trip across the country come from various sources: ticket stubs and other archival material in SSSB.

Descriptions of Louisville being built like a wheel and what it was like in terms of segregation in general in 1938 come from TKM. For a full discussion of segregation and the social history of public swimming pools in America, the definitive book is Jeff Wiltse, *Contested Waters: A Social History of Swimming Pools in America* (Chapel Hill: University of North Carolina Press, 2010). Wiltse deals largely with Mainland pools. SSCT contains a recounting of Sakamoto's shock at not being met at the train

Section Notes

station and being less than welcomed in general in Louisville, as does Sakamoto's letter home, "Soichi Sakamoto Tells of Arrival in Kentucky," *MN*, 8/13/38.

Throughout the experience of the 3YSC, the team is treated with confusion by those who don't understand or who haven't categorized Asian-Americans as African-American or Caucasian. Without the old standard of "one drop," everywhere Japanese-Americans traveled or lived in the Mainland United States in the years during which the events of this book take place, the swimmers presented conundrums that led to ad hoc decisions about whether they would be allowed in the water.

Details of the flood in Louisville one year before the Lakeside meet appear in "All Louisville Darkened as Power System Fails," *NYT*, 1/25/37; "Fire in Louisville Fought by Blasts," *NYT*, 1/27/37; and "Cracked Buildings at Louisville Peril," *NYT*, 1/29/37. The political situation reflected in the poisoning of Happy Chandler is recounted in "Chandler Illness Laid to Poisoning," *NYT*, 6/26/38.

The brief history of football pigskin "zealots" comes from Charles Fountain, *Sportswriter: The Life and Times of Grantland Rice* (New York: Oxford University Press, 1993).

Biographical details and descriptions about Bob Kiphuth and descriptions of Payne Whitney are from: Peter Kennedy, *The Life and Professional Contributions of Robert John Herman Kiphuth to Yale Competitive Swimming* (PhD diss., Ohio State University, 1973).

Descriptions of Mike Peppe are from Jesse Abramson, "US Swim Team For Olympics Will Eclipse '36 Berlin Winner," *NYHT*, 4/8/46.

Kiphuth's record at Yale, including Harvard's win to break the Yale streak, is discussed in "Yale Suffers First Defeat," *NJ*, 3/15/37. PK also discussed in an interview with me the rocky relationship between Mike Peppe and Bob Kiphuth, but he argued that each man had a "heart of gold" and, he said, for all their foibles and petty skirmishes with each other, they were loved without reservation by their swimmers.

The description of Ralph Flanagan's modified American crawl is described by John Lodge in "Science Sets New Sports Records," *Popular Science Monthly*, 3/38. I find the description of Flanagan's "stroke" rather vague, frankly, and I believe that Lodge is referring as much to the entire crawl movement, including the kick, as he is the arm movement when describing the "stroke." He conflates "stroke" with the event. I have no reason to believe, however, that Soichi Sakamoto would have had access in March of '38, or even later, to this article.

A note regarding Halo Hirose's performance in Louisville: Hirose also swam the 100-meter freestyle and placed fifth behind a field that included Peter Fick of Philly and NYAC at number one, Otto Jaretz, and then Bill Neunzig of Ohio State.

Steve Forsyth's anger with regard to what he thinks of as Kiphuth's hegemony appears in "Swim Coach Complains," *NYT*, 7/31/38, with additional information a year later in Forsyth's article written as an as-told-to piece with Phil R. Sheridan, entitled "We Haven't Begun to Swim," in the *Saturday Evening Post*, 7/22/39. Other material about Forsyth appears in Dick Faris, "Scene Through the Sports Eye," *MN*, 7/22/39. Information about the outcome of the Louisville meet is in "Kiefer Sets U.S. Long-Course Mark in National Medley Swim," *NYHT*, 8/1/38; and the meet program itself, inked in by HH and courtesy SHH.

SS in SSCT accounts with some embarrassment how unabashed he was in getting film at Louisville. All details of Flanagan's stroke method appear in Steve Forsyth's *Saturday Evening Post* article mentioned above. It is Pete Kennedy who comments about Kiphuth competing with Eleanor Roosevelt and others in terms of travel. Announcements of the Germany junket appear in Jesse Abramson, "AAU to Send Swimming Team to Germany Terminating Rift," *NYHT*, 4/28/38; and "Swim Team to Tour Europe," *NYHT*, 6/25/38. Accounts of the Germany trip come from newspaper accounts, primarily those reprinted in the *NYT* in the month of August that year, but HHHY provides his own account both in that interview and in a letter home published in the *Maui News*. A note regarding the Kiphuth junket: in addition to swimmers, he took along two divers, Al Patnik of OSU and Elbert Root of the Detroit Athletic Club.

SHH has provided programs for most of the Germany meets, in addition to some German newspaper articles, cartoons, and other memorabilia that serve as the basis of information about the trip. Bob Kiphuth recounts the Germany trip in *Amateur Athlete* magazine, 10/39. Details about Halo's lying about his family are from SHH and JO.

Part Three

Epigraph is from Shakespeare, *Julius Caesar*, act 4, sc. 3, 218–24.

CHAPTER EIGHT: *Down Under*

Details of Keo Nakama's invitation to visit Australia appear in "Permission Granted to Make Trip," *MN*, 11/19/38. The trip itself and the wild reaction of the Australians to Nakama are chronicled in "Nakama Tells of His Trip in Letter to Maui Coach," *MN*, 1/14/39; "Australians Like Nakama; Kiyoshi Tells Experiences," *MN*, 1/28/39; Harry M. Hay, "Untold Facts About Kiyoshi Nakama and Robin Biddulph," *Referee*, 1/26/39; "Nakama Wins the Heart of All Australia," *MS*, 3/14/39; and W. P. Corbett, "Hawaiian Swimmer Is 'Human Shark,'" which is an unattributed and undated clip from an Australian newspaper from SSSB. For information on Duke Kahanamoku's own travels in Australia as they were reported at the time, please see the various biographies (Nendel, in particular), but especially helpful to me were articles from the period of time, such as "Kahanamoku Kick Latest in

Swimming," *NYT*, 2/14/16, in which the Australians have carefully studied DK's form, how he stays low in the water, how his arm and leg movements are completely separate from one another, and rather than the Australian way of "slapping the water" from the knees down, how he employs a fluid flutter kick.

The critical reaction to Nakama's having "skipped the ship" on 3/15/39 appear in "Nakama's Return from Australia Is Delayed," *MN*, 3/18/39; and Wallace Hirai, "Kiyoshi Nakama Praised by Australian Official," *NJ*, 3/15/39. My understanding of Damkroger's duplicitousness comes from SSCT and from comparing newspaper articles at the time that indicate always a March 30 departure date from Sydney with an arrival roughly two weeks later. Why Sakamoto—and Damkroger—would have been at the pier on the fifteenth is inexplicable otherwise, since Damkroger is the person who handled all travel arrangements; had something changed, he would have informed Sakamoto, which it appears he did. The shock of the press afterward and the fact that they blame Sakamoto suggests he was set up. Descriptions of the day of Nakama's actual return on April 12 and his condition appear in "Nakama, Uncertain at First, Decides to Enter Swimfest," *NJ*, 4/12/39; Wallace Hirai and Louis Leong Hop, "Nakama's Back; Tired, but Willing to Swim," *HSB*, 4/12/39. A note: on two of the photographs in SSSB, the date marked is April 13; that means the photographs would have been taken a day *after* Nakama returned, and unless they are staged, my opinion is that Sakamoto or someone else merely wrote the wrong date. Details of Nakama's remarkable performance in the trials that night and in the meet are in Wallace Hirai, "Gilbert Ching Cracks Junior Pool Marks; Nakama Places," *NJ*, 4/13/39; Kenneth Hamai, "Four More Records Broken in Hawaiian Indoor Swimfest," *NJ*, 4/14/39; and "Maui Scores Grand Slam at AAU Swimming Meet," *MS*, 4/18/39.

As in earlier chapters, the details of Sakamoto's training regimen appear in numerous sources, including written and oral forms, newspaper articles, and were confirmed in my own interviews. These include: JTCT; CMCT; BS; and KA. Criticism of Sakamoto's strenuous training regimen appears in various newspaper articles, but primarily Wallace Hirai, "Local Aquatic Aces: Aren't They Being Overworked," *NJ*, 6/8/39; Sakamoto himself recounts the painful occasions when Damkroger called him down to his office in Wailuku for conversations with Bud Crabbe and Robert Hughes in detail in SSCT and quotes the men extensively.

CHAPTER NINE: *Youths of the Sea*

Details about June 12, 1939, Kamehameha Day, are in newspaper articles from both Maui and Oahu, principally, "Stein Named Speaker; Kam," *MS*, 6/2/39 "Floats, Pa-u Riders Mark Kam. Parade," *NJ*, 6/12/39.

Section Notes

Georgia O'Keeffe's remembrances of downtown Wailuku, the shops, and the car rental experiences are recounted by Patricia Jennings and Maria Ausherman in *Georgia O'Keeffe's Hawaii* (Kihei, HI: Koa Books, 2011). Plaques on-site at the Lahaina prison and *Exploring Historic Lahaina* (Honolulu: Watermark, 2001), are the sources for information on the "Stuck-in-Irons-Place," and the latter was helpful with regard to the feel of life in Lahaina in the early nineteenth century. I've used the 1910 census to find the location of Sakamoto's childhood home on the "Road to Maalaea Bay" and Sakamoto's own account of living across from the prison SSCT; I have yet to determine which house in particular they lived in, but *MN* and *MS* are full of materials about properties and plats owned or mortgaged by the Sakamoto family. Early accounts of Kahului Harbor, its danger, the dredging of it, and its currents appear in "Work Starts on Construction Breakwater Project," *MN*, 7/13/17.

The wreck of the *Mae West* and the drownings are recounted in "Girl Drowned, Two Missing in Maui Tragedy," *NJ*, 6/13/39; "One Dead, Two Missing as Launch Swamps at Kahului," *HA*, 6/13/39; "1 Dead; 2 Lost in Sea Tragedy," *MS*, 6/13/39; "Body of One of Missing Men on Maui Recovered," *NJ*, 6/15/39; "Bodies of Two Missing Men Recovered," *MS*, 6/16/39; "Body of Benzo Sakamoto Found," *NJ*, 6/16/39; "Bodies Recovered Near Breakwater, 4th Victim Found," *MN*, 6/17/39; my interview with Blossom Young is the source of all the personal material about that day.

Details about the Pirie meet that takes place when Sakamoto is back on Maui appear in Wallace Hirai, "Nakama Beats Pirie in 400; Fast Times Feature Meet," *NJ*, 6/16/39; Hirai, "Pirie, Nakama Swim to Spectacular Tie in 200; Former Record Broken," *NJ*, 6/17/39; and "Hirose Outsprints Pirie in Century," *NJ*, 6/18/39. Sakamoto's advertisement for the redo of the Pirie meet appears in "Swimming Meet: See Bob Pirie and K. Nakama Re-Swim Their Dead-Heat Race," advertisement, *MS*, 6/20/39.

CHAPTER TEN: *The Coup*

Details about the finances of the 3YSC and the ACHA takeover appear in Maui Shinbun, "4 Swimmers & Coach Will Go to Nat'ls Tuesday," *MS*, 6/27/39; "Maui Swimming Team Assured $800 by HJCC for National AAU Meet," *MS*, 7/4/39; "Maui Natators Will Compete in National AAU Swimming Meet," *MS*, 7/7/39; "Seven Valley Islanders to Go to National Swim Meet," *NJ*, 7/7/39; "Five Swimmers to Compete in National Meet," *MN*, 7/8/39, "Valley Isle Natators Set for Nationals," *NJ*, 7/11/39; "$456.85 More Needed for Swimmers," *MS*, 7/14/39.

Fujiko's letters aboard the *Empress of Canada* are in the SSSB. Descriptions of the Katsutani family appear in SSCT; FKCT; ticket stubs provide the framework for the story of Fujiko's journey to Des Moines, as do the actual affidavits from stewardesses, SSSB; her reaction to being misunderstood as Japanese and not American appears in "Hawaiian Tank Star Insists She's—U.S. Citizen and Not Japanese," *Des Moines Sunday Register*, 7/30/39; Des Moines meet results are from "Hawaiian Nears Mark," *Des Moines Tribune*, 7/29/39; Brad Wilson, "'Kids Dominate AAU Swim Meet," *Des Moines Sunday Register*, 7/30/39; and "Katsutani Wins National Swim Title," *NJ*, 7/31/39.

The Detroit '39 Men's Nationals trip is chronicled variously in letters home from E. L. Damkroger; from materials in the SSSB, including stubs and programs from the various entertainments to which Damkroger took the children; from Detroit newspapers and Maui newspapers, principally, "Soichi Writes of Maui Swim Squad," *MN*, 8/5/39; "Damkroger Writes from San Diego," *MS*, 8/11/39; "Maui Swimmers in Heavy Training Before AAU Meet," *MN*, 8/26/39; "Damkroger Again Writes an Interesting Letter," *MS*, 8/28/39; "Damkroger Writes Again Before Meet," *MS*, 9/1/39; George E. Van, "Hawaiians Team to Beat in Swim Meet," *Detroit Times*, 8/26/39; "Maui Natators Win National AAU Meet Team Championship," *MS*, 8/28/39; Laurence Johnson, "Men's Swimming Championships," *Amateur Athlete*, 10/39; Wallace Hirai, "Kiyoshi Nakama Explains Why He Lost," *NJ*, 10/18/39. The reaction of the children to the places they visit appears in JTCT.

Descriptions of the Ecuador trip come principally from "Soldiers on Guard in Panama Transit," *NYT*, 10/11/39; and Michael Peppe, "U.S. Swimmers Win Pan American Championships," *Amateur Athlete*, 11/39.

Sakamoto's reaction to the 1939 cancellation of the games in Helsinki and his account of the Studebaker raffle scandal come from SSCT; and his contributions in 1939 are chronicled in "Soichi Sakamoto Did Most for Hawaii Sports in 1939," *HH*, 1/1/40; details of the Snowman's Hop—with the snowflake effect coming from the mirrored ball—come from programs from SHH and also appear in the "3YSC News," December 1939.

Part Four

"A tide in the affairs of men" is from Shakespeare, *Julius Caesar*, act 4, sc. 3.

CHAPTER ELEVEN: *A Season of Flame*

"Winged Foot," "splashers," "known skill," and details of cocktail lounge party are from Arthur Daley, "US Olympic Swim Squad Picked Despite Slim Chances for Games," *NYT*, 4/8/40. Sakamoto's response to the list of potential Olympic athletes after the Daley article appears in SSCT; Sakamoto gives voice to the fact quite erroneously, unfortunately, that because at least six of his swimmers might have been chosen for the US Olympic Men's Swim Team, that he would have been chosen as head coach. Given Bob Kiphuth's tenure, it is unlikely. Sakamoto's reasoning for why he'd be chosen: "Majority rules." See SSCT.

Kukkonen's "the abnormal situation prevailing between the great powers" is from "Pan America Meet Slated in Summer as Finland Calls off Olympics," *NYHT*, 4/4/40.

"Junkers transports—with bomb racks exposed like wolf fangs" and "menacing flying wedges at less than 2500," are from Grantland Rice, *The Tumult and the Shouting: My Life in Sport* (Berkeley: University of California Press, 1954), 251; "imagined community of millions," "friendly rivalry," and "to reinforce the sense that they all belonged together" are from Eric Hobsbawm, quoted in James Nendel, *Duke Kahanamoku: Twentieth-Century Hawaiian Monarch* (PhD diss., Pennsylvania State University, 2006). Avery Brundage's response to the cancellation of the Games, in particular his desire to name teams, comes from Avery Brundage, "Olympic Tryouts," *Amateur Athlete*, 4/40; and descriptions of meetings of various American Olympic committees to decide on those teams are in an untitled editorial in *Amateur Athlete*, 6/40. The story of Sakamoto's invitation to Bob Kiphuth appears in "B. Kiphuth Is 3YSC Member," *MS*, 2/6/40; "under auspices of the Alexander Community House Association" is from "HC&S Wins Swimfest," *MS*, 6/14/40. See also "7 point Policy," under auspices of the Alexander Community House Association, Subcommittee on Policies; for more information about the Alexander House Settlement Association and history, please see http://www.angulohawaii.com/newsletters/apr2008nl.php; "Maui Will Be Title in AAU Games," *MN*, 2/21/40.

"Hall of Fame" and details about Mary Sakamoto's contributions to the team are included in "Coach Soichi Sakamoto and Kiyoshi Nakama Honored at AHCA Dinner," *MS*, 9/2/38; and are also widely referenced in "Missus," an unattributed article about Mary from Keith Arakaki's Hawaii Swim Legacy website. The article frequently appeared in the program for the Keo Nakama swim meets in the years that Coach Sakamoto was still alive.

The details of Mary's struggle on the trip to Portland are found in a variety of sources, including her letters home reprinted in Maui newspapers. Materials about the trip itself are in "Arrangements to Sail on SS *President Taft*: Swimmers to Leave for National Meet," *MS*, 7/30/40; and in the ship manifest of *President Taft*, 8/1/40. Descriptions of the forest fires in Portland at the time appear in CMCT; "Bad Forest Fire Season Feared," *LAT*, 7/21/40; "Fireworks Start 70 Blazes in Pacific Northwest Forests," *LAT*, 7/5/40. My description of the forest comes from "Twenty Five Thousand Acres of Forest Ablaze," in *Forest Fires, 1940–1949*, British Pathé Films video. Description of Jantzen Beach Park comes specifically from the online site pfxhistory.com. Locals' reactions to the girls (i.e., the questions about grass skirts and huts) appear in Mary Sakamoto's letter home of August 15, 1940, written from Portland Auto Camp, reprinted as "Mrs. Mary Sakamoto of Maui Girls Swim Team Writes of Experiences," *MN*, 8/31/40. Sources for detail about the specifics of the Women's National Championships appear in James D. Richardson, "Women's Swimming," *Amateur Athlete*, 9/40; "Maui Girl Wins Swim," unattributed clip from BSE, 8/17/40; and "Maui Girls Place 4th in AAU Meet," *MS*, 8/20/40.

CHAPTER TWELVE: *Santa Barbara*

The story of the voyage to Santa Barbara and descriptions of team experience appear in "Pre Meet Experiences of Swim Stars Told in Letter by Team Coach," *MN*, 7/13/40. Description of Coral Casino and pool and parts of Santa Barbara in 1940 appear in "Holidays in Santa Barbara," *NYT*, 12/8/40. Descriptions of the meet in Santa Barbara appear in "Coach Sakamoto Desc. 1st part of meet, 3rd, 4th, 5th places finishes," *MN*, 7/6/40. The way Smith describes his negative reaction to San Francisco in great detail, including his quotations, are in BSCT. Sakamoto's impressions of Smith are from SSCT.

CHAPTER THIRTEEN: *Mr. Smith Comes to Maui*

There are numerous sources for biographical material on Bill Smith, much of it delightfully contradictory. Soichi Sakamoto and the 3YSC swimmers offer their remembrances of Smith in KNCT; SSCT; and HHY. Other biographical materials derive from BSCT; BS; SSCT; Alexander MacDonald, "Twinkle, Twinkle, Aquastar," *Collier's*, 8/23/41; and "Boys in the News," *Boys' Life*, 41.

The observation of the children diving from the ships is from an essay by Jack London reprinted in Michael N. Willard, "Duke Kahanamoku's Body," in *Sports Matters: Race, Recreation, and Culture*, ed. John Bloom and Michael N. Willard (New York: New York University Press, 2002), but it is originally from Jack London, *In Hawaii* (London: Mills and Boon, 1918).

Specific materials on the stonewall gang and the beachboys are to be found in "Oral Histories of Waikiki: John C. Ernstberg, 76, Former Beach Boy Musician and Retired City and County Lifeguard," Oral History Project, Social Science Research Institute, University of Manoa, 1985. Primary source materials on the Massie case, including the transcript of the proceedings, appear in http://darrow.law.umn.edu/trialpdfs/MASSIE_CASE.pdf.

Biographical details of Harvey Chilton are rich and begin as early in the news as 1897, when he's described in the *Honolulu Evening Bulletin* as a model choirboy, 11/6/97; we begin to see his criminal life as early as the late 1890s and into the beginning of the 20th century: (*Hawaiian Star*, 12/17/19; assault and battery charges, *HSB*, 5/4/03; and then burglary). Deliciously, columnist Wally Hirai describes Chilton in the *Hawaii Times* in 1927 in an unattributed clipping from BSE. An article praising Chilton and his career appears in *HSB*, 7/21/13; "New Hawaiian Swimmer: Warren Kealoha," *NYT*, 7/20/19; and see Don Watson, "Honolulu Finds Successor to Duke," *LAT*, 8/10/30.

Smith's observations of Sakamoto's relocation to Maui appear in BS; and BSCT. MH told me the story of how BS asked for help in convincing both Coach Sakamoto and BS's father.

Announcement of Benny Castor's job is in Isao Tanaka, "In the Realm of Sports," *MN*, 4/16/41.

Bill Smith's remembrances of the first inquisition from SS are from BS, as is the story of the declination of BS's nickname from "Brother" to "Brother Bill" to "Brada" to "Brala" to "La-La."

Bill Smith's impressions and all quotations regarding the Sakamoto home, the island of Maui, Soichi Sakamoto's obsessive attention to his car, "A-1 condition"; details of the "We Stick It Club"; and Smith's initiation into the 3YSC and impression of Keo and Halo appear in two places: BS; and BSCT.

Halo Hirose's bitterness about Sakamoto, in particular his lack of academic oversight, comes from HHHY; and the Bob Kiphuth quote is from the back of the drawing owned by SHH.

CHAPTER FOURTEEN: *Blitzkrieg*

Stories of evenings at the Sakamoto house and the intensity of the daily training come from BS; BSCT; and SSCT; Bill Smith's improving times in the spring of 1941 are chronicled particularly in *MS* between 3/40 and 5/40. Keo Nakama's appendicitis, hospitalization, and predictions about the races in which he was supposed to have participated are mentioned in "UH Maui Swimfest Tomorrow: Nakama Unable to Come Because of Appendectomy," *MS*, 4/25/41. Lead-ins to meet are in "Maui Team to Compete in Hon. Meet," *MS*, 5/2/41. The extraordinarily detailed workout that Sakamoto gives to Bill Smith Jr. is in Alexander MacDonald, "Twinkle, Twinkle, Aquastar," *Collier's*, 8/23/41. Accounts of the world record marks Bill Smith sets appear in "Sets Three US Swim Marks," *NYT*, 5/11/41.

MacDonald, "Twinkle, Twinkle, Aquastar," is a rich source of the Smith myth. So is Harold Classen, "Typhoid Started Swim Career: Hawaiian Champion Went to Water After Attack at Age 12," *Tuscaloosa News*, 8/3/41. Stanley Brauninger's reaction to Smith's record-breaking appears in Bob Considine, "Mr. Smith Goes to St. Louis," King Features Syndicate, 8/29/41, clip from BSE.

Section Notes

The notion of a sportswriter needing to get out of the game if he has no heroes is in Mark Inabinett, *Grantland Rice and His Heroes: The Sportswriter as Mythmaker in the 1920s* (New York: New York Times Books, 1986), quoting Ira Berkow in *Red: A Biography of Red Smith*. "Malolo" (Flying Fish) is a term freely used to describe Bill Smith, but it seems to start in May of 1941.

Mary Sakamoto describes the Maplewood experience in MSCT and depicts the situation as familial. Chic Miyamoto and other girls also talk about how "Missus" would allow the children to share their feelings: CMCT; FKCT; later Sakamoto swimmer Jerry Miki also describes in great detail Sakamoto's desire not to show his feelings and his desire for his swimmers to hide theirs.

Details of the Maplewood experience from the Mauiites' point of view are included in Grace Crockett, "Maui Swimmers Comment on Fine Hospitality," *MN*, 8/23/41; the description of the arrival in Maplewood and the ensuing parade, CMCT. One key article depicts the "island" lifestyle, including food and Mary's shopping as seen by a Midwesterner: Dent McSkimming, "It's Kau Kau Time for Hawaiian Swimmers," *St. Louis Dispatch*, 8/41 (undated clipping from BSS). Stories about hitchhiking are in CMCT; and the Maplewood, Missouri, meet program of 8/41 provides heat and finals information.

Details of the heats and races at the Maplewood meet itself are to be found in "Billy, 'Kiyo,' Win Swim Titles," *NJ*, 8/9/41; "Maui Swimming Team in Third AAU Victory," *MN*, 8/13/41; "Hawaiians Mop Up in Title Swims; Lee Second in Dives," *LAT*, 8/11/41; "3 Boys Win 2 Titles Each at Nationals," *MS*, 8/12/41; "Smith Shatters Makino's 800-meter World Record," *HH*, p. 3, date unknown; BSS; Maplewood meet program, FK; "Islanders Break Swim Records," *NYT*, 8/10/41; "Smith of Hawaii Wins Title," *NYT*, 8/10/41; "Hawaiians Mop Up in Title Swims," *NYT*, 8/11/41; "Maui Swim Team in Third AAU Victory," *MN*, 8/13/41; the story of "Keo" Keshner appears in an article of that name on the Hawaii Swim Legacy website.

Details of the High Point, North Carolina, race—and the social events the girls attended—come from meet program, FK; "Retains Medley Title," *MN*, 8/20/41; "Maui Mermaid Retains Medley Championship," unattributed clip from SSSB, 8/15/41; and in "Maui Mermaid Misses Record by 4/10th Sec," unattributed clip from SSSB, 8/16/41. The stories of the trip to New Orleans come from Grace Crockett, "Maui Swimmers Comment on Fine Hospitality" (a reprint of her letter home), *MN*, 8/23/41. Articles that depict both the West Coast meet and the nation's response to the 3YSC's triumph at Maplewood include "Malolos," *Time*, 8/18/41; "Boys in the News," *Boys' Life* magazine, 8/41; "Honolulu King of the Water," *Newsweek*, 8/14/41; Dick Hyland, "Behind the Lines," *LAT*, 8/18/41; Pacific Coast meet materials from Hyland, "Island Tank Belies Duke's Pessimism," *LAT*, 8/22/41; "Hawaiians Set Swim Record," *LAT*, 8/24/41; Hyland, "Hawaiian Natators Win 11 of 12 Events," *LAT*, 8/25/41.

Section Notes

The background about the increasing pressure on AJA in the Maui community is found in "Fingerprinting 1941 and Registration of Aliens Starts Soon," *MS*, 8/16/40; advertisement, *MS*, 8/22/41; "Rally Turns out a Huge Success," *MS*, 8/26/41, is but one example of how, in this period, the AJA community on Maui, as on the Mainland, endeavored to show its support and loyalty through rallies such as those. The story and details, including the songs sung, in Marian Anderson's Maui concert appear in "Noted Singer Is Given Huge Ovation," *MS*, 6/28/40; other kinds of activities on the island pre–December 7, 1941, appear in local newspapers in articles such as "The Doll and Kimono Pageant Is Huge Success," *MS*, 9/16/41.

All details of Bill's remembrances of 12/7/41 appear in BSCT; Duke Kahanamoku's exclamation appears in biographer Sandra Kimberley Hall's book *Duke: A Great Hawaiian* (Honolulu: Bess Press, 2004); and Keo Nakama's story of his experience that day in Columbus appears in KNCT. HH tells his story in HHHY. Other details about the day are in *MN*: "War Extra Editions," including "Japanese Planes Attack: Game Off" (fourth ed.), 12/8/41. The arrests of Maehara and Miura, plus all of the changes in Maui on that evening, come largely from John Tsukano, *Bridge of Love* (Honolulu: Hawaii Hosts, 1985); general details of that night are in the documentary *Great Grandfather's Drum*, directed by Cal Lewin, 2011; and Spencer Shiraishi, *Plantation Life and Beyond: Adventures of a Boy Scout, Swimmer, Coach and Boy Scout Leader* (Kahului, Maui/Lexington, Kentucky: CreateSpace, 2010). Details about Hawaii in general under martial law come from: Jeffrey Rogers Hummel, "Not Just Japanese Americans: The Untold Story of U.S. Repression During 'The Good War,'" *Journal of Historical Review* 7, no. 3 (Fall 1987); and articles in *MN* throughout December. *MN* Centennial Edition, 2000, contains very detailed information about the significant changes on the island. HH's account of 12/7/41 is in HHHY.

Part Five

CHAPTER FIFTEEN: *Go for Broke*

The book I've relied on most is John Tsukano's *Bridge of Love* (Honolulu: Hawaii Hosts Press, 1985), in large part because Tsukano belonged to the 3YSC. The book is an extraordinary compendium of materials, with photographs of every unit in the 442nd and 100th, lists of those who served in those units, their rank and their medals. I've also cross-referenced with the swimmers' own accounts and with registries of Pu'unene veterans. While Tsukano was trained as a journalist, the book is less a traditional history than a personal scrapbook; hence, some of the quotations from it are difficult to source. The book includes delightful stories of misunderstandings between kotonks and buddhaheads, the questioning of the phrase "go for broke" as it might have been used in that famous battle and Tsukano's vivid descriptions of battle, the way that soldiers traveled in the dark, were careful of the sounds of their dishes, and more. Spencer Shiraishi's book *Plantation Life and Beyond: Adventures of a Boy Scout, Swimmer, Coach and Boy Scout Leader* (Kahului, Maui/Lexington, Kentucky: CreateSpace, 2010) is excellent on the ordinary details of "talk story," the building of trenches, the bayonetting of straw men, and the practical matters of becoming a grunt, including keeping dirt out of one's rifle. There are other excellent histories on the 442nd, especially documentation on multiple websites: http://www.the442.org; http://442sd.org; http://www.100thbattalion.org/history/japanese-american-units/442nd-regimental-combat-team/; 442nd RCT The Hawaii Nisei Veterans' Project, University of Hawaii, from which I have used the interview with Katsugo Migo of Maui: http://nisei.hawaii.edu/page/home; and Densho.org has an excellent overview on the subject.

The Pu'unene soldier, Barney Hijiro of McGerrow Camp, another one of Soichi Sakamoto's former sixth-grade students was among them. Hijiro, of I Company, singlehandedly destroyed enemy machine guns in the rescue of the Lost Battalion, and he was later awarded the Medal of Honor for his frontline service.

3YSC swimmers' own accounts of their wartime experiences are in Conybeare's CT, but also in the following: Charlie Oda, "The Contributions of Mussolini" (college essay, University of Hawaii English composition class); and videos from the Hawaii Nisei Veteran's Project at http://nisei.hawaii.edu/page/home. Jose Balmores also chronicles his service in the Philippines, though more briefly, in his own essay for his UH composition class, "My Army Career" (English 101R, Themes #10 and #11), SHH.

JT confirms that Sakamoto wrote letters to the boys like a "dotting [*sic*] father," but I have not been able to locate any except for the photo from HH collection. I'm certain they exist in individuals' archives.

Details about the New Orleans swim meet are from CO and an unattributed BSE clipping, 8/24/48; SHH has provided the girls' pictures and inscriptions from Halo Hirose's collection.

Adolph Kiefer provided many details to me about the Navy swim-training program, as did Bill Smith. "What good [is] a 5-man gun crew, if one of those 5 couldn't swim and fell in? With one man down drowned, what good [is] a 5-man weapon?" is a direct quotation. See also Donald W. Rominger Jr., "From Playing Field to Battleground: The United States Navy V-5 Preflight Program in World War II," *Journal of Sport History* 12, no. 3 (Winter 1985), for an overview of the use of sports programs in boot camps.

Section Notes

The comic book I've referred to is "Human Fish, Bill Smith, Hawaiian Swimmer," *True Sport Picture Stories*, 5/44. BS recounts his Navy career in his interviews with me. Charlie Oda narrates his wartime experience both in CO and in the Hawaii Nisei Veterans' Project. HHHY recounts the story of the Fifth Army Games in Rome.

Details of combat seen by the 442nd and 100th in June 1944 come largely from John Tsukano, *Bridge of Love* (see citation above).

CHAPTER SIXTEEN: *Home Front*

Details of a changed Maui come from many sources: Spencer Shiraishi, *Plantation and Beyond: Adventures of a Boy Scout, Swimmer, Coach and Boy Scout Leader* (Kahului, Maui/Lexington, KY: CreateSpace, 2006); details about Sakamoto moving to coach at the university are from SSCT.

Notice of KN disqualification as amateur appears in "Nakama Disqualified as Sports Job Holder," *LAT*, 3/16/46. KN's experiences with racism during the war are from KNCT and the account of the 1942 meet at Yale, "Kiefer Twice Cuts World Swim Mark to Capture Title," *NYT*, 4/5/42. Halo Hirose tells the story of Keo's collapse after the Chouteau race in HHHY. A tragic note: on September 7, 1944, the *New York Times* announced the death, two days prior, of First Lieutenant Rene Auguste Chouteau, age 23; he was serving in the Marine Corps as a flight instructor when he was killed in an accident at the Naval Air Station in Pensacola, Florida.

The story of KN's efforts in swimming as an instructor and the life he saved appears in "Kio Nakama, OSU Swim Champ, Saves Life of Sailor," Ohio News Bureau, Cleveland, 9/13/43, reprinted on the Hawaii Swim Legacy website.

The story of the Outrigger debacle appears in "Honolulu Club Bars Noted Nisei Swimmer," *LAT*, 12/1/45; also reprinted in the *Pittsburgh Courier* on the same date; also see "Outrigger Apologies to Nakama," *MN*, 11/21/45.

Creation and description of Keo Nakama Swim Meets described in KNCT; SSCT; and a variety of other sources, including meet programs reprinted on Hawaii Swim Legacy Website. Perhaps the most comprehensive I have found is in the sixty-second annual invitational program, in which Sakamoto details how the meet came about. Other information can be found in Red McQueen, "Ho'o Mali Mali (Kid 'Em Along): Nakama Meet Proves Need of 50 Meter Tank," *HA*, 6/46.

The description of the changing environment in the postwar period for international swim meets is in "Lend-Lease Is Not Dead—Sports Does It in a Big Way," *WP*, 12/16/46. The story of Halo's trip to Paris appears in "Bill Smith to Swim in Paris Meet," *MN*, 6/7/46; "Jany Victor in Swim," *NYT*, 8/31/46; "Hirose First in

Swim," *NYT*, 11/11/46; "A mon ami Halo" and "Amore, Bilal," SHH; "Hirose Cops Two Swim Events in French Meet," *MN*, 9/7/46; and in SHH and HHHY.

The issue of broken time is discussed extensively in Janie Hampton, *The Austerity Olympics: When the Games Came to London in 1948* (London: Aurum Press, 2008), but is also discussed in primary source articles as early as 1947. I have used "Broken Time Pay for Athletes Is Gaining Support in England," *NYT*, 3/21/47; and "Pay Issue Put Off by Olympic Body," *NYT*, 6/10/47.

CHAPTER SEVENTEEN: *Detroit, Redux (1948)*

The descriptions of various Detroit swimmers including Joe Verdeur appear in Arthur Daley, "Water Boy," *NYT*, 4/5/48; and Jim Nendel, "New Hawaiian Monarchy: The Media Representations of Duke Kahanamoku, 1911–1912," *Journal of Sport History* 31, no. 1 (Spring 2004), describes the various swimming events in the early days of the modern Games.

JM provides the quotation "You goin' tank today?" He has written vivid e-mails to me describing his experiences as a youngster in Waikiki. I rely on those e-mails for a sense of perspectives of the children from what Jerry calls the "slums" as they looked on while SS trained his University swimmers and Detroit-bound swimmers at the Nat.

The story of the invitation from Bob Kiphuth appears, in part, in "Sakamoto to Olympics Drive Opens," *MN*, 4/24/48.

Description of the city of Detroit years later, TS; the description of Jimmy McLane appears in Art Daley, "The World's Best Swimmer." Other key articles include George E. Van, "Hawaiians Team to Beat in Swim Meet," *Detroit Times*, 8/26/39; "Maui Natators Win National AAU Meet Team Championship," *MS*, 8/28/39; and Laurence Johnson, "Men's Swimming Championships," *Amateur Athlete*, 10/39. See also Wallace Hirai, untitled, *NJ*, 10/18/39.

Tales of the trip to Ecuador appear in "Soldiers on Guard in Panama Transit," *NYT*, 10/11/39.

Michael Peppe, "U.S. Swimmers Win Pan American Championships," *Amateur Athlete*, 11/39; and the colorful detail of drinking and carousing come from a delightful Adolph Kiefer telephone interview.

CHAPTER EIGHTEEN: *Goals and Sacrifices*

All of the descriptions of London, the prep for the Games, and the opening of the Games is described in two sources: The Olympic Report of 1948; and Janie Hampton, *The Austerity Olympics: When the Games Came to London in 1948* (London: Aurum Press, 2008). Lord Burghley's speech is recounted both in Hampton and in OR48.

Section Notes

Bill's experience in London is told in part in his two letters to Peedee Riley on "Wednesday," no date, one of which describes the uniforms of the US team; the other describes his preparation for and success for the 400-meter race: dated August 4, 1948, BSE.

George Puscas is the denigrating sportswriter in "Whale Tests Olympic Pool," *Detroit Free Press*, 6/48 clip from BSE.

The Official Report of the Organising Committee for the XIV Olympiad (London: Organising Committee for the Fourteenth Olympiad, 1948), provides descriptions of the Smith 400-meter race and also the 4x200 relay. Statistics about the Games, including heat times and order of swimmers in the 4x200, are all from http://www .sports-reference.com/olympics/, accessed 7/15/2015.

These articles have been essential in telling the story of the heats and finals in both the 4x200 relay and the 400-meter relay: Soichi Sakamoto, "Smith Real Threat in 400 Swim: Sakamoto," *HSB*, 7/26/48; Charles Grumwich, " 'Ukulele' Bill Smith Wins 400 M. Swim," unattributed clip from BSE, 8/4/48; Arthur Veysey, "U.S. Team Sets Olympic Swim Relay Record," *CT*, 8/7/48; "Holds Out First-Stringers," *NYT*, 8/3/48.

Friday, September 29, 1961

The detailed account of KN's crossing of the Molokai Channel appears in unattributed author, "Second Annual Keo Nakama Swimming Invitational 8/20–8/31/47" meet program, SHH; KA; and appears reprinted as "Keo Nakama" on the Hawaii Swim Legacy website, as do KA, "I Still Call Him Coach" (undated); Lin Clark, "Molokai Channel," *HSN* (undated), reprinted on Hawaii Swim Legacy site; Ilima Loomis, "Pioneer in Swimming Nakama Dies at 91," *MN*, 9/18/01; other supporting materials are in SSCT and KNCT.

Three-Year Swim Club Members

The following is a list of Maui swimmers who either swam in the ditch with Soichi Sakamoto, who are confirmed "originals" from the classroom in June 1937, or who are confirmed as swimmers for the 3YSC during the years 1937 and 1941 from newspaper articles listing meet participants and from photographs. The list is not meant to be complete or definitive, however. Even in consulting with living members of the 3YSC, it has been difficult to assure that the names and spellings printed in the papers are correct or if the records are incorrect. I welcome corrections, additions, and clarifications to the list in the future. I think it's only fair to include in a list of Sakamoto's swimmers those who swam for him in the ditch, in the meets between 1932 and 1936. I also include those who swam with Sakamoto on the Maui High swim team and the Pu'unene School champions in 1936–1937.

Abe, Hiroko
Alfonso, A.
Ambrose, ?
Anzai, Nobuo
Apau, Carolina
Apo, Claudia
Arakawu, S.
Araki, N.
Asavalia, ?
Austin, Martha
Bal, B.

Balmores, Jose
Balmores, Remy
Brandt, Dutch
Brandt, Fred
Castor, L. "Benny"
Ching, Bertha
Coke, Beverly
Coleman, Marjorie
  "Tootsie"
Collinger, P.
Crabbe, E. "Bud"

Demura, M.
Eberle, Wallace
Ebisu, L.
Ebisu, Rikio.
Enomoto, T.
Fukada, H.
Fujinaka, Henae
Fukahara, K.
Ginobag, E.
Ginoza, Seiji "Mike"
Gushi, Bunichi

Three-Year Swim Club Members

Hamada, Tatsuo
Hamai, K.
Hanada, Y.
Hashimoto, B.
Higa, Kimiko
Higa, T.
Higashi, R.
Higashida, Yoshie
Higuchi, Mitzuko
  "Mitzi"
Higuchi, Yoshio
Hiranaga, H.
Hirose, Takashi
  "Halo"
Honda, Asaji
Honda, S.
Hoshino, George
Hughes, Robert E., Jr.
Hughes, Donald
Imada, Takeo
Imamura, Matao or
  Mitsugi
Inada, N.
Ishikawa, Kotoro
  "Emerick"
Ito, I.
Iwasaki, Yoshio
Jenkins, D.
Kamimoto, K.
Kaminoto, Y.
Kanemitso, K.
Katahara, K.
Katayama, N.
Katayama, Yoshitugi

Katayama, Yushinaga
Katsutani, "Fred"
Katsutani, Fujiko
  "Fudge"
Katsutani, S.
Kaumeheiwa, L.
Kawasaki, Yoshie
Kenechike, K.
Kim, Jack
Kitagawa, Takeshi
  "Giant"
Kitagawa, Takeo
  "Tucock"
Kuniyoshi, S.
Kurosa, K.
Lufkin, Lucia
Machida, T.
Maehara, Michie
Maehara, R.
Marnie, Jim
Matsueda, I.
Matsui, K.
Matsui, Yoshizuku
  "Zuke"
Matsuura, T.
Mihara, J.
Miho, Katsugo
Miyajima, Isamu
Miyamoto, Chieko
  "Chic"
Mizuki, H.
Moniz, Mary
Mukai, Hiroto
Mukai, K.

Mukai, Shiro
Murakami, T.
Murata, T.
Nakagawa, Teruko
  "Lulu"
Nakagawa, M.
Nakagawa, Y.
Nakama, Bunmei
  "Bunny"
Nakama, Kiyoshi
  "Keo"
Nakama, Tsunao
Nakama, Yoshio
Nakamine, K.
Nakamura, Kazue
Nakamura, M.
Nakamura, Yukko
Nakano, Tadao
  "Mac"
Nakashima, M.
Nakasone, Hisashi
Nakasone, Tsyano
  "Dynamite"
Nakayama, S.
Neunzig, Bill
Niimi, K.
Nishimura, S.
Nitta, N.
Nouchi, C.
Nouchi, W. L.
Oda, Isamu
  "Charlie"
Oda, Matsy
Ohta, ?

Three-Year Swim Club Members

Okamura, T.
Okazaki, T.
Ono, Takashi
Otsuka, ?
Peacock, Jack
Perez, Sibio
Purdy, Hiaka Ann
Purdy, William
Richardson, Wayne
Roffey, Virginia
Sakamoto, Kagiko
Sakamoto, Natalie
Sato, H.
Sato, M.
Sato, Takeo.
Senso, K.
Shibata, A.
Shibuya, Masao
    "Chow"
Shibuya, Toshio
Shibuya, Yoshio
Shigehara, Charlotte
Shigehara, Takeo
Shigetani, Hiroshi
Shimoda, ?
Shiraishi, Spencer
Shiramizu, Tamiyo
Shokiyo, T.
Smith, Bill
Sodetani, T.
Souza, ?
Sugahara, Nobuko

Sugino, Kay
Suzuki, F.
Suzuki, Miyoshi.
Suzuki, S.
Tachikura, S.
Tagami, S.
Taguchi, S.
Takahashi, Masawa
Takahashi, Stella
Takahashi, Tumio
    "Frank"
Takamatsu, T.
Takeyama, Toyoko
    "Toyo"
Tanaka, T.
Teruya, N.
Tokunaga, N.
Tokunaga, Takashi
Tomita, K.
Toyota, Doris
Tsukano, Mitsuo
    "Pachi"
Tsukano, Toshio
    "John"
Tsukano, Tsugio
    "Shangy"
Uchida, S.
Uchida, U.
Uchida, Y.
Ueki, Eleanor
Urago, Asako
Urago, Satoru

Voss, Henry
Wakamatsu, T.
Walker, Pat
Watanabe, Sukumo
Wong, Faith
Yamada, Hisashi or
    Masashi
Yamada, Tsugio
    "Tsuke"
Yamamoto, W.
Yamaoka, M.
Yamashita, H
Yamashita, Shiro
    "Tommy"
Yamashita, Toshio
Yanagada, ?
Yanagi, S.
Yasutomi, Jeannette
Yokouchi, Masaru
    "Pundy"
Yokouchi, S.
Yoshida, Hideo.
Yoshimura, Matsue
Yoshina, Avano
Yoshinaga, T.
Yoshino, Doris
Yoshizawa,
    Hiroshi
Young Goon,
    Blossom
    "Blackie"
Yun, Anna

*Mahalo Nui Loa/*Thank You

This book exists not because I was passionate enough to write it, but because so many people have been so large-hearted in helping me find my way in doing so. When I asked for the permission of the living members of the 3YSC to try to piece this story together, I also asked them to forgive me in advance for the ways in which I knew I'd fail them, the thousand glaring flaws in the final work, the oversights, and the harm that I was sure to do in the conjuring of ghosts. Though they told me not to fret too much—even joked about it—I worried then and worry still. And I take full responsibility for my failings.

Just as I once trespassed on the grounds of the Camp 5 pool, in reconstructing the story of the Three-Year Swim Club I have engaged in varying degrees of trespass, physical and spiritual, traveling in a world that could never be my own, and in the land of others' precious memories. I am grateful to all who have allowed me to tread on such sacred ground.

Keith Arakaki inherited from Soichi Sakamoto the Hawaii Swim Club, and he maintains the Hawaii Swim Legacy project, and he single-handedly runs the annual Keo Nakama Invitational Meet. It was Keith who guided me from the very beginning when I began to ask the most basic of questions, and it was he who connected me to those who could provide firsthand details about the 3YSC and Coach Sakamoto.

Ivanelle Hoe swam with Coach Sakamoto at the University of Hawaii. Among other achievements, she set a world record in the 100-meter butterfly in 1955 and won the 200-meter breaststroke event in the 1957 US Women's Indoor National Championships. Her story, and the story of Sakamoto's second generation of women's swimmers—including Thelma Kalama and Evelyn Kawamoto—deserve their own book.

Ivanelle has been a bridge between those early days and Sakamoto's later life. In her pretty garden, beneath pendant guava and avocado trees, she made it possible for me to interview original members of the club— nonagenarians enthusiastic to share their extensive memories of the early days. She was close to both Coach and Missus at the end of their lives, picking seaweed with Mary during her last illness, and visiting Coach regularly and marveling at the contraptions he continued to invent—no longer for swimming, as it turns out, but for housework! Ivanelle qualified for the Olympics, but by the ill luck of the draw wasn't chosen in her event; she deserves a gold medal for her swimming, her kindness, her personal bravery, and her abidung community service to the Special Olympics.

Blossom Young and Pachi Tsukano filled in so many missing pieces of the first years of the club, identifying teammates in old photographs, and remembering the words of the 3YSC songs, at least one of which Pachi himself composed. Their humility about their major contributions to and participation in the early club years was striking; neither would admit to how central they were to the club's success.

Bill Smith, the club's two-time gold medal winner, opened his home to me, as well as his memory, and spent hours and hours reminiscing about his particular part in the story, the other members who were no longer living, and his life with Coach on Maui. His memories of Sakamoto in the grim years after the canceled Olympics and during the war were essential to my understanding, at least in part, of the ways in which Sakamoto demonstrated his grief; and Smith's recollections of life with Missus helped to explain the ways in which Sakamoto had embraced American mores but still adhered to a very traditional Japanese notion of gender roles in the home.

In interviews with Bill and the other elder members of the club, I tried to be sensitive to the fact that I might be tiring them out with my barrage of questions day after day. Once, when I visited him at the senior residence community in which he and Moana lived, I asked him to tell me honestly if I was asking too much of him; in perhaps one of those most meaningful and touching gifts anyone could give in response, he replied: "No. It's amazing.

You're helping to remember." I'm grateful there was something that this project could give back to him.

The Smith family surprised me in another way as well. After inquiring of them if they had any archival materials they would be willing to let me look over, they emerged from a back room lugging brown shopping bags filled with memorabilia and scrapbooks and, on faith, urged me to take them, examine them, and digitize them for my own use. Sono Hirose Hulbert, daughter of Halo, did the same; she emerged from her garage with materials so voluminous that they filled an 8-foot-long red duffel bag she allowed me to carry back to the Mainland. I experienced that level of generosity and trust with all of those I interviewed, even when I thought they had good reason not to turn over such valuable and irreplaceable materials, if only for a time, to someone who was, just a short time before, a complete stranger.

People told me that Charlie Oda's memory was going, but in an extensive interview with him, he knew what he was talking about. He brought to life for me the rich, felt details of his past in the water, in camp, and in battle. I will say that his one error of remembrance is his claim that he wasn't one of the "originals." He wasn't in Sakamoto's classroom on June 7, 1937, at the first meeting, but records show that he'd been swimming with Sakamoto since 1936. That's my only correction to the record. I'm grateful to him for bearing with me on the phone.

Like Sono Hirose Hulbert, who spent hours upon hours with me, analyzing her father and sharing stories about the Hirose clan, Lee Matsui, son of Fujiko Katsutani, was willing to spend several afternoons with me on Maui, during which we talked heart-to-heart about his bittersweet experience of learning about his mother's swim career only later in her life. It's a testimony of his love for her that he, too, was willing to share her mementos with me and to bear the complexity of her experience as a girl and a woman in the 3YSC.

While not a member of the club himself, Adolph "Sonny Boy" Kiefer swam alongside the 3YSC in many lanes across the world, and he loved them like brothers. He, too, came from humble origins and learned to swim in a ditch. I think I've never met a more enthusiastic nonagenarian by phone. Just like his fans in the 1930s and 1940s, I fell immediately in love with him.

I'm indebted to him for his enthusiastic remembrance of Keo Nakama, Halo Hirose, and Bill Smith in particular, and their time together in the Navy.

Gaylord Kubota, scholar and founding director of the Alexander and Baldwin Sugar Museum in Pu'unene, gave me my first sense of the larger historical context for the 3YSC—both the poverty and the dignity of the men and women and children who lived in the camps and who worked on Maui's vast sugar plantations. I first saw the history of Japanese-American immigration to Maui and camp life through Gaylord's eyes—and his vision was spot-on, comprehensive and balanced. I have appreciated his good cheer and steadfast support while I have been working on this project.

It was Jan Prins, director of the Aquatic Research Laboratory at the University of Hawaii and founder of Swim Hawaii, who first explained to me in layperson's terms how far ahead of the curve Soichi Sakamoto was as a coach of technique and in developing training methods. With patience, Jan schooled me in fluid dynamics and the ways that the human body propels itself through water. It was he who convinced me—though he might not have said this himself—that Sakamoto was a genius, a glorious amateur who, with few resources but common sense and a sense of purpose, moved swimming along by decades. Once I heard what Jan had to say, I knew for certain that someone had to shout Soichi Sakamoto's name from the mountaintops, sharing the man's achievements with others.

When Chris Conybeare directed the 1984 documentary *Coach*, he couldn't have known how significant the transcripts from his interviews would prove to me later and how valuable they are to future researchers. In addition to being a filmmaker, Chris is the North Star at the University of Hawaii's Center for Labor History. The oral histories he conducted for that half-hour documentary provide to all of us a living record of one man's labor of love and the effect it had on children of the working poor in the late 1930s. I am grateful to Chris for his willingness to share all of the extant interviews, and I hope he'll find a way to preserve the invaluable tapes. The full transcripts deeply inform this book.

Brian Niiya has been my touchstone as I've attempted to represent even a fraction of the experience of Americans of Japanese ancestry in the twentieth century. His work at densho.org, a nonprofit organization that began with the mission of documenting oral histories from Japanese-Americans who were incarcerated during World War II and has grown into so much more, is essential, passionate, and unprecedented. His writing on the intersection between sport and the lives of Nisei reveals the extraordinary and resilient strategies by which—even in the face of exclusion, prejudice, and literal imprisonment—Nisei came to and experienced athletics. Brian breaks it down. It's not about simple upward mobility and not just about playing a game while waiting for social justice on a larger playing field. I appreciate the nuances of his views. I also thank Larry Hashima for his guidance in looking at similar phenomena of complex, strategic, and life-saving empowerment in the Japanese-American community, including his delightful discussion of George Takei's musical, *Allegiance*.

Erik Jensen generously introduced me to that moment in twentieth-century history when sports moved from a paradigm of exhaustion to a modern paradigm in which the body is seen as a mechanism. Sakamoto was at the forefront of this movement without knowing it. He understood the body as motor, and Erik made it clear to me why Sakamoto met such resistance—no pun intended—to his training regimen.

Bill Woolsey helped me to understand the ways in which Coach Sakamoto literally saved children's lives, including his own.

Peter T. Young, who runs two websites—ImagesofOldHawaii.com and totakeresponsibility.blogspot.com—is an eclectic cultural historian whom I much admire and on whom I have called many a time. He's been a patient e-mail correspondent, and he's helped me again and again to resolve matters of fact with regard to everything from early twentieth-century public education in Hawaii to the secret real-estate deals that led to today's Waikiki. And he was willing to do the footwork of checking up on some architectural info I needed. Above and beyond the call of history.

I came to David Davis late in my project, but his new biography of Duke Kahanamoku and his depth of knowledge about the man fill in important gaps in the accepted narrative of Kahanamoku's life while allowing us to continue to honor and, more deeply than ever, respect him.

There are so many other unsung, behind-the-scenes archivists, researchers, and experts behind this book's material: Bruce Wigo, director of the

International Swimming Hall of Fame, regaled me with tales about old-fashioned aquacades, and he pointed me in the direction of *Swimming in Japan*—a 1935 book (International Young Women and Children's Society/ Tetsutaro Hasegawa) that, had I not read it, would have seriously under-mined my credibility in writing this one. Jeff Wiltse, the preeminent histo-rian of the social history of swimming pools in the United States, guided me in understanding the history of natatoriums and also the swimming pools on the Mainland. It was good to talk about how the segregation of pools in one place does and does not line up with the segregation in the other. A great topic for a future academic researcher.

Tim Wise, Yale swim coach; and Pete Kennedy, former Yale swimmer and Kiphuth biographer, worked with me endlessly to understand the Kip-huth legacy with kindness, and they tolerated, as much as they could, my presentation of Kiphuth through the eyes of Sakamoto. Pete showed me how much Kiphuth and Sakamoto were in fact alike, although, of course, also worlds apart. Pete's own biography of Kiphuth will set the story straight on Kiphuth's legacy. The late Peter Daland, USC swim coach, agreed, before his death, to disagree with me about the relative importance of Kiphuth and Sakamoto in the history of competitive swimming. I do, however, thor-oughly agree with Daland about his statement that swimmers *are* the great-est people in the world.

Frank Deford gave me the sportswriter's thumbs-up that I needed at just the right time in my research, and so many others' enthusiasm made me enthusiastic and better educated about all matters of things large and small. Larry Gerlach taught me about "Gee Whiz" journalism, which led me to understand that Hawaii inherited that voice about a decade later and to see the ways in which Mainland sportswriting created larger-than-life figures out of Bill Smith and the other members of the 3YSC. Tracy K'Meyer guided me in my understanding about 1930s Louisville, and Tom Sugrue did the same for me about the 1930s and '40s in Detroit.

The book would be far less rich in delicious maritime and travel detail without the help of the indefatigable Michael Grace of cruiseliner.com. Michael's eclectic past includes having written for *The Love Boat*. I could call on Michael day or night to help me sort out ticket stubs and train schedules and to teach me about what it was like to fly commercial in 1939. I'm grateful also to the extraordinary people at Streamliner Schedules, *Wooden Boat* magazine, and folks like Paul Adsett, Barry Fritz, and Brian Chernik, who taught me how to work a vintage 16-mm movie camera.

Colin O'Connor of the Steiner Aquatic Center in Salt Lake City spent patient hours teaching me to swim again, if on dry land. And Jen See gently corrected me about technical issues like splits, long and short course races, pacing, and other matters counterintuitive to an outsider. I'm still learning.

Mahalo to others with similar special knowledge: Donna Ventura at HC&S and Linda Howe, formerly at HC&S and now at Matson CO, provided background on the Big Five. I promised Linda that in exchange for her help, I would remind readers that swimming in the ditches on Maui is forbidden today.

Thanks to Ilima Loomis for reading early versions of this material and for sharing her enthusiasm for the men and women of the 3YSC. Rich Lucas dove into the dusty yearbooks of Old Maui High and came up with gems, including the graduation photo and bio of Benzo Sakamoto that broke my heart and made so much of his tragic life make sense. The late Hiroshi Yamauchi helped me better and more subtly understand the life and contributions of Halo Hirose.

The time I spent with Mitzi Higuchi and the late Spencer Shiraishi at the downtown Wailuku McDonald's talking about the 3YSC was the best anybody in the world has spent at Mickey D's Formica tables. Mitzi shared with me the story of that fateful day when it was she who first informed Sakamoto that his brother was lost at sea, and Spencer was patient as I asked so many questions about camp life. I thank both of them for their stories, and I commend their persistence and pleasure in pursuing the scratch-off coupons that allowed them to meet every morning in the same venue.

Wallette Pellegrino spent time with me on Maui identifying buildings and people in Wailuku and Waikapu from old photos. Virgie Haines helped me understand more about Camp 5 life. Sam Kadotani remembered Boy Scout life on Maui, and Judge Andrew Sato generously shared his reminiscences, which was especially kind on a day of so much dental work. Thanks to both Les Vida Sr. and Les Vida Jr. for allowing me into their home at the spur of the moment, in spite of what might have been a wiser course of an overabundance of caution with a reporter; and also to Barbara Kikuchi, owner of the Waikapu on 30 restaurant, the former site of the Tokuichi Sakamoto store, for her embrace of the Sakamoto family history, and also for the best mixed plate on the island.

Lee Tonouchi's play, though loosely based on fact, was in spirit helpful, especially in reminding me to honor the sound of the children's voices and their daily use of pidgin in the story. Carol Wilcox was kind enough to sign off on my layperson's understanding of Maui's extensive ditch system after I'd read her monumental book, *Sugar Water*. Ted Nagata was a thoughtful commentator at both the beginning and the end of the project. Hiroko Hashitani kindly translated Benzo's obituary and various newspaper accounts of the June 1939 wreck of the *Mae West*. Warren Shibuya spent generous time on Maui with me, helping me to understand Camp 5 and how the machines worked at the Camp 5 pool.

Gail Ainsworth Bartholomew single-handedly and exhaustively indexed a hundred years of the *Maui News*; without that resource, I would have no book. Similarly, Susan Brusik, Rose-Marie Walton, and the magically invisible crew at Interlibrary Loan at the University of Utah treated me kindly no matter what crazy, obscure, rare book or manuscript I requested or what hard-to-find roll of microfiche I wanted from far-flung archives. I am grateful to Lorraine Crouse at the University of Utah's special collections. On the other side of the equation, working with Susan was Cheryl Ogawa at special collections at the University of Hawaii at Manoa; Cheryl made the requested material fly all the way across the Pacific and the Internet to me in Utah.

John Fox, in-house historian at the FBI, was helpful in far more than just my FOIA requests, as were the volunteers at the LDS Family History Library in Salt Lake with genealogical work and Sanborn mapping. Bert Granberg and Jaime Yu helped with my forensic mapping of the ditches and the long-gone camps. Tiffany Glasgow helped me understand typhoid in the early twentieth century. Kelli Nakamura was generous in sharing information with me from her own research on Maui internment camps. I was happy to come upon Donna Ching and the friends of the Natatorium who, in spite of the idiosyncrasies of the Nat, love and treasure it, as it should be. Ken Nelson was my early guide to the history of the 442nd.

Researching and sourcing and sleuthing photographs for the book was a tremendous effort, and I'm grateful to a number of people for patiently combing through their archives to determine provenance. These include Ivonne Schmid of the International Swimming Hall of Fame. Philip Barker, historian of the British Olympic Association, helped me deeply to research the origins of 1948 Olympics photos and the complicated consortium to which the rights belonged. Zachary Durham of Yale Athletics, who led me to archival photographs of Kiphuth. And a special thank-you to Tod Tsukano, who helped me track down pictures of his father, John, and his uncles, Pachi and Shangy.

The hospitality of the University of Utah was essential to my research. Vince Pecora first made it possible for my affiliation as a scholar in residence; Marc Hoenig had to deal with the paperwork every year and did so with a smile. Alfred Mowdood made me feel at home and welcomed as a researcher; and Alison Regan, head of Education Services, gave me not only a desk and help with parking but the great company of Linda St. Clair, Dale Larsen, Lindsay Hansen, and Adriana Parker. Geralyn White Dreyfous made getting away possible.

I would not have been able to sustain this project without the kindness of two women in particular—Suzanne Sato and Maizie Cameron Sanford— to whom I was a stranger but who embraced me, no questions asked, as a guest in their homes and who both became my friends. I am truly indebted to them for so much. Among other things, Suzanne introduced me to the pleasures of cold sake, and Maizie stayed patient with me at the beach Kihei while I fretted over what I decided was a hurricane and what she knew was just another passing tropical storm. Both have also been great guides in terms of following down leads and sources. Smart, kind cookies both. Thanks to Ira Rubinfeld, who shared his time-share points; and Darcy and Jim Iams for good company in Honolulu.

Both Sonny Tanabe and Jerry Miki, swimmers for Sakamoto in the 1950s, spent countless hours with me in their homes, on the phone, and via e-mail. Each was willing to answer questions 24/7. Sonny, whose knowledge of Hawaiian watersports is encyclopedic, was always willing to call up his fellow Olympians and ask clarifying questions. Jerry Miki's sweetness, sincerity, and love of Coach gave me more insight than anyone else into Sakamoto's psychology, and, as a talented writer of prose, he conjured up so many of the images that became central to the story. In terms of the politics of the club, the underlying but subtle radicalism of Sakamoto, Jerry kept me in line in presenting it to a larger audience. Bill Woolsey, another of Sakamoto's swimmers, told me how Coach literally saved children's lives.

Thank you to Eric Hinderaker for early on pointing me toward the foundational literature on sugar production and the particular economy and social structure it has required. Laura Johnson made it possible for me to research this book to the deepest degree possible by opening the door for me to scholarly resources I would otherwise not have been able to access.

Kudos to the fast fingers of Cristina Grossau for the hundreds of pages—and hours—of interview transcription. Thank you to Anne Holman and Betsy Burton of the King's English bookstore in Salt Lake City. Enormous thanks to Dr. Fiona Halloran for pinch-hitting on reader's guide questions.

Roz Lightfoot and Holly Buland of the Alexander Baldwin Sugar Museum on Maui continually surprised me with their generosity and professionalism in sharing their extensive archives with me. Thank you to Kevin Higa for guidance about his grandfather. To Michael Martone, thank you for your kindness and support and to former colleagues Bryant Simon, Christy Desmet, and Roxanne Eberle for referrals to other historians and quick answers to literary questions. I am grateful to Terry Orme, Lisa Carricaburu, and Anne Wilson for putting up with me as a long-form writer at the *Salt Lake Tribune*; and to Jessica Ravitz, now of cnn.com; and to Anna Cekola, a dear friend with tremendous patience.

It takes a village to write a book and raise a family at the same time. There are so many people in my life, and in the lives of my husband and my children, who have helped make this book possible. Thank you to Val Burnett, Dawn Houghton, Mary Lawlor, Kathy Gundersen, Susan Chortkoff, and Gail Sanders for always asking how the project was going: every time they did so, I felt both understood and honored.

To the "it-takes-a-village" people at Rowland Hall, thank you, thank you,

Mahalo Nui Loa/Thank You

thank you for helping us raise and teach our children well—Katie Schwab, Erika McCarthy, Chuck White, Linda Tatomer, Kody Partridge, Sofia Gorder, Deborah Mohrman. It's a partnership, and I'm astonished at how much you've become a part of our family and how warmly you've welcomed us into yours and into the community. Thank you to Linda Hampton and Ryan Hoglund for all of their support to my husband in his work. Dearest thanks to those others who have been there for our whole family in times of need: my brother-in-law Dan Dinsmoor, Laura Brockbank, Missy Alder, and Merritt Stites. Thank you to the Borgenicht family for being there for ours. I don't know if you know how much you mean to us. My gratitude to Kelly Wilson.

My office overlooks the beautiful spring garden of Marge Gunn. I am grateful to her in all seasons. Other neighbors have come through in a pinch: Tish Archuletta, David Lester, Andrea Globokar, Ray Barnson.

Thank you to my sister Karen Checkoway and her husband, Carlos Reyes, for the offer of quiet space and the wonderful visits my children were able to make to them.

I am grateful always to my teachers through the years—to the late Monroe Engel, Grace Mojtabai, Jane Smiley, James Alan McPherson, and Stephen Dixon.

Thank you to Bill Fulton, who's probably the only person on earth who knows full well why it's a big deal that I wrote this book and *not* the other one. My brother Neal taught me on our previous film project how to grow up and just get things done. And my in-laws, George and Mary Ellen Thomsen, for their enduring love and support.

To my agent Eileen Cope: thank you for standing by me all these years and for finding this story in the first place. Enormous thanks to Jimmy Franco, Elizabeth Kulhanek, and Anne Twomey at Grand Central. And to my editor Deb Futter: thank you for seeing the beauty and humanity in this story, for shedding real tears over the lives of these men and women, for appreciating my sometimes infuriating passion about it, but believing we could find a way through everything as a team. Carolyn Kurek read the manuscript with a perspicacity that surprised and delighted me; I am grateful to her for where she was able to catch my goofs. Sarah Malik was my

*Mahalo Nui Loa/*Thank You

research assistant in the last half-year of this project; I wish I had known her sooner; her dedication, good humor, and meticulous work made the last 100-yard stretch down the straightaway so much better. This book wouldn't exist without her constancy.

My daughters Abby and Sophia were more than patient with me, even when they returned home from school or rehearsal or saxophone practice to find on my office door the infuriating sign: "The Writer Is Working/Sleeping/Thinking." Abby completed high school during the time I wrote this book, and Sophia grew more and more into her wonderful, creative, and very clever self. And what do I say about my glorious husband? Thank you, Lee—Laurence Woodward Thomsen—for absolutely everything that is good in my life. Dear Reader, you should count yourself lucky if you have found a person half as good as he to accompany you through your own life. He is my first in everything, morning and night; and he is my truest reader and editor. Nothing I write goes out into the world without passing "the husband test"—an understanding of the point at which one's labor is reasonably ready to be abandoned. I simply adore the man, and I love the family we have worked so hard to build together. It is, remarkably, the one we said we always wanted.

Index

Index

Index

Index

Index

Index

Index

Index

Index

Index